LAW, LORDSHIP AND TENURE:
The Fall of the Black Douglases

LAW, LORDSHIP AND TENURE:
The Fall of the Black Douglases

Alan R. Borthwick &
Hector L. MacQueen

THE
STRATHMARTINE
PRESS

First published in 2022
by The Strathmartine Press Ltd.

2, Kinburn Place,
St Andrews
KY16 9DT
www.strathmartinetrust.org

ISBN: 978-0-9955441-2-3

Copyright © Alan R. Borthwick and Hector L. MacQueen 2022

The right of Alan R. Borthwick and Hector L. MacQueen to be identified as the authors of this work has been asserted by them in accordance with the Copyright, Designs and Patent Act, 1988.

All rights reserved. No part of this publication may be reproduced, stored, or transmitted in any form, or by any means, electronic, mechanical or photocopying, recording or otherwise, without the express written permission of the publisher.

Typeset and printed by Wordzworth

Cover Image: Portrait of James II,
from the *Diary of Georg von Ehingen*, c.1460
(Stuttgart, Wuerttembergische Landesbibliothek,
Cod. hist. qt. 141, fol. 97)
Cast of the seal of the 8th earl of Douglas
(Laing seal casts, NRS RH17/1/247)

Dedicated with gratitude and affection to
the memory of three Scottish Medievalists

Sheriff Peter Grant Brass McNeill QC
3 March 1929–22 April 2011

Dr Athol Laverick Murray
8 November 1930–24 August 2018

and

William David Hamilton Sellar MVO
27 February 1941–26 January 2019

Contents

Preface ix

Abbreviations xi

Chapter 1 Introduction 1
The Problem Stated 1
The Law 10
The Black Douglases 21

Chapter 2 Regency, Council and the Earls of Douglas 1437–51 35
Regency in Scotland before 1437 36
Regency 1437–49 51
The Eighth Earl of Douglas and the Regency Government 59
The 1449 Transumpt and Its Immediate Aftermath 64
The End of the King's Minority 69
The Eighth Earl Abroad 72

Chapter 3 The Fall of the House of Douglas 75
Introduction 75
The Settlement of 1451 79
Wardenship of the Middle and Western Marches 82
Ettrick and Selkirk Forest 85
The Earldom of Wigtown 86
Stewarton 90
Analysis of the Trial and Its Aftermath 98
Explaining the Killing of the Eighth Earl? 103

Chapter 4 The Coshogle Case — 113

Coshogle and the Brieve of Mortancestry — 113
Drumlanrig: Barony in Regality — 117
The Blair Claim to Coshogle — 120
The Loranes — 125
The Nithsdale Context — 128
The Douglases of Drumlanrig (and Hawick) — 133
Hawick and Sprouston — 139
The Crisis of 1451 and Afterwards: Regaining Hawick and Coshogle — 142

Chapter 5 The Blarmade Case — 145

Introduction — 145
Hamilton of Cambuskeith v Maxwells of Calderwood — 147
The Barony of Crawfordjohn — 153
The Hamiltons of Cambuskeith — 156
The Maxwells of Calderwood — 159
What Lay behind the Litigation in the 1460s? — 166
Conclusions — 169

Chapter 6 Conclusions — 173

Violence, Law and Society — 173
Regency — 176
The Eighth Earl's Conduct 1444–51 — 178
Calling the King to Account — 181
Law and Tenure in the Localities — 188

Appendix — 197

(a) NLS: Ch. 951 — 197
(b) NLS Adv Chs B. 1316, 1317 — 206
(c) NLS: Acc 7043 Adamton charters No 16/2 — 210
(d) NLS Acc 7043 Adamton No 16/1 — 214

Bibliography — 217

Index — 237

Preface

This book began life some years ago as what was intended to be a contribution to a collection of essays in honour of a leading scholar of medieval Scotland. The study rapidly grew; and a first instalment was published in a Stair Society Miscellany in 2015. Completing the work for the contribution to the essay collection increasingly meant leaving much material either severely abbreviated or omitted altogether. A growing realisation that we were beginning to develop a new understanding of the relationship between the earls of Douglas and the kings of Scots in the fourteenth and (especially) the fifteenth centuries led us eventually to decide to attempt this book. It incorporates both the article published in 2015 and the one finally published in the essay collection in 2022; but we hope that otherwise the book does not bear too many traces of its content's divided past.

It is important to stress that the book is intended to be, not a comprehensive study of the minority of King James II and its aftermath, or of the Black Douglases in the fourteenth and fifteenth centuries, but a reinterpretation of key events leading up to the fall of the Douglases in 1455, some of them reaching back to a time over a century earlier. The principal analytical tool throughout is the law relevant to these events and the specific meaning and significance of the documents (which is often a legal question) that evidence them.

In writing this book we have incurred many intellectual debts, not least to the works of those with whom from time to time in what follows we venture to disagree; notably those of Steve Boardman, Michael Brown, Christine McGladdery, Michael Penman and Roland Tanner. We are also grateful to the anonymous reviewer of a first draft who provided thought-provoking comments resulting in some significant improvements to our argument. Claire Hawes and Cynthia Neville have kindly allowed us to refer to their unpublished work. Other friends and colleagues too numerous to name individually have generously answered questions, supplied materials and references, and pointed us towards sources we might otherwise never have found. We are grateful to them all. Our dedication is a gesture of gratitude to three particular friends who are no longer with us but who would, we think, have enjoyed this book even if they disagreed with its arguments. Staff at the National Library of Scotland and the National Records of Scotland have also been patient and helpful to us in our researches. Opportunities to present interim conclusions at the conference 'Living with the Law: Society and Legal Dispute c.1200–1700' held at the University of St Andrews 27–29 June 2016; at the Legal History section of the Annual Conference of the Society of Legal Scholars held at Queen Mary University London 4–7 September 2018; and at the Annual General Meeting of the Stair Society held on 17 November 2018, and the discussion which followed all these presentations, were and are much appreciated.

We must finally record our thanks to our spouses who have tolerated this rival for our attention for too many years.

Alan Borthwick and Hector MacQueen
EDINBURGH, MARCH 2022

Acknowledgment

The map on p. 130 was drawn by Bryan Harper Titus, based on MacQueen, Hector, Ward, Pauline, Macdonald, Stuart (2016), South of Scotland Castles of the 15th Century, dataset [University of Edinburgh] https://doi.org/10.7488/ds/1392. It also appears in Boardman, S., and Ditchburn, D., (eds), *Kingship, Lordship and Sanctity in Medieval Britain: Essays in Honour of Alexander Grant* (Woodbridge, 2022) p. 195.

Abbreviations

AB III	*Illustrations of the Topography and Antiquities of the Shires of Aberdeen and Banff*, ed. Robertson, J. (Aberdeen, 1847–69)
ADA	*Acta Dominorum Auditorum: The Acts of the Lords Auditors of Causes and Complaints*, ed. Thomson, T. (Edinburgh, 1839)
ADC	*Acta Dominorum Concilii: The Acts of the lords of Council in Civil Causes*, eds Thomson, T. and others (Edinburgh, 1839, 1918, 1993)
APS	*The Acts of the Parliaments of Scotland*, eds Thomson, T. and Innes, C. (Edinburgh, 1814–75)
AHCAG	*Archaeological and Historical Collections relating to Ayrshire and Galloway*, ed. Cochran-Patrick, R.W. (Ayr, 1878–99)
Ayr Friars Chrs	*Charters of the Friars Preachers of Ayr* (AHCAG, 1881)
Bracton	*Bracton De Legibus et Consuetudinibus Angliae*, ed. Woodbine, G. E., trans Thorne, S. E., (Cambridge, MA, 1968-77)
CDS	*Calendar of Documents relating to Scotland*, eds Bain, J. and others, 5 vols (1881–1996)
CPL	*Calendar of Papal Letters to Scotland of Benedict XIII of Avignon: 1394-1419*, ed. McGurk, F. (Edinburgh, 1976)
CPR	*Calendar of Papal Registers Relating To Great Britain and Ireland*, eds Bliss, W.H. and others (1893-)

CSSR	*Calendar of Scottish Supplications to Rome*, eds Lindsay, E.R. and others (Edinburgh and Glasgow, 1934, 1956, 1997, 2017)
Chron Bower	*Scotichronicon by Walter Bower*, eds Watt, D.E.R. and others (Aberdeen and Edinburgh, 1993–98)
Chron Fordun	*Johannis de Fordun, Chronica Gentis Scotorum*, ed. Skene, W.F. (Edinburgh, 1871–72)
Chron Wyntoun	*Original Chronicle of Andrew of Wyntoun*, ed. Amours, F.J. (Edinburgh, 1903–14)
Craig, *Jus Feudale*	*Jus Feudale Tribus Libris Comprehensum by Thomas Craig of Riccarton* (Edinburgh, 1655; Leipzig, 1716; Edinburgh, 1732); trans. Lord Clyde (Edinburgh, 1933); ed. and trans. Dodd, L. (Edinburgh, 2017–)
Dunf Reg	*Registrum de Dunfermelyn*, ed. Innes, C. (Edinburgh, 1842)
ER	*The Exchequer Rolls of Scotland*, eds Stuart, J. and others (Edinburgh, 1878–1908)
Family of Rose	*Genealogical Deduction of the Family of Rose of Kilravock*, ed. Innes, C. (Edinburgh, 1848)
Foedera	*Foedera, Conventiones, Litterae et Cuiuscunque Generis Acta Publica*, ed. Rymer, T., Record Commission edition (London, 1816–69)
Fraser, *Buccleuch*	Fraser, W., *The Scotts of Buccleuch* (Edinburgh, 1878)
Fraser, *Carlaverock*	Fraser, W., *The Book of Carlaverock* (Edinburgh, 1873)
Fraser, *Douglas*	Fraser, W., *The Douglas Book* (Edinburgh, 1885)
Fraser, *Melvilles*	Fraser, W., *The Melvilles Earls of Melville, and the Leslies Earls of Leven* (Edinburgh, 1890)
Fraser, *Menteith*	Fraser, W., *The Red Book of Menteith* (Edinburgh, 1880)

Fraser, *Pollok*	Fraser, W., *Memoirs of the Maxwells of Pollok* (Edinburgh, 1863); OR Fraser, W., *The Cartulary of Pollok-Maxwell* (Edinburgh, 1875)
Glanvill	*Tractatus de Legibus et Consuetudinibus Regni Anglie qui Glanvilla Vocatur*, ed. Hall, G. D. G., (London, Edinburgh, Lagos and Nairobi, 1965)
Glasgow Reg	*Registrum Episcopatus Glasguensis*, ed. Innes, C. (Edinburgh, 1843)
Haddington Chrs	*Charters and Writs concerning the Royal Burgh of Haddington. 1318–1543*, ed. Wallace-James, J.G. (Haddington, 1895)
HES	Historic Environment Scotland
HMC	Historical Manuscripts Commission
Justinian, *Institutes*	*Justinian's Institutes*, ed. Krueger, P., trans. Birks, P. and McLeod, G., (London, 1987)
Laing Chrs	*Calendar of the Laing Charters 854–1837*, ed. Anderson, J. (Edinburgh, 1899)
Laws of Medieval Scotland	*Laws of Medieval Scotland: Legal Compilations from the Thirteenth and Fourteenth Centuries*, ed. Taylor, A. (Edinburgh, 2019)
Morton Reg	*Registrum Honoris de Morton*, eds Thomson, T. and others (Edinburgh, 1853)
NGR	National Grid Reference (Ordnance Survey)
NLS	National Library of Scotland
NRAS	National Register of Archives for Scotland
NRS	National Records of Scotland
ODNB	*Oxford Dictionary of National Biography*, accessible online at https://www.oxforddnb.com/
Paisley Reg	*Registrum Monasterii de Passelet*, ed. Innes, C. (Edinburgh, 1832; Edinburgh, 1877)

Pinkerton, *History*	Pinkerton, J., *The History of Scotland from the Accession of the House of Stuart to that of Mary; with Appendices of Original Papers* (London, 1797)
RMS	*Registrum Magni Sigilli Regum Scotorum*, eds Thomson, J.M. and others (Edinburgh, 1882–1914)
RPS	*Records of the Parliaments of Scotland*, accessible online at https://www.rps.ac.uk/
Rot Scot	*Rotuli Scotiae in Turri Londinensi et in Domo Capitulari Westmonasteriense Asservati*, eds Macpherson, D. and others (1814–19)
RCAHMS	Royal Commission on the Ancient and Historical Monuments of Scotland
Scots Peerage	*The Scots Peerage*, ed. Balfour Paul, Sir J. (Edinburgh, 1904–14)
Scottish Formularies	*Scottish Formularies*, ed. Duncan, A.A.M. (Edinburgh, 2011)
Stirling Chrs	*Charters and other Documents relating to the Royal Burgh of Stirling AD 1124–1707*, ed. Renwick, R. (Glasgow, 1884)
Wigtownshire Chrs	*Wigtownshire Charters*, ed. Reid, R.C. (Edinburgh, 1960)
Wigtown Charter Chest	*Charter Chest of the Earldom of Wigtown*, ed. Grant, F.J. (Edinburgh, 1910)

Chapter One
Introduction

The Problem Stated

'Fiction', declares the historical novelist Hilary Mantel in the third of her 2017 Reith lectures, 'if well written, doesn't betray history, but opens up its essential nature to inspection. When fiction is turned into theatre ... the same applies: there is no necessary treason'.[1] She goes on:

> [W]ithout art, what have you, to inform you about the past? ... if we crave truth unmediated by art we are chasing a phantom. ... We need historians, not to collect facts, but to help us pick a path through the facts, to meaning. We need fiction to remind us that the unknown and unknowable is real, and exerts its force.[2]

The three James plays written by Rona Munro, which premiered at the Edinburgh International Festival in August 2014, paint powerful images of kingship and lordship in later medieval Scotland, and raise questions about the characters, motivations and personal interactions of the major figures in the period.[3] In particular, what led the 21-year-old King James II on 22

---

[1] Mantel, H., 'Resurrection: The Art and Craft: Adaptation', in BBC Radio 4, *Remarkable Minds: A Celebration of the Reith Lectures* (London, 2019), p. 19.
[2] Ibid., pp. 27–28.
[3] Munro, R., *The James Plays* (London, 2014). See the comments made by McGladdery, C., *James II*, 2nd edition (Edinburgh, 2015) [McGladdery, *James II*], pp. 250–51.

February 1452 to 'stert sodanly ... with ane knyf' at William, eighth earl of Douglas, (only a few years older than his assailant) 'and straik him in at the colere and down in the body'? The near-contemporary Auchinleck chronicle has so much other circumstantial detail about the king's attack – for example, that it took place in the 'inner chalmer' at Stirling castle around 7 in the evening after the king and earl had 'dined and supped' together – that its account commands credibility. The king was joined in the assault by Patrick Gray, who struck the earl on the head with a pole-axe 'and strak out his harnes' (i.e. brains); thereupon 'the gentillis that war with the king gaf thaim ilkane a straik or twa with knyffis', leaving the earl's body with 26 wounds altogether.[4]

It is difficult, however, to believe that such a killing was being planned, at least when the king previously gave his written assurance of the earl's safety in joining him at Stirling.[5] Nor can the immediate trigger mentioned in the Auchinleck chronicle, the earl's refusal to comply with the king's insistence that he break his band of mutual support with the recently rebellious earl of Ross and the unreliable earl of Crawford, be the whole story behind the attack. The king being joined in the assault on Douglas by the others in the room with the knives at their belts, with Gray perhaps snatching the pole-axe down from the wall of the 'inner chalmer' where the assault took place, or from the hands of a guard at the door, was however most likely driven by their instinctive calculation, even in the heat of the moment, of the better side to take, rather than any pre-meditated conspiracy. How much then stemmed from the situation of two hot-tempered young men falling into evening argument after dining and supping together in the company of

---

[4] All quotations in this paragraph from *Auchinleck Chronicle*, f 114v (as per McGladdery, *James II*, p. 265). On the source in general, see McGladdery, *James II*, pp. 210–21, seeing it as generally accurate and useful, censorious of James II but not necessarily pro-Douglas, and in need of careful use alongside other available primary sources. For 'harnes', see https://dsl.ac.uk/entry/dost/harnis. The king had the previous day invited the earl 'to the dynere & to the supper', apparently two separate meals. The chronicle's 'sowpit' seems to refer to the latter meal, but the verb 'soup' has the meaning, not only of supping together, but also of taking in (sipping) liquids. It can also mean to soak or saturate. See https://dsl.ac.uk/entry/dost/soup_v_1, https://dsl.ac.uk/entry/dost/soup_v_2 and https://dsl.ac.uk/entry/dost/soup_v_4.

[5] See further below, Chapter 3, text accompanying notes 112–14.

others, with perhaps at least some strong drink having been taken and all concerned having knives to hand?[6]

Rona Munro's dramatisation of the event highlights the king's fears for himself, which were surely deep-rooted after traumatic childhood experiences of sudden and violent death. Born on 16 October 1430, between the ages of six and ten the boy James would have heard, in probably terrifying circumstances, about the grisly assassination of his father, King James I, in the drains of the Blackfriars at Perth on 21 February 1437; perhaps witnessed the brutal executions of the killers a few weeks later;[7] and, finally, almost certainly been present when in November 1440 the teenaged William, sixth earl of Douglas, his younger brother David, and (three days afterwards) their friend Sir Malcolm Fleming of Cumbernauld and Biggar were 'put to deid' following the 'Black Dinner' and at least some semblance of a trial at Edinburgh castle.[8]

The problem for the historian as distinct from the dramatist is how far beyond traditional documentary sources to go in search of explanations and understanding of events like the king's killing of the earl of Douglas or, indeed, the Black Dinner. Some approach the question by viewing all interactions between kings and their nobility, and amongst the nobility themselves, as necessarily reflective of continuous contests for political dominance or raw power; but is this necessarily so in every case? What had James II to gain from killing the earl in such a sudden and violent fashion? Hindsight and the knowledge that just over three years later the house of Douglas would be toppled completely from its place at the very pinnacle of the Scottish nobility by the forces of the king makes it tempting to detect motive and purpose in

---

[6] The famous image of James II from the *Diary of Georg von Ehingen*, datable to c.1460 and reproduced on the cover of this book, shows him with hands on a dagger hanging from a belt round his waist. It seems unlikely, however, that Patrick Gray carried a pole-axe around with him. See further McGladdery, *James II*, pp. 221–22.

[7] Connolly, M., '*The Dethe of the Kynge of Scotis*: A New Edition', *Scottish Historical Review* lxxi (1992), pp. 46–69 [Connolly, '*Dethe of the Kyng of Scotis*'], pp. 63–68.

[8] *Auchinleck Chronicle*, f 121r-v (McGladdery, *James II*, p. 274) is the only near-contemporary account of this mysterious event. McGladdery, *James II*, pp. 237, 242, 245–48, traces the elaborations of later writers on the subject. See further below text accompanying notes 91–104.

what happened. But at the time of the assault, the king's actions laid him open at the very least to charges of abusing his own hospitality, and risked, not only dividing his kingdom internally, but also exposing himself and the kingdom to international condemnation and sanctions such as papal excommunication. Moreover, as we will see in the course of this book, the king had available other means of bringing troublesome subjects like the earl to heel; there was no need for him to resort to crude physical assault and homicide as the answer to the problems posed by the earl of Douglas.

Sir John Fortescue, the Chief Justice of England, exiled to Scotland with his king (Henry VI) in 1461, subsequently declared that the king of Scots reigned by 'political and royal government'; that is to say, not like the king of France, by royal fiat alone, but like the king of England, one guided 'by the wisdom and counsel of many'.[9] Fortescue's perception has been unconsciously echoed by recent Scottish historians of the middle ages. Thus, in his study of King Alexander III (1249–86), Norman Reid argues that '[c]ollaborative rule by king and aristocracy was a long-standing and integral element of the culture of Scottish kingship'.[10] He builds on the insights developed by Alice Taylor for the twelfth and thirteenth centuries, challenging, as she puts it, the 'fallacy of the notion that royal and aristocratic power serve fundamentally different interests (the "public" and the "private" respectively) and thus are structurally opposed forces of political power'.[11] This book too will argue, as did also Alexander Grant from the 1970s on, that (as Fortescue bears contemporary witness) this interdependence of king and aristocracy is as true of the fourteenth and fifteenth as it is for the earlier centuries studied by Reid and Taylor.[12] But the book will show further that there must also be sensitivity to the existence of the ordinary and the routine as part of the individual ties involved in kingship, lordship, governance and landownership:

---

[9] Fortescue, Sir John, *De Laudibus Legum Anglie*, ed. Chrimes, S.B. (Cambridge, 1949, repr 2011), pp. 32–33; idem, *The Governance of England, otherwise called The Difference between an Absolute and a Limited Monarchy*, ed. Plummer, C. (Oxford, 1885), p. 112.

[10] Reid, N.H., *Alexander III 1249–1286: First Among Equals* (Edinburgh, 2019), p. 37.

[11] Taylor, A., *The Shape of the State in Medieval Scotland, 1124–1290* (Oxford, 2016), p. 3.

[12] Grant, A., *Independence and Nationhood: Scotland 1306–1469* (London, 1984) [Grant, *Independence and Nationhood*], pp. 147–70.

'the system, so to speak, lying behind those ties [which] has tended to be taken for granted'.[13]

Law was (and is) part of the underlying system and routines of governance and should not be contrasted with the realities of social and political practice. Rather, for later medieval Scotland we should think about concepts of 'legal consciousness' and the 'constitutive' role of law in social relations and organisation developed by legal historians elsewhere as well as by sociologists of law.[14] 'Broadly speaking, legal consciousness refers to the way that people – individuals and collectives of legal actors and lay people – perceive, and act in relation to, law'.[15] The sociologist Simon Halliday, elaborating on the application of Anthony Giddens' notion of 'practical' (as distinct from 'discursive') consciousness, adds to the idea of legal consciousness the thought that it is manifest more in what people do than in what they say or can articulate, orally or otherwise: it is 'a form of tacit or background knowledge connected to what people do as purposive agents'.[16] The US legal historian Robert W Gordon, also drawing on ideas of legal consciousness, notes that 'law is partly constitutive of social life, because law distributes powers and immunities, and because all social actors internalise and enact legal identities and roles'.[17] Earlier, he had also written:

> ... law figures [not only] as a factor in the power relationships of individuals and social classes but also ... is omnipresent in the very marrow of society [in] that law-making and law-interpreting institutions have been among the primary sources of the pictures

---

[13] Grant, A., 'Service and Tenure in Late Medieval Scotland, 1314–1475', in Curry, A. and Matthew, E. (eds), *Concepts and Patterns of Service in the Later Middle Ages* (Woodbridge, 2003), pp. 145–79, 145 [Grant, 'Service and Tenure']. See also the same point put differently in Grant, A., 'To the Medieval Foundations', *Scottish Historical Review* 73 (1994), pp. 4–24, 6.

[14] See Fisk, C.L., '&: Law_Society in Legal History Research', in Dubber, M.D. and Tomlins, C., (eds), *The Oxford Handbook of Legal History* (Oxford, 2018) ch 26.

[15] Kennedy, C., 'Sociology of Law and Legal History', in Přibáň, J., (ed.), *Research Handbook on the Sociology of Law* (Cheltenham, 2020), pp. 31–42, 32–33.

[16] Halliday, S., 'After Hegemony? The Varieties of Legal Consciousness Research', *Social and Legal Studies* 28 (2019), pp. 859–78 at 863; citing Giddens, A., *The Constitution of Society* (Cambridge, 1984), pp. xxiii, 49.

[17] Gordon, R.W., 'Critical Legal Histories Revisited: A Response', *Law & Social Inquiry* 37 (2012), pp. 200–15, 208.

of order and disorder, virtue and vice, reasonableness and craziness, realism and visionary naiveté and of some of the most commonplace aspects of social reality that ordinary people carry around with them and use in ordering their lives.[18]

None of this should be taken as meaning that law is necessarily in step with society, or indeed that society is in step with the law. Rather the argument is that law is integral to society, one of the key ways through which society realises itself and by which its members understand their individual relationships with each other in relation to the myriad of their social affairs. Law is a social and often political product but its formation, development and application is dependent upon an infinite variety of social and political factors, the relative force of which varies from time to time and place to place.

Below elite levels it is hard indeed to detect legal consciousness of this kind in later medieval Scotland, but some significant contemporary sources manifest association of good government and social peace with enforcement of the law and justice. The leading lawbook of the period, *Regiam Majestatem*, followed Roman law and the earlier English treatises, *Glanvill* and *Bracton*, in saying that 'royal majesty' should be armed not only for the defence of the realm against rebels, but also with 'laws governing his peaceful subjects and people'.[19] Writing about the reign of James I in the 1440s the praise of the dead king composed by Walter Bower, abbot of Inchcolm abbey and royal counsellor, focused not only on James' personal qualities but also on the vigour with which he pursued justice through law:

> This man was a patron of peace, and a most weighty deviser of laws ... The law was available to all while he was alive, with crime buried, theft then lay low, dishonour did not remain unpunished.[20]

---

[18] Gordon, R.W., 'Critical Legal Histories', *Stanford Law Review* 36 (1984), pp. 57–126 at 109. For a critical assessment of Gordon's approach, see Tomlins, C., 'Historicism and Materiality in Legal Theory', in Del Mar, M. and Lobban, M., (eds), *Law in Theory and History: New Essays on a Neglected Dialogue* (Oxford, 2016), pp. 57–83.

[19] *Regiam Majestatem*, prologue (*APS*, i, p. 597; Stair Society vol 9, 57); see also Justinian, *Institutes*, proemium; *Glanvill*, prologus; *Bracton*, introduction.

[20] *Chron Bower*, viii, pp. 334–35; also ibid., pp. 256–57 (noting of the legislative

CHAPTER ONE: INTRODUCTION

Bower also expressed a wish that James' son would prove to be 'a similar king in the future',[21] and this hope was evidently shared in his minority government. In 1440 a Council General indicated a determination to enforce the law in which the young king was to play an active part.[22] In 1445 James II probably took an oath in Parliament that he would govern

> ... eftir the lawis and custumis of the realm; the law, custume and statutis of the realm neyther to eik nor to myniss without the consent of the thre estatis, and na thing to wirk na use tuiching the commoun proffit of the realm bot consent of the thre estatis; the law and statutis maid be my forbearis keip and use in all punctis, at all my power, till all my leigis in all things...[23]

After the king had assumed active authority at the head of government in 1450 his first Parliament set out a comprehensive legislative statement under which not only was justice to be done so that 'general peace be proclaimed and kept throughout the realm', but also the means provided by which it was to be made available, in particular to 'the pure pepill that lauboris the grund'. 'Juste men ... at kennys and minister evinly justice alsweill of the grete als the smal' were crucial to this process.[24] The general peace would mean that 'al man may travel surely and sickirly in marchandice ande uthir wayis in al placis throu the lande swa that na man nede til have assouerans of uthir bot the kingis pece be souer til al man'.[25] If justice in this vision was

---

activity of James I that 'some of it would have served the kingdom well enough for the future if they had been kept').

[21] Ibid., pp. 334–35; also at 216–17 (directly addressed to the young king and pointing out that 'the laws of the state are most certainly a comfort to human life, a help to the weak, a restraint on tyrants. It is from them that security comes and conscience can enjoy freedom').

[22] *RPS* 1440/8/2-4.

[23] *RPS* 1445/3. See further the *RPS* pop-up note on this material; Lyall, R.J., 'The Medieval Scottish Coronation Service: Some Seventeenth Century Evidence', *Innes Review* 28 (1977), pp. 3–21, 9–11, 15–16; Tanner, R., *The Late Medieval Scottish Parliament: Politics and the Three Estates, 1424–1488* (East Linton, 2001) [Tanner, *LMSP*], pp. 112–13. We discuss this and other similar oaths in Chapter 6, text accompanying notes 31–43; see also Chapter 2, text accompanying notes 20, 28 and 39.

[24] *RPS* 1450/1/12-30.

[25] *RPS* 1450/1/12.

primarily corrective rather than distributive it was nonetheless for the good of society as a whole.

As the medievalist John Hudson further remarks, law both shapes and is shaped by social practices and by the aims and acts of individual participants. Hudson rightly observes that 'the many functions of law' include

> not just that which may spring most readily to mind, the punishment of offences and the prevention and settlement of disputes, but also others such as attempting to increase the predictability of the future; giving ideological underpinning to authority and social order; controlling allocation of resources; facilitating and legitimising certain acts or states, and thereby concealing the exercise of power.[26]

Nor is law always necessarily prescriptive or prohibitive in its aims and effects: it can also be 'used to give force to arguments within a considerably more fluid process of dispute and settlement'.[27] Claire Hawes has further contended in an important unpublished paper that the principles, structures and values shaping and defining political relationships in later medieval Scotland included the law. Indeed, law can be seen, as we ourselves will argue further below, as part of the constraints on political action that Hawes characterises as the 'common knowledge' generated in the 'public domain' constituted by the performance of 'legal rituals'.[28] This includes, not only the public proclamation of new law and the public penalisation (and exoneration) of suspect persons discussed by Hawes, but also, we suggest, the law as commonly applied in regularly recurring non-criminal settings and

---

[26] Hudson, J., *The Oxford History of the Laws of England Volume II 871–1216* (Oxford, 2012), p. 4.

[27] Ibid.

[28] Hawes, C., 'Reassessing the Political Community: Politics and the Public Domain in Fifteenth-Century Scotland', unpublished paper delivered at the Colloquium on *Legal Culture in Medieval and Early Modern Scotland*, held on 16–17 December 2019. An earlier version was delivered at the Scottish Legal History Group meeting on 1 October 2016. Gordon, 'Critical Legal Histories', pp. 95–96, comments that 'cultural anthropology of this kind' is 'potentially one of the most exciting and fruitful sources of new insights about law', while lamenting its under-development in legal history scholarship.

the processes of civil litigation, especially in disputes over the ownership and possession of land.

Another important idea raised by recent writing on late medieval England is that of 'common legalities', 'widespread practices aimed at producing explicitly legal effects'.[29] While the concept has been deployed primarily in the context of law as a way of understanding non-elite society in England, it will be suggested in this book that it can also be used to understand the elite society of land-owners and nobility in Scotland. They too went through certain acts and actions in and (more often) out of court – marriage, grants of land and security for debt, the creation of other written agreements, the use of standard forms of process and documentation – which were designed to have long-term effects in ways that went beyond the parties and their immediate social (and political) situations. In this way, the law was 'bound into a wider ethic of associational life', part of the way individuals moved in the course of living together.[30]

Law has also to deal with social and political dislocations and even shocks resulting from what might be unanticipated or unexpected incidents of life in general or simple mishaps, rather than from the pursuit of any participant's political advantage or other objectives. An accident killed James II himself, aged just 29,[31] as another had befallen his predecessor, Alexander III, in 1286. In each case a child under 10 years old was left as the heir to the throne. How was the kingdom to be led meantime? The question became even more acute when a king, whether minor or adult, was absent long term from his kingdom, as with David II and James I. Again, when royal marriage had yet to produce an heir, or had not produced the male heir which was the preferred outcome, how might plans be laid to cover all the contingencies that might arise? At the other end of life, kings like Robert II and Robert III in their relative old age became physically and perhaps mentally unable to discharge the twin burdens of kingship, defence of the realm and the administration of law and justice. In this situation too arose questions of how the lack of an effective king might be handled and the stability and good governance of the kingdom

---

[29] Johnston, T., *Law in Common: Legal Cultures in Late-Medieval England* (Oxford, 2020), p. 7.
[30] Ibid., p. 270.
[31] McGladdery, *James II*, pp. 202–03.

maintained. The law, we will argue, provided at least some of the answers in these kinds of case.

The Law

The law in operation in medieval Scotland was a combination of the secular, resting ultimately on the authority of the king, and the ecclesiastical, based upon the spiritual authority of the Church headed by the pope. The most significant element for the purposes of this book was the secular law about landholding and succession to land, relating to the inevitable fact of death and the need for orderly transmission of property to the survivors of any deceased person, especially land. At the social levels with which we will be mainly concerned, land was typically held by way of grant from a superior in return for service. That service might be military but by the fourteenth century was most often either financial or nominal.[32] The ultimate superior was the king. While the hackneyed image of the feudal pyramid descending from the king at the apex to the mass of the people at the base does not reflect all social or political realities, we will see in what follows that tenurial structures had by no means lost all significance in the later middle ages.

When a landholder died, the successor would generally be the firstborn legitimate son.[33] With twin sons, the first to be born was to be preferred for the purposes of inheritance, as with James, ninth earl of Douglas, against his twin Archibald, earl of Moray, in 1452.[34] But James II became king in 1437 because his elder twin Alexander failed to survive much beyond birth.[35] If a deceased landholder had no surviving offspring, the inheritance passed to collaterals: the next youngest brother first, or to sisters where there was no such brother.[36] In the absence of a son, the land would

---

[32] Grant, 'Service and Tenure', pp. 149–61.
[33] On succession, see Sellar, W.D.H., 'Succession Law in Scotland – A Historical Perspective', in Reid, K.G.C., de Waal, M., and Zimmermann, R., (eds), *Exploring the Law of Succession: Studies National, Historical and Comparative*, (Edinburgh, 2007), pp. 49–66, especially 51–57.
[34] *RMS*, ii, no. 301. See further text accompanying note 112 below.
[35] *Chron Bower*, viii, p. 262.
[36] See Irvine Smith, J., 'Succession', in Paton, G.C.H., (ed.), *An Introduction to Scottish Legal History*, (Edinburgh, 1958) [*ISLH*], pp. 208–21, 209–10.

pass to any legitimate daughters to be partitioned between them should there be more than one. But any title of honour held by the father, such as earl or baron, would in such circumstances normally pass to the eldest of the daughters;[37] titles, including that of the monarch, were indivisible, while the Great Cause of 1290–96 giving John Balliol the kingship of the Scots, also established that the kingdom itself was an indivisible unity.[38]

These examples apart, female inheritance held at least two risks: division of the land for multiple daughters, and, with only one daughter, it being carried away into another family or kindred in the event of her marriage. Hence the development of the tailzie or entail, the grant which displaced the ordinary rules of succession by defining in advance a sequence of inheritance in which only a male would take. This also manifests the freedom which a current landholder had to deal with his land, including its transfer to others as well as the definition of its future inheritance, at least if he got the consent and confirmation of his superior to what he wanted to do. A landholder may also have had greater freedom to deal with the land he himself acquired (conquest) rather than inherited (heritage); it was not uncommon, for example, to grant such conquest lands to younger sons.[39]

Succession to the Crown itself in the period covered by this book was governed by a tailzie established by Parliamentary statute passed in 1373 under Robert II (1370–90).[40] The statute sought 'to avoid as far as possible

---

[37] *The Court Book of the Barony of Carnwath 1523–1542*, ed. Dickinson, W.C. (Edinburgh, 1937), introduction, pp. xxxi–vi.

[38] *Edward I and the Throne of Scotland 1290–1296: An Edition of the Record Sources for the Great Cause*, eds Stones, E.L.G. and Simpson, G.G. (Glasgow, 1978).

[39] See *Regiam Majestatem* Book II title 17 (*APS*, i, 613; Stair Society vol 9, II, 20); Craig, *Jus Feudale*, 1.10.26 (London, 1655, p. 59; Leiden, 1716, p. 105; Edinburgh, 1732, p. 79; Clyde translation 1933, i, p. 164; Stair Society vol 64, pp. 258–9). For a contemporary example of use of this term, see *Auchinleck Chronicle*, f 117r (McGladdery, *James II*, p. 267): 'Item that samyn moneth and yere [*i.e. May 1454*] Sir George of Crechtoun resignit all his conquest lands in the kingis handis and maid him his aire'. Although this triggered a rebellion by George's heir James it seems that the former's action was not illegal.

[40] *RPS* 1373/3. A valuable discussion of the background to the 1373 Act is Penman, M., '*Diffinicione successionis ad regnum Scottorum*: Royal Succession

the uncertainty of the succession and the evil and harm which happens and has happened in very many places, kingdoms and regions in past times from the succession of female heirs'. It provided for succession through the male lines of the king's six legitimate sons, starting with the eldest and providing for a move to the next male line upon the failure of male heirs in the first. By the time of James II's accession in 1437, however, he was the lone surviving descendant of Robert II in the direct male line, raising the question of who was to succeed him should he die without a male heir; a real possibility, given that he himself was not yet seven years old, and childhood was a vulnerable time even in otherwise favourable political conditions. The 1373 tailzie provided that upon such total failure of male heirs the succession would open to females; but who was that to be?

In October 1448 the king's eldest surviving sister, Isabella, and her husband, Francis, duke of Brittany, who had married in 1442, were recognised by treaty with the king of Scots as his heirs-presumptive should he die childless.[41] There were five other sisters, of whom the oldest, Margaret, was born in 1424, while the others in order of birth (although the precise dates are unknown) were Isabella, Joanna, Eleanor, Mary and Annabella.[42] Margaret married the Dauphin of France in 1436, but died in 1445 without issue of the marriage.[43] Judging from oblique references in the negotiations for that French marriage,[44] Margaret had at least two other sisters by July 1428, i.e. Isabella and Joanna, both of whom would therefore have been older than James II. Joanna, who was betrothed to the earl of Angus

---

in Scotland in the Later Middle Ages', in Lechaud, F. and Penman, M., (eds), *Making and Breaking the Rules: Succession in Medieval Europe, c.1000-c.1600* (Turnhout, 2008), pp. 43–59.

[41] NRS: SP7/13/1.

[42] Downie, F., *'She is but a woman': Queenship in Scotland 1424–1463* (Edinburgh, 2006) [Downie, *Queenship*], pp. 125–26. See also Downie, F., "'La voie quelle menace tenir': Annabella Stewart, Scotland, and the European Marriage Market, 1444–56', *Scottish Historical Review* lxxviii (1999), pp. 170–91; also Laing, D., 'Historical Notices of the Family of King James the First of Scotland, chiefly from information communicated by John Riddell, Esq, Advocate', *Proceedings of the Society of Antiquaries of Scotland* 3 (1862), pp. 88–101.

[43] McGladdery, *James II*, pp. 72, 206 note 56.

[44] Downie, *Queenship*, p. 38.

in 1440, remained unmarried despite living at the French king's court from 1448 to 1457, when she returned to Scotland to marry the earl of Morton. There may have been a view before the birth of a male heir in 1452 that the king's sisters, as potential heirs to the Crown, should not become close to members of the domestic nobility. That potential to inherit the Crown may also have made the king's sisters more attractive propositions in the marriage market for the upper echelons of European royalty and aristocracy.

Despite the recognition of Isabella's claim in 1448, there might still have been an argument, founded on the principle that succession always descends where it can,[45] that the oldest of the king's three younger sisters (Eleanor) was to be preferred against either Isabella or Joanna. In 1448, Eleanor too acquired a powerful husband in Duke Sigismund the Rich of Austria-Tyrol, who might have wished to push her claim to the Scottish Crown had an opportunity arisen. Isabella lived until c.1495, however, while Eleanor died in 1480. In 1444, it should be noted, their younger sister Mary married Wolfaert van Borselen, son and heir of Henry, lord of Veere, Sandenburg, Flushing, Westkapelle, Domburg and Bronwershaven, admiral to Philip, duke of Burgundy. Wolfaert's naming as earl of Buchan upon this marriage is perhaps of some significance in the context of the royal succession.[46] Also in 1444 Annabella, youngest of all the king's sisters, was betrothed to Louis, count of Geneva, second son of the duke of Savoy. But the marriage never took place, and the betrothal was annulled in 1456. Annabella did not return to Scotland until 1457, when she married the son of the king's lieutenant in the north, the earl of Huntly.[47] By then, there was no further cause for doubt on the question of the Scottish succession, however, as the king and his wife, Mary of Gueldres, had begun to produce children: a daughter (Mary) in 1451, whose claim would have defeated those of any of her aunts; and then a male heir (later James III) in May 1452.

---

[45] Sellar, 'Succession Law', p. 53.
[46] On the royal prerogative to create earls, see below, text accompanying notes 76–80.
[47] Downie, 'Annabella Stewart', passim. On Huntly as king's lieutenant in the north see further Chapter 3 below text accompanying note 120.

LAW, LORDSHIP AND TENURE: THE FALL OF THE BLACK DOUGLASES

The Kings of Scots and their relations 1370-1460

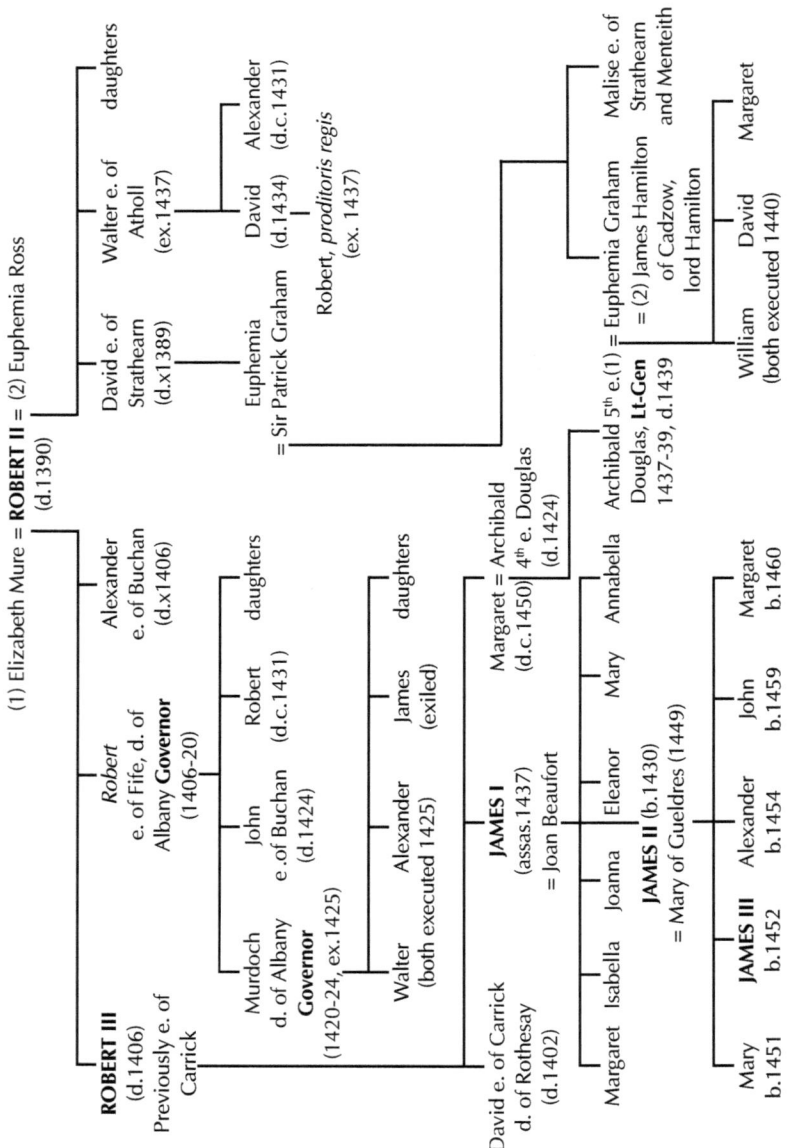

CHAPTER ONE: INTRODUCTION

Upon a non-royal landholder's death, the incoming heir had to be identified through a process of service begun by brieve of inquest, a written royal command addressed to the sheriff of the area where the lands lay, requiring him to hold an inquiry on the matter through an inquest (or jury) of locals.[48] While the process was primarily inquisitorial, it could become contentious where the heir's identity was uncertain; and there was a procedure by which the king's council could strike down an inquest's decision for error.[49] A well-known example is a decision in 1457 overturning in the interests of the king a 1438 verdict in a case about the lands of the earldom of Mar.[50] The case has been said to represent a 'perversion of the procedure';[51] but actually, whatever the merits of the actual decision, it shows the king pursuing a disputed matter through the forms of the law, while the case for his opponent, Robert Erskine, was far from clear-cut.[52]

Once identified, the heir would generally be liable to make some payment or render (casualty) to the superior, in order then to be entered into the land (or infeft) by the latter by the giving of sasine, the handing over to the entering heir of symbols of the land being taken up.[52a] Just as with inheritance tax today, these liabilities were an incentive to avoid transfer through inheritance if possible. One device to this end was to make a grant to one's heir while still alive but reserving what was known as the *liberum tenementum* (frank tenement in Scots) for the remainder of the grantor's life. He was thus able to continue much as before, while the heir had the comfort of knowing there would be no relief payable on his ancestor's death.[53] Grants in blench ferme (i.e. for some purely token or symbolic return, commonly only if requested by the superior) were often a means by which the grantor waived his entitlement to the casualties in advance,

---

[48] *Scottish Formularies*, A22, E11, B51-B55, TCa5, La1.
[49] Willock, I.D., *The Origins and Development of the Jury in Scotland* (Edinburgh, 1966), pp. 234–43.
[50] *AB III*, iv, pp. 205–13.
[51] Willock, *Jury*, p. 234; see also Macdougall, N.A.T., *James III*, 2nd edn (Edinburgh, 2009), p. 21; McGladdery, *James II*, pp. 190–91.
[52] See Borthwick, A.R., 'The King, Council and Councillors in Scotland, c.1430–1460', 2 vols (Edinburgh University PhD, 1989) [Borthwick, 'Council'], vol 1, pp. 87–91, 210–18.
[52a] See further Simpson, A. R. C., 'Earth and Stone: History, Law and Land through the Lens of Sasine', in Combe, M. M., Glass, J. and Tindley, A., (eds), *Land Reform in Scotland: History, Law and Policy* (Edinburgh, 2020), pp. 113-53, especially at 113-26.
[53] Dickinson, W.C., 'Freehold in Scots Law', *Juridical Review* 57 (1945), pp. 135–51.

15

frequently as a mark of especial gratitude to, and favour of, the grantee.[54] While at first sight this might seem inconsistent with the superior's long-term interests, it may have been balanced by that party's power to impose a non-entry fine if, when the time came, the grantee's heir took too long to seek infeftment from him.[55] The death of a landholder who was also a superior triggered the need of those who had held of him to seek confirmation of their titles with the incoming heir, possibly becoming liable to another relief in the process.

Another key point in succession law was that bastards – children born of parents not married to each other – could not inherit land or titles.[56] This did not however prevent them from receiving land and titles in other ways from their parents (usually the father, in practice) or, indeed, others. The status of bastardy – or to put it another way, the question of legitimacy – was fundamentally dependent on the law of marriage, laid down and controlled by the Church. Marriage was easy, constituted by the parties' exchange of present consent thereto (*sponsalia per verba de praesenti*), whether or not in the face of the Church or with parental consent; or by a promise of future marriage followed by copulation (*sponsalia per verba de futuro subsequente copula*).[57] But in land-owning society marriage was not generally about affective relationships (incidentally explaining something of the prevalence of bastardy) but rather

---

[54] Grant, 'Service and Tenure', pp. 157, 160–61.

[55] Nicholson, R., 'Feudal Developments in Late Medieval Scotland', *Juridical Review* 18 (1973), pp. 1–21, 19–20; Madden, C., 'Royal Treatment of Feudal Casualties in Late Medieval Scotland', *Scottish Historical Review* lv (1976), pp. 172–94, 181–84.

[56] See generally Grant, A., 'Royal and Magnate Bastards in the Later Middle Ages: The View from Scotland', in Bousmar, É., Marchandisse, A., Masson, C. and Schnerb, B., (eds), *La bâtardise et l'exercice du pouvoir (XIIIe–début XVIe siècle)* (Lille, 2015), pp. 313–67 [Grant, 'Bastards']; Marshall, S., *Illegitimacy in Medieval Scotland 1100-1500* (Woodbridge, 2021).

[57] *ISLH*, pp. 71–74; see also Parker, H., '"In all gudly haste': The Formation of Marriage in Scotland, c.1350–1600' (University of Guelph PhD, 2012), especially chapter 2; Helmholz, R.H., 'The Medieval Canon Law in Scotland: Marriage and Divorce', in Godfrey, A.M., (ed.), *Miscellany VIII* (Edinburgh, 2020), pp. 95–112. Cohabitation with habit and repute of marriage was evidence of an exchange of marital consent, not an independent form of constituting marriage. See further Sellar, W.D.H., 'Marriage by Cohabitation with Habit and Repute: Review and Requiem?', in Carey Miller, D.L. and Meyers, D.W., (eds), *Comparative and Historical Essays in Scots Law: A Tribute to Professor Sir Thomas Smith QC* (Edinburgh, 1992), pp. 117–36.

about the creation of alliances and the control of land.⁵⁸ The man who married a land-owning wife acquired a title to and control of her lands which, however, expired on her death unless a child was born alive to the couple, in which case the husband's title lasted for his rather than the wife's life (courtesy). But the lands would ultimately pass to the wife's heirs. Not quite equally, the wife who married and survived a land-owning husband was entitled to life enjoyment of a third (terce) of her deceased spouse's land, which third went to his heir only on her death. Again these rules might be evaded: for example, by a grant to husband and wife jointly (conjunct infeftment) and the longer liver of the two, often linked with provisions for the inheritance of the children begotten by the couple (frequently the males only), as distinct from any other legitimate issue either party might have by virtue of previous or later marriages.

There were other important rules on the legal capacity of persons. An heir under the age of 21 was said to be in minority, or non-age, and capable of owning but not of dealing with the inherited property. The superior of the land held for military service was entitled to hold it in ward until the majority of the heir. Wardship enabled the superior to administer the property and treat it as his own so long as his acts did not prejudice the inheritance. With other tenures legal processes existed for the determination of who should be tutor of the minor and his lands; usually the nearest agnate (male blood relative) aged 25 or over, or some other person able to look after another's property properly.⁵⁹ Once the heir reached majority at 21 (or 'full age'), he had four more years (the *quadriennium utile*) to review and strike down the prejudicial acts of those who had managed his minority. 25 was therefore the 'perfect age' in the sense that thereafter the heir was not only fully capable of self-management, but also completely bound by what he had not previously denounced.

The age of marriage was less demanding than that of landownership, however: puberty (14 for boys, 12 for girls), with the further possibility of marriage at a still earlier age *si malitia suppleat aetatem* (malice supplies age, i.e. parties' wicked intent might overcome their youthful incapacity), or if the couple homologated their union after reaching the requisite ages.⁶⁰

---

⁵⁸ See Parker, H., 'Family, Finance and Free Will: Marriage Contracts in Scotland, c.1380–1500', *Scottish Archives* 18 (2012), pp. 10–24.
⁵⁹ *Scottish Formularies*, A32-3; E15, 28, 58; B65, 66, 75, 78, 79; TCa12-14; La5.
⁶⁰ *ISLH*, p. 75.

The pope might grant relief from other limits upon marriage, such as the parties being within the forbidden degrees of consanguinity of affinity. The papal dispensation which enabled James, ninth earl of Douglas, to marry the widow of his dead brother, William the eighth earl, in 1453 narrated how the latter had contracted marriage with her *per verba de praesenti* although she was related to him in the second and third degrees of kindred and was below the marriageable age and her twelfth year but not ignorant of the relationship. These pre-dispensation defects were not cured by William's attempt at consummation of a marriage which, however, had no legal existence at the time.⁶¹ The marriage of first cousins once removed William and Margaret had therefore also required a papal dispensation, granted on 24 July 1444, quite possibly some time after the parties' initial exchange of consent.⁶² And of course, as this narrative confirms, medieval teenagers might have sexual relations in or out of marriage, with children of their own as a possible consequence (although not in the case of William

---

⁶¹ *CPR*, x, 130 (27 February 1453). On Earl James' un-canonical marriage to his dead brother's widow, see too *The History and Cronicles of Scotland by Robert Lindesay of Pitscottie*, ed. Mackay, A.J.G., 3 vols (Edinburgh, 1899), i, p. 101 ('Lord Douglas send to the paipe for ane dispensatioun to marie his brotheris wyfe quhome ane great part of the landis fell throw deceis of hir husband besyde the landis that apperteinit to hir in herietage quhilk he could be na maner of way obtein and thairfoir withtout law or ony respect to god or goode conscience he tuik and marieit his brotheris wife to the effect forsaid').

⁶² For the dispensation of 24 July 1444 for William and Margaret, 'to preserve peace and concord amongst the couple's parents, kindred and friends', see *CSSR*, iv, no. 1045 and *CPR*, ix, 467. Assuming the supplication was made after the seventh earl's death any parental discord must have been between his widow Beatrix Sinclair and Margaret's mother Euphemia Graham (who had remarried in 1441 with Sir James Hamilton of Cadzow, soon to become the first Lord Hamilton). The dispensation also incidentally narrated that the couple were 'said to be the greatest nobles and barons of the whole kingdom of Scotland.' A much later story that Earl William had gone through a ceremony of marriage with Margaret before their papal dispensation had been received is narrated in *David Hume of Godscroft's The History of the House of Douglas*, ed. Reid, D., 2 vols (Edinburgh, 1996), ii, pp. 346–47. See further Sellar, W.D.H., 'Marriage, Divorce and the Forbidden Degrees: Canon Law and Scots Law', in Osborough, W.N., (ed.), *Explorations in Law and History: Irish Legal History Society Discourses, 1988–1994* (Blackrock, 1995), pp. 59–82.

and Margaret).[63] We shall see a number of examples of these kinds of possibility in what follows.

All this, it should be emphasised, was mundane, everyday law, known and followed throughout the later medieval period, and as such 'common knowledge', in Hawes' terminology.[64] It underlies the vast bulk of the documentation which is the basis of our knowledge of landed society in medieval Scotland. Like its equivalents today, it was capable of being used and applied mechanistically and without any dispute arising except, perhaps, about the amount of time and laborious documentation involved. There were means of evading some of the rules, such as conjunct infeftment of husband and wife together with a tailzie in favour of the male children begotten between them. But again like its equivalents today each aspect of the process did generally embrace the interests of more than one person at a time – notably the superior and the person holding land of him, perhaps especially when one or other of them was a minor – and potential for conflict arose whenever these interests clashed.

While judicial process was also often mechanistic, as for instance in the service of uncontested heirs or the appointment of tutors, it was further available for the resolution of disputes. Long before the fifteenth century, forms of action existed for typical cases about land, which mostly arose in relation to claims about possession and inheritance. In particular the brieve of mortancestry, which was the starting point for the cases examined in Chapters 4 and 5 below, was an action in the court of the justiciar, brought where the pursuer claimed to be the lawful and nearest heir of either a parent, uncle, aunt, sibling or grandparent who had died vest and in sasine as of fee (i.e. heritably) of certain lands which, however, were now being held by the defender. The amount of time which might be needed to go back to the title of, in particular, grandparents partly explains why the mortancestry assize had to consist of 'older' men, whose memories could be expected to reach sufficiently far into the past.[65]

---

[63] See further on the whole subject of child marriage Parker, H., "'At thair perfect age': Elite Child Betrothal and Parental Control, 1430–1560', in Nugent, J. and Ewan E., (eds), *Children and Youth in Premodern Scotland* (Woodbridge, 2015), pp. 173–86.

[64] See above, text accompanying note 28.

[65] MacQueen, H.L., *Common Law and Feudal Society in Medieval Scotland* (Edinburgh, 1993, repr 2016) [MacQueen, *CLFS*], p. 168; *Scottish Formularies*, A20, B106, TCa19; see also ibid., La27, La38.

A final introductory point is that laws, legal documents and courts indicate the presence of lawyers, or at least of people knowledgeable in the law. They might be skilled in the production of documents that would achieve their intended legal effects. Or they might be articulate and persuasive in the presentation of arguments about procedure, the significance of evidence oral as well as written, and the application of the law to any contested set of facts. In our case studies we can see parties representing themselves, but also others using procurators and pre- or pro-locutors, some of them churchmen but many others being of the laity.[66] While it is open to debate whether such advocates were professional lawyers in the sense of advocacy being their primary means of earning a living, it can scarcely be doubted that we must see as such the notaries who drew up the instruments through which we know about the cases today.[67] Notaries public, who had multiplied in Scotland since 1300, were appointed by imperial or apostolic (i.e. papal) authority to produce documents which by their style, witnessing by others and application of the notary's distinctive sign manual could thereafter be taken as authentic records, whether that was of an event which had occurred (such as the proceedings and decision of a court or in an arbitration) or of the content of another document produced for the purpose before the notary. The notarial instrument was not necessarily conclusive proof, but the burden of disproving what it appeared to evidence would lie on the other side of the argument. This is a crucial point in the present work.

Chapter 2 of this book looks first at the law's answers to the problem of the incapable king, suggesting that these assist considerably in understanding

---

[66] On this terminology see Finlay, J., *Men of Law in Pre-Reformation Scotland* (East Linton, 2000), pp. 9–11; MacQueen, *CLFS*, p. 76; Simpson, A., 'Men of Law in the Aberdeen Council Register? A Preliminary Study, circa 1450–1460' *Juridical Review* (2019), pp. 136–59 [Simpson, 'Men of Law']; Simpson, A.R.C., 'Andrew Alanson: man of law in the Aberdeen Council Register, c.1440-c.1475?', in Armstrong, J.W. and Frankot, E., (eds), *Cultures of Law in Urban Northern Europe: Scotland and Its Neighbours c.1350-c.1650* (London, 2020), ch 13. See further Borthwick, 'Council', pp. 238 note 137, 288–301, 309 note 124.

[67] On notaries, see Scott, W., 'William Cranston, Notary Public c.1395 to 1425, and Some Contemporaries', in MacQueen, H.L., (ed.), *Miscellany VII* (Edinburgh, 2015), pp. 125–32 [Scott, 'William Cranston, Notary Public']; Durkan, J., 'The Early Scottish Notary', in Cowan, I.B. and Shaw, D., (eds), *The Renaissance and Reformation in Scotland: Essays in Honour of Gordon Donaldson* (Edinburgh, 1983), pp. 22–40; and Simpson, 'Men of Law', pp. 147–48.

what happened during the long minority of James II (from 1437 to 1449). Two case studies in Chapters 4 and 5 illustrate issues about landholding, orderly succession to land and mechanisms for the resolution of disputes, whether by courts or arbitrators. Both parts are held together, however, in their provision of vital context for the relationship of the earls of Douglas, first with the kings of Scots from 1400 to 1455, and second with those who held land of the earls in the same period. New light is thereby thrown upon the long lead-up to the fall of the house of Douglas in 1455, explored in depth in Chapter 3, and its aftermath. This may also tell us something about the question with which we began, the reasons behind the killing of the eighth earl by James II in 1452.

The Black Douglases

It is helpful to the discussions which form the main substance of this book to give a brief account of the so-called 'Black' Douglases and their rise to prominence as the most powerful family below the Crown in the first half of the fifteenth century.[68] Their fortunes were based initially upon the rewards for services rendered to King Robert I (1306–29) in his successful struggle to maintain Scottish independence from England. The king's companion, Sir James Douglas ('the Good Sir James'), died in 1330. His heir, William, was killed in 1333 at the battle of Halidon Hill and left no issue. Sir James did, however, have an illegitimate son, Archibald, who would live until 1400 and be known as Archibald 'the Grim'. Also killed at Halidon was Sir James' half-brother, Archibald, then guardian of the kingdom; but he did leave an heir in William.

William became lord of Douglas upon the resignation in 1342 of Hugh 'the Dull', brother of the Good Sir James and Archibald, but a priest. This resignation was accompanied by a tailzie, granted by David II on 29 May, over the lands formerly pertaining to the Good Sir James, in favour of William lord of Douglas and the lawful heirs male of his body, whom failing (after various other possibilities) Archibald 'the Grim' (despite his illegitimacy).[69]

---

[68] See generally Brown, M., *The Black Douglases: War and Lordship in Late Medieval Scotland 1300–1455* (East Linton, 1998) [Brown, *Black Douglases*]; also McGladdery, C., 'The Black Douglases, 1369–1455', in Oram, R.D. and Stell, G.P., (eds), *Lordship and Architecture in Medieval and Renaissance Scotland* (Edinburgh, 2005), pp. 161–87.

[69] *RRS*, vi, no. 51.

In 1354 the king erected into a regality all the lands which William lord of Douglas had received from his father Archibald and from the Good Sir James via Hugh the Dull.[70] The 1342 tailzie and the 1354 grant of regality not only unified the succession to and administration of the Douglas estates at the relevant times, but would also be crucial documents in some of the later events discussed in this book.

The Black Douglas earls of Douglas

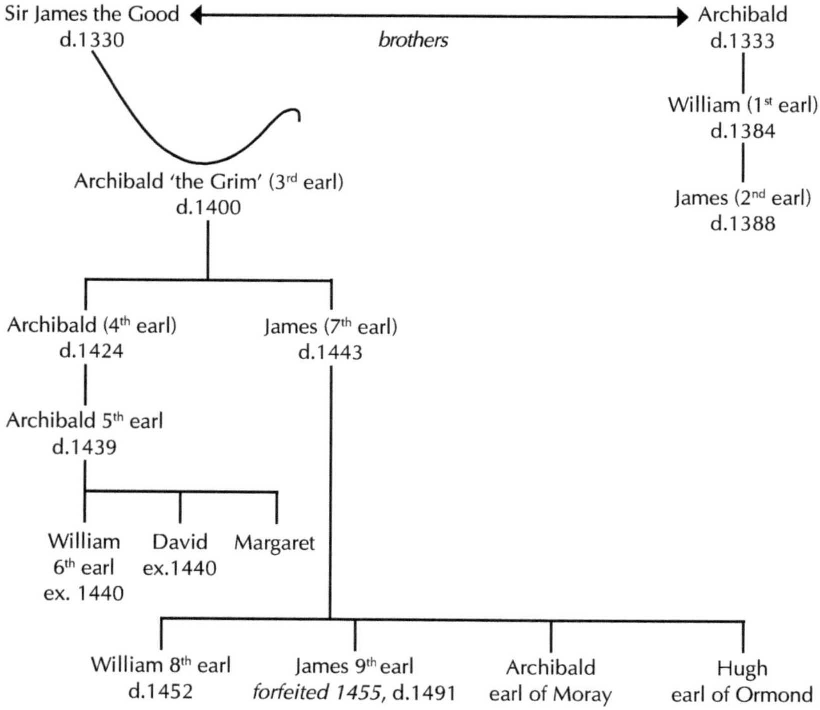

```
Sir James the Good  ←———— brothers ————→  Archibald
    d.1330                                  d.1333
                                              |
                                         William (1st earl)
                                            d.1384
                                              |
      Archibald 'the Grim' (3rd earl)    James (2nd earl)
              d.1400                        d.1388
        ┌───────────┴───────────┐
  Archibald (4th earl)     James (7th earl)
       d.1424                 d.1443
         |
  Archibald 5th earl
       d.1439
    ┌────┬────┬────┐
 William  David  Margaret
 6th earl ex.1440
 ex. 1440

   ┌──────────────┬──────────────┬──────────────┐
 William 8th earl  James 9th earl   Archibald        Hugh
     d.1452      forfeited 1455, d.1491  earl of Moray  earl of Ormond
```

Symbol indicating illegitimate birth

---

[70] *RMS*, i, app 1, no. 123.

CHAPTER ONE: INTRODUCTION

In 1358 William was created the first earl of Douglas,[71] and held the earldom until his death in 1384. The creation was significant in that the title was not linked to any particular territory. William was succeeded as earl in 1384 by his son, James, who was, however, killed at the battle of Otterburn in 1388 and left no heir, male or otherwise. It was at this point that the tailzie of 1342 came into play in helping Archibald the Grim to acquire the lands of the Douglas earldom, albeit not without dispute from Sir Malcolm Drummond, the husband of Earl James' sister Isabella (already countess of Mar in her own right by descent from her mother). The decision of Parliament in Archibald's favour on 7 April 1389 has been criticised as of at best dubious legality.[72] But Parliament actually said nothing about the title of earl, which Archibald had been using since January.[73] Rather, in a grand inquest procedure in the presence *inter alia* of the sheriffs in whose bailiaries the lands in question lay, Parliament held Archibald to be entitled to them all in terms of the tailzie. The outcomes of brieve of inquest processes previously raised by Sir Malcolm Drummond, which had presumably gone the other way, were annulled.[74] Any alternative claims, said Parliament, were to be pursued by way of pleadable brieve rather than by brieve of inquest.[75] As a matter of the construction of the 1342 tailzie, the conclusion in favour of Archibald the Grim was indubitably correct.

The tailzie of course pre-dated the earldom and Archibald's claim to the title of earl as distinct from the earldom lands was certainly controversial at the time because of his bastard status.[76] Its ultimate success may be explicable because the king had some sort of prerogative to appoint earls, which was not

---

[71] *RMS*, i, app 2, no. 1222.
[72] See e.g. Boardman, S., *The Early Stewart Kings: Robert II and Robert III 1371–1406* (East Linton, 1996) [Boardman, *Early Stewart Kings*], p. 166; Brown, *Black Douglases*, pp. 82–87 (although the suggestion that the notarial transumption of the tailzie by Archibald in 1392 shows that 'doubts were still being raised about its validity' is untenable; the opposite is more likely the case); Grant, 'Bastards', pp. 333–34.
[73] Grant, 'Bastards', p. 333 note 112.
[74] *RPS* 1389/3/8; see also *RPS* 1389/3/9-11.
[75] *RPS* 1389/3/14. This appears to be an invocation of the rule that no-one was to be put out of their heritage except through process begun by pleadable brieve, for which see MacQueen, *CLFS*, ch 4.
[76] See Grant, 'Bastards', p. 334, quoting the contemporary Froissart, J., *Ouevres*, ed. Kervyn de Lettehove, J.C.M.B., t 13 (Brussels, 1871), p. 256.

entirely tied down by the ordinary rules of succession.[77] Alexander Grant has argued persuasively that 'royal or official approval must have been required before a man could become an earl', although such approval was more or less automatic where the earldom was acquired by inheritance.[78] Approval was made manifest by way of a public ceremony of 'belting' by the king. A charter of creation was unnecessary unless there was also a grant of lands as well as the title. Women might become countesses as the heirs of earls, but well before the end of the fourteenth century their husbands did not generally become earls.[79] So even if Isabella of Mar had been recognised as countess of Douglas her husband, Malcolm Drummond, would probably have been at best lord of the earldom.

No doubt in favouring Archibald the Grim over Isabella and her husband a political decision was being made, recognising the considerable power, authority, loyalty and experience of a candidate who already held at least the lands of an earldom (of Wigtown) as well as, perhaps, his leadership of the Douglas kindred following the death of Earl James and his direct descent from the heroic Good Sir James. But the only doubt there could have been as to legality was about the decision-making capacity of a king (the aged Robert II) who was under the guardianship of his second son Robert earl of Fife (whose decision it may therefore actually have been).[80] Hereafter, however, the lands covered by the tailzie were regarded as

---

[77] Note here the 1444 appointment of Wolfaert van Borselen as earl of Buchan upon his marriage to the king's sister Mary (above, text accompanying note 45).

[78] An unsuitable heir might be deprived of his earldom, to judge from the example of Malise Graham, who was denied his hereditary earldom of Strathearn by James I (although compensated with the much lesser earldom of Menteith). Malise went on to be a hostage in England for the king's ransom from 1427–1453. Donaldson, G., *Scottish Kings*, 2nd edn (London, 1977) [Donaldson, *Scottish Kings*], p. 85, suggests that Malise was 'infirm either mentally or physically'; but he survived until 1490.

[79] See Grant, A., 'The Higher Nobility in Scotland and their Estates, c.1371–1424' (University of Oxford DPhil, 1975), pp. 8–11. See also Grant, A., 'Earls and Earldoms in Late Medieval Scotland (c.1310–1460)', in Bossy, J. and Jupp, P., (eds), *Essays presented to Michael Roberts* (Belfast, 1976), pp. 24–40, 27–28; and Grant, A., 'The Development of the Scottish Peerage', *Scottish Historical Review* lvii (1978), pp. 1–27 [Grant, 'Scottish Peerage'], p. 6; Grant, *Independence and Nationhood*, pp. 122–23.

[80] See further below Chapter 2, text preceding note 27.

somehow forming the earldom's landed core with succession to the earldom going with them.

By the time he acquired the earldom of Douglas Archibald the Grim had long been married to Joanna Murray of Bothwell, who brought to him and their heirs extensive lands previously pertaining to the Murrays of Bothwell. Her identity has been disputed. Until quite recently, it was generally thought that she had somehow gained the lands through an earlier marriage to Sir Thomas Murray of Bothwell, an understanding that cast doubt on the lawfulness of Archibald's acquisition.[81] Alternative views, however, are that Sir Thomas was actually Joanna's father, and his wife a different Joanna Murray (of Drumsagard);[82] or that Archibald's Joanna was actually Sir Thomas' heir as well as his widow.[83] Either way she therefore inherited the Murray of Bothwell estates, which thereby came under Archibald's control and then descended to the Douglas heirs of that marriage. Such interpretations are to be preferred to those suggesting that the rules of inheritance were somehow bent in relation to the Bothwell estates to benefit Archibald as the king's man he undoubtedly was.[84] Either is consistent with the fact that no contemporary doubt appears to have been cast on the lawfulness of Archibald's control of the lands as Joanna's husband, or about their descent to the heirs of their marriage after his death.

In his own right Archibald also acquired a string of offices and lands, including the Wardenships of the Western and Middle Marches, the earldom of Wigtown

---

[81] *Scots Peerage*, ii, pp. 130–31; Brown, *Black Douglases*, pp. 56–57; Penman, M.A., *David II, 1329–71* (East Linton, 2004) [Penman, *David II*], pp. 270–71.

[82] For this theory, see McAndrew, B., 'Heraldic Investigations anent early Murray Genealogy', *Proceedings of the Society of Antiquaries of Scotland* 140 (2010), pp.145–64, at 154–59. The theory gains some support from the verse of *The Buke of the Howlat*, ed. Hanna, R. (Woodbridge, 2014), lines 547–59, which say that Archibald married a 'douchter' of 'ane callit Murray the riche', who was 'his deir air / Of all his tressou[r] untald, towris and townis'.

[83] This view is developed by Grant, 'Bastards', pp. 331–32 note 105. On the whole question see also Maxwell Findlater, A., 'Arms and the Man, But Which Man? A Look at Early Murray Arms', *The Double Tressure* 26 (2003), pp. 50–69 and ensuing correspondence between the author and Bruce McAndrew printed in *The Double Tressure* 27 (2004), pp. 46–51.

[84] For such views see e.g. Brown, *Black Douglases*, p. 56; Penman, *David II*, p. 270.

and its lands west of the River Cree, and Galloway between the Rivers Cree and Nith. By virtue of the latter two grants, he generally designed himself as lord of Galloway.[85] All his lands and offices were held on a hereditary basis but never tailzied. No problem for the unity of the Douglas estates resulted from this so long as the earls continued to produce male heirs to take both the tailzied and untailzied estates. Archibald the Grim was succeeded by his eldest son, another Archibald, who became fourth earl in 1400; likewise the latter's eldest son and heir (also Archibald) became fifth earl on his father's death in 1424, and he was succeeded in 1439 by his son and heir William (who was, however, a minor).

Between 1419 and 1424 both the fourth earl and his heir led large Scottish contingents in France in support of the French king against his English opponent, with the fourth earl being made duke of Touraine and lieutenant-general of the French king's army in reward for his services not long before his death at the battle of Verneuil, and his son becoming count of Longueville before succeeding to his father's duchy too.[86] But a momentous occurrence during the wars in France was the repeated refusal of the Scots forces and their leaders to comply with the orders to desist their involvement on the French side which came from their own king, James I.[87] The context was that he had been held in English captivity from 1406, and by 1419 was co-operating with the English king in efforts to hasten his own release.[88] The disobedience of

---

[85] See *RRS*, vi, no.451 and *RMS*, i, no.507. The earliest surviving seals of Archibald the Grim show, as a supporter of his arms, the figure of a standing wild man or savage, possibly representing his lordship of Galloway (Fraser, *Douglas*, ii, p. 551). This figure became a central feature of the seals of his successors as earl as well as other kin members, while under the eighth and ninth earls he was rendered as the kneeling image to be seen in the illustration on this book's cover (see Fraser, *Douglas*, ii, pp. 551-4; Laing seal casts, NRS RH17/1/247).

[86] On the French military adventures of the fourth earl and his son, see Brown, *Black Douglases*, pp. 214–23; Brown, M., 'French Alliance or English Peace? Scotland and the Last Phase of the Hundred Years War, 1415–53', in Clark, L., (ed.), *The Fifteenth Century VII: Conflicts, Consequences and the Crown in the Late Middle Ages* (Woodbridge, 2007), pp. 81–99, especially at 86–91.

[87] See Sumption, J., *Cursed Kings: The Hundred Years War IV* (London, 2015), chapters xvi–xviii.

[88] Brown, M., *James I* (Edinburgh, 1994) [Brown, *James I*], pp. 22–24; Penman, M., 'The Lion Captive: Scottish Royals as Prisoners of England, c.1070–c.1424', *Quaestiones Medii Aevi Novae* 20 (2015), pp. 413–34 [Penman, 'Lion Captive'], 428–33.

the Scots (in effect a denial of James' kingship) may account in part for the distance at which the fifth earl was kept by the king after his final return to his kingdom in 1424, despite the fourth earl having taken active and probably critical steps in 1421 and again in 1423 to procure the king's release.[89]

When the fifth earl died of the plague in 1439 (by when he was lieutenant-general of the kingdom for the minor James II[90]), he too had a minor son and heir, William. As already noted, the still-minor William and his younger brother David were executed after the 'Black Dinner' at Edinburgh in November 1440, with Malcolm Fleming meeting the same fate three days later.[91] There are indications that the trial which preceded this was presided over by the 10-year-old king himself.[92] It is also possible that the earl's great-uncle, James ('the Gross') Douglas of Balvenie, presided or was otherwise involved as justiciar (perhaps of the whole realm and not just south of Forth).[93] He was a younger son of Archibald the Grim, brother of

---

[89] The significance of the Scots' refusal to obey their king and to continue to fight for the French king as a denial of James I's kingship is discussed in Hunt, K., 'The Governorship of Robert Duke of Albany (1406–1420)', in Brown, M. and Tanner, R., (eds), *Scottish Kingship 1306–1542: Essays in Honour of Norman Macdougall* (Edinburgh, 2008), pp. 126–54 [Hunt, 'Governorship'], 137–38; Lord Sumption, 'Anglo-Scottish Relations, 1290–1513, and the Beginnings of International Law', in Godfrey, A.M., (ed.), *Miscellany VIII* (Edinburgh, 2020), pp. 1–12 at 11. See also Chapter 6 text accompanying note 45. For the efforts of the fourth earl ('an ambitious and flexible politician') to obtain King James' release from captivity, see Brown, *James I*, pp. 23, 27, 31; Brown, *Black Douglases*, pp. 219–20; Brown, 'French Alliance', pp. 88–90. For another view of the fourth earl, see Macdonald, A.J., 'Profit, Politics and Personality: War and the Later Medieval Scottish Nobility', in Brotherstone, T. and Ditchburn, D., (eds), *Freedom and Authority: Historical and Historiographical Essays presented to Grant G Simpson* (East Linton, 2000), pp. 118–30, 128–30 (recognising political acumen alongside 'gluttony' for power, money and war).

[90] See further Chapter 2 below, text accompanying notes 66–68.

[91] See text accompanying note 8 above.

[92] See the comment in the Coupar Angus MS of Bower's *Scotichronicon* that the sixth earl was executed '*apud Castrum Puellarum rege pro tribunali puero tunc decenni*' (*Chron Bower*, viii, p. 262 note l). Note also the reference in another chronicle to the trial being held before 'James the second beand Justice' (BL, Royal MS 17 DXX, f 307).

[93] The reference to the trial being held before 'James the second beand Justice' (mentioned in the preceding footnote) has also been interpreted as meaning

the fourth earl, and since 1437 earl of Avondale.[94] But it is most likely that, whoever presided, the trial took place in an assembly of the Three Estates, again exercising their supervisory role in relation to the king's business at a time of minority. The subsequent executions certainly headed off any possibility of the sixth earl becoming regent upon attaining his majority. Perhaps more significantly, they brought the earldom of Douglas itself to James the Gross by virtue, ultimately, of the 1342 royal tailzie in favour of heirs male of the lands and offices that had once pertained to the Good Sir James.[95] As the ultimate gainer from the whole episode, Earl James is thus often seen as its real instigator, manoeuvring to achieve titles and lands for himself and his heirs.

A puzzle is, however, that if the sixth earl's crime was any form of treason, the full pains of that crime – life and limbs of the convicted traitor at the king's pleasure, disinheritance in perpetuity and forfeiture of moveables – were not exacted against the earl's estates, allowing them to pass instead to James the Gross as the lawful heir.[96] A near-contemporary statement in a Burgundian chronicle source does declare that the great lords of the kingdom were reacting to a conspiracy between the sixth earl and his co-accused to dispossess

---

James, second earl of Douglas of that name (MacQueen, H., 'Tame Magnates? The Justiciars of Later Medieval Scotland', in Boardman, S. and Goodare, J., (eds), *Kings, Lords and Men in Scotland and Britain, 1300–1625: Essays in Honour of Jenny Wormald* (Edinburgh, 2014), pp. 93–117 [MacQueen, 'Tame Magnates?'], 106–07. But at the time of the trial James Douglas of Balvenie, earl of Avondale, had yet to become earl of Douglas.

[94] On the creation of the earldom of Avondale in 1437 (but without any more precise date), see *Joannis de Fordun Scotichronicon cum Supplementis et Continuatione Walteri Boweri Insulae Sancti Columbae Abbatis*, ed. Goodall, W. (Edinburgh, 1759), ii, p. 541). The earliest reference to Balvenie as earl of Avondale is dated 10 May 1437 (Argyll Muniments, Inveraray: Bundle 1107). The creation was therefore most likely the work of the lieutenant-general but probably the new young king gave his consent and participated in the belting of the new earl, if we may judge from the absence of any subsequent challenge to the title or its descent to the heirs of James the Gross.

[95] See text accompanying note 69 above.

[96] *Regiam Majestatem* IV, 1. The Douglas lordship of Annandale was not forfeited in 1440, however, but lapsed to the Crown of which it had been held because the original grant thereof in 1409 was to the fourth earl and the lawfully begotten heirs male of his body (*RMS*, i, no. 920); the line failed on the execution of the sixth earl.

the young king.⁹⁷ This might mean that the three accused were thought to have had some idea of wresting control of the king's person from his then custodians (the Livingstons).⁹⁸ But as noted in *Regiam Majestatem* I, 1, an exceptional feature of treason by comparison with other crimes was that it could be perpetrated by purpose (*de proposito*) as much as by deed (*pro facto*), i.e. conspiracy was enough even if no action had been taken to implement it. Nonetheless, whereas the near-contemporary Auchinleck chronicle is explicit that the assassins of James I were 'put to ded ... for tresoun', there is no such specificity in its entry on the same folio dealing with the Black Dinner executions.⁹⁹

Some significant hesitation was also apparent on the part of Chancellor Sir William Crichton (also the keeper of the castle within which the executions had taken place) before in March 1441 he issued brieves of inquest for the service of Malcolm Fleming's son and heir Robert to his father and mother's extensive lands around Scotland.¹⁰⁰ If forfeiture was under consideration as an alternative possibility, Malcolm may have been seen as the leader of any plot there might have been. The three days that elapsed from the execution of the Douglases to that of Fleming is not explained in the Auchinleck chronicle,¹⁰¹ although it is probably significant that in August 1443 Sir Alexander Livingston of Callander (head of the family with custody of the young king) purged himself upon oath in the presence of four bishops and Robert Fleming of having given any council, assistance or consent to the death and slaughter of Malcolm Fleming.¹⁰² That suggests that there might have been relevant deliberations involving others during the three-day interval. Robert had already succeeded, however, in contesting the sentence of death against his father before, first, the sheriff depute of Linlithgow, then James the Gross as justice-general south of Forth early

---

⁹⁷ Jean de Wavrin, *Recueil des Chroniques et Anchiennes Istories de la Grant Bretagne à present nommé Engleterre*, eds Hardy, W. and E.P.C.L. (London, 1864–91, repr Cambridge University Press, 2012) iv, pp. 213–14. The fourth volume of the *Chroniques* was probably produced between 1446 and 1455.

⁹⁸ On the Livingston custody of the king's person from 1439, see further Chapter 2 below, text accompanying notes 79–81, 98.

⁹⁹ *Auchinleck Chronicle*, f 121r-v (McGladdery, *James II*, p. 274).

¹⁰⁰ *Wigtown Charter Chest*, no 25.

¹⁰¹ *Auchinleck Chronicle*, f 121v (McGladdery, *James II*, p. 274).

¹⁰² *Wigtown Charter Chest*, no 29.

in 1441, and seems to have completed the process of being served as his father's heir by 1444.[103]

The finger of suspicion pointed at Earl James for his possible role in the executions of his great-nephews is thus countered somewhat by his role in the finding that Malcolm Fleming's death had been unlawful. It is hard to see how that was possible if he had presided over the latter's conviction with the Douglas brothers. Nothing similar to the Fleming inquest survives in connection with the deaths of the sixth earl and his brother. But the possibility that a general miscarriage of justice in relation to all three convicted men was subsequently recognised should not be altogether ruled out. This would explain the non-forfeiture of the Douglas as well as the Fleming estates as well as, perhaps, the absence now of any record of the trial proceedings. The record of a false judgement, especially one of treason, might well have been destroyed in a ritual making clear the absence of any taint that it would otherwise cast in future. We will see that something similar may have happened in the 1450s when Sir Alexander Livingston, convicted of treason and forfeited with others of his kindred in 1449–50 in a trial of which no record now survives, was subsequently pardoned by the king and restored to his lands (if not his offices).[104]

The Black Dinner executions introduced issues about female succession for the first time in the Douglas line descended from Archibald the Grim.[105] The general heir was the fifth earl's daughter Margaret, and the untailzied estates thus fell to her and became separated from the earldom and its lands, which were now in the hands of James the Gross. Upon the latter's death in 1443, he was succeeded by his still-minor eldest son, William the eighth earl, who

---

[103] For all the foregoing see *Wigtown Charter Chest*, nos 26–28.

[104] See further Chapter 2 below, text accompanying notes 153–58. For an example of the destruction of the record of a rescinded court judgement in 1380, see *Moray Reg* no 159. *Auchinleck Chronicle*, f 122r-v (McGladdery, *James II*, p. 275) notes that the Livingstons were 'forfaltit' and that Alexander's son and heir James was 'put to deid' along with his cousin 'Robyne' (Robert) 'baith togidder on [Edinburgh] castellhill their heidis striking of'. McGladdery, *James II*, p. 219, points out that it was Alexander's younger son Alexander, not James, who was executed.

[105] There had of course been an issue about the possibility of female succession (by Isabella, countess of Mar) on the death of her brother Earl James in 1388.

would become the victim of James II's homicidal attack in 1452. William was succeeded by his brother, James, who became the ninth and last earl of Douglas: his earldom and he were forfeited in June 1455 after an unsuccessful uprising against the king earlier that year.[106]

As we have already seen, Earl William and Earl James each and successively married their cousin Margaret under papal dispensation as part of an effort to re-unify the Douglas estates divided by the death of her brothers, but neither marriage produced any offspring.[107] In Earl James' case a dispensation was also required to allow him to marry his dead brother's widow, her previous marriage having put him in a relationship of affinity with Margaret. Moreover, the earl had previously committed fornication with another woman within the second and third degrees of kinship with Margaret, thereby creating a further relationship of affinity requiring papal dispensation to make the marriage lawful. That any fertility difficulties suggested by the lack of offspring for either marriage lay with the two earls is supported by the issue produced by Margaret's third and final marriage, with John Stewart, earl of Atholl (half-brother of the king), while Earl James' second marriage, to Anne Holland when in exile in England after 1455, was also childless.[108]

Earl William's need to gain a papal dispensation to marry his cousin may also be part-explanation of an apparent departure from his father's anti-papal position in the schism of the Church which, after a long run-in from 1434, took place in 1439 as a result of the Council of Basle.[109] Earl James the Gross had been a prominent supporter of the conciliar movement in the Church, successfully seeking through that support to have William's younger brother, James, appointed as bishop of Aberdeen by the anti-pope Felix V in 1441, and then in 1442 (but this time unsuccessfully) translated to become bishop of St Andrews.[110] There is no sign of any support of Basle by Earl William, and from his succession as earl in 1443 he was part of a regency government

---

[106] See *RPS* 1455/6/2, 1455/6/6, and Chapter 3 below, text accompanying notes 109, 133-34.

[107] See above, text accompanying notes 61 and 62.

[108] Borthwick, A.R., 'Douglas, James, ninth earl of Douglas and third earl of Avondale c.1425–1491', *ODNB*.

[109] See generally Burns, J.H., *Scottish Churchmen and the Council of Basle* (Glasgow, 1962) [Burns, *Scottish Churchmen*].

[110] Burns, *Scottish Churchmen*, pp. 71, 78–79.

which, perhaps steered by Bishop James Kennedy of St Andrews and William Turnbull, vicar of St Giles in Edinburgh as well as keeper of the privy seal, moved steadily towards reconciliation with the pope and the reunification of the Church.[111]

After their father's death, the new earl's brother James, who had studied Arts at Cologne, gave up his ecclesiastical career (for which probably his university studies were significant preparation) and was recognised as his brother's heir-presumptive in 1447. This was by virtue of a decree of Master Nicholas de Otterburn, official of St Andrews in Lothian, interponing his court's authority to an indenture between the brothers that James was older than his twin brother, Archibald, who had been earl of Moray since 1445. The decree, which received a royal confirmation, was issued after evidence from 'certain good women' together with the brothers' mother.[112] There is nothing to suggest that this process involved anything more than a formal clarification of the facts of the matter (as distinct from, say, being an exercise in heir-switching). It may have been a precaution arising from the failure to that date of Earl William's marriage to produce any children, never mind a male heir, and to avoid any possibility of intra-familial dispute should that situation continue until the earl's death. By February 1449 James, now the Master of Douglas as his brother's heir-presumptive, and two others were facing a challenge from three Burgundian knights (led by Jacques de Lalain) in the lists at Stirling, with all six being knighted by James II before the tournament began.[113] The culmination of the brothers' renunciation of their father's position in relation to the Church would be their triumphant pilgrimage together to Rome in 1450–1 to participate in the celebration of the papal jubilee.[114]

This summary account of the fortunes of the Black Douglases from the 1320s to 1455 has not only provided important context for what follows in this book but also illustrates the operation of the common law rules about succession to

---

[111] Burns, *Scottish Churchmen*, pp. 60–85; Tanner, *LMSP*, pp. 101–07.
[112] *RMS*, ii, no. 301.
[113] See generally Borthwick, 'Douglas, James, ninth earl of Douglas and third earl of Avondale c.1425–1491'; Stevenson, K., *Chivalry and Knighthood in Scotland, 1424–1513* (Woodbridge, 2006) [Stevenson, *Chivalry and Knighthood*], pp. 52–3, 72–76.
[114] See further on the earl's pilgrimage Chapter 2 below, text accompanying notes 161–70.

land and titles in later medieval Scotland. There is no need to see these rules as being sidelined or bent in the rise of Archibald the Grim through either the Bothwell marriage or his accession to the lands of Douglas by virtue of the tailzie of 1342; or indeed in the 1447 declaration that James was the elder of the twins born to the seventh earl and his wife. With the award of the title of earl to Archibald the law of the possible may have developed to meet a situation without direct precedent, but that is what often happens in the non-legislative evolution of a customary or common law system.[115] In any event a prerogative of the king in relation to the appointment of earls was probably being exercised, but in doing so a new precedent was being set. The recognition of bastards as earls occurred in at least two other cases before the end of the reign of Robert III: in 1397 George Douglas, first earl of Angus (a son of William first earl of Douglas), and, in 1404, Alexander Stewart, earl of Mar (a son of Alexander Stewart, earl of Buchan, lord of Badenoch and so grandson of King Robert II).[116] Both came to their titles through marriage to a countess but whether they could have done so before 1389 was probably moot until then.

Where the law may perhaps have been abused was in the mysterious events surrounding the Black Dinner in 1440. Our inability to determine why the minor sixth earl and his brother were executed still leaves strong suspicions that matters were engineered by James the Gross (possibly with the assistance of William Crichton) to promote his own and his descendants' interests; suspicions that may have been shared by contemporaries outside the innermost circles of government. But we cannot tell with any absolute certainty; and

---

[115] Edward Bruce's bastard Alexander Bruce became earl of Carrick in 1333, probably under Edward Balliol's regime, although it was subsequently confirmed by Sir Alexander Douglas as Guardian of Scotland; but Bruce's death at Halidon Hill in the same year brought an end to what may well have been a situation that could only be finally settled by King David II when he attained majority. See Grant, 'Bastards', pp. 328–30.

[116] See Grant, 'Bastards', pp. 338–43; Marshall, *Illegitimacy*, 182, 185. There was perhaps room for doubt about the legitimacy of both Robert III and Alexander Stewart, earl of Buchan, as each had been born before their parents' subsequent marriage (Grant, 'Bastards', pp. 318–19, 322–24, 341; Marshall, *Illegitimacy*, 100-6); but this must be set against Scots law's general acceptance of the canon law doctrine of legitimation by subsequent marriage (Marshall, *Illegitimacy*, 26-7, 34-41, 110-6).

the declaration that Malcolm Fleming had been unlawfully killed as well as the absence of any forfeitures of the convicted men's lands raises important questions, not only about Fleming's guilt, but also about that of the Douglas brothers. The absence of any forfeiture of the executed men's estates and titles, and of any record of their trial and conviction, may instead suggest that their executions were subsequently recognised as having been miscarriages of justice. We cannot take it that the law must have been ignored, abused or bent by men interested only in acquiring land and power; instead we must use the law to analyse the evidence that we do not have alongside that we do. At the very least it can then be seen that there are important questions to be considered; and even if in the end we can only speculate about the answers to those questions, at least proper boundaries have been set within which to confine our inquiry.

Chapter Two
Regency, Council and the Earls of Douglas 1437–51

This and the following chapter consider carefully the governance of Scotland following the assassination of James I in early 1437. This provides crucial context, not only for the killing of the earl of Douglas in 1452, but also for the final fall of his house in 1455. Much of what took place in government thereafter up to the achievement of full age by James II in October 1451 has traditionally been presented as the unhappy result of factionalism amongst a nobility whose members sought power and its fruits mainly for themselves.[1] We argue, however, that a fuller understanding can be obtained through analysing what happened as the operation of regency government as it had developed in Scotland since the thirteenth century. This does not mean that the individual nobles involved in the regency always placed the general interest above their own; in particular this was probably not true of the eighth earl of Douglas. But the system had ways of holding to account those who misused the authority they enjoyed in regency governments. In Chapter 3 this will be shown in operation in the treason trial before Parliament undergone by the earl in the summer of 1451 as the king approached his legal full age. A full understanding of this event also requires analysis of the relationship between the king and the earl's predecessors stretching back to the accession of James I (also as a minor and, moreover, one in captivity in England) in 1406. It will then be seen that the

---
[1] See e.g. Tanner, *LMSP*, p. 91; McGladdery, *James II*, chs 2–4; Brown, *Black Douglases*, ch. 12.

actions of James I in relation to the earls of Douglas, especially after his return to Scotland in 1424, were not necessarily over-concerned with legalities; at least one question left by his active rule is how the king himself might be held to account for what he did. This is also a question for James II after the killing of the eighth earl. While this latter point will also be assessed in Chapter 3, the wider question of the accountability of the king in general is addressed in Chapter 6. In this chapter, however, the focus is on the principles of regency government in later medieval Scotland and, latterly, on the role played in it by the eighth earl of Douglas. We will see him emerge at the end of the minority of James II as apparently high in royal favour and widely recognised as Scotland's leading noble, until a sudden and dramatic fall upon his return from a pilgrimage to Rome that was also a diplomatic mission on the king's behalf.

Regency in Scotland before 1437

We begin with a discussion of the law and practice of regency in medieval Scotland up to the reign of James I. With this background, it is possible to see the minority of James II as an exercise in the traditional forms of regency established since the thirteenth century, albeit a somewhat special case. It is over half a century since the late Peter McNeill became the first to explore the subject of regency in any depth.[2] The term 'regency' did not come into use until the sixteenth century, however, and is used here merely as a convenient omnibus term for the office variously described from the thirteenth through the fifteenth centuries as 'guardian', 'lieutenant' and 'governor'. Relatively little reference has been made to McNeill's article since its publication, despite the problem of a king being incapable of government by virtue of minority, senility or absence prevailing for around 170 of the 425 years between the

---

[2] McNeill, P.G.B., 'The Scottish Regency', *Juridical Review* 12 (1967), pp. 127–48 [McNeill, 'Scottish Regency']. A very valuable recent study which, however, makes no mention of McNeill's work is Reid, N. and Penman, M., 'Guardian-Lieutenant-Governor: Absentee Monarchy and Proxy Power in Scotland's Long Fourteenth Century', in Pechaud, M. and Penman, M., (eds), *Absentee Authority Across Europe* (Woodbridge, 2017), pp. 191–218 [Reid and Penman, 'Guardian-Lieutenant-Governor']. See also Brown, M., "Lele consail for the comoun profite': Kings, Guardians and Councils in the Scottish Kingdom, c.1250–1450', in Rose, J., (ed.), *The Politics of Counsel in England and Scotland 1286–1707* (Oxford, 2016), pp. 45–61 [Brown, 'Lele consail'].

death of David I in 1153 and the 1578 majority of James VI. Nor was any treatise ever written before 1707 on the matter of regency in Scotland; so, as McNeill remarked, 'we are left to deduce the law from practice'.[3]

From just such an exercise McNeill identified three kinds of arrangement that prevailed between 1286 to 1580, each analogous but not exactly equivalent to the classes of tutor or guardian in private law (i.e. in ordinary family rather than royal and public life). Each, as McNeill argued, is borne out by pre-1500 evidence. We do not think, however, that McNeill saw a static or pre-existent 'law of regency' applied automatically as each case arose;[4] rather, law and practice evolved together within a generally understood framework of ideas and principles, analogous to but necessarily not the same as the private law tutor or guardian. Regency is an excellent example of how a customary or common law system develops in response to the specifics of particular contingencies.

First, a monarch might nominate a regent in advance of his own demise (an equivalent to the tutor testamentar), who would prevail against other possible claimants. The major example before 1460 was the 1318 appointment of Thomas Randolph as guardian of the kingdom should Robert I die with his heir still a minor. The heir was to be any male child to be lawfully begotten by the king, whom failing Robert Stewart (born 1316), son of the king's daughter and her husband Walter Stewart. In the event, when Robert I died in 1329 his heir was his five-year-old son David. The appointment document of 1318 was clear that the king himself nominated Randolph, with a 'whom failing' provision in favour of Sir James Douglas ('the Good Sir James'). But the nomination was made with the unanimous assent of the whole community, and published as an ordinance of Parliament. Moreover, 'the bishops, abbots, priors and others of the clergy in their way according to law, and also the earls, barons, knights, freeholders and others of the community performed a great oath for the observing of all and singular foregoing things without deceit, fraud, pretence or evil character in future times, having touched God's holy Gospels and the relics of the saints'.[5] But the nomination was made with the

---

[3] McNeill, 'Scottish Regency', p. 127.
[4] Contra Blakeway, A., *Regency in Sixteenth Century Scotland* (Woodbridge, 2015), pp. 19–22.
[5] *RPS* 1318/30. See further Chapter 6 below, text accompanying note 35.

unanimous assent of the whole community, and published as an ordinance of Parliament. Randolph was the king's 'dearest nephew'; but that relationship arose because his mother was a half-sister of Robert I through the first marriage of the king's mother, Marjorie, countess of Carrick, to Adam of Kilconquhar, the king being a product of her second marriage to Robert Bruce of Annandale. There was no question of Randolph having any claim to the Crown, therefore, while Douglas had no blood relationship at all to his king.[6] The 1318 appointment did not cover the contingency of Douglas predeceasing Randolph, however; hence perhaps some of the wrangling amongst both clerical and lay magnates at Perth which followed Randolph's death on 20 July 1332, Douglas having been killed in battle in Spain on 25 August 1330.[7]

In the absence of an effective nomination, 'the next person entitled to the office of regent was the person (being adult) who *at law* was the next in succession, as the nearest agnate'.[8] The nearest agnate was the king's nearest male blood relation. There never was a female regent at law before 1460.[9] The difficulty in 1332 was that the now king David's nearest agnate, his cousin and next in line to the throne, Robert Stewart, was himself still a minor and as such incapable of regency.

McNeill's third category of regency arose if there was neither nomination nor a capable person entitled in law as the nearest agnate. In such cases, 'a regent was *given* to the realm by a gathering of notables representative of the realm': normally a group of 'such persons as for the time were best suited to represent the realm or carry out the needs of the time'.[10] Such regents were equivalent

---

[6] We do not share 'the inescapable sense that these Bruce-era decisions merely pay lip-service to estates' expectations': see Reid and Penman, 'Guardian-Lieutenant-Governor', p. 207.

[7] For the wrangling, see *Chron Fordun*, I, p. 354; II, p. 346.

[8] McNeill, 'Scottish Regency', p. 129 (emphasis in original).

[9] While Mary of Guelders certainly fulfilled the traditional role of a queen mother in the royal minority which followed the death of James II in 1460, i.e. as custodian of the person of the boy James III (see further below, text accompanying notes 74–77), until her death in 1463 she also took a much more active and leading role in general regency government than any of her predecessors ('the gouernyng ... [and] keping of the kinrik', according to the Auchinleck chronicle (McGladdery, *James II*, p. 273)). See further Downie, *Queenship*, p. 136; also chapter 9, especially at pp. 169–74.

[10] McNeill, 'Scottish Regency', p. 131.

to private law's executors dative or the tutors dative (both appointed by court process), and there might be more than one at a time, acting together. The classic example is the Guardians appointed by the community of the realm in 1286 after the death of Alexander III.[11]

But the appointment after Randolph's death in 1332 fell to Donald, earl of Mar, nephew of Robert I, third in line to the throne, and the king's nearest capable agnate. It is clear, however, that he was appointed by the Three Estates rather than having any entitlement from his closeness in blood to the king. The major reason for the wrangling reported amongst the estates before his appointment was probably about Donald's long and strong connections with the English Crown and the Balliols;[12] the principle favouring the nearest available male relative must ultimately have prevailed over such countervailing considerations. Ten days later, probably desperate to prove himself to the community of the realm, Donald led the Scots into battle at Dupplin Moor and was killed in the resultant rout of his forces. His son and heir, Thomas, was probably not yet five years old, and certainly unable to take up his father's short-lived role.[13] Following Donald's death, therefore, another appointment had to be made by the Three Estates.

Those now chosen for the office of regent were a series of individuals who were not agnates of the minor king (although there was generally some link with the king's father and his major supporters). They were rather amongst the military leaders of the Scots forces battling with the supporters of Balliol and the English at the time. The office was something of a poisoned chalice for the appointees, however.[14] Sir Andrew Murray of Bothwell (husband of Robert I's sister Christian) held the position for less than a year before his capture by the English at Kelso in April 1333. His joint successors, Sir Archibald Douglas (half-brother of the Good Sir James who had been the alternate guardian appointed back in 1318) and John Randolph, earl of Moray (son of Thomas Randolph), were respectively killed at the battle of Halidon Hill in July 1333 and captured by the English in the Marches in July 1335.

---

[11] See Reid and Penman, 'Guardian-Lieutenant-Governor', pp. 191–205.
[12] *Chron Fordun*, i, p. 354; ii, p. 346.
[13] On Donald and Thomas, earls of Mar, see Watson, F., 'Donald, eighth earl of Mar (1293–1332)', *ODNB*.
[14] For further detail and citation of sources for the period 1332–57, see Reid and Penman, 'Guardian-Lieutenant-Governor', pp. 209–14.

By that time, the king's cousin and heir-presumptive, Robert Stewart, although still a minor, had nonetheless joined Randolph in office. This was perhaps seen as some form of apprenticeship; it came to an end, however, by the end of the year. By then ransomed and released, Sir Andrew Murray returned to office and held his position until his resignation in 1338. Although Robert Stewart turned 21 on 2 March 1337, it was the following year before he became sole regent. This was as the king's nearest agnate and heir-presumptive, rather than as an appointee of the Three Estates. Robert then held office until June 1341 when King David (by then 17) returned from France (where he had been sent to safe keeping in 1334). Stewart resumed office after David was taken into English captivity in October 1346. This regency lasted until David's release and return to his kingdom in November 1357.[15]

During this turbulent period, the regent, whether nominated or appointed as nearest agnate or appointed by the Three Estates, largely ceased to be designated as *custos* (guardian) and became instead *locum tenens* (lieutenant, or placeholder).[16] This may have been initially because the person entitled to be 'guardian' (Robert Stewart) was himself as a minor incapable of the role. By 1338, when Robert did finally assume office, the absent king was in his fourteenth year and the notion of 'guardian' in these circumstances may have seemed less appropriate than that of 'placeholder', so recently established during the incapacity of both king and lawful guardian of the realm. One to act in the king's place in his majority was even more necessary later when he was suffering involuntary absence from the kingdom because held in captivity in England. Reid and Penman suggest that the lieutenant's powers were perhaps 'lesser' than those of a guardian.[17] But the terminology developed, we suggest, mainly to meet emerging new situations for the exercise of authority in regency situations.

Use of the nomenclature of lieutenancy developed further when in the reigns of Robert II and Robert III (1371–1406) regency had to be deployed to deal with the new problem of the living, present, but disabled or mentally incapable adult king.[18] In the case of Robert II, in November 1384, because 'the lord king

---

[15] On David's absences from his kingdom, see Penman, 'Lion Captive', pp. 419–28.
[16] See Reid and Penman, 'Guardian-Lieutenant-Governor', pp. 209–10.
[17] See Reid and Penman, 'Guardian-Lieutenant-Governor', p. 210.
[18] See also Boardman, *Early Stewart Kings*, chs 5, 6 and 8; Boardman, S., 'Coronations, Kings and Guardians: Politics, Parliaments and General Councils,

himself is unable on each occasion to be attentive continually to the execution of justice and the law of his kingdom in person', his heir and nearest agnate, then John, earl of Carrick, was appointed by king and council to 'cause execution of common justice throughout the realm', albeit under the supervision of king and council.[19] Carrick, touching the holy gospels, took an oath, along with all others present, to implement the ordinances, which were to endure for a period of three years. But nowhere in this process is he formally designed or appointed as 'lieutenant'.[20] In June 1385, he presided over a meeting of General Council as 'eldest son and lieutenant of our same lord king'; but this may mean no more than that he was standing in for the incapable king at the meeting.[21]

Carrick's position was clearly subject to the direction of General Council, which in April 1385 ordained –

> that he personally attack the northern regions with all possible haste, supported by an appropriate and sufficient force of men, and secured by prudent and faithful counsel, ... he should devise, ordain, procure and decree, and without any delay, sparing no person, he should actively pursue ways and means in which or through which those malefactors and caterans and their accomplices, and also their receivers, might be effectively pursued ... or in other ways ... to cause them to be punished ... with the proviso that such punishment as is to be imposed should be due and appropriate for their demerits and should provide hereafter an example for the rest.[22]

1371–1406', in Brown, K.M. and Tanner, R.J., (eds), *The History of the Scottish Parliament volume I: Parliament and Politics in Scotland 1235–1560* (Edinburgh, 2004), ch 4; Brown, 'Lele consail', pp. 57–59. Robert II already had 'lieutenants' in the northern parts of his kingdom (his son, Alexander Stewart of Badenoch, later earl of Buchan, appointed October 1372: *RMS*, i, no. 556), and in Argyll (Gillespic Campbell, appointed heritably in 1382: Argyll Muniments, Inveraray: Bundle 1107, a notarial instrument of 10 May 1437 transuming hereditary grant of royal lieutenancy to Gillespic Campbell of Lochawe in 1382; see further below, note 70).

[19] *RPS* 1384/11/4.
[20] *RPS* 1384/11/16, 17. See further on the oaths taken by Carrick and the others present Chapter 6 below, text accompanying notes 31–43.
[21] *RPS* 1385/6/1.
[22] *RPS* 1385/4/3. See also *RPS* 1385/4/9, in which General Council gives another order to Carrick to issue letters of command 'without delay' in ongoing judicial proceedings.

General Council here was guiding Carrick in his assigned role as the executive arm of justice in the kingdom.

At a meeting of General Council on 1 December 1388, more than three years since his initial appointment, Carrick gave up or was deprived of his authority by a king and council 'above all wishing to guard against the dangers which threaten at present by an invasion of their enemies in the marches', but also concerned about 'great and numerous defects in the governing of the kingdom'.[23] This may have been the final outcome of events the previous February when, it has been suggested, Carrick procured the arrest by David Fleming of a king not only unable to administer justice but also 'unwilling or unable, to take a personal lead in Anglo-Scottish warfare' despite a truce with England being due to expire on 19 June.[24] How long the king's arrest lasted is not known. The December meeting in Edinburgh followed the prorogation of an earlier one begun at Linlithgow on 18 August. The Edinburgh meeting agreed that the 'age' of the king (now 72) and the 'infirmity' of Carrick (he had apparently been previously lamed, possibly crippled, by the kick of a horse and must also have been at least 50 years of age[25]) meant the inability of either, not only to deal effectively with failures of justice, but also to lead personally in the event of war. The non-renewal of the truce with England had already been followed by a number of private military sallies south, notably that leading to the battle of Otterburn on 5 or 19 August and the death there of the second earl of Douglas. It seems quite possible, however, that the prorogation of the Linlithgow meeting had resulted from the occurrence of Carrick's accident during the meeting; it was made 'by reason of the lord earl of Carrick'.[26]

---

[23] *RPS* 1388/12/1.

[24] See Boardman, 'Coronations, Kings and Guardians', p. 107, citing Bodleian Library Oxford, MS Fairfax 23, f 16. We are grateful to Professor Boardman for showing us his copy of this MS. See also *Liber Pluscardensis*, i, p. 347; ii, p. 262, narrating that James Douglas of Balvenie justified his slaughter of Fleming in 1406 on the ground that he was one of the principal actors in the arrest (*ad capcionem*) of Robert II. See further Chapter 6 below, text accompanying note 28.

[25] *Chron Bower*, vii, p. 442. *Chron Wyntoun (Amours)*, vi, pp. 338–39 (*Chron Wyntoun (Laing)*, iii, p. 40), says that Carrick 'wes nocht fery as he was won', i.e. he was not as active as he once was (see https://dsl.ac.uk/entry/dost/fery). For Carrick's birth before 1340, see Boardman, S., 'Robert III (d.1406)', *ODNB*.

[26] As suggested by Nicholson, R., *Scotland: The Later Middle Ages* (Edinburgh, 1974), p. 199. For the Linlithgow meeting see *RPS* 1388/8/.

CHAPTER TWO: REGENCY, COUNCIL AND THE EARLS OF DOUGLAS 1437–51

The record of the Edinburgh meeting also adds to the age of the king and Carrick's infirmity the then minority of Carrick's own firstborn son and heir David as all together the sum of explanation for the appointment of Carrick's younger brother, Robert, earl of Fife, to replace him, but as guardian (*custos*) rather than lieutenant of the kingdom.[27] Fife was to act under the king, and his firstborn, and the latter's son and heir, to put justice into effect and keep the law internally, and to defend the kingdom with the king's force against those attempting to rise up as enemies. This went further than Carrick's assignment to the purely internal matters of justice; in the shadow of conflict with England, Fife was also to engage in the defence of the realm against foreign enemies. He must have been seen as physically better able than his brother to discharge that role. In combining leadership in war and the administration of justice he was clearly the guardian of the kingdom.

Fife's appointment was not for an indefinite period: it was 'to last until [*the king's*] firstborn son recovers from his infirmity by God's grace or until *his* [i.e. Carrick's] firstborn son and heir arrives at the ability of governing his office according to and by the determination of the council of the kingdom'. Fife's conduct in office was also to be subject to annual review in full Parliament or General Council. All subjects and lieges of the king were to take an oath of fealty to the guardian during the term of his office (after which, Bower adds, the prelates and magnates were also sworn to support him in office and to give him faithful counsel), while the king further

> commanded the chancellor in full council, from the consent and deliberation of the council, that he shall release whatsoever letters under the king's seal which the guardian and council, by one consent, may command touching common utility, and [touching] the common ordinance to be made by his council for the governance and defence of the kingdom.[28]

---

[27] Writing over 50 years later, Bower says that the king 'desired [Fife] to be called governor' rather than guardian (*Chron Bower*, vii, pp. 442–43) but this is not borne out by the record, albeit it suggests that nomenclature was important.

[28] See for the foregoing *RPS* 1388/12/1 and *Chron Bower*, vii, pp. 442–43. The form of the oath of fealty may have followed that to the king as set out in *RPS* 1445/6, on which see Chapter 1 text accompanying note 23 and Chapter 6 text accompanying notes 31–43. Compare the oaths taken in 1385 on the occasion of Carrick's appointment to act in the stead of his father in the administration of justice: above, text accompanying notes 19–20.

Giving Fife the ability to use the royal seal was an important mark of the authority he was to enjoy as regent, albeit under the oversight of the king's council.

Whether or not all this amounted to a 'series of palace coups or irresistible transitions'[29] as distinct from a response to a general crisis further compounded by an unfortunate accident, it does look like a decision about the leadership of the kingdom responding to current needs in a manner consistent with existing general principles. King and council also moved decisively ten days later against one of the major targets for contemporary concern, Alexander Stewart, earl of Buchan and lord of Badenoch, removing him from office as justiciar north of Forth because 'he had not performed in that office where and when he ought to have done, and where it seemed that for anyone else to hold the office of justiciar was useless to the community'.[30]

Fife continued as guardian after his incapable brother's succession to the throne as Robert III in 1390, and held the office until 1393. By then, the new king's eldest son, David, although still a minor, was playing an increasingly active role in government (for example, as justiciar in 1392 aged just 14[31]) and Scottish adherence to the long Anglo-French truce agreed in 1389 showed no signs of breaking down. The greatest threat to the kingdom had passed for the foreseeable future, and the young heir stood in much less need of protection until he came of full age in 1399. In 1398, having been hitherto earl of Carrick, he became duke of Rothesay, while his uncle Robert became duke of Albany. In January 1399, in line with what had been laid down back in 1388,[32] Parliament appointed Rothesay as 'lieutenande', albeit only for three years.

Like his father and uncle before him, Rothesay's regency was to be exercised under the supervision of council (whose 21 members were however specially

---

[29] Reid and Penman, 'Guardian-Lieutenant-Governor', p. 214.
[30] *RPS* 1388/12/3. The editors of *RPS* suggest in a pop-up, 'The final clause of the sentence seems to be defective. The correct sense may be "... and where others were held to administer the office of justiciar it was useless to the community"'. On Buchan, see Grant, A., 'The Wolf of Badenoch', in Sellar, W.D.H., (ed.), *Moray: Province and People* (Edinburgh, 1993), pp. 143–61; Boardman, S., 'Lordship in the North-East: The Badenoch Stewarts I: Alexander Stewart, Earl of Buchan, Lord of Badenoch', *Northern Scotland* xvi (1996), pp. 1–29.
[31] *ER*, iii, p. 311. See further MacQueen, 'Tame Magnates?', p. 101 note 65.
[32] See above, text preceding note 27.

chosen for the task).³³ This measure was perhaps partly a response to Rothesay's youth and perceived impetuosity; but it is worth noting that the same Parliament criticised 'the mysgouvernance of the reaulme and the defaut of the kepynge of the common law [which] sulde be imputit to the kynge and his officeris'.³⁴ The king, however, 'for seknes of his persoun may nocht travail to governe the realme na restreygne trespassours and rebellours'.³⁵ That this may have caused issues about the king's susceptibility to whoever approached him even when his brother was guardian is, however, hinted at in a provision in Rothesay's appointment:

> at the kynge be obliste that he sal nocht lette his office na the execucioun of it be na contremandmentis as sumqwhile has bene seyne; and gife ocht be done in the contr[ary] be lettres or ony other maner throch oure lorde the kyngis byddynge, that contremandment be of na valu na of effect, na the forsaid lieutenant be nocht haldyn tyl ansuere suylke contremandmentis na be nocht essoynyhet thruch vertu of thaim that he doys nocht his office etc ...³⁶

It does not look as though Rothesay's lieutenancy had any lesser powers than Fife's guardianship: he was to have

> fwl powere and commissioun of the kyng to governe the lande in althynge as the kynge sulde do in his persoun gife he warre present; that is to say to punys trespassours, til restreygne trespassis and to trete and remitte [*presumably with foreign powers such as England*³⁷] ...³⁸

Moreover, Rothesay was to take an oath modelled on that taken by the king at his coronation:

> [and to] be sworne til fulfyl efter his power all the thyngis that the kynge in his crownyng wes suorne for til do to haly kyrke and the

---

³³ *RPS* 1399/1/3. See Brown, 'Lele consail', p. 45.
³⁴ *RPS* 1399/1/2.
³⁵ *RPS* 1399/1/3.
³⁶ *RPS* 1399/1/3.
³⁷ See *RPS* 1399/1/10, where Rothesay and others are to 'trete' for peace with England and the establishment of a 28-year truce.
³⁸ *RPS* 1399/1/3.

pepyl, syn in to thir thyngis he is to ber the kyngis powere, that is to say the fredume and the rycht of the kirke to kepe wndamyste, the lawys ande the lowablez custumes to gerre be kepit to the pepil, manslaerys, reiferis, brynneris and generaly all mysdoeris thruch strynthe til restreygnhe and punyse, and specialy cursit men, heretikis and put fra the kyrke at the requeste of the kyrke to restreygne.[39]

A plausible suggestion may be, therefore, that by this time the nomenclature of 'lieutenant' was seen, not as showing some sort of lesser authority than a guardian's, or as reflecting the time-limited nature of an appointment,[40] but rather as simply more apt than 'guardian' for a son acting in effect in his adult father's place while the latter still lived.

The importance of the regent's council even when the regent was the king's heir-apparent is shown by the fate of Rothesay and his lieutenancy. Late in 1401, with the end of his three-year term approaching, he was arrested and imprisoned by Sir John Ramornie (a member of the special council appointed for him in 1399[41]) and Sir William Lindsay of Rossie (brother of another of the appointed councillors, David, earl of Crawford). In the General Council meeting of May 1402 which followed Rothesay's subsequent death in custody the previous March, it was held that the arrest and imprisonment were justified by the 'public good' (*pro publica utilitate*), and for that reason did not constitute any crime of lese majeste (*lese majestatis*) against the king. Nor was Rothesay's death to be seen as any crime; it had occurred through divine providence and not otherwise, and murmurings against the duke of Albany, the earl of Douglas and other participants were to cease, under the pains of the law.[42] Writing not quite fifty years later, the chronicler Walter

---

[39] RPS 1399/1/3. Compare the oath that James II may have taken in Parliament in June 1445 (*RPS* 1445/3) and see Lyall, R.J., 'The Medieval Scottish Coronation Service: Some Seventeenth Century Evidence', *Innes Review* 28 (1977), pp. 3–21, 16; and further text above accompanying notes 19–20 and 28; Chapter 6 below, text accompanying notes 31–43.

[40] As suggested by Reid and Penman, 'Guardian-Lieutenant-Governor', p. 210 (see also ibid., p. 215), and McNeill, 'Scottish Regency', p. 131.

[41] Described as a counsellor of the king, bold in spirit, highly eloquent, and in difficult cases *prelocutor regis* and a *causidicus disertissimus* (a very eloquent pleader) (*Chron Bower*, viii, p. 40).

[42] RPS 1402/5/1.

CHAPTER TWO: REGENCY, COUNCIL AND THE EARLS OF DOUGLAS 1437-51

Bower stated that Rothesay had begun to spurn the advice of his council and give himself up to the frivolity which had marked his earlier youth; the council had tendered a collective resignation to the king who had thereupon commanded his brother, the duke of Albany, to effect the lieutenant's arrest and incarceration 'until after punishment by the rod of discipline he should know himself better'.[43] There is certainly evidence of Rothesay's arbitrary and possibly unlawful conduct of his office, which may have contributed as much to his arrest as the hostility and ambition of his predecessor as lieutenant.[44]

Albany probably succeeded to Rothesay's role as lieutenant in 1402; certainly he is designed as 'lieutenant' of the king and as presiding in that capacity at a General Council held at Linlithgow in April 1404.[45] This meeting saw the king (seemingly of his own volition rather than with the advice of his council) formally appoint Albany as lieutenant once again, and for a period of two years, for which he was to be given a commission prepared by the chancellor.[46] The title emphasised continuity with the role previously discharged by Rothesay and, perhaps, continued discomfort with the idea of guardianship when the king was an adult and present in the kingdom. From 1402 Rothesay's younger brother and Albany's nephew James (born in 1394 and appointed earl of Carrick in 1404[47]), became the king's heir, albeit an incapable one through minority,

---

[43] *Chron Bower*, viii, pp. 38–39 (*donec virga discipline castigatus seipsum melius cognosceret*).

[44] For further discussion of the fall and death of Rothesay, generally pointing a finger of suspicion at Albany and others, but showing also maladministration in the lieutenancy, see a number of writings by Boardman: *Early Stewart Kings*, chapter 8; 'The Man Who Would Be King: The Lieutenancy and Death of David, Duke of Rothesay, 1378–1402', in Mason, R. and Macdougall, N., (eds), *People and Power in Scotland; Essays in Honour of T C Smout* (Edinburgh, 1992), pp. 1–27; 'Stewart, David, Duke of Rothesay, (1378–1402)', *ODNB*; 'A Saintly Sinner? The Martyrdom of David, Duke of Rothesay', in Boardman, S. and Williamson, E., (eds), *The Cult of Saints and the Virgin Mary in Medieval Scotland* (Woodbridge, 2010), ch 5. The line of these writings is followed by Brown, 'Lele consail', pp. 58–59, and Reid and Penman, 'Guardian-Lieutenant-Governor', pp. 215–16.

[45] *RPS* 1404/1.

[46] *RPS* 1404/4.

[47] *HMC Mar and Kellie*, i, p. 7. The charter is also printed in Dickinson, W.C., 'An Inquiry into the Origin and Nature of the Title Prince of Scotland', *Economica* 11 (1924), pp. 212–20 [Dickinson, 'Inquiry'], 214. See further Chapter 3 below, text accompanying note 72.

and the title of guardian might not have been inapt for Albany had a still-minor James succeeded his father in normal circumstances. But in 1404 as lieutenant Albany was given 'the power of doing all that he might do for the rule and governance of the people, for the defence of those who are enemies of the people of England, and for the suppression of transgressors within [the kingdom], and for all and singular things, both in peace and in war, which it pertained to the lord king to do'. In other words, he had all the powers of a guardian.

A fresh issue to be dealt with by way of the council-appointed regent-dative approach was presented on the death of Robert III in 1406. His son and heir James had been captured by the English three months before his father's demise, and he remained imprisoned south of the border. No coronation was therefore possible (unlike the situation with David II in the 1330s). The kingdom with a living, minor, but uncrowned absentee king needed a regent; and the solution was supplied by the appointment of the highly experienced Robert, duke of Albany, not as guardian, but as 'governor'. The new title may have reflected the all but unprecedented nature of the situation and the vice-regal powers that Albany needed to exercise for the uncrowned king (although these do not seem to have included the power to convene Parliaments).[48] But his appointment followed the established principle that the regent was the nearest agnate (in this case, the uncle) of the king unable to act. That continued to be the case when Murdoch Stewart, the duke's son and the king's cousin, inherited both the Albany title and the office of governor on his father's death in 1420, with James now in his majority but still held captive in England and uncrowned.

A number of general observations made by McNeill, primarily on the basis of later evidence, clearly hold good for the period from 1329 to 1406. His argument from sixteenth-century evidence that '[w]hatever the right of a regent to

---

[48] McNeill, 'Scottish Regency', p. 129. See further Hunt, 'Governorship', pp. 127–35. She argues inter alia that there was a precedent in the recognition of Margaret of Norway as queen without being inaugurated as such, the Guardians ruling as representatives of the *regia dignitas* and not in her name. The difference may have been that Margaret had not been inaugurated, was not detained by a hostile kingdom, was very young indeed, and in the end died *en route* to Scotland from Norway. See further Reid, N., 'Margaret 'Maid of Norway' and Scottish Queenship', *Reading Medieval Studies* viii (1982), pp. 75–96.

his office his legal title appears—at least in the more sophisticated records of the fifteenth century and after—to have been an Act of Parliament confirming the regent in office',[49] is borne out by our analysis above and Karen Hunt's demonstration that fourteenth- and early fifteenth-century regents depended on the authority given by the Three Estates (whether in Parliament or General Council).[50] Hunt also argues that, from the time of Robert II on, the king or his regent had a 'secret' or 'inner' advisory council appointed by the Three Estates, the role of which was to offer advice 'for the good of the common weal'.[51] Michael Brown notes further that the use of lieutenancy in the reigns of Robert II and Robert III 'had a very strong conciliar character'.[52] Our discussion has shown in particular the significance of the regent's council for Rothesay's lieutenancy.

McNeill goes on to say: 'Like any other custodian or guardian of an estate, the regent had all the powers which were necessary for the proper management of that estate—always subject to certain qualifications'.[53] He had powers over the monarch, the realm and the lieges. McNeill notes the way in which politics might sway the policies of the regent; '[b]ut all these political activities could only operate within the law which governed the regency'.[54] Hunt highlights that the regent had always to act under the eye of the Three Estates, which could take its authority away from an unfit person (as in the case of Robert II's lieutenant in 1388 and probably Rothesay in 1401).[55]

Further, McNeill argued, '[t]hese powers of a regent were qualified by the fact that he was a trustee for the crown and that at the end of his term of office he was required to hand over the realm intact and to give an account of his stewardship before he was entitled to be discharged'. Moreover:

> [A]s an incident of the king's 'lesage', the child had the power when he attained twenty-one and thereafter during the *quadriennium utile* to review all the transactions made by him or on his behalf during

---

[49] McNeill, 'Scottish Regency', p. 131.
[50] Hunt, 'Governorship', pp. 130–34.
[51] Hunt, 'Governorship', pp. 133–35 (quotation from ER, iii, p. 589).
[52] Brown, 'Lele consail', pp. 45–61, 58.
[53] McNeill, 'Scottish Regency', p. 133.
[54] McNeill, 'Scottish Regency', p. 138.
[55] Hunt, 'Governorship', pp. 130–34.

his minority, including grants 'be our tutouris and governouris for the tyme'. Generally, he could revoke any contract or alienation which was 'maide in prejudice or hindering of the croun', whether or not the regent concurred in the transaction ... [A] transaction between king and regent was especially suspect. Again, the various statutes prohibiting alienation of crown property without certain necessary consents were equally applicable to the acts of a regent as to the acts of a king.[56]

McNeill also deals with the name in which the regents exercised their authority, noting that up to and including the Albany governors, they did so in their own name rather than that of the king. The Albanys' use of their own name in gubernatorial *acta* was therefore a reflection, not of regal ambition, but of established custom and practice.[57] Further, as Hunt remarks, the gubernatorial great seal struck in 1406 was 'a necessary and practical prerequisite to good government, ... not a personal assumption of the royal prerogative'.[58] Normally a king's great seal was broken on his death and a new one struck after the inauguration of his successor. But since James I remained uncrowned, no such new great seal could be struck for him; hence the need for the governor to have his own great seal. As Hunt also notes, Albany's great seal had similarities to previous royal ones; but in addition 'there are elements indicative of Albany's non-royal status'.[59] The practice of regents using their own name ceased after the execution of the second Albany in 1425; thereafter, when regencies arose, the regent acted in the name of the king.[60] In particular, all royal documents issued in the minority of James II ran in the king's name, not that of any lieutenant-general or other responsible officer.[61]

Unless otherwise limited, the office of regent lasted as long as the incapacity or inability of the king in whose name the regent acted; 'in the case of minority [*according to sixteenth-century practice*], the regency lasted until the monarch

---

[56] McNeill, 'Scottish Regency', pp. 134–35.
[57] McNeill, 'Scottish Regency', pp. 136–37.
[58] Hunt, 'Governorship', p. 128.
[59] Hunt, 'Governorship', p. 128. This point seems not quite taken by Reid and Penman, 'Guardian-Lieutenant-Governor', pp. 216–17.
[60] McNeill, 'Scottish Regency', pp. 135–36.
[61] Borthwick, 'Council', vol 2, Appendix A, pp. 398–417.

CHAPTER TWO: REGENCY, COUNCIL AND THE EARLS OF DOUGLAS 1437–51

was twelve years complete'.[62] How far this was either law or practice in the later medieval period is doubtful. The 1318 appointment of a guardian for any minor successor of Robert I simply stated that the office was to last 'until it seems to the community of the kingdom or the greater and more sensible part [thereof] that the ... heir of the same lord king, as aforesaid, is capable of the government of the kingdom and the people'.[63] David II in fact assumed active kingship in 1341 at the age of 17, and Rothesay may have been seen as 'capable of government' from the end of his pupillarity in 1392 had his father died then or later in the 1390s.

Regency 1437–49

Peter McNeill did not discuss in any detail the regency situation which arose upon the assassination of James I on 20 February 1437. Although the young James II was crowned at Holyrood on 25 March (meaning that his great seal could be struck, and that Parliaments could thereafter be held as well as general councils[64]), a regent was clearly needed. Following the executions of Walter Stewart, earl of Atholl, and his sons for their part in the killing of James I, the new king's nearest male relative in the lines descended from the legitimate sons of Robert II, to whom the Crown had been entailed by statute in 1373,[65] was either Archibald, fifth earl of Douglas, son of James I's sister Margaret, or Malise Graham, earl of Menteith, son of Robert II's granddaughter Euphemia.[66] The link of both men to the royal house thus came through

---

[62] McNeill, 'Scottish Regency', p. 137.
[63] *RPS* 1318/30.
[64] The distinction between 'parliament' and 'general council' has been little mentioned in recent literature. See Hannay, R.K., 'On 'Parliament' and 'General Council'', *Scottish Historical Review* xviii (1921), pp. 157–70, reprinted in *The College of Justice: Essays by R K Hannay* (Edinburgh, 1990), pp. 217–30. Core differences seem to have been whether or not the presence of the king was required, the formalities of prior notice and its length of time, the fencing or not of the assembly as a court, and jurisdiction in treason trials.
[65] *RPS* 1373/3. See above, Chapter 1, text accompanying note 40.
[66] A useful genealogical table illustrating the relationships can be found in Donaldson, *Scottish Kings*, p. 67; and see discussion at ibid., pp. 84–85. Pace Macdougall, N., *James III*, 2nd edn (Edinburgh, 2009) [Macdougall, *James III*], pp. 5–6; McGladdery, *James II*, p. 106; and Brown, M.H., 'Graham, Malise, third Earl of Strathearn and first Earl of Menteith (1406x13–1490)', *ODNB*,

a female rather than a direct male descendant of Robert II. So even if these male lines of descent failed, neither Douglas or Menteith had any immediate claim to the Crown, with the sisters of James II being the heirs-presumptive should he die without issue.[67] Malise had also been a hostage in England for James I's unpaid ransom since 1427. No question of seeking his return to become regent seems to have arisen. Instead, and in line with McNeill's third category of regency (by appointment of the Three Estates rather than as the next in succession to the Crown), Earl Archibald, much the older of the two men and also the king's oldest near agnate, became 'lieutenant-general' of the kingdom.[68]

The significance of the earl's regency title (neither guardian nor governor) is probably that he was acting in the stead of a king who had been crowned and was present in the kingdom, but who was not yet capable of rule.[69] The label of 'general' may also have been to distinguish the office from the Campbells' royal lieutenancy in Argyll, renewed in the person of Duncan Campbell of Lochawe around 10 May 1437; and, perhaps, from the lieutenancy of the lord of the Isles in the northern parts of the kingdom.[70] Such harnessing of local power to royal

---

Donaldson does not argue that Malise was to be preferred to James II as king, only that the question of who would be the latter's heir must have been very live throughout his minority and indeed as long as he remained without lawful issue.

[67] See discussion in Chapter 1, text accompanying notes 41–47 above. Donaldson, *Scottish Kings*, p. 85, is wrong to suggest that Earl Archibald was heir-presumptive to James II.

[68] Tanner, *LMSP*, p. 78, places the earl's appointment as the work of a Parliament held on 25 March 1437; cf McGladdery, *James II*, p. 13 ('almost certainly, at a meeting of the three estates in a General Council which took place around 6 May [1437]'). We think it unlikely that this overrode the wish of James I that his queen should be his regent, as suggested by Brown, 'Douglas, James, of Balvenie', *ODNB*. Such an appointment would have been unprecedented (see above, text accompanying note 9). Earl Archibald was born c.1391, while Earl Malise was born in 1406.

[69] See discussion of the word 'lieutenant' in text accompanying notes 16–21, 32–40 above, and notes 70–73, and 78.

[70] For the Argyll lieutenancy, see Argyll Muniments, Inveraray: Bundle 1107 (notarial instrument of 10 May 1437 transuming hereditary grant of royal lieutenancy to Gillespic Campbell of Lochawe in 1382; witnessed by, inter alia, James Douglas, earl of Avondale and lord of Balvenie, Robert Stewart, lord of Lorn, and Alexander Livingston of Callendar). Boardman, S., *The Campbells*

CHAPTER TWO: REGENCY, COUNCIL AND THE EARLS OF DOUGLAS 1437–51

authority in a relatively remote area of the kingdom made good practical sense in the context of ordinary as well as minority government. It had already happened, as previously noted, in the reign of Robert II, and also under the Albany Governors and James I, for both of whom Alexander Stewart, earl of Mar, acted as lieutenant in the north.[71] James I also appointed two *custodes* of Kintyre and Knapdale in August 1430, giving them extensive judicial and other powers in the territories for seven years.[72] Their period of office may be linked to Duncan Campbell's successfully reclaiming the king's lieutenancy in Argyll in May 1437.

Roland Tanner suggests that Douglas was to govern with the aid of the Council, noting that 'several documents and acts from his period of government reflect the extent to which lieutenant and Council were meant to work together for the common weal'.[73] This is again consistent with the principles of regency as analysed by both McNeill and Hunt. So too is the queen mother's custody of her son and residence at Stirling castle, along with an annual income of 4,000 merks, probably granted to her by the Three Estates at the same time.[74] McNeill remarked that the regent did not have custody of his ward: 'as in private law, it was regarded as too dangerous to combine custody of the child

---

1250–1513 (Edinburgh, 2006), p. 159 note 2, says that 'The notarial instrument was probably intended to assist Duncan in pleading his case for a restoration of the lieutenancy before the royal council.' Campbell obtained a further notarial instrument of the 1382 grant on 13 May 1439, shortly after the fifth earl's death: Glasgow Univ [Scot Hist Dept] Argyll Transcripts, vol. 2, s. d. 13/5/1439). On the lord of the Isles as lieutenant in the north, see below note 78.

[71] See above, note 18; and further M. Brown, 'Regional Lordship in North-East Scotland; The Badenoch Stewarts II: Alexander Stewart Earl of Mar', *Northern Scotland* xvi (1996), pp. 31–53, 41 (citing what is now *RPS* 1429/4/2 (which refers to '*Quo die consensum fuit et statutum ut omnes et singuli fugientes a rege vel alio quocunque eius locum tenente punientur sicut rebelles publici et notorii*') and *Family of Rose*, p. 128). In November 1420 Governor Murdoch Stewart duke of Albany promised Mar letters patent 'of power to be steadhaldande [*i.e. locum tenens, placeholder*] till him' in north-east Scotland (Fraser, *Menteith*, i, p. 261 (also *AB Ill*, iv, pp. 181–82 – where the source is given as Pinkerton, *History*, i, pp. 454–55 – where the source is a Balfour transcript, BL: Harleian MS 4694 f 22); also Brown, 'Regional Lordship', p. 39).

[72] *RMS*, ii, no. 163. For context see Brown, *James I*, p. 135.

[73] Tanner, *LMSP*, p. 80 (citing *APS*, ii, p. 32; NRS: GD350/1/949; Fraser, *Melvilles*, iii, no. 31). See also Tanner, *LMSP*, p. 85; McGladdery, *James II*, pp. 15–16.

[74] Tanner, *LMSP*, pp. 79–80; McGladdery, *James II*, pp. 14–15.

with the administration of his estate'.[75] Instead, '[l]egal custody was the right of the nearest cognate who was usually the queen mother'.[76] McNeill added that 'the physical custody was usually exercised by the house of Mar', but in 1437 the earldom of Mar was vacant following the death of Alexander Stewart in 1436 and would remain so throughout the minority.[77]

Earl Archibald's death from plague in June 1439 when his own heir, William, was still a minor and therefore incapable of acting as any kind of regent created a situation without any direct precedent in recent Scottish history. In principle, the matter was one for the Three Estates to handle. But there is no evidence that any new 'lieutenant-general' or other kind of regent was appointed, although Duncan Campbell of Lochawe continued as king's lieutenant in Argyll, and Alexander, lord of the Isles, in the north, for the rest of the minority.[78] The first known business of the General Council after the earl's death was at a meeting in Stirling in September 1439, where the focus was on depriving the queen mother of her rights of custody over the king following her clandestine marriage to the 'Black Knight' of Lorne, James Stewart.[79] Alexander Livingston of Callander, who with his sons (James and Alexander) and Sir William Cranston had previously arrested and incarcerated the queen mother and her new husband, now took over her role with its appurtenances. This 'citizens' arrest' and deprivation of office were not necessarily the illegalities perceived by recent writers on the affair.[80] The queen mother had

---

[75] McNeill, 'Scottish Regency', p. 134.
[76] McNeill, 'Scottish Regency', p. 134.
[77] McNeill, 'Scottish Regency', p. 134. For the Mar earldom, see Borthwick, 'Council', pp. 87–90.
[78] For examples of use of the title of king's lieutenant in the parts of Argyll by Duncan Campbell of Lochawe (dates 4/8/1442; 20/2/1447; 1/12/1448 and 20/11/1450), see Glasgow Univ [Scot Hist Dept] Argyll Transcripts, vol 2 (very good copies made by the antiquarian tenth Duke of Argyll); NRS: RH6/325; RMS, ii, no. 346. See further Boardman, Campbells, pp. 82–83, 99, 109, 125, 141, 146–47. For the lord of the Isles as lieutenant in northern parts, see CSSR, iv, nos 510, 522, 684, 735, 813 (king's lieutenant various dates 1439–41).
[79] The marriage was presumably established by clear evidence of the parties' exchange of present consent or per verba de futuro subsequente copula, since there had hardly been time to establish marital consent by cohabitation with habit and repute.
[80] Brown, Black Douglases, pp. 257–58; Tanner, LMSP, p. 92; McGladdery, James II, p. 24. The perception of illegality may derive from the apparent

without consent of the Three Estates subjected herself to a man not of the royal house, and her fitness for the custody of the king was thereby undermined. The queen mother's recognition of this in an 'appoyntmente' dated 4 September, acknowledging that Livingston and his allies had acted 'of gude zele and motife and of grete truth and leaute that was in tham ... anerly for the safety of our soveryn lord, the worship of hir persone and the common gude of the reaume', may have been forced upon her; but it was witnessed by significant numbers of representatives of each of the Three Estates (including the still-minor new earl of Douglas), reflecting their traditional supervisory role in times of royal minority.[81]

A possible understanding of the notoriously unclear governmental arrangements that prevailed in Scotland from late 1439 on is then that the Three Estates at least initially opted not to appoint any one individual as regent in succession to Earl Archibald and to proceed instead with the regency council which must have already existed. The lack of adult and capable earls or representatives of the royal blood would have been an important factor in this decision;[82] any conflict over entitlements or choices between possible contenders as regent were also thereby avoided. There was also perhaps the lack of any significant external threat to the kingdom, in particular from an England pre-occupied with the final stages of the Hundred Years War in France and led by a king who 'showed not the slightest aptitude for warfare and government'.[83] An absence of concern about English aggression may have been reinforced by a nine-year truce negotiated from November 1437, agreed by March 1438, and in force

---

reference in a 1450 statute speaking of 'crimes committit ... again [the king's] derrest modir of gud mynde' (*RPS* 1450/1/13). But this phrase appears in only two of the six MSS of the 1450 legislation (i.e. NLS: Adv. 25.4.15, and Lambeth Palace Library: MS 167), and its authenticity as part of the original statute cannot be beyond doubt. See further the Notes on the Sources for the Parliaments of Scotland, 1424–1466 (The manuscript sources for legislation, 1424–1466) on the *Records of the Parliaments of Scotland* website (*http://www.rps.ac.uk*); and below, text accompanying notes 155-57.

[81] *RPS* 1439/9/1.
[82] Borthwick, 'Council', pp. 43–46, also notes the loss through death by 1439 of several men experienced in the council of James I.
[83] Powell, E., 'Lancastrian England', in Allmand, C.T., (ed.), *The New Cambridge Medieval History VII c.1415–c.1500* (Cambridge, 1998), pp. 457–76 [Powell, 'Lancastrian England'], 466.

from 1 May that year.[84] The major foreign policy issue confronting the kingdom at the end of 1439 was thus which if any position to take in the schism of the Church brought about by the Council of Basle and its assertion of authority over the pope. While this created serious divisions in the Scottish Church, it did not pose any immediate threat to the king himself.[85]

Roland Tanner draws attention to regular and quite frequent meetings of the Three Estates, mostly in General Council, from early 1440 until early 1444, from which he suggests that 'the Estates continued to have a recognised right to oversee the minority government'.[86] But it would not have been practical to run the government of the country on the basis of such meetings alone. The impression gained from reading through the documents showing the work of the administration before 1450 is of a more direct involvement of a smaller number of councillors in the general business of government.[87] A sense of an active conciliar concern in routine administration may be derived from the Exchequer Rolls also.[88] What might be termed an inner council having more or less regular membership and involvement in government is discernible over the remainder of the minority, although the active members certainly varied from time to time.[89]

Amongst the nobility, Earl Archibald's uncle, James Douglas of Balvenie, had already become earl of Avondale and 'justiciar of the whole realm of Scots generally constituted' early in his nephew's lieutenancy. Tanner suggests that 'Balvenie ... was clearly to act as [the fifth earl]'s right hand man';[90] and this

---

[84] Dunlop, A.I., *The Life and Times of James Kennedy Bishop of St Andrews* (Edinburgh, 1950) [Dunlop, *Bishop Kennedy*], pp. 22, 349 (*Foedera*, x, pp. 688–95; *Rot Scot*, ii, pp. 306–10).

[85] See generally Burns, *Scottish Churchmen*, especially at pp. 60–85; Tanner, *LMSP*, pp. 101–07.

[86] Tanner, *LMSP*, pp. 93–112 (quotation at 93).

[87] Borthwick, 'Council', p. 94. See also Brown, M., 'Public Authority and Factional Conflict: Crown, Parliament and Polity, 1424–1455', in Brown, K.M. and Tanner, R.J., (eds), *The History of the Scottish Parliament volume I: Parliament and Politics in Scotland 1235–1560* (Edinburgh, 2004) [Brown, 'Public Authority'], pp. 123–44, 131–35. Note also Brown, 'Lele Consail', pp. 60–61.

[88] Borthwick, 'Council', p. 95.

[89] See for the key personnel in the minority government 1437–49 Tanner, *LMSP*, pp. 107–21; McGladdery, *James II*, pp. 86–92, 108–09.

[90] Tanner, *LMSP*, p. 79.

CHAPTER TWO: REGENCY, COUNCIL AND THE EARLS OF DOUGLAS 1437–51

was probably because, although his position at court had certainly faded under James I, he had lengthy prior experience of the demands of government.[91] His nephew's death in 1439 did not deprive Balvenie of his prominence in the regency government, which was reinforced by his becoming the seventh earl of Douglas in 1440 after the Black Dinner. But he fell out of the circles of power in the course of 1441 and 1442 after the defeat of his conciliarist position in relation to the schism in the Church.[92]

Another prominent figure in the regency administration from 1439 on was Alexander, lord of the Isles, earl of Ross. As we have already seen, he at least claimed to be the king's lieutenant in northern parts, paralleling the role of Campbell of Lochawe in Argyll in the west.[93] Alexander was certainly justiciar north of Forth from 1439 until his death in 1449.[94] Sir William Crichton, chancellor 1439–44 and again 1447–53, was another figure of central significance who was sufficiently important to survive the sentence of outlawry which cost him the chancellorship in 1444, and then to return to office in 1447.[95] By virtue of his office Crichton had custody of the great seal, without which in particular no Crown grant of land could be made. From March 1441 to August 1443, he signed with the word 'Cancellarius' the tag of virtually all great seal charters, perhaps part of a system devised to ensure that during the minority such charters were not issued only in the interests of one part of the regency government.[96] Alongside Crichton as keeper of the privy seal from 1440 on (and after the minority's end, although until no later than November 1452) was Mr William Turnbull, consecrated as bishop of Glasgow in April 1448. Together the appointments of Crichton and Turnbull ensured that the system of royal seals lay beyond the control of any faction within the minority government, with the effect that it formed an important brake on the undue distribution of land.[97]

---

[91] Borthwick, 'Council', pp. 45–46.
[92] Tanner, *LMSP*, pp. 105–06. See further on Earl James' conciliarist position Chapter 1 above, text accompanying notes 109 and 110.
[93] See above, text accompanying note 78.
[94] MacQueen, 'Tame Magnates?', p. 107.
[95] On Crichton's career, see Borthwick, 'Crichton, William of that ilk, first lord Crichton', *ODNB*; Borthwick, 'Council', pp. 125–30. James Bruce, bishop of Dunkeld, was chancellor in the interval between Crichton's two spells in office.
[96] Borthwick, 'Council', pp. 92–93.
[97] Borthwick, 'Council', pp. 91–94.

Most significant of all in the regency government, however, was Alexander Livingston of Callendar who became a dominant figure following his dramatic arrest of the queen mother in 1439.[98] We can speak of 'the Livingston revolution' thereafter. Throughout the rest of the minority family members and associates gained numerous offices and financial concessions from the Crown such that it is hard to find any document which has a royal connection and is more than a simple brieve where there is no mention of anyone with the surname Livingston.[99] Of particular significance was Alexander's son James becoming the king's custodian by 1445 and probably from 1442 at latest.[100] Further, only Crichton the chancellor witnessed more royal documents in the minority (122) than Alexander Livingston's 119 appearances in that role.[101] Alexander also succeeded the seventh earl of Douglas as justiciar south of Forth by 1444. In September 1449, a few months after the death of the lord of the Isles, Alexander was possibly exercising the office of justiciar throughout the kingdom as he then appears as justiciar of 'Scotia'.[102] The end of the minority was signalled by the king's overthrow of the Livingstons while Alexander was in England on diplomatic business in the autumn of 1449.[103] Alexander would remain in exile while other members of his family were executed or imprisoned.

A further significant development during the minority was the emergence of the title 'lord of parliament' for a group of, initially, around 20 men.[104] The title seems to have entitled them to individual summons to Parliament when convened. These lords were primarily drawn from the 'greater barons', i.e. those holding three or more baronies without having earldoms or provincial lordships, and outweighing lesser barons not only in terms of land and wealth

---

[98] On Alexander Livingston, see Borthwick, 'Council', pp. 58–62, 81–82.

[99] Borthwick, 'Council', p. 60. See also ibid., pp. 61–80 for detailed analysis of the sources to support these conclusions.

[100] Borthwick, 'Council', p. 61; see further Appendix C, sv Keeper of the King's Person. The post of custodian may have been linked to James' position as captain of Stirling castle, which he held from 1442 at latest: Borthwick, 'Council', Appendix D, sv Stirling.

[101] Borthwick, 'Council', p. 82.

[102] *CDS*, iv, no. 1216 (dated 18 September 1449 at Durham).

[103] Ibid.; Borthwick, 'Council', pp. 58–62, 81–82, 89. See further below, text accompanying notes 103, 151-56.

[104] Grant, 'Scottish Peerage', pp. 11–27; Tanner, *LMSP*, pp. 82–86, 116–18.

but also political significance. In other words, they were figures who needed to be involved in and by the regency government. Decisions at meetings of the Three Estates, whether as Parliaments or General Councils, would be far more effective with these lords on board. They may or may not have been part of the inner council as it developed through the 1440s: William Crichton became lord Crichton, for example, but Alexander Livingston was never a lord of parliament. But the support of the lords of parliament for the inner council was generally important. In particular they would have been crucial in maintaining what Roland Tanner shows was the consistent policy of the Three Estates during the period between 1439 and 1449: overseeing and controlling alienation of the royal estates, preventing abuse of royal resources, protecting the king's rights and ensuring the continuing administration of justice in the kingdom.[105] Much of this, of course, would also have been the role of the Three Estates in relation to the supervision of any individual regent had one been appointed.

The Eighth Earl of Douglas and the Regency Government

The succession of William as eighth earl of Douglas in 1443 was probably the next crucial event for the minority government and its suggested inner council. Christine McGladdery remarks that from 1445 'the next four years would be dominated by William 8th earl of Douglas and his close allies'.[106] Michael Brown writes that 'Earl William's appearances as a councillor of the king from 1444 to 1449 were designed to secure his personal ascendancy in the minority regime', and adds: 'Earl William and his brothers claimed a place at the royal council table as the king's greatest subjects, his 'natural' advisers, the heirs, not of James I's servant [*i.e. James the Gross*], but of Robert I's right hand [*i.e. the Good Sir James*]'. Roland Tanner describes the period from 1444 until September 1449 as 'the Douglas supremacy', and argues that a Douglas-Livingston alliance was behind the overthrow of Crichton as chancellor in 1444; that the lords of parliament were augmented with Douglas friends and allies in 1445; and that in the same year the young king took an oath in Parliament only to change the law or act for the common profit of the realm with the consent of the Three Estates. Further,

---
[105] Tanner, *LMSP*, pp. 81, 87–88, 94, 96, 111, 114.
[106] Tanner, *LMSP*, p. 115.

Earl William's younger brothers Archibald and Hugh became earls (of Moray and Ormond respectively).[107]

The 1445 Parliament, which began in Perth before moving to Edinburgh, was clearly a significant occasion. It was the first gathering to be so named in the reign since the king's coronation in March 1437, and the king according to one document sat *'pro tribunali in regali habitu et maiestate'*.[108] A civil war was almost over (William lord Crichton was readmitted to the governing council immediately afterwards);[109] new earls and lords of parliament were appointed;[110] upon papal authority a custom by which kings claimed the moveables of deceased bishops was set aside, while the procedure for removing treasonous bishops was confirmed;[111] and treason trials were held alongside other judicial acts.[112] Lords of the articles were appointed, perhaps for the first time, although very little legislation seems to have been produced.[113] Probably responding to the king's oath, the prelates took an oath of fealty to him, while the barons offered their sworn homage and fealty, both groups undertaking to keep the king free from harm and to give him good counsel.[114] The occasion was a major event, therefore, when the 'community of the realm' actively sought a general reconciliation under a still young but

---

[107] Tanner, *LMSP*, pp. 107–18. See also McGladdery, *James II*, pp. 45–48, 53–54, 58–61; and, for the king's oath, Chapter 1 above, text accompanying note 23.

[108] For the 1437 coronation Parliament, see *RPS*, 1437/3/1 and 2. For the king sitting *pro tribunali* in 1445, see *RPS*, A1445/10.

[109] Tanner, *LMSP*, p. 115; McGladdery, *James II*, p. 58.

[110] Tanner, *LMSP*, p. 117; McGladdery, *James II*, p. 59.

[111] *RPS*, 1445/9.

[112] *RPS*, 1445/7 and 8; A1445/11.

[113] Angus Archives, Montrose burgh records, M/W1/4/11 (a notarial instrument, 30 June 1445, made before reverend and venerable fathers in Christ, noble and potent lords, and honourable burgh commissioners, deputed by the king and the Three Estates in Parliament to decide on the articles). For the legislation passed in 1445, see *RPS*, 1445/2 ('parliament concludit and decretit that all and sindri landis, possessiounis and movables of the quhilk of gude mynde king James [I] quham Gode assolye, fadir til our soverane lorde that now is, the day of his decese had in possessioune pessable, sal abide and remayn withe oure said soverane lorde that now is in sic lik possessioune as his fadir broukit thaim, undemandit and unpleyit of ony man befor ony juge wythein the realme on to the tym of his lauchful age'). Note that this attributes no active legislative role to the king himself.

[114] *RPS*, 1445/4-6. The king's oath is at *RPS*, 1445/3.

maturing king, Parliament being the only real place where such a significant occurrence could take place.

We are, however, cautious about any general Douglas 'dominance', 'ascendancy' or 'supremacy' in the regency government from 1444 on. For example, while the belting of the eighth earl's younger brothers as earls was probably carried out by the minor king under the tutelage of his council, Archibald was most likely the beneficiary of an earlier marriage with Elizabeth Dunbar, one of the co-heiresses of the Moray earldom, a marriage in which the seventh rather than the eighth earl may, however, have been the key mover: a document of 1441 shows him then acting as tutor to the girls.[115] Given that Archibald's twin James was at that point set on an ecclesiastical career, a good marriage may have been seen as the best way of promoting the younger twin's future interests as well. It is, however, significant for later events that Elizabeth was the younger of the two sisters. The older, Janet, who might have been thought to have the better claim to the earldom title on ordinary principles,[116] was married to Sir James Crichton, the son of the then out-of-favour and former chancellor, William lord Crichton. The growing power and influence of the eighth earl at the time may well therefore be detectable in the Moray title going to his brother rather than the son of one who was probably his enemy. But this outcome was one which, as we shall see in the next chapter, would fall under review after the earl's death in 1452.[117]

Further, while it may be accepted that Earl William was regularly at court and active in government, witnessing 83 charters there between July 1444 and January 1452, it would be unwise to see him as continually present. That of course need not mean that his influence was limited; but matters affecting his estates clearly demanded considerable attention from him as well. Moreover, an examination of the occurrences of the eighth earl in documents affecting his own estates leads to the conclusion that his position even there was not in the least as secure as might be expected.[118] It is certainly true that a basic issue for the eighth earl was the reunification of the Douglas lands. As already noted, the 1342 tailzie in favour of male heirs did not carry with it all the Douglas

---

[115] NLS Dep.175 Box 184 no 2.
[116] See Chapter 1 above, text accompanying note 37.
[117] See further Chapter 3 below, text accompanying note 92.
[118] Borthwick, 'Council', p. 144. See also ibid., p. 148.

lands. The estates and offices acquired by Archibald the Grim during his highly successful career *before* he became third earl of Douglas, in particular those of the earldom of Wigtown and the lordship of Galloway between the Rivers Cree and Nith, remained unentailed and open to inheritance by females.[119]

As a result, on the execution and non-forfeiture of the sixth earl in 1440 the untailzied estates went to his minor sister, Margaret, the 'Fair Maid of Galloway'. Although Earl William was designing himself 'lord of Galloway' by 20 August 1443,[120] his marriage with Margaret did not take place until 1444. This may have been when he attained majority and when she reached the marriageable age of 12, but it was certainly a union of cousins within the forbidden degrees of the canon law which therefore required a papal dispensation.[121] While the marriage did not by itself reunite the Douglas territories, any heir born of it would inherit them all; and meantime the eighth earl could control his minor wife's as well as his own estates. No heir had been produced by 1447, however; this was when his mother and 'certain good women' declared that of the twin boys James and Archibald who were her next-born sons James was the elder and therefore the heir to Earl William should the latter not father any children.[122] Margaret's heir should she outlive her husband but not have any children with him, it should be noted, was most probably her oldest male cousin and brother-in-law.

In Chapter 4 we explore in detail Earl William's attempts to assert a regality and consequent superiority in the barony of Hawick, held by the Douglases of Drumlanrig by virtue of a grant made by the fourth earl of Douglas in 1407, and where the eighth earl's claim must have begun with his wife's right to the untailzied Douglas lands.[123] He seems, however, to have been already

---

[119] See above Chapter 1 text accompanying notes 71–83.
[120] *Laing Chrs*, no. 122.
[121] See Chapter 1 above, text accompanying note 62. For the age of marriage, see Chapter 1 above, text accompanying note 60.
[122] *RMS*, ii, no. 301 (royal confirmation under the great seal dated 9 January 1450 of an indenture made at Edinburgh on 25 August 1447 between James and Archibald Douglas *'fratres gemellos'* before their mother and William, earl of Douglas). See further Chapter 1 above, text accompanying note 112.
[123] Borthwick, A. and MacQueen, H., 'Three Fifteenth-Century Cases', *Juridical Review* 31 (1986), pp. 123–51 [Borthwick and MacQueen, 'Three Fifteenth-Century Cases']; Borthwick, 'Council', pp. 145–46; Chapter 4 below.

infeft in the lands of the barony of Hawick in his own right in 1446 (i.e. after he had attained majority).[124] Another example of the earl's acquisitiveness was his exercise of lordship in all Galloway from at latest 1447, occupying its chief residence at Threave, making land grants and authorising regalian judicial proceedings in his own name and on each side of the Cree.[125] This probably followed a resignation of the lands to the earl by Margaret, duchess of Touraine and countess of Galloway, widow of the fourth earl (and sister of James I).[126] She had held lifetime rights in the lordship of all Galloway by virtue of a royal grant of 1426, made after the fourth earl's death two years before, and probably as a special favour from her royal brother.[127] The grant consolidated what had been the originally two separate grants of the earldom of Wigtown and the lordship of Galloway between the Rivers Cree and Nith to Archibald the Grim.[128] Although the countess herself did not die until late 1450 or 1451, her resignation to the eighth earl may well have been made not long after he succeeded to the earldom in 1443; possibly when he reached his majority in 1444.

Further, on 2 February 1450, 'before the three estates of the realm in full parliament', the king granted to Earl William the *maritagium* of Margaret Douglas, daughter of the late Earl Archibald, 'with all the lands, rents, fermes and possessions which justly and according to the laws of the realm ought to pertain to the same *maritagium*'.[129] Given that the earl was already married to Margaret, the significance of this grant was not so much the power to control her marriage (although there was perhaps implicit royal and parliamentary

---

[124] *ER*, ix, p. 659 (index to Responde Books); Fraser, *Buccleuch*, ii, no. 38 (23 July 1446).

[125] *RMS*, ii, no. 383 (grant of lands at Isle of Whithorn in regality, made at Threave 1447); Fraser, *Carlaverock*, ii, no. 38 (brieve of perambulation on the marches between the lands of Sweetheart Abbey and the neighbouring lord of Kirkconnell at the estates of Airds in Kirkcudbright-shire, described as within the regality of Galloway 1448).

[126] See *RMS*, ii, no. 309, discussed further below, text accompanying note 143–44.

[127] *RMS*, ii, no. 47.

[128] See further below, Chapter 3, text accompanying notes 44–49. Note too the claim made around 1450 that the king 'gaif [Galloway] to the Douglas [*i.e.* Archibald the Grim], heretable ay [*i.e. always*]': *The Buke of the Howlat*, ed. Hanna, R. (Woodbridge, 2014), lines 560–72, discussed in the editor's introduction at ibid., 41–42.

[129] *RMS*, ii, no. 315.

blessing for what had already happened in that regard) as the control of her inheritance until she came of age. The grant was thus an insurance policy against any doubts that might be harboured about the earl's entitlements as merely the husband of a still-minor bride.

Earl William's acquisitive policy was not invariably successful: for example, his failures between 1445 and 1450 to get the sixth earl's widow, Jean Lindsay, to abandon most of her other claims to terce in exchange for help in gaining terce in Annandale (which had lapsed to the Crown on her husband's execution without male heirs of his body) and to find her a new husband.[130] Probably in 1448, he joined with his wife and the duchess of Touraine and countess of Douglas (possibly in reciprocation for the latter's resignation of Galloway) in writing to King Charles VII of France in pursuit of any rights they might have in the late fourth earl's landed interests in France. The claim was swiftly and not unsurprisingly knocked down by the French king on the Salic law grounds that Earl William was not a male descendant of the fourth earl.[131] But even these unsuccessful ventures help make clear Earl William's overall strategy of regaining control of his family's estates as well as his self-confidence in petitioning a foreign king and seeking deals with others who had no particular reason to trust him or his family.

The 1449 Transumpt and Its Immediate Aftermath

In January 1449, with the minority government and the Livingstons still operative, a transumpt[132] embodied in a royal charter was made of seven fourteenth-century documents lying at the root of the Douglas title to various lands.[133] No fewer than the first four of the seven related to Galloway. The first three of these related to the earldom of Wigtown (i.e. Galloway west of the

---

[130] NRS: RH6/321. See further Dunlop, *Bishop Kennedy*, pp. 34, 130; Borthwick, 'Council', p. 145.

[131] *Letters and Papers Illustrative of the Wars of the English in France, temp. Henry VI*, ed. Stevenson, J. (London, 1861), i, pp. 20, 21; Fraser, *Douglas*, iii, pp. 374–79.

[132] A transumpt is an authenticated copy of another document, normally executed by a notary public under his declaration and sign manual.

[133] NLS: Ch 951; NRS: GD212/1/10 (Maitland Thomson transcript); *Wigtown Charter Chest*, no. 30 (1681 inventory summary). See Appendix (a).

River Cree): one David II's grant of the earldom to Thomas Fleming in 1367; another Robert II's 1372 grant of the earldom to Archibald upon Thomas' resignation as earl; and the third the same king's confirmation of contracts previously made by Thomas to sell the earldom to Archibald. The fourth Galloway document was the grant by David II to Archibald the Grim of the lands between the Rivers Cree and Nith, i.e. eastern Galloway. As already noted, none of these lands were amongst the tailzied Douglas territories; further, none of them had descended to Earl William amongst the Balvenie estates.

Plate 1: NLS Charter 951
(Courtesy of the National Library of Scotland)

The three other documents transumed[134] were, in order, a David II grant of Hawick with Sprouston (both in Roxburghshire) to Thomas Murray the pantler (i.e. of Bothwell) dated 1358; a record of an inquest of 1320 into the regality of Sprouston; and a Robert I grant to his cousin William Murray of half the tenement of Stewarton in Ayrshire, made in 1321. All the lands concerned were ones that had been acquired by Archibald the Grim before he became the third earl of Douglas, and were thus also not amongst the tailzied Douglas estates or the Balvenie part of the inheritance. The lands linked to the Murrays had come to Archibald via his marriage with Joanna Murray of Bothwell around 1360.[135]

An inquiry into at least some of the unentailed Douglas lands stemming from Archibald the Grim was clearly in train by 1449, although at whose instigation is not made explicit by the transumpt.[136] Its character is unique, not only for the reign of James II, but also for his predecessor's. It is not a confirmation, simply an inspection *ad futuram rei memoriam*. Any transuming notary remains unnamed, and there is no notarial sign manual. While the transumpt was drawn up in the king's name and his great seal was to be used for its authentication, the seals of a number of witnesses were also appended to it (although only seal tags have survived). All the named witnesses were active in the minority government at the time as well as having links to the Douglas earls.

William Turnbull, bishop of Glasgow, had been keeper of the privy seal since 1440; his initial rise to prominence had, however, been under the patronage of the fourth and fifth earls of Douglas.[137] Alexander Lindsay, earl of Crawford, by this time had probably entered the band with the eighth earl and the earl of Ross which in February 1452 would become the immediate bone of

---

[134] Transume means to make an authenticated copy of a document. This would normally be executed by a notary public under his declaration and sign manual.

[135] See above Chapter 1 above, text accompanying notes 81–84 for the marriage of Archibald and Joanna; and further below Chapter 3 text accompanying notes 63–66 on the acquisition of Stewarton.

[136] The underlying process may have been akin to that discussed by Maxtone Graham, R.M., 'Showing the Holding', *Juridical Review* 2 (1957), pp. 251–69. See also MacQueen, *CLFS*, pp. 120–22.

[137] See further Durkan, J., *William Turnbull Bishop of Glasgow* (Glasgow, 1951) [Durkan, *William Turnbull*], pp. 19–27.

contention in the fatal clash between the king and Earl William.[138] We have already met Alexander Livingston of Callendar, knight.[139] Mr James Lindsay was a former secretary to the eighth earl who had become provost of the collegiate church of Lincluden, founded by Archibald the Grim c.1400.[140] Robert Livingston, the comptroller, was one of the family beneficiaries of the Livingston revolution.[141] A significant absentee, however, was Chancellor Crichton, by whose authority alone the great seal could have been appended to the transumpt. In January 1449 he was abroad on important government business, helping to negotiate with Philip, duke of Burgundy, the king's marriage to Mary, daughter of Arnold duke of Gueldres, and remained there until the spring.[142]

While Earl William did not witness the transumpt, it is inconceivable that he was unaware of its making. The original documents had apparently been inspected and their authenticity confirmed by the presence of royal seals

---

[138] Cox, J., 'The Lindsay Earls of Crawford: The Heads of the Lindsay Family in Late Medieval Scottish Politics, 1380–1453' (Edinburgh University PhD, 2009), pp. 200–35. See further below, Chapter 3, text accompanying notes 115–19.

[139] See above, text accompanying notes 98–103.

[140] On Lindsay's 'eccentric career', see Borthwick, 'Council', pp. 154–57.

[141] Borthwick, 'Council', pp. 68–70.

[142] Also involved in the marriage embassy were John Ralston, bishop of Dunkeld, and Nicholas Otterburn, official of St Andrews and canon of Glasgow (McGladdery, *James II*, p. 75). Sir George Seton was of the party too: see *Scots Peerage*, viii, pp. 575–76; McGladdery, C.A., 'Seton family, per c.1300-c.1510', *ODNB*. See further Brown, M.H., 'War, Marriage, Tournament: Scottish Politics and the Anglo-French War, 1448–1450', *Scottish Historical Review* xcviii (2019), pp. 1–21 [Brown, 'War, Marriage, Tournament'], 6–12. The official register of the great seal is deficient for much of the 1440s. While there are no registered charters for the period from April 1445 to December 1449 (*RMS*, ii, no. 289, the charter there stated to be dated 17 December 1447, should be regarded as dated 1444), we know that charters and other documents continued to be issued under the great seal, including for the year from June 1448 when Crichton was absent from the realm as ambassador. No-one in particular is known to have had custody of the great seal in Crichton's absence (see Borthwick, 'Council', pp. 414–19). This is similar to the lengthy absence from Scotland of John Cameron, bishop of Glasgow and James I's chancellor, who was working on the king's behalf before the Council of Basle and Pope Eugenius IV from 1433 to 1437 (Brown, M.H., 'Cameron, John (d.1446)'). Great seal documents continued to be issued despite Cameron's absence.

as well as the absence of suspicious erasures or other vices. Such access would have required the earl's cooperation. The transumpt witnesses were generally amongst his allies and supporters in government. Further, there appears to have been at least one favourable consequence for him in the grant made to him in a Parliament on 26 January 1450, under which he received the whole province of Galloway on both sides of the River Cree (i.e. the earldom of Wigtown and the lordship between Cree and Nith) as a single unit. The grant was preceded by a resignation to the king by the earl, confirming that he was seen as already holding the lordship of Galloway. As noted above, Earl William styled himself 'lord of Galloway' from at least 20 August 1443; he first appeared as a Crown charter witness with this designation on 3 January 1448.[143] The 1450 grant was made with 'the mature deliberation and full consent of the three estates of the realm in full parliament'. The full consent was probably needed because this grant certainly had elements in diminution of the royal estate. It seemed to perpetuate the consolidation for the fourth earl's widow, Countess Margaret, of what had been originally two separate grants. Further, the regality jurisdiction now given over the whole was greater than the baronial rights over each of the parts which, as the 1449 transumpt showed, Archibald the Grim had originally received from David II.[144] There was no mention of the fact that the heritable rights in the Galloway lands were, as with Hawick and Sprouston, those of the earl's wife Margaret, and so pertained to him only through that marriage.

On the same day in Parliament the earl further received a royal grant of Ettrick and Selkirk Forest (again with 'the mature deliberation and full consent of the three estates of the realm in full parliament'), having previously resigned the lands to the king.[145] The Forest had been amongst the Douglas estates erected into a regality for William, lord of Douglas, by David II in 1355.[146] Now in 1450 the Forest was granted back to the eighth earl, not only in regality, but also *in regaliam*, a phrase meaning, as we will explain further below, with the

---

[143] *RMS*, ii, no. 309; Brown, *Black Douglases*, p. 288; above, text accompanying note 120; NLS: Acc. 5976 Box 6 bundle 55 no. 11.
[144] This is discussed further and in more detail in Chapter 3, text accompanying notes 46–49.
[145] *RMS*, ii, no. 308.
[146] *RMS*, i, app 1, no. 123.

king's full rights.[147] The king further granted to the earl 'any right pertaining to him [*the king*] by virtue of any resignation or donation made by the late Archibald earl of Douglas to King James [*I*]'; another piece of phraseology to which we will revert in Chapter 3.[148]

As already noted, shortly before the Parliament began, there was issued a royal confirmation of the 1447 indenture affirming who was the elder of the earl's immediate younger twin brothers and therefore his and (separately) his wife's heir if there was no issue of their marriage.[149] During the Parliament itself Earl William was granted, not only the *maritagium* of his still-minor wife as noted above, but also some lands that had previously been forfeited by James Dundas for treason.[150] But all these successes, mostly consolidating and extending the earl's authority over the estates in question, must have been offset by the absence of any resolution of the position relating to the other estates mentioned in the 1449 transumpt, namely Hawick and Sprouston on the one hand, and Stewarton on the other. We will see in Chapter 4 that with Hawick in particular, the position was being keenly contested by its baron, William Douglas of Drumlanrig, and that this was closely linked to Sprouston.[151] As will also emerge more clearly in Chapter 3, Stewarton too was the subject of competing claims that plainly remained unresolved in early 1450.[152] In the investigation and re-granting of the earl's titles which clearly began to take place within royal government early in 1449, there is apparent a desire to sort out a chaotically uncertain and variable situation in the untailzied Douglas territories in particular, most probably at the instigation of the eighth earl himself. But the goal was not a readily achievable one in all cases, since other interests were engaged.

The End of the King's Minority

All the grants actually made in January 1450, however, show Earl William in favour with a king now exercising full personal authority at the head of

---

[147] See Chapter 3 below, text between notes 42 and 43, and text accompanying notes 72–73.
[148] See Chapter 3 below, text following note 42.
[149] See text accompanying note 122 above.
[150] *RMS*, ii, nos 316 and 317.
[151] See Chapter 4 below, text accompanying notes 81, 110, 118, 121.
[152] See Chapter 3 below, text from note 57 to 87.

government. The king had married Mary of Gueldres on 3 July 1449 before moving to oust the Livingstons in late September, and assume full regal authority, even although yet to achieve his full age of 21. The Livingstons' previous closeness to Earl William does not seem to have affected the latter's position at this point; indeed, the Dundas estates which the earl received in the 1450 Parliament were forfeited as a result of James Dundas' association with the Livingstons.[153] In May 1450 Earl William was granted more lands forfeited by Dundas and members of the Livingston family.[154]

The justification for the overthrow of the Livingstons is not expressed in surviving contemporary records. Something may be gleaned from the remission (i.e., pardon) granted to James Livingston and his father Alexander in Parliament in August 1452, which refers to the process against the Livingstons and their associates in the Parliament at Edinburgh in January 1450.[155] The remission states that it was made notwithstanding certain acts or decreets given before in councils general or parliament, especially one which said that anyone placing hands on the king, the queen, the prince or the king's castles, committed treason without any remission. This last must refer to another act passed in the Parliament of January 1450 laying down that

> gif ony man as God forbeid commit or dois treson agaynis the kingis persoune or his majeste or rise in feire of were agaynis hym or lais handis in his persoune violently of quhat age the king be of young or aulde, or resettis ony that ar convict of tresoune or that suppleis thaim in help, red or consale, or that stuffis the housis of thaim that ar convict of tresoune and haldis thaim agayn the king, or at stuffis housis of thare awin in furthiring of the kingis rebellis,

---

[153] Borthwick, 'Council', p. 155, suggests that while Douglas did not fall from royal favour alongside the Livingstons he ceased to be fully accepted in court circles after their fall. The evidence – some eclipse of Douglas associates on the king's council after September 1449 – is, however, circumstantial.

[154] *RMS*, ii, no. 357.

[155] NLS: Adv Ch B.1316 and 1317 (two versions, nearly identical texts). See Appendix (b). There is nothing in the surviving record and other evidence of the Parliament held in January 1450 (*RPS* 1450/1) to reflect proceedings there against the Livingstons or their associates. See further on the remission Borthwick, 'Council', pp. 101–02, 115 note 134; Borthwick, A.R., 'Livingston, Alexander, of Callendar (b.c.1375, d. in or before 1456)', *ODNB*.

or at assailyeis castellis or placis quhar the kingis persoune sal happyn to be, witht oute the consent of the thre estatis, sal be punyst as traytouris, etc.[156]

While the king avenging the 1439 arrest of the queen mother and the transfer of his own custody to James Livingston may or may not have also been part of the story,[157] any personal rancour against James did not prevent the latter's ultimate remission. As with the Black Dinner trial, the records of any proceedings against the Livingstons may have been destroyed when the judgement against them was rescinded by the remission. The likeliest cause for the Three Estates' acceptance in 1450 of what had happened to the Livingstons the year before is a perception, whether or not justified, of abuse of the powers of regency in the minority government in the self-advancement of the family and its allies. It is certainly striking that Livingston associates as well as the Livingstons themselves were swept from government after September 1449, while others such as Chancellor Crichton and Bishop Turnbull remained firmly in position.[158]

Personal tragedy befell the king and his wife on 19 May 1450 when their firstborn, but premature, child lived for only six hours.[159] This must once again have raised questions about who was to succeed if James II were to die childless. The king and queen would not produce a son until May 1452; he was presumably the prince referred to in the Livingston remission later that year. Although the royal couple had three further boys between 1454 and 1457 (plus two girls, one born in the spring of 1451 and the other by 1460), the death of the second of these boys in infancy further demonstrated the uncertainties with which even royal parents had to live in the middle ages.[160]

---

[156] *RPS* 1450/1/24. See also 'A Letter of James III to the Duke of Burgundy', ed. Armstrong, C.A.J., *Scottish History Society Miscellany VIII* (Edinburgh, 1951), in which c.1471 James III king of Scots tells the duke about the statute enacted in his father's reign making it treason to seize the king's person without parliamentary sanction. The context is the king asking the duke to cease his support of the exiled Boyds who had themselves seized custody of the minor king in a coup in 1466 (Macdougall, *James III*, pp. 69–72).
[157] See above text accompanying notes 79–81, 100.
[158] Borthwick, 'Council', pp. 62–76, 101–04 (collapse of Livingston power), 121–54 (Crichton family and associates beneficiaries of patronage after 1449).
[159] *Auchinleck Chronicle* f 122v (McGladdery, *James II*, p. 275).
[160] Macdougall, *James III*, p. 20.

The Eighth Earl Abroad

In October 1450 Earl William departed abroad with his brother James, his close associate Sir James Hamilton, and various others, first, to celebrate the papal jubilee in Rome, and also to hold diplomatic meetings en route in Burgundy, France and (on the way back) England.[161] The trip was not just 'to restore credit at the papal curia lost by his father's association with Basle' or to achieve 'the wider goal of recovering the influence of his family across western Europe'.[162] John Law's early sixteenth-century chronicle (possibly derived from a now lost part of the contemporary Auchinleck chronicle) says that the earl's trip was made with the king's licence and good will.[163] We also know from a notarial instrument dated 7 June 1451 that the earl then claimed to stand 'under the king's respite', by which the court action against him by William Douglas of Drumlanrig in relation to Hawick (and Sprouston) was suspended.[164] From the evidence of legal formularies, this respite was most probably a royal grant of immunity from any legal action against the earl while he was absent from the kingdom on (significantly) the king's business (rather than his own alone).[165] It had most likely been granted to the earl before he set out for Rome in October 1450, albeit probably having to be renewed after his return to Scotland in April 1451 to allow him to take part in Anglo-Scottish truce negotiations in England that were set up at around the same time.[166] Law's account is thus corroborated by the evidence of legal form: the trip's purpose apart from

---

[161] The earl and his party reached Lille on 12 October 1450: Dunlop, *Bishop Kennedy*, p. 124 note 3. The journey involved pleasure alongside business: see Ditchburn, D., *Scotland and Europe: The Medieval Kingdom and Its Contacts with Christendom, 1214–1560* (East Linton, 2000) [Ditchburn, *Scotland and Europe*], p. 138; Stevenson, *Chivalry and Knighthood*, pp. 78–79, 115–16.

[162] Brown, *Black Douglases*, p. 287. Cf Grant, *Independence and Nationhood*, p. 192.

[163] John Law, *De Cronicis Scotorum Brevia*, Edinburgh University Library MS DC.7.63 (relevant extracts printed in *ER*, v, pp. lxxxv-vi). See also McGladdery, *James II*, pp. 227–29 on the relationship of Law's text to the *Auchinleck Chronicle*.

[164] NRS: AD1/53.

[165] For letters putting *in respectu* all actions and complaints against a person going abroad *on the king's business* until his return, see *Scottish Formularies*, A65, B90.

[166] See further Chapter 3 below, text accompanying notes 5–6.

the celebration of the papal jubilee was diplomacy on behalf of the king. Even Earl William could hardly have risked a prolonged absence from the kingdom in 1450-1 without such royal blessing, given what had happened to Alexander Livingston just over a year before.

In three papal supplications granted between January 1450 and May 1452 Earl William is designed as the 'guardian of the kingdom', in one as 'Great Guardian of the kingdom of Scotland'.[167] The earliest of these supplications must have been submitted in the course of 1449, with the others being written before the earl's death in February 1452. It is not improbable that they were all produced before October 1451, while King James II remained technically a minor. The claim to be 'great Guardian of the kingdom' has been downplayed: '[it] seems to indicate his duties as warden of the Marches'.[168] That dismissal is, however, based on the fifth earl describing himself as 'great guardian of the marches of Scotland' in letters to the pope and the French king in 1418 and 1423 respectively.[169] While Earl William was of course hereditary warden of the western and middle marches, following in the footsteps of Archibald the Grim, the claims to be guardian of the kingdom as well should not be so readily brushed aside. By 1450 the earl was at least of full age and clearly involved in the still-minor king's government, indeed probably representing him abroad on the journey to Rome and back. Again, while there probably was never any grant of regency powers to him alone by the Three Estates, the earl's social and political status was certainly higher than that of any other survivor of the minority government of the 1440s.

The earl's party left Rome on 6 February 1451, and towards the end of that month was awaited in England, where Garter King of Arms was to meet the earl and escort him to the presence of King Henry VI.[170] The earl's reappear-

---

[167] *CSSR*, v, nos 310, 462 and 466. The earl is also designed as 'defender of the kingdom' in another supplication dated 15 January 1444 (*CSSR*, iv, no. 987), when he was still a minor himself.

[168] *CSSR*, v, no. 310; Brown, *Black Douglases*, p. 287; McGladdery, *James II*, p. 71; Tanner, *LMSP*, p. 112 note 115.

[169] See Brown, M., 'The Scottish March Wardenships (c.1340-c.1480)', in King, A. and Simpkin, D., (eds), *England and Scotland at War, c.1296-c.1513* (Leiden, 2012), pp. 203-29 [Brown, 'Scottish March Wardenships'], 219 (citing Archives Nationales, Paris, J677, no. 20; *CSSR*, i, p. 8).

[170] *CDS*, iv, no. 1231; McGladdery, *James II*, p. 104.

ance in Scotland may have been by 7 April 1451[171] rather than towards the end of the month as suggested by Brown.[172] The earl certainly issued documents at Jedburgh between 26 April and 6 May, however.[173] Two months later, however, his political position had deteriorated sharply. In a Parliament held in Edinburgh in late June and early July, Earl William 'put him body landis and gudis in the kingis grace at the Request of the qwene and the thre estatis'.[174] Something had clearly happened to sour previously good relations between king and earl. This will be explored in the next chapter.

---

[171] *ER*, v, pp. lxxxv–vi, quoting Law's chronicle (above, note 163) as the source for the date in a footnote.

[172] Brown, *Black Douglases*, p. 290 and note 11, citing *HMC*, xii, app 8, no. 201, which, however, notes only a charter by James Douglas brother german of William, earl of Douglas, on 29 April 1451. Since James had accompanied William on his trip to Rome, however, it is certainly likely that they returned together as well.

[173] *HMC Home*, nos 80, 126 and 201; NRAS859 (Home), Box 131/1.

[174] *Auchinleck Chronicle* f 114r (McGladdery, *James II*, p. 265).

Chapter Three
The Fall of the House of Douglas

Introduction

The causes of the rupture between James II and the eighth earl of Douglas in 1451 have been the subject of much discussion. Recent writing shows a broad consensus that the still newly married king, probably acting with the support of the Burgundian connections made as a result of the marriage, and the advice of his councillors William Crichton and William Turnbull, began to move against the earl during the latter's absence from Scotland in the autumn and winter of 1450–51. The need to fulfil a promised dowry for his new wife was probably a major motivating factor.[1] The king was active in the borders and the south-west during the period and this has been interpreted as manoeuvring to enlist supporters against Douglas ('strategy … to win over the leading men of the communities of the south-west',[2] 'probing weak areas of Douglas lordship … a significant design … to proffer the enticements of direct royal lordship'[3]) in order to stake a claim to the earldom of Wigtown. Another significant event (albeit one mentioned only by sixteenth-century chroniclers and not corroborated by any more contemporary source) was the taking and razing by royal forces of Craig Douglas, a small fortification in the Ettrick Forest

---

[1] See generally Brown, *Black Douglases*, pp. 288–90; McGladdery, *James II*, pp. 101–06; Tanner, *LMSP*, pp. 128–29; Brown, 'War, Marriage, Tournament', pp. 17–20.
[2] Brown, *Black Douglases*, p. 289.
[3] McGladdery, *James II*, p. 103.

('a symbolic gesture to Douglas of the assertion of royal authority with which he was now obliged to come to terms'[4]). In this view, the king's suspicions may also have been raised by the returning earl's apparently tarrying with the English king en route for home, and his brother James possibly negotiating for the release of the hostage Malise Graham, earl of Menteith, with his distant claim to the Crown, at a time when the king still did not have a male heir.

All this speculation around the king's actions in the winter of 1450–51 and their possible significance is, however, somewhat inconsistent with the earl's appointment by 17 April 1451 (over a week after his return to Scotland) as one of a Scottish embassy of eleven altogether to go to Newcastle under the English king's safe conduct to discuss with English commissioners breaches of the Anglo-Scottish truce agreed the previous June.[5] This was to lead on to further negotiations in London for the renewal of the truce, anticipation of which most probably explains the further English safe conduct issued to the earl and 34 of his retainers (plus 60 or 70 further members of the *comitiva*) on 12 May.[6]

It is also, to say the least, left unclear by modern historians whether and how all this relates to an entry in the Auchinleck chronicle that has been rightly described as curious, cryptic, incomplete and undated:[7]

> thai cryit him luftennent and sone efter this thai worthit als strange as euer thai war and at this tyme thai gat the erllis sele to consent to the trewis and Incontinent thai send furth snawdoun the kingis herrod to lundoune to bynd wp the trewis and als fast as Sir Iames of douglas gat wit in herof he past till londone Incontinent and quharfor men wist nocht redelye bot he was thar with the kyng of yngland lang tyme and was mekle maid of.[8]

It is probably right to think that this entry refers to the early spring of 1451, since the immediately following entry relates the summons of Earl William

---

[4] McGladdery, *James II*, p. 104.
[5] *Rot Scot*, ii, pp. 344–45.
[6] *Rot Scot*, ii, p. 346; *CDS*, iv, no. 1232.
[7] McGladdery, *James II*, pp. 104–05.
[8] *Auchinleck Chronicle* f 114r (McGladdery, *James II*, p. 264).

before Parliament in June and the outcome there. But it would be helpful to know to whom 'thai' refers, especially those who were proclaiming someone as lieutenant. This need not mean that the person so proclaimed (very probably the earl) was performing any regency role of the kind discussed in the previous chapter. Instead he was to act in the king's place for a purpose, probably in relation to business regarding the truce.[9] This would also have been consistent with the earl's office as warden of the middle and western marches. 'Thai worthit [*i.e. grew*] als strange as ever thai war' has been read as referring to the earl and king's growing mutual hostility,[10] but it more likely means that whoever 'thai' were (and they were most probably king and earl), they were growing as strong (rather than as strange) as ever they had been, leading to the earl putting his seal to the draft truce and with the king sending Snowdon Herald off to negotiate its finalisation in London.[11] There the latter was speedily joined by the earl's brother James. This last piece of information was not widely known (in Scotland?). But James was with the king of England for a long time and was made much of there.

James Douglas' presence with Henry VI in the summer of 1451, escorted by Garter King of Arms, is attested in the English records, as also that of Snowdon Herald.[12] The nine-year Anglo-Scottish truce of 1438, agreed

---

[9] McGladdery, *James II*, p. 105, notes that 'the term 'luftennent' does appear in other places in the Auchinleck Chronicle carrying the meaning of the king's representative.' A discharge granted to James, master of Douglas, dated 1 June 1450 and mentioned in an instrument of 17 May 1473 also refers to the 'high and mighty lord James master of Douglas, lieutenant etc' (*sic*) (NRS: GD158/72); it is unclear to what position in 1450 this might refer, and the date seems too early to relate to what is referred to in the Auchinleck chronicle.

[10] Brown, *Black Douglases*, p. 290; Tanner, *LMSP*, p. 129. McGladdery, *James II*, p. 105, reads the phrase as meaning that the Douglases were as strong as ever.

[11] See *https://dsl.ac.uk/* for 'worth' and 'strang'.

[12] *CDS*, iv, nos 1236, 1242 (for a full text of the latter see *Issues of the Exchequer being payments made out of His Majesty's revenue from King Henry III to King Henry VI inclusive (1216–1461) with an appendix*, Record Commission (London, 1837), pp. 471–73). The 'Sir James Douglas' in question is unlikely to have been the alternative 'Sir James', Sir James Douglas of Ralston; the level of hospitality involved was above his social status. For the role of heralds as messengers, escorts and envoys, see Stevenson, K., 'Jurisdiction, Authority and Professionalisation: the Officers of Arms of Late Medieval Scotland', in Stevenson, K. (ed.), *The Herald in Late Medieval Europe* (Suffolk, 2009), ch. 4.

when the fifth earl was lieutenant-general,[13] had expired on 1 May 1447 and was not immediately renewed, ushering in what Michael Brown terms 'the most intensive border conflict for at least thirty years' over the period from September 1448 to August 1449.[14] A new temporary truce commenced in the latter month and (after James II had assumed active government in Scotland) was eventually extended at the pleasure of each king, subject to 180 days' notice.[15] Earl William was appointed as a conservator of this truce along with the earl of Angus, reflecting their roles as wardens of the western, middle and eastern marches.[16] The truce was ratified by James II on 9 June 1450,[17] but negotiations for the more permanent arrangement must have continued. A new three-year truce was certainly concluded at Newcastle on 14 August 1451.[18]

The earl of Douglas was, however, probably embroiled in his Parliamentary process by mid-May, which is when the summons to Parliament would have been sent out.[19] It seems unlikely therefore that he was able to make use of the English safe conducts issued to him on 17 April and 12 May, the first of them explicitly to let him travel to Newcastle or Durham and therefore probably to help conclude the new truce.[20] Moreover, the Scottish king and the royal administration had been continuously based at Edinburgh castle from early March through to the time the truce was concluded in August.[21] Long before the Parliament began in June, therefore, government business requiring

---

[13] See Chapter 2 above, text accompanying note 84.
[14] Brown, 'War, Marriage, Tournament', pp. 3–5.
[15] *Foedera*, xi, pp. 229, 231–33, 236–40, 247–55. See also *CDS*, iv, nos 1212, 1215 and 1216.
[16] *Rot Scot*, ii, pp. 337–41; *Foedera*, xi, p. 253. Note too the statute passed by the Scottish Parliament in January 1450 following the overthrow of the Livingstons and the king's assumption of active personal authority, ordaining the wardens to appoint deputes and officers for whom they would be answerable 'fore the keeping and observing of the trewis' (*RPS* 1450/1/14).
[17] *Foedera*, xi, p. 271.
[18] *Rot Scot*, ii, pp. 347, 354; *Foedera*, xi, pp. 293–301.
[19] Tanner, *LMSP*, p. 129, notes that in order to begin on 28 June Parliament must have been called no later than 19 May.
[20] *Foedera*, xi, pp. 283, 284.
[21] All crown documents between 9 March and 21 August 1451 were issued from Edinburgh (Borthwick, 'Council', Appendix A, nos 438–518). The king himself was certainly present in the castle on 10 June: see *Dunf Reg*, no. 437.

lengthy and fairly continuous discussion within the royal administration was clearly in hand. Relations with England, and how to provide the new queen's dowry, were no doubt high on the agenda throughout; but so too may have been the approach of the king's formal majority and the rights that would then arise to review and revoke the acts of his minority, including the conduct of those who had managed the kingdom during the minority (amongst them the possibly quite unsuspecting earl of Douglas).

The Settlement of 1451

Our analysis of what went wrong between King James and Earl William starts from the settlement that began to be reached between king and earl in July 1451. This is surely the best evidence of what had been in dispute in the first place. It will be recalled that the earl had put his 'body, landis and gudis in the kingis grace' at the request of the queen and the Three Estates (presumably gathered in Parliament). According to the Auchinleck chronicler, the king thereupon

> grantit [the earl] all his lordshippis agane outtane the erldome of wigtoun That is to say Galloway fra the watter of Cre west... and stewartoun ... and charterit him now of all the laif of his lordschippis and gaf him and all his a fre Remission of all thingis bygane to the day forsaid.[22]

Parliamentary records and the great seal register confirm that the earl did indeed receive new royal grants of many of his lands from the king on 6 July, but these did not include the earldom of Wigtown, its associated lands of Galloway west of the River Cree, or the Ayrshire estate of Stewarton.[23] All of these, it will also be recalled, had been included in the 1449 transumpt discussed in the previous chapter; if the underlying inquiry to that document had been initiated in the earl's interest, by the summer of 1451 it was being used against him. The final piece of the settlement jigsaw seemed to fall into place on 26 October 1451, however, when Earl William was granted the

---
[22] *Auchinleck Chronicle* f 114r (McGladdery, *James II*, p. 265).
[23] See also *RPS* 1451/6/5-11; *RMS*, ii, nos 463, 464, 466–72, 474–82. Stewarton is NGR: NS 419 458.

previously withheld Wigtown earldom with the lands of western Galloway and (separately) Stewarton (with neighbouring Dunlop), the latter of which had also been part of the inquiry ongoing in 1449.[24]

Historians have generally seen the immediate outcome of the 1451 crisis as a triumph for the earl of Douglas and a humiliation for a still weak and dependent king.[25] In particular the king is supposed to have wanted the earldom of Wigtown to complete his queen's dowry, with his concession of the earl's entitlement a symptom of his political weakness in the face of the earl. But, as we shall see, even after Earl William's death at the hands of the king and the renunciation of the king's lordship by the earl's brother and heir, the Wigtown earldom was not immediately conferred on the queen. Instead, it continued to be a major negotiating chip for the king in dealing with his victim's vengeful brother. Closer analysis suggests that the whole settlement process with the eighth earl in 1451 was much more like a carefully staged assertion of dominance by the king, completed significantly just 10 days after he achieved his full age of 21 on 16 October. The process was moreover conducted at a time when a new Anglo-Scottish truce was being concluded in a process in which Earl William was supposed to be playing a leading role. His absence from the discussions about the truce at Newcastle was surely conspicuous; his naming as one of the conservators of the truce in the document finalised on 14 August came only after the conclusion of the major part of the Scottish parliamentary process.[26]

By no means all the lands of the earl seem to have been involved in that process: at least the re-grants in 1451 represented only part of the Douglas estate, mostly (although not entirely) from the untailzied portion. Moreover,

---

[24] For the grants see *RMS*, ii, nos 502–03.
[25] Grant, *Independence and Nationhood*, p. 193 (James II 'had to back down … must have been bitterly humiliated'); McGladdery, *James II*, p. 107 ('humiliating climb-down'); Brown, *Black Douglases*, p. 291 ('Douglas had faced down the king'); Tanner, *LMSP*, p. 129 ('sign of the king's failure'); J Cox, 'The Lindsay Earls of Crawford: The Heads of the Lindsay Family in Late Medieval Scottish Politics, 1380–1453' (Edinburgh University PhD, 2009), p. 233 ('move designed to emphasise James II's authority which probably failed … a major victory for earl William'). But cf Grant, A., 'To the Medieval Foundations', *Scottish Historical Review* 73 (1994), pp. 4–24, 10 note 28, hinting at the line of inquiry followed below.
[26] *Foedera*, xi, p. 300.

at least some of the re-grants curbed the earl's previously acquired powers significantly. First, the previous grant of all Galloway in January 1450 must have been rescinded by the reinstatement of the division between the lands east and west of Cree while, as we will see in more detail below, the 1450 grant of Ettrick and Selkirk Forest was re-cast in a fashion that took back an important part of the authority and power it had conferred upon the earl. Further, there were significant variations in the language of the grants actually made. While most were expressed as simple confirmations, five – Ettrick and Selkirk Forest, the wardenship of the west and middle marches (twice over, the second being on 8 July), and two of Galloway east of Cree (both, puzzlingly, on 6 July) – were given 'with the mature deliberation and full consent of the three estates of the realm in full parliament'. This suggests that these lands and offices (as well as the then still withheld Wigtown earldom and Stewarton) were at the heart of whatever the issues were that had put the earl in the king's disfavour and brought him in disgrace before the Parliament.

Finally, the grants over which Parliament was expressly said to have 'deliberated' in July 1451, whether of lands or offices, all declared that they were made –

> notwithstanding (*non obstantibus*) any statutes, decreets, constitutions or ordinances of any parliaments or general councils in the king's minority or at other times which might detract from the foregoing grant in the future, and notwithstanding any crimes being the cause or occasion of forfeiture or treasonous acts perpetrated by the said William or his uncle the late Archibald earl of Douglas or any of his predecessors before the present day.

The reference in the first 'notwithstanding' clause is presumably to legislation of the minority reflecting the consistent policy of the Three Estates from 1437 to 1449, focused on the preservation of the royal estate from alienations. The concern must have been that these acts, an inquiry into which had been authorised in the Parliament held early in 1450,[27] might derogate from the grants now being made by a king still in minority in July 1451. The second 'notwithstanding' clause, with its reference to crimes giving rise to forfeiture in addition to treason committed by Earl William must link to the remission for the earl 'and all his ... of all thingis bygane' mentioned in the Auchinleck chronicle. This

---

[27] *RPS* 1450/1/21.

suggests accusations of serious misconduct by the earls during the whole period of the minority from 1437 on, and a process of review by the Three Estates of their actions during the regency. But the remission headed off any possibility of the Douglas family now sharing the forfeitures, exiles, imprisonments or executions which had befallen the Livingstons nearly two years before.

In addition, Earl William's predecessors as earl were mentioned as possible perpetrators of treasonous acts, with the fourth earl (Archibald, who held the title from 1400 to 1424) being specifically named. This is therefore an indication that the Parliament had under particular review the conduct of Earl Archibald during the period during which King James I was absent from the kingdom and also, for a considerable part of that time, a minor. There was at least one precedent from the reign of Robert I that a dead man could be accused and found guilty of treason, with the consequent sanctions against their estates falling upon his successors.[28] The accusation against Earl Archibald was thus one with potentially serious repercussions for the eighth earl and his heirs.

Some further sense of what was at stake in mid-1451 may be gleaned from study of the history of the various estates and offices over which Parliament deliberated and their administration in the hands of the Douglases over the previous century, and in particular the period from the accession of the absent King James I in 1406. We take each of these estates and offices in turn.

Wardenship of the Middle and Western Marches

The history and nature of the offices of wardenship in the middle and western marches certainly shows why they had become particularly contentious between king and earl. While Archibald the Grim had been the first Douglas to hold these offices, and they had then descended to the third and fourth earls, James I appears to have deprived the fifth earl of at least the middle march and possibly the western one as well.[29] Given the reference in the re-grants of 1451 to the possible treason of the fourth earl, these deprivations may have been due as much to the latter's conduct in office as that of the fifth earl. Further, a Parliament held in 1430 passed with the king's authority 'statutis ordanit for the

---

[28] Penman, M., *Robert Bruce King of the Scots* (New Haven, 2014), p. 222. The deceased accused in 1320 was Roger Mowbray of Barnbougle and Dalmeny.

[29] Brown, 'Scottish March Wardenships', pp. 219–21.

marches', an extensive and unprecedented codification of what had hitherto been a customary law.[30] On 18 December 1448, however, as Anglo-Scottish conflict on the border intensified following the lapsing of the truce in May 1447, Earl William had in his own name and by his own authority as warden issued at Lincluden (in Nithsdale) a new edition of the 'statutis and use of merchis in tym of were [*i.e.* war]'. This made no reference to the king's 1430 statutes and instead purported to 'put in wryt the statutis, ordinancis, and use of merchis that wes ordanit to be kepit in blak Archibald of Douglas dais and Archibald his sonnies dayis', i.e. from 1364 to 1424, before the active reign of James I began.

These Lincluden laws declared treasonous a number of wrongs when committed in the Marches jurisdiction, and concluded with the statement that –

> … all uther thingis that ar nocht now put in writ quhilkis ar pointis of were usit of befoir in tyme of werefar salbe rewlit be the Wardane and his counsall and be the eldest and maist worthy bordouraris that best knawis of the auld use of merche in all tymis to cum.[31]

While the Lincluden statement of the laws went no further than the 1430 statutes in making breaches of march law treason, it also amounted to Earl William's strong reassertion of his family's hereditary claim to the office and, perhaps above all, its autonomy and independence of the king and his parliament, at least in time of war.

Quite possibly, however, this claim had been first renewed by the fifth earl when lieutenant-general between 1437 and 1439. Purported exercise of wardenship jurisdiction may have been the trigger for the formal but forceful protest made before the lieutenant-general and his council in 1438 by the 'venerable' Egidia Stewart, dowager countess of Orkney and in her own hereditary right lady of Nithsdale (and so also its warden), when she denied their authority to hold justice and chamberlain ayres 'or any court' in her

---

[30] *RPS* 1430/32-53. See further Brown, 'Scottish March Wardenships', pp. 220–21; Tanner, *LMSP*, pp. 47–48. The statutes refer five times to the warden having a 'lieutenant': *RPS* 1430/34, 35, 38, 41 and 45.

[31] For the text see *APS*, i, pp. 714–16. See further Neilson, G., 'The March Laws', in *Miscellany I* (Edinburgh, 1970), pp. 12–77, 39–46; Brown, 'Scottish March Wardenships', pp. 221–22.

lordship.[32] If so, Egidia's claim was to the autonomy of her own wardenship jurisdiction; but she was also denying any claim of the fifth earl to a superior jurisdiction across the whole west march. Comital challenge to the assertion of royal authority over the warden of the marches as represented by the actions and legislation of James I may thus have been amongst the 'crimes being the cause or occasion of forfeiture or treasonous acts' of the fifth as well as the eighth earl; and possibly the fourth as well.

It is indicative of the significance attached to the king's ultimate authority over law in the marches that, after the fall of the ninth earl in 1455, king and parliament in August –

> statuyt and ordanyt that in tym to cum thar be na wardanis on the bordoris maid in fe and heritage, and that the wardanis hav na power to knawe the poyntis of tresone saufande the poyntis quhilkis ar neidfull for the confirmatioun of the trewys, ande sa that the wardane court intromet nocht with ony thing that efferis to dittay of the justice.[33]

The limitation of the warden's power to declare what constituted treason, and of his jurisdiction in relation to that of the justiciar, points to what the wrongdoings of Earl William in the role had been. A number of further acts about the marches were also promulgated in Parliament in October the same year, greatly reducing the leadership role of the warden in the region.[34]

---

[32] Fraser, *Douglas*, iii, no. 403.

[33] *RPS* 1455/8/4.

[34] *RPS* 1455/10/2a-15. See further Neilson, 'The March Laws', pp. 48–51; Brown, 'Scottish March Wardenships', pp. 223–24. One consequence of the reduced power of the wardens may have been the possibility of the king (rather than the warden) appointing a lieutenant for the region of the marches: see *HMC Various Collections V, Hay of Duns*, p. 11 (a bond of manrent dated 8 March 1456 in favour of James II by James Tweedy of Drummelzier, which refers to Tweedy making his house ready for the king and his lieutenant whenever required, and if the lieutenant has entry to the house in the king's name he will deliver it back to Tweedy on his departure). Note, however, the lieutenants of the warden referred to in the legislation of 1430 (above, note 30). It should also be noted, however, that the Lincluden text of 1448 was added to the traditional thirteenth-century *Leges Marchiarum* in the manuscript collections of 'auld lawes' compiled and kept by later lawyers: see *Laws of Medieval Scotland*,

Ettrick and Selkirk Forest

Behind the 1451 grant of Ettrick and Selkirk Forest lies a somewhat similar history of expanding Douglas claims being made at the expense of the king. The original grant to the Good Sir James had been to the office of the king's chief forester.[35] But John Gilbert notes that King Robert I also began a trend of granting out the lands in forests and in effect separating them from his forest rights: 'a practice which led to the situation where the holder of the lands of the forest came to regard the forest as his own even though he did not hold forest rights'.[36] The Forest had been amongst the estates erected into the over-arching regality for William, lord of Douglas, by David II in 1355.[37] The whole grant was in fee and heritage, but the holding was also '*in liberam varrenam*', i.e. the right to control the hunting of lesser game, which may have been the only specifically forest right actually given away by the king at this point.[38]

The administration of the forest, which included the appointment of subordinate officers and the holding of courts at which the forest and other laws were applied, seems to have proceeded apace under the earls' control in the fourteenth and fifteenth centuries.[39] At the same time the lands in the forest were increasingly granted or leased out by the earls to produce revenue, not all of which seems to have found its way into royal coffers. That position may have been challenged by King James I after his return to Scotland in 1424, and so once again the administration of the fourth earl may have been a royal target at this time. The king can be found asserting his superiority in the Forest in 1426 when he confirmed grants of forest lands and offices made by the fifth earl both before and after he became earl in 1424.[40] The king also exercised

---

pp. 383–86. On this aspect we have also benefited from an unpublished paper delivered at the Colloquium on *Legal Culture in Medieval and Early Modern Scotland*, held on 16–17 December 2019: Neville, C.J., 'The Manuscript Tradition of the Medieval *Leges Marchiarum* Treatise'.

[35] *RMS*, i, app 1, no. 38 ('*infra forestam nostram de Selkirk de qua* [*Jacobus dominus de Douglas*] *est officiarius noster*'); see also *RRS*, v, nos 288, 329, 330.
[36] Gilbert, J.M., *Hunting and Hunting Reserves in Medieval Scotland* (Edinburgh, 1979), p. 33.
[37] *RMS*, i, app 1, no. 123.
[38] Gilbert, *Hunting and Hunting Reserves*, pp. 208–11.
[39] Gilbert, *Hunting and Hunting Reserves*, pp. 40, 129–30, 136–39.
[40] *RMS*, ii, nos 58, 59.

the right to graze the royal sheep in the Forest.[41] Dr Gilbert remarks that the king may have reasserted royal forest rights in Ettrick: 'Possibly no free forest grant of Ettrick was ever made to the Douglases and so, in theory, the king could still claim forest rights there'.[42] The fifth earl's resignation or donation to the king, mentioned in the 1450 re-grant to Earl William in Parliament, may have been part of this royal effort to regain control.

But the 1450 re-grant had not only emphatically reversed that previous transaction between king and fifth earl, but also extended the earl's powers in the forest beyond regality to *in regaliam*. This was clearly a claim to kingly authority in the Forest that effectively excluded the king altogether. It was this last phrase which disappeared from the 1451 re-grant, although Earl William did get the lands of the Forest heritably and 'in free and special regality' along with a renewal of the king's renunciation of the rights flowing from the fifth earl's resignation or donation to his father. The royal objection was not to the earl's exercise of jurisdiction in the Forest but to the purported exclusion of the king.

After the final fall of the earl of Douglas in 1455, Parliament laid down that certain lordships and castles were to be annexed perpetually to the Crown, not to be given away to anybody without the 'avyse deliverance and decret of the thre estatis and of the hail parliament, ande for gret seande [*obvious*] and resonable cause of the realme'. Amongst the lordships so annexed were 'the lordschip of Ettrik Forest with all boundis pertenyng tharto'.[43]

The Earldom of Wigtown

The grant of the earldom of Wigtown with its lands was made on 26 October 1451: crucially, after the king reached full age ten days before. This meant that the grant was irrevocable, not being an act of minority. The grant was preceded by a resignation of earldom and lands by Earl William, perhaps implying that he already claimed to be in possession of them. The grant was said to be made 'with the full and mature deliberation of the three estates of the realm in full parliament'. It is probably not to be inferred from the absence

---

[41] *ER*, iv, p. 576.
[42] Gilbert, *Hunting and Hunting Reserves*, p. 40.
[43] RPS 1455/8/2.

this time of reference to its assent and consent that Parliament dissented from them, but rather that with a fully adult king its agreement was no longer required to make the grant as secure as possible. The grant of the earldom also included the *non obstantibus* clause, however, with, as already quoted, its reference to Earl William's predecessors and especially the fourth earl.

The power of the adult king to strike down the detrimental transactions of his guardians during his minority must explain why the 1450 grant of all Galloway (without any reference to the Wigtown earldom) was replaced by, first, the grant of Galloway east of Cree in July 1451 and, second, a grant of the seemingly more contentious earldom and its lands west of Cree on 26 October.[44] The fundamental point was surely an emphatic reaffirmation that there were two separate estates, which were not to be unified as a single massive lordship in a strategically crucial region. Both were, however, granted in regality, indicating that the earl's holding such privileges in the area was not by itself objectionable.

What may have been most in issue in 1451 therefore was whether the eighth earl had any claim at all to the title of earl of Wigtown. Judging from the inclusion in the 1449 transumpt of three documents relating to the earldom,[45] that may have been the earl's first step in making that claim; or it may have been a claim that he revived when his ambition to enjoy a single lordship over all Galloway was thwarted in June 1451. The earldom had been created by King David II in 1341 for his foster-father (*alumnus*) Malcolm Fleming and gave him in effect the whole of the sheriffdom of Wigtown as well as its head burgh 'in as free regality as any regality is most freely possessed or held in our whole kingdom'.[46] In February 1372, however, Malcolm's grandson Thomas sold the whole earldom to Archibald the Grim in return for 'a certain and notable sum of money' in Thomas' 'great and urgent necessity'.[47] The sale was confirmed by Robert II the following October, but neither the sale nor the confirmation charter made any mention of either the title of earl (as distinct from the earldom) or regality jurisdiction. Instead, the sale simply gave Archibald jurisdiction '*cum furca et fossa sok et sak toll et teme infangandtheffe et outefangandtheffe*', i.e.

---

[44] *RMS*, ii, nos 471, 503.
[45] See Chapter 2 above, text accompanying notes 132–33.
[46] *RMS*, i, app 1, no. 119.
[47] *RMS*, i, no. 507.

baronial rather than regality jurisdiction. This was because when Thomas was made earl by David II in January 1367 the regality jurisdiction was withheld because 'for certain causes [it was] to remain in suspense'.[48] Whatever these certain causes may have been, Archibald Douglas' take-up of the earldom did not involve the regality's renewal in his hands.[49] But the 1451 grant may have been seen more as lifting that long ago suspension rather than as extending a previously more limited jurisdiction.

Archibald the Grim himself made little, if any, use of the title earl of Wigtown and, perhaps, was never entitled to do so. Until he succeeded to the Douglas earldom in 1389, he generally preferred to be designed primarily as lord of Galloway (presumably by virtue of his holding the territory on each side of the Cree, albeit by distinct grants). His heir, the fourth earl, does not seem to have used the Wigtown title either. It appeared therefore to have fallen into abeyance until in 1419 it was revived for the fourth earl's heir Archibald (later the fifth earl) as one of the leaders of the Scottish armies in France. The suggestion that this was to give him greater status in the eyes of the French, or at least equal status alongside his co-commander and brother-in-law, John Stewart, earl of Buchan, seems plausible. This use of the title ceased again, however, upon the younger Archibald succeeding his father in 1424 and the return of James I to Scotland in the same year.[50] There was no further sign of it until its reappearance in the crisis of 1451.

The 1451 royal grant explained that Earl William was to hold the earldom and its lands 'as freely as the late Archibald earl of Douglas, grandfather of [William] (*i.e. the third earl*) or Archibald uncle of [William] (*i.e. the fourth earl*) or any of his predecessors held the earldom and lands'. This should

---

[48] *RMS*, i, no. 250; *RRS*, vi, no. 368.

[49] For further detail and discussion see Oram, R.D., 'The Making and Breaking of a Comital Family: Malcolm Fleming, First Earl of Wigtown, and Thomas Fleming, Second Earl of Wigtown', *International Review of Scottish Studies* 42 (2017), pp. 1–58, especially at 16–18, 45–49. Note also *Scotland and the Flemish People*, eds Fleming, A. and Mason, R. (Edinburgh, 2019), ch. 12.

[50] The fifth earl's one appearance as earl of Wigtown in James I's active rule is in a royal confirmation dated 8 January 1425 of a charter by his nephew Archibald earl of Wigtown and lord of Eskdale (dated 2 December 1423), itself confirming a charter of 18 July 1423 granting Trabroun to John Heriot (*RMS*, ii, no. 13). The final royal confirmation may have been to remove any doubt about the validity of Heriot's holding of Trabroun.

be seen as first an acknowledgement that the earldom and its lands were indeed part of the untailzied Douglas inheritance from Archibald the Grim despite his immediate descendants' non-use of the title. The one thing that their freedom may not have given the fourth earl, however, was the power while he still lived to pass the title of earl on to his heir unless he had consent from the king himself. We have already noted Alexander Grant's argument that royal or official approval, manifested by a public ceremony of 'belting', was needed to make a man an earl, although such approval was automatic where the earldom was acquired by inheritance.[51] No charter of creation was needed unless there was also (as in the establishment of Wigtown in 1341) a grant of lands as well as the title. The making (and un-making) of earls was thus an exclusively royal prerogative or privilege. Even if the Governor Albany consented to the adoption of the title by the fourth earl's heir in 1419, that was not necessarily enough to make his use of it lawful, since it had not involved the absent king at all.[52] This purported creation of an earl without royal consent may then have been the treasonous act of the fourth earl making his name especially relevant in the *non obstantibus* clause deployed in the grant in October 1451. But after his father's death, the fifth earl of Douglas could have legitimately claimed the title of earl of Wigtown, even if he chose not to do so and indeed may never have been formally recognised as such by James I (but perhaps only because from May 1426 Margaret Stewart, the earl's mother and the king's sister, was in liferent possession as countess of the lands and jurisdiction of the earldom along with the rest of Galloway).

Finally, all this background may also be part of the explanation for the deferral of the recognition of Earl William as also earl of Wigtown until the king attained majority and with it the unbridled capacity to belt a man as earl. Perhaps that ceremony was carried out contemporaneously with, or not long after, the grant on 26 October 1451. Earl William was designed as earl of Wigtown in witnessing two royal confirmations at Edinburgh on 13 January 1452, while a fortnight later he designed himself as earl of Douglas, Wigtown and Avondale (his father's original earldom) as well as lord of Galloway in

---

[51] See Chapter 1 above, text accompanying notes 77–78.
[52] In this respect in particular it may have been unlike the creation of Archibald the Grim as earl of Douglas in 1389 even although the then king (Robert II) was subject to the guardianship of his second son Robert earl of Fife (later also Governor as duke of Albany and still holding that office in 1419).

making a grant of lands in the sheriffdom of Wigtown.[53] His brother's recognition as earl of Wigtown, if it took place, did so in 1453.[54] There is no reason or evidence in all this for the supposition made by some, that the king coveted the Wigtown earldom in order to confer its lands upon his queen as part of her dowry or had unlawfully seized or confiscated it after the death of Countess Margaret at the end of 1450 or the beginning of 1451.[55]

The earldom certainly disappeared again in 1455, when 'the hail lordschipe of Galloway with sik fredomes and commodities as it hais thir dayis togiddir with the castell of the Treife' (Threave) was annexed to the Crown in the same manner as Ettrick Forest.[56] This must have included the estates of both the lordship between Cree and Nith and the earldom of Wigtown. There was to be no revival in different hands of the old Douglas power in Galloway any more than in the Forest or indeed the Wardenship of the Marches. The Wigtown earldom would not be revived until 1606, when it was granted to John, lord Fleming of Cumbernauld. This doubtless explains why the transumpt of 1449 with the fourteenth-century documents recording the transfer of the earldom from John's ancestor Thomas to Archibald the Grim found its way into the charter chest of the Fleming earls of Wigtown, there to be inventoried in 1681.[57]

Stewarton

As with the Wigtown earldom, the grant of the estate of Stewarton was made on 26 October 1451, after the king reached full age. The grant was again preceded by a resignation of the estate by Earl William and said to be made 'with the full and mature deliberation of the three estates of the realm in full parliament'. But this time the royal grant did not include the *non obstantibus* clause. No treason to the king by Earl William or any of his predecessors was involved in the background to the problem with Stewarton.

---

[53] *RMS*, ii, nos 522, 523; *RMS*, iv, no. 796; *RMS*, v, no. 2319; *Stirling Chrs*, no. 21; *Haddington Chrs*, pp. 18–21 *Wigtownshire Chrs*, no. 136.
[54] See below, text accompanying note 95.
[55] Cf McGladdery, *James II*, pp. 102–03, 108, 111, 113; Brown, *Black Douglases*, pp. 290–92; Tanner, *LMSP*, pp. 128–33.
[56] *RPS* 1455/8/2; and see above text accompanying note 43 for Ettrick Forest.
[57] *Wigtown Charter Chest*, no. 30; see Chapter 2 above, note 133.

CHAPTER THREE: THE FALL OF THE HOUSE OF DOUGLAS

There are various clues to the nature of the difficulties involved. Most important is that the grant itself declares that the earl had resigned the lands to the king in the latter's capacity as steward of Scotland. Next, the 1449 transumpt had included a 1322 charter of Robert I granting William Murray half the tenement of Stewarton by the boundaries made by him and his elder brother Patrick.[58] This suggests that Patrick, having possibly inherited the whole of the estate, still retained the other half of Stewarton at this point. William was to perform half a knight's service, with Patrick again presumably liable for the other half.

Then there are two almost identical royal grants of lands said to be in the lordship of Stewarton to Alexander Hume on 20 July 1451 (i.e. when the ultimate fate of Stewarton had still to be decided), but in the first of which the king reserved 'le Mote de Castletoun' as a messuage (i.e. its lord's principal dwelling in the estate and its symbolic head place or *caput*[59]), while in the second he erected and incorporated the lands into the barony of Langshaws.[60] The first of these grants was, however, all but a carbon copy of a grant made to Hume by the eighth earl dated 24 August 1444, save that the reservation of 'le Mote' was made for the earl.[61] Finally there is the Auchinleck chronicler's additional comment that the initial withholding was with the exception of 'Pedynnane' (Pettinain, Lanarkshire), 'of the quhilk the erllis moder had conjunct feftment'.[62]

We can begin with the Robert I charter of 1322, which raises the possibility that Stewarton thereby not only was or became, but in the fifteenth century also remained, a lordship the lands of which were divided between two different proprietors. A divided lordship might explain why Stewarton seems often to have been held along with other lands, in particular neighbouring Dunlop: it was to replicate the value of what had been before the division (whenever that occurred) a full knight's fee.

---

[58] *RRS*, v, no. 468, from NLS: Ch 951. Note also *RMS*, i, app 2, no. 338.
[59] See *https://dsl.ac.uk/entry/dost/messuage*.
[60] *RMS*, ii, nos 484–85.
[61] Fraser, *Douglas*, iii, no. 412.
[62] *Auchinleck Chronicle* f 114r (McGladdery, *James II*, p. 265). Pettinain is NGR: NS 954 430.

Next is the question of what if any relation existed between Patrick and William Murray, on the one hand, and on the other Joanna Murray, marriage with whom brought to Archibald the Grim extensive lands, including Stewarton.[63] Patrick and William can be linked to the later family of Murray of Cockpool, which in the fifteenth century 'bore arms which were practically the same as those of the house of Bothwell'.[64] While this 'can hardly be adduced as sufficient proof of their descent from a common Murray stock',[65] it would seem most likely that the Douglas interest in Stewarton was in succession to that of Thomas Murray of Bothwell and Joanna, however it had reached Thomas from (most probably) William rather than Patrick Murray. It is also likely that it continued to be an interest in only half the estate, with the other half remaining in the hands of some other branch of the Murray family descended from Patrick Murray. Meanwhile Pettinain, having previously belonged to Maxwells, appears to have come to yet another Murray family during the reign of David II.[66]

The 1451 reference to the 'steward of Scotland' is not the first such in relation to Stewarton. In 1410 the fourth earl of Douglas obliged himself to give his estate of Stewarton to his daughter Elizabeth and her prospective husband John Stewart, earl of Buchan, upon their marriage.[67] John was the younger son of the Governor, Robert Stewart, duke of Albany, and the marriage indicated the increasingly strong links between the houses of Stewart and Douglas at this point. In May 1413, the Governor received the earl's resignation of Stewarton and also Ormsheuch and granted them both to John and Elizabeth jointly and to their heirs (whom failing, the heirs male of John, whom failing the heirs of the earl). They were to hold 'of the steward of Scotland' and his heirs as the

---

[63] See Chapter 1 above, text accompanying notes 81–83.
[64] *Scots Peerage*, i, pp. 214–16 (quotation at ibid., p. 215).
[65] Ibid., p. 215.
[66] Robert I grants Pettinain to Eustace Maxwell (*RMS*, i, app 2, no. 278); Herbert Murray gets Pettinain from David II on forfeiture of Herbert Maxwell (ibid., 1155); David II grants half of barony of Pettinain to Herbert Murray (ibid., 1210); charter of Pettinain to Herbert Murray by David II (ibid., 1227). Note also *RRS*, vi, no. 123A (David II instructs chancellor in March 1352 to make grant of Pettinain, forfeited by the late Herbert Maxwell, to Alexander Stewart, knight, and the lawful heirs male of his body, to be held for the service of four armed men and four archers).
[67] NRS: GD86/9, referred to in Fraser, *Douglas*, i, p. 380.

CHAPTER THREE: THE FALL OF THE HOUSE OF DOUGLAS

earl had previously held of the king, and were to perform to the steward 'the services used and wont (*debita et consueta*)' for the land'.[68]

Stewarton 1322-1455

Held of the king of Scots to 1404, thereafter of the prince and steward of Scotland
Halved by 1322

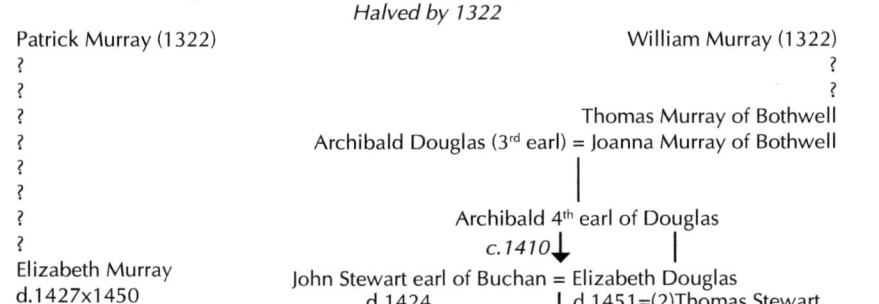

```
Patrick Murray (1322)                                    William Murray (1322)
?                                                        ?
?                                                        ?
?                                        Thomas Murray of Bothwell
?                        Archibald Douglas (3rd earl) = Joanna Murray of Bothwell
?                                                        |
?                                        Archibald 4th earl of Douglas
?                                             c.1410 ↓        |
Elizabeth Murray         John Stewart earl of Buchan = Elizabeth Douglas
d.1427x1450                      d.1424              d.1451=(2)Thomas Stewart
       |                                                  =(3)William Sinclair
       |                                                  earl of Orkney
       |              1427  →                             |
James Douglas of Balvenie = Beatrix Sinclair     Margaret = George lord Seton
7th earl of Douglas     | countess of Douglas
                    ____|____
                   |         |
            William 8th earl  James 9th earl
              of Douglas       of Douglas

——— inheritance
——→ grant
```

Five months later, in November, the Governor issued a set of further grants to the couple. Dunlop was given on terms virtually identical to those of the Stewarton/Ormsheuch grant just summarised, save that this time it was said that the earl had previously held of the steward of Scotland.[69] Also granted was Traboyack in the earldom of Carrick, with the holdings of both the couple and the earl described as being 'of the earl of Carrick' (a title associated with the king's eldest son from the reign of Robert II on).[70] Finally but separately granted were the lands of 'Tulchfraser' in the sheriffdom of Stirling and the barony of Tillicoultry in the sheriffdom of Clackmannan. In both of these the

---

[68] *RMS*, i, app 1, no. 945.
[69] *RMS*, i, app 1, no. 946.
[70] *RMS*, i, app 1, no. 947. See Chapter 2 above, text accompanying notes 19–26, 32, 47.

holdings were of the king and for present purposes we need concern ourselves no further with either.[71]

The title 'steward of Scotland' was a comparatively recent one in 1413, seemingly established in 1404 by King Robert III for his sole remaining son James with a charter granting him as *'senescallo Scotiae'* all the hereditary lands of the Stewarts – the baronies of Renfrew, Cunningham (where Stewarton was located), Kyle Stewart, Ratho (Mid-Lothian) and Innerwick (East Lothian) – plus the islands of Bute, Arran and the Cumbraes, the lands of Cowal and Knapdale, all the lands of the earldom of Carrick and, finally, the lands of Kyle Regis. The grant was made for the prince's lifetime only, but *'in liberam regalitatem seu regaliam'*.[72] Professor Dickinson argued convincingly that here *regalitatem* and *regaliam* were not mere synonyms but a reference to distinct concepts of 'regality' and 'royalty', and that the king's son and heir to the Crown was being granted lands to hold as his father governed the rest of Scotland, i.e. effectively as a separate kingdom within the kingdom.[73] This was the origins of the Principality of Scotland, with its holder being the Prince of that Principality. But the title 'Prince of Scotland' did not come into use until the reign of James III. Before that the holder was simply 'steward of Scotland' in relation to the Stewart lands and earl of Carrick in relation to that earldom's lands (such as Traboyack). Dickinson went on to argue that when James I became king he held both these titles and the accompanying lands *in cumulo*, and suggested that since his was only a lifetime right it must have lapsed upon his assassination in 1437.[74]

We can certainly see from this analysis that the fourth earl of Douglas must have been granted the lands of (half of) Stewarton and Ormsheuch by the king before 1404 but gained Dunlop and Traboyack only after the death of Robert III in 1406. From either May or November 1413 all were held of the captive but uncrowned James I in his capacities as steward of Scotland or earl of Carrick. We can now also see, however, that once the king was back in Scotland and his son and heir was born in 1430, the former must have renewed his father's 1404 grant in favour of that son and heir at least

---

[71] *RMS*, i, app 1, nos 948, 949. The Governor reserved a liferent (*liberum tenementum*) of Tillicoultry to himself.
[72] The charter is printed in Dickinson, 'Inquiry', p. 214.
[73] Ibid., pp. 215–16.
[74] Ibid., pp. 216–18.

in relation to the Stewartry, and thereby begun to develop the later position also identified by Dickinson, that the king held the relevant lands (including Stewarton) as steward only when there was no (male?) heir to the Crown.[75] It is not clear whether this also held good for the earldom of Carrick. While Traboyack was also amongst the estates regranted to Earl William in July 1451, there was no apparent reference to the superiority of the earl of Carrick.[76] But in Stewarton Earl William had resigned to the still son-less king in his capacity as steward of Scotland.

All this still leaves open, however, the question of how Stewarton had become Earl William's to resign, since the fourth earl had apparently given up all right to the lands in 1413 unless the marriage of his daughter to John Stewart, earl of Buchan, failed to produce an heir or, indeed, John alone was unable to do so. But John's marriage had actually produced a daughter, Margaret, who, albeit possibly very young indeed at her father's death with his father-in-law at the battle of Verneuil in France in 1424, survived to marry around 1436/37 a seeming Douglas supporter in George later first lord Seton.[77] Margaret was probably still alive in 1451; her husband's second marriage did not take place until the late 1450s.[78] Margaret was not immediately relevant, however, as there was still the continuing interest of the widowed Elizabeth Douglas as survivor under the conjunct infeftment with the earl of Buchan. She too lived until some time in 1451, having re-married, first, Sir Thomas Stewart, bastard son of Alexander Stewart, earl of Mar, and then, by 1432, William Sinclair, third earl of Orkney.[79]

---

[75] Ibid., p. 216.
[76] *RMS*, ii, no. 463.
[77] There are four instances linking Seton to the Douglases in 1437. On 8 and 12 June he was at Wigtown with Margaret, countess of Douglas (widow of the fourth earl), witnessing first a charter of lands in Galloway and then its confirmation by the countess (NRS: CS7/430 f 289v–290r). On 2 November Seton issued a charter at Seton over land in Tranent, with one witness being William Sinclair, earl of Orkney, himself linked to the Douglases by marriage to the fourth earl's daughter (NLS: MS 1010 f 98). Another charter over land in Haddington was issued by Seton on 20 November, but at the Douglas stronghold of Threave (NLS: MS 1010 f 36). For the marriage between Seton and Margaret, which required papal dispensation, see *ER*, vi, p. cvi.
[78] *Scots Peerage*, viii, p. 576 (vouching *RMS* but undated). Seton's second wife was Christian Murray, probably of Tullibardine (ibid., 14 May 1473).
[79] *Scots Peerage*, ii, p. 265; iii, pp. 167–68; Crawford, B.E., *The Northern Earldoms:*

In January 1427, just over three years after their marriage, Earl William's parents, James Douglas of Balvenie and Beatrix Sinclair (sister of William, earl of Orkney), received from James I two simultaneous but distinct grants of Stewarton and Pettinain (Lanarkshire) in conjunct infeftment. Both estates had been resigned to the couple by an Elizabeth Murray who, however, retained each of them *pro tempore vite liberum tenementum*, i.e. a lifetime interest.[80] In making the grant of Stewarton (but not Pettinain) the king acted as steward of Scotland, of whom the lands were also to be held. Beatrix was to continue to enjoy these lands should Balvenie predecease her, with the final destination being in favour of Balvenie's lawful heirs whomsoever. Pettinain was likewise granted heritably.

The identity of Elizabeth Murray is, however, mysterious. It is suggested that she must have been a descendant of the Murray family that had owned the non-Douglas half of Stewarton along (perhaps) with Pettinain. If Countess Beatrix's conjunct infeftment in Pettinain had become operative on the ground, as the reference to it in the Auchinleck chronicle suggests, the probability must be that Elizabeth Murray had died some time before 1451. Thus, whatever the original rationale for the 1427 transaction may have been, by mid-1451, and probably for some time before, it had become a basis by which the whole estate of Stewarton together with Pettinain could be re-united in the hands, ultimately, of the earl of Douglas. That he had persuaded his mother to resign to him her entitlements in Stewarton very shortly after he inherited the earldom (leaving her, however, with Pettinain) is suggested by his charters of lands in the lordship of Stewarton made to Gilbert Kennedy of Dunure on 20 April 1444 and to Alexander Hume on 24 August 1444.[81] There is no sign in any of this, however, of recognition of the special position in Stewarton as a whole of 'the steward of Scotland', i.e. the young king himself.

Once again, therefore, we see Earl William claiming lordship without much if any apparent reference to royal superiority or other possible rights in the lands in question. We need not doubt that Countess Beatrix supported, not only her eldest, but also her second son (James), who would become ninth

---

Orkney and Caithness from AD 870 to 1470 (Edinburgh, 2013), p. 354. For the death of Elizabeth Douglas before 1452 see *ER*, v, p. 516; vi, p. 268.

[80] *RMS*, ii, nos 77, 78. See further Chapter 1 above, text accompanying note 53.

[81] NRS: GD25/1/33 (Kennedy; copied from a transumpt made 3 December 1454 (NRS: GD25/1/61)); Fraser, *Douglas*, iii, no. 412 (Hume).

earl after his brother's death; in 1455 she was forfeited with the latter and fled into exile in England, not dying until 1463. It is improbable, however, that as a couple Beatrix's sister-in-law (Elizabeth Douglas) and brother (William Sinclair, earl of Orkney) were equally or, indeed, at all supportive of their ambitious and much younger nephews. Sinclair, who had once been close to his brother-in-law, the seventh earl, was apparently alienated by the eighth earl's claims to Galloway and to wardenship jurisdiction in his mother Egidia Stewart's lordship of Nithsdale.[82] His ultimate loyalties became apparent from his acceptance of the positions of the king's chancellor and justiciar south of Forth in the period immediately before and after the ninth earl's final overthrow in 1455.[83] His rupture with the Douglases can only have been exacerbated, if indeed it was not actually begun, by the eighth earl's behaviour in relation to Stewarton. Likewise with George Seton and his wife Margaret Stewart, no matter their previous Douglas connections. Seton was to appear as a lord of parliament by 1452, amongst those accepting the king's lack of guilt in killing the eighth earl, and going on to be prominent in the governments of James II and III.[84]

Both Stewarton and Pettinain seem to have been treated as royal estates after 1455.[85] A particularly interesting illustration of the transitional issues involved in this appears from a sasine of the 20 merks lands of 'Padynane' given in favour of Matthew Johnstone on 19 November 1455, following a chancery precept, and according to the king's charter thereof. The king's mair of the sheriffdom of Lanark gave the sasine, at the tenement and *mansio* of Andrew Clerisone, then existing in the said lands. Johnstone took the *mansio* as his messuage, or chemys, and the rest of the said lands beyond the messuage called 'lie Westerraw'. It seems that he then summoned the tenants and leased their lands to them. A few witnesses are specifically named, and the notary records in addition the presence of 'many others to the number of 40 persons'.[86] This probably relates to the account given by Hume of Godscroft's

---

[82] See above, text accompanying note 32.
[83] Brown, *Black Douglases*, pp. 238, 247, 255, 260, 262, 263; McGladdery, *James II*, p. 38; MacQueen, 'Tame Magnates?', p. 108; Crawford, *Northern Earldoms*, pp. 356–60.
[84] *Scots Peerage*, viii, pp. 575–76; McGladdery, 'Seton family, per c.1300-c.1510', *ODNB*.
[85] For Stewarton see e.g. *RMS*, ii, nos 912, 1200, 1258, 1325.
[86] NLS: Acc 12189 (cartulary of Westraw and Pettinain), page 1.

History of the House of Douglas of the aftermath of Arkinholm where it is narrated that the lord of Carlyle and laird of Johnstone each got half of the £40 lands of Pettinain as a reward for their capture of the earl of Ormond.[87] The sasine shows Johnstone choosing his messuage, and then, after being infeft, confirming the tenants in their leases.

Analysis of the Trial and Its Aftermath

On the analysis just given, it was not so much the king's as Earl William's position that was in at least potential serious peril in the summer of 1451. He stood accused not only of abuse of his extensive authority in the Scottish borders and Galloway during the king's minority but also of possible treason for which he underlay the judgement of king and Parliament. The treason essentially lay in the exercise of and claims to powers amounting to the exercise of kingship. Earl William's long-dead uncle and cousin, the fourth and fifth earls, lay open to similar charges; and in effect all three men were called to account before the Three Estates gathered with the king in Edinburgh in June 1451. The symbolic significance of what happened in Parliament was the clear assertion of the king's authority over the eighth earl, underscored by the process being strung out for months until after another potently symbolic moment, the king's attainment of full age on 16 October. But he and whoever was advising him – most probably the chancellor William Crichton and Bishop Turnbull prominent amongst them, given the technical document-based nature of many of the charges against the earl[88] – certainly did not want the latter's removal from the corridors of power and influence. The earl was eventually allowed to keep his lands and offices, but with the associated powers and jurisdiction defined largely as they had been at the death of James I (the most significant exception being James II's renewal of his 1450 renunciation of the fifth earl's resignation or donation of his forest rights to James I). The overall objective thus was to show the power of Douglas firmly harnessed under the king's hand, not its destruction.

---

[87] *David Hume of Godscroft's The History of the House of Douglas*, ed. Reid, D., 2 vols (Edinburgh, 1996), ii, pp. 434–35.

[88] This may be the origin of the 'rumour' articulated some 70 years later by the chronicler John Law that Turnbull plotted with Crichton and his cousin George to kill the earl: *ER*, v, p. lxxxv, note. There is a lack of any contemporary direct evidence for such a plot.

CHAPTER THREE: THE FALL OF THE HOUSE OF DOUGLAS

That this continued to be the aim of royal policy even after the killing of Earl William is clear from the king's cautiously conciliatory handling of the earl's angry and vengeful brother James after February 1452. A month after the killing, still known as 'Sir Iames of douglas erll Iames second son' [i.e. *of James the Gross*], he came to Stirling town cross with his younger brother the earl of Ormond as well as the lord Hamilton and some 600 men to 'blow out' upon the king and his lords, i.e. declare them outlaws for 'foule slaughter'; an act which Ranald Nicolson was surely right to see as a ceremony of *diffidatio* (i.e. a formal defiance of the king and withdrawal of the fealty otherwise owed to him).[89] During a Parliament at Edinburgh in June 1452 he and his allies took their defiance even further:

> thar was put on the nycht on the parliament hous dure Ane letter wnder Sir Iames of douglas sele & the sele of the erll of Ormond & Sir Iames hammiltonnis declynand fra the king sayand that thai held nocht of him nor wald nocht hald with him.[90]

It is consistent with this renunciation of the superior lordship of the king of Scots that later in June 1452 James was seemingly ready to do homage to the English king, by whom he was named as earl of Douglas.[91] His brother Archibald had however been deprived of the earldom of Moray, because James Crichton, married to the elder of the two co-heiresses to the earldom (Janet Dunbar), was belted earl of Moray in the Parliament of June 1452, seemingly retaining the title until his death in 1454.[92]

---

[89] *Auchinleck Chronicle* f 115r (McGladdery, *James II*, p. 265). See Nicholson, R., *Scotland: The Later Middle Ages* (Edinburgh, 1974), p. 360. *Diffidatio* is the withdrawal of fealty because the superior (in this case the king) has failed in his corresponding duty to be faithful to the vassal: see Craig, *Jus Feudale*, 2.11.1-8, 33 (London, 1655), pp. 207–09, 215; (Leiden, 1716), pp. 379–83, 394–95; (Edinburgh, 1732), pp. 284–86, 294; (Clyde translation 1933), i, pp. 583–88, 607). The last citation is a passage making clear that the king is no exception to the general rule of mutual faith.

[90] *Auchinleck Chronicle* f 115v (McGladdery, *James II*, p. 266). See also Hawes, 'Reassessing the Political Community', on Douglas' public defiance of the king, although the suggestion that the blowing out at Stirling was merely a 'parody of the horning ritual' seems to us to under-state his intentions.

[91] *Rot Scot*, ii, p. 358.

[92] *Auchinleck Chronicle*, f 115v (McGladdery, *James II*, p. 266); Borthwick, A.R., 'Crichton, William of that ilk, first lord Crichton', *ODNB*, commenting of James

The initial response of the Scottish king to the Douglas renunciation of his superiority was therefore almost certainly that all the earl's lands remained in the hands of the king while those of Sir James and his adherents were automatically forfeited. A possible consequence can be found later in the same month, when the king granted lands within Stewarton to Gilbert lord Kennedy, in terms identical to those the same grantee (then Gilbert Kennedy of Dunure) had received from the eighth earl in April 1444.[93] Sir James Douglas also received a safe conduct as earl of Douglas from the English king on 22 September 1452, but it is not clear that use was ever made of this facility.[94] The situation in Scotland had changed over the preceding summer months.

An 'appoyntement' between the king and 'James Earle of Douglas' in August 1452 shows that negotiations were well under way between them by then. The king must already have recognised James as earl.[95] For his part, the new earl renounced claims to the earldom of Wigtown and the lands of Stewarton, feud with those who had been art and part in the slaughter of his brother, and any power to eject those holding on tacks and mailings within the earl's lands. The

---

that 'While there has been doubt about the status of this grant, he is clearly styled earl on a number of occasions, though he certainly did not transmit his title to his son.' James' wife survived until 1494x1506 and the title was hers, not his; and all the couple's sons predeceased her (*Scots Peerage*, iii, p. 64). There is also some suggestion that James had earned the displeasure of the king just before his death: 'Sir Iames lord of Crechtoun decessit at Dunbar and it was haldin fra the king a litill quhile and syne gevin till him' (*Auchinleck Chronicle* f 112v (McGladdery, *James II*, p. 270 – see also ibid., p. 146)). James II granted the earldom to his third son David in 1456 but he died just over a year later and there were no further royal grants of the earldom until 1501 (*Scots Peerage*, vi, p. 311). It is significant that after 1452 the new countess of Moray renewed grants previously made by her sister as countess to their illegitimate half-brother Alexander Dunbar of Westfield (NRS: GD466 (formerly NRAS3094)). For Archibald Douglas' marriage to the younger co-heiress Elizabeth Dunbar and his belting as earl in the 1445 Parliament, see Chapter 2 above, text between notes 115 and 117. The 1455 forfeiture of Archibald Douglas labels him as '*pretensus*' earl of Moray (*RPS* 1455/6/6).

[93] NRS: GD25/1/53 (royal charter to Gilbert lord Kennedy); NRS: GD25/1/33 (earl's charter of same lands to same grantee April 1444, copied from a transumpt made 3 December 1454 (NRS: GD25/1/61)). Cf the Dunbar of Westfield charters referred to in the previous footnote.

[94] *Rot Scot*, ii, p. 359.

[95] On 27 August 1452 the king confirmed a grant by James earl of Douglas: *RMS*, ii, no. 503.

nearest the 'appoyntement' comes to the question of what the earl now held of the king is when he undertook 'to do to our said soverane lord, honor and worship in als far as lyes in my power, I havand sic sovertie as I can be content of reason for safety of my life'.[96] This is not the language of a vassal addressing his lord superior, and it seems unlikely at this point that Earl James had been served as his brother's heir in the Douglas estates as distinct from receiving the title of earl. If the king's objective had from the beginning been to acquire the earldom of Wigtown for the queen's dowry, this was the moment to take it; but that did not happen. The earl was however styling himself 'lord of Galloway' as well as by his other main titles on 14 October and 1 November 1452.[97]

The Lanark bond granted by the earl to the king in January 1453 did not quite re-establish the earl's acceptance of the king's lordship but showed the king moving to accept his claims. Writing in his own hand, and designing himself as 'James erle of dowglas', the earl undertook to give the king 'my manrent [*here to be read, it is suggested, as meaning 'homage'*[98]] and my service' at the next general council when the king was to give him lawful entry and possession of both the Wigtown earldom and Stewarton (showing incidentally, however, that the king was now content to let the earl be infeft in these estates).[99] It is also indicative of a settlement between king and earl that the former supported the latter's supplication for the papal dispensation needed to allow him to marry his dead brother's widow Margaret (granted on 27 February 1453).[100]

Little survives, however, to show what transpired at the General Council held in March 1453.[101] There is no evidence of Earl James being thereafter

---

[96] Tytler, P.F., *The History of Scotland from the Accession of Alexander III to the Union* (Edinburgh, 1845) iii, p. 503 (Letter M).

[97] NRS: GD10/14; *HMC 11th Report*, App 6, Hamilton, no. 14.

[98] Cf Wormald, J., *Lords and Men in Scotland: Bonds of Manrent 1442–1603* (Edinburgh, 1985), pp. 14–20, especially at 17; also ibid., pp. 152, 450. See further Grant, 'Service and Tenure', pp. 175–77; Grant, 'To the Medieval Foundations', p. 10 note 28.

[99] Brown, M., 'The Lanark Bond', in Boardman, S. and Goodare, J., (eds), *Kings, Lords and Men in Scotland and Britain, 1300–1625: Essays in Honour of Jenny Wormald* (Edinburgh, 2014), pp. 227–45 [Brown, 'Lanark Bond'], prints the text of the bond as an appendix.

[100] *CPR*, x, pp. 130–31 (27 February 1453); see also Chapter 1 note 61.

[101] *RPS* 1453/1; *The Parliaments of Scotland: Burgh and Shire Commissioners*, ed Young, M.D. (Edinburgh, 1992–93), ii, p. 750; Tanner, *LMSP*, pp. 139–41.

designed as earl of Wigtown (or of the queen being endowed with the earldom instead). Nor does he appear as a witness to any crown charters in 1453 or afterwards: 'he remained a fringe figure'.[102] But by 17 April 1453 Earl James had been appointed by the king as an ambassador to the English king to negotiate a renewal of the truce between the two kingdoms.[103] He received a new safe conduct from the English king on 22 May 1453, and sealed a four-year truce at Westminster on 23 May 1453.[104] The earl was also named as one of the Scottish conservators of the truce, along with his brother, the earl of Moray, as well as the earl of Crawford, both also previously hostile to the king.[105] Perhaps then the whole business of the 1453 truce suggests successful efforts by the king of Scots since the summer of 1452 to bring his previously disaffected nobility within the fold of his supporters, albeit still keeping them at some distance from court.

Another example of the same royal thinking may be the trip to England of Earl James' close associate, James lord Hamilton, for which he (along with James Livingston) received an English safe conduct at the beginning of January 1453.[106] That was renewed on 22 May 1453, just before the conclusion of the truce; but the purpose by then for Hamilton and the others named in the safe conduct was to go on pilgrimage to the 'threshold of the Apostles', i.e. Rome.[107] Hamilton's initial objective in January was, however, most probably not the truce concluded on 23 May but the release of his brother-in-law Malise, earl of Menteith, from the hostage status in which he had been held in England since 1427. If so, the release and return of Malise to Scotland later in 1453 may not have been so

---

[102] Borthwick, A.R., 'Douglas, James, ninth earl of Douglas, and third earl of Avondale (c.1425–1491)' *ODNB*.

[103] *Rot Scot*, ii, p. 367; *CDS*, iv, no. 1249.

[104] *Foedera*, xi, pp. 326, 337. James also appears as 'earl of Douglas' at ibid., p. 327 and, again in connection with the business of the truce, in *Rot Scot*, ii, 367. For the whole text of the truce see also ibid., pp. 326–37.

[105] *Foedera*, xi, p. 334. See also *CDS*, iv, no. 1257. On Crawford see further text between notes 116, 119–21 below.

[106] *Rot Scot*, ii, p. 359.

[107] *Rot Scot*, ii, p. 362. See also *CDS*, iv, no. 1254. That Hamilton made the trip and returned via England may be suggested by ibid., no. 1266, in which on 19 February 1454 Garter King of Arms is to receive his expenses in attending Lord Hamilton at London and elsewhere for five weeks and more. Garter had also been sent to the Scottish Marches to ask certain appointments of the earl of Douglas.

much a veiled threat to the king of Scots as his favouring settlement of an old grievance that might help create greater political unity in the kingdom. There is certainly no sign of the returned Malise making any claim to the Scottish crown (or of it being made for him by others) for the remainder of a long life.

By early 1455, however, Earl James could be taken, as Michael Brown has shown,[108] to have broken other terms of the settlement with the king and thus to have deprived himself once more of whatever he held from the crown. The path to the final fall of the house of Douglas later that year, and the subsequent mixture of forfeitures, exile and executions for the ninth earl, his family and remaining adherents, had opened up. Malise, earl of Menteith, it may be noted, was present at the Parliament which finally forfeited the Douglases in June 1455.[109]

Explaining the Killing of the Eighth Earl?

We finish this chapter with some speculations about links between the events of summer 1451 and the king's killing of Earl William early the following year. In our view, the accusations against the earl in 1451 were primarily to do with his self-aggrandising activities and excessive claims of authority as well as, possibly, his misuse of his position in the regency administration. But these posed no threat to the king's personal safety or security. Earl William aspired to enjoy the highest levels of autonomy within his extensive territories and responsibilities, and (perhaps) to be first among the king's counsellors; but not to be king himself. There must have been a serious blow to his self-esteem in finding himself summoned before the king and the Three Estates for treason and abuse of power, with the possibility of forfeiture, imprisonment and even execution therefore before him; even if at the request of the still new and pregnant queen and the Three Estates he already stood in the king's grace.[110] While this probably meant that the parliamentary proceedings were more symbolic than threatening, with settlement and remission always in prospect as well, the overall context and the lack of support for him in Parliament, cannot have been comfortable for the earl.

---

[108] Brown, 'Lanark Bond', pp. 242–43.
[109] *RPS* 1455/6/6.
[110] *Auchinleck Chronicle* f 114r (McGladdery, *James II*, p. 265).

He seems nonetheless to have remained in and around court after October 1451. He witnessed crown charters at Stirling on 9 November (probably still there after his recovery of Stewarton and the earldom of Wigtown at the Parliament on 26 October), and on 26 December (at Edinburgh); then six more such charters at Edinburgh between 11 and 13 January 1452.[111] He was, however, not invariably a witness to royal charters at this time, so his attendance at court was not constant. The earl's possible unease at a royal summons to attend the king and his lords at Stirling again in February is apparent in its being accompanied by 'a special assouerans and respite' under the privy seal as well as being subscribed in the king's own hand.[112] According to the Auchinleck chronicle, the document stated that 'all the lordis that war with the king that tyme war oblist suppose the king wald brek the band forsaid that thai suld let it (i.e. *prevent it*) at thare powere'.[113] The same source adds that, when James Douglas and his retinue 'blew out' against the king and his counsellors at Stirling town cross in March 1452, he also showed 'all their seles ... on ane letter with their handis subscrivit', before having the document dragged through the town at the tail of a horse. That can have done it little good as evidence of wrongdoing to be used again in future. But the existence and substance of a royal protection for the earl in coming to the king at Stirling is confirmed by Parliament's finding in June 1452 that the day before his death the earl had publicly renounced all 'respites and other assurances' given him by the king.[114]

The eighth earl's need for such extensive reassurance before coming into the king's presence suggests that he did not see the events of summer 1451 as his triumph over or humiliation of the king, nor indeed that good relations had been fully restored between the two men by the settlement achieved by October 1451. It also shows that from experience the earl feared the king's hot temper and his now councillors – with considerable justification, as events would show. Amongst other causes of apprehension for the earl must have been his bond with the earls of Ross and Crawford, which may only very recently have come to the notice of king and council.

---

[111] *RMS*, ii, nos 507, 522–23, 1863; *RMS*, iv, no. 796; *RMS*, v, no. 2319; *Stirling Chrs*, no. 21; *Haddington Chrs*, pp. 18–21.
[112] *Auchinleck Chronicle* f 114v (McGladdery, *James II*, p. 265).
[113] Ibid. For the meaning of 'let', see *https://dsl.ac.uk/entry/dost/let_v*.
[114] *RPS* 1452/6/1. See further Tanner, *LMSP*, pp. 137–38.

CHAPTER THREE: THE FALL OF THE HOUSE OF DOUGLAS

As Sandy Grant was the first to point out, one result of the ousting of the Livingstons in 1449 had been a rising in the north of the kingdom in March 1451, led by John, lord of the Isles and earl of Ross (married to a daughter of the forfeited James Livingston).[115] Earl William was of course absent from the kingdom at this time, and there seems to have been no contemporary suggestion that Ross had invoked the bond in any way, if indeed it was known about or remembered beyond the original parties themselves: Douglas had probably entered the bond with John's father (who died in 1449) and Crawford around 1446.[116] Although the bond must have been either heritable or renewed between Douglas and the younger Ross,[117] Dr Grant suggested that the relationship of the two was 'probably strained' in 1450–51; perhaps because of the former's acceptance of, if not participation in, the Livingstons' downfall.

It is therefore conceivable that the bond's existence only came (or returned) to the notice of the king and his advisers after the parliamentary proceedings against Douglas during the summer and autumn of 1451; perhaps as late as the end of January or the beginning of February 1452.[118] Another possibility advanced by Dr Grant in a further subsequent article is that, like a number of charters entered by the lord of the Isles in the fifteenth century, the bond did not include the otherwise conventional phrasing excepting the king from those against whom the parties' mutual service and support could be due; this may be supported by a note by the seventeenth-century antiquarian, Sir James Balfour of Denmilne, of a bond dated 7 March 1445/46, with the earl of Douglas 'solemly suering ane offensiue and defensiue league & Combinatione against all none excepted (not the king him selue) with the

---

[115] Grant, A., 'The Revolt of the Lord of the Isles and the Death of the Earl of Douglas, 1451–1452', *SHR* lx (1981), pp. 169–74. The conclusions of this short article are essentially followed by Brown, *Black Douglases*, pp. 270, 291–94; and McGladdery, *James II*, pp. 91, 108–11. See also Tanner, *LMSP*, pp. 131–32.

[116] See the discussion in Brown, M., 'The Great Rupture: Lordship and Politics in North-east Scotland', *Northern Scotland* 5 (2014), pp. 1–25 [Brown, 'Great Rupture'] at 15–20.

[117] On heritable bonding, see Wormald, *Lords and Men*, pp. 63–66 (noting only a few examples in the fifteenth century, but finding heritability much more common in the sixteenth).

[118] Brown, 'Great Rupture', pp. 16–19, argues that in 1446 the bond was designed to regulate the exercise of lordship in the north-east by each of the three parties and not as any challenge to the Crown. It took on a different look, however, in the changed political circumstances of 1451–52.

Earle of Craufurd & Donald Lord of the Iles'.[119] Whether or not that was the case, the king can have felt little but serious threat in an un-renounced bond between one who had recently rebelled (Ross), another who had recently been on trial for treason (Douglas), and a third (Crawford) against whom royalist forces were to take successful armed action at Brechin as soon as May 1452.[120] Crawford may indeed have been forfeited in the Parliament of June 1452 (although if so it must have been rescinded quite soon after) and on his death in September 1453 was 'callit a rigorous man and ane felloun … richt inobedient to the king'.[121]

---

[119] See Grant, A., 'Scotland's 'Celtic Fringe' in the Late Middle Ages', in Davies, R.R., (ed.), *The British Isles 1100–1500: Comparisons Contrasts and Connections* (Edinburgh, 1988), pp. 118–41 at 131 (citing *Acts of the Lords of the Isles*, eds Munro, J. and R.W. (Edinburgh, 1986), nos 19, 21, 61 and 96, which are however all charters rather than bonds; cf ibid., no. 45, for the note by Balfour of Denmilne, which is accepted as authentic in Grant, 'To the Medieval Foundations', p. 10 note 28. See also Brown, 'Great Rupture', p. 15.

[120] For the battle of Brechin, in which Crawford's opposite number was Alexander, earl of Huntly, who 'displayit the kingis banere and said It was the kingis action and he was his luftennend' (*Auchinleck Chronicle* f 123v [McGladdery, *James II*, p. 276]), see McGladdery, *James II*, pp. 129–30. McGladdery's suggestion that Huntly appropriated the title of lieutenant (ibid., p. 172) seems misplaced. He also appears as king's lieutenant (in the north?) in the marriage contract dated 20 May 1455 between him and his son George, on the one side, and on the other Elizabeth Dunbar, countess of Moray and widow of the Douglas earl killed at Arkinholm on 1 May (NRS: GD44/13/10/3, a poor transcript of which is printed in *Spalding Club Miscellany*, vol 4, pp. 128–31). Omitted text includes the following: 'sen the lords last passing out of Murra, sen they were in the way of treaty, and at our soveran lord, and him [i.e. Huntly] as lieutenant and he sall mak them to be assover[…]….'. For earlier king's lieutenants in the north see Chapter 2 text accompanying note 78.

[121] *Auchinleck Chronicle* ff 112r-v, 115v (McGladdery, *James II*, pp. 266, 270) ('rigorous' here possibly meaning 'harsh, severe, cruel' – see *https://dsl.ac.uk/entry/dost/rigorous*). See also Cox, 'Earls of Crawford', p. 250. As McGladdery (*James II*, p. 142) points out, if Crawford was forfeited in the June 1452 Parliament, the sentence must have been rescinded before May 1453 when he became one of the conservators of the Anglo-Scottish truce sealed at Westminster at that time (above, text accompanying notes 103–05). There is evidence for this rescission and reversion of previously forfeited Crawford estates from the king to the earl in a charter and later sasine in NRAS387, Kinloch-Smythe of Balhary, unsorted MSS. See also *ER*, v, pp. c-ci for the earl's claims to moneys from the customs.

When therefore the king 'chargit' Earl William 'to breke the forsaid band' and the earl replied that 'he mycht nocht nor wald nocht', suspicions and fears that probably reached back to the assassination of the king's father, and were very likely fuelled by at least some consumption of alcohol, must have surfaced in the violent reaction described at the beginning of this book. When Parliament conducted what it claimed to have been an objective inquiry detached from the king himself in June 1452, its report spoke in terms of the earl's persistence in treasonous conspiracy with other great men of the realm as justifying his death:

> [If] the aforementioned late William earl of Douglas ... had any respites or other sureties from the said most excellent king on the day preceding his death, those respites and sureties were expressly renounced before a multitude of barons, magnates, knights and nobles, and furthermore, from the letters and evidences sealed with the seal of the said late Earl William, being read through in parliament, and other clear deductions and proofs, it is openly established concerning the bonds and conspiracies made and initiated by the said earl with certain great magnates of the realm, in oppression and offence of the most serene royal majesty, and the public rebellions frequently perpetrated by him, his brothers and accomplices, and also after many flattering persuasions made both by the king and by various barons and nobles for agreeing and assisting the king against his rebels to the said Earl William on the day of his death, shameless obstinacy of such a degree having been displayed to the serene lord the king and other wicked acts having also been perpetrated by him, he is considered to have procured and produced the occasion of his death.[122]

In the concluding sentence of this verdict, however, there is a significant echo of the language used in the standard brieve of inquest into whether or not a homicide was committed by 'forethocht felony'. The brieve commanded the inquest to determine whether the accused killed the victim

---

[122] *RPS* 1452/6/1 (editors' translation slightly adjusted).

in anger in the heat of the moment and not through murder or forethocht felony; and whether and in what respect he [the deceased] gave him occasion and cause for his death arising out of anger in the heat of the moment foresaid or otherwise; and what were the general circumstances of the death and the cause of the death ...[123]

Parliament's finding was therefore that the killing of the earl did not arise from any premeditation on the king's part but was the result of the latter's just anger 'occasioned and caused' by the earl's 'shameless' persistence in *lese majeste*. That conclusion did not render the king free from all blame, however; provocation merely qualified the blameworthiness of the conduct that had resulted provided that any honourable person would have so responded. The outrage of a king directly confronted with a subject's refusal to give up treasonous associations was such an explanation of his consequent actions. His anger-driven reaction was an honourable response to the dishonouring words of the earl. Hence the killing, even if it was what the king intended at the moment of action, was not murder but homicide in hot blood, or by 'chancemedley' (*chaudmelle*). The killer should therefore not be punished in his person but instead be subject to an obligation to compensate, or 'assyth', the kindred of his victim.[124] And as the late David Sellar argued, the king's subsequent

---

[123] Scottish Formularies, pp. 55 (E14), 149–50 (B68).

[124] For the significance of the distinction between 'chaudmelle' and 'forethocht felony', see Sellar, W.D.H., 'Forethocht Felony, Malice Aforethought and the Classification of Homicide', in Gordon, W.M. and Fergus, T.D., (eds), *Legal History in the Making: Proceedings of the Ninth British Legal History Conference, Glasgow 1989* (London, 1991), pp. 43–59; Sellar, W.D.H., 'Was it Murder? John Comyn of Badenoch and William, Earl of Douglas', in Kay, C.J. and Mackay, M.A., (eds), *Perspectives on the Older Scottish Tongue* (Edinburgh, 2005), pp. 132–38, 136–37. Sellar gives further grounds for supposing the king's actions not to be by forethocht felony. Note also Armstrong, J.W., '"Malice" and motivation for hostility in the burgh courts of late medieval Aberdeen', in Armstrong, J.W. and Frankot, E., (eds), *Cultures of Law in Urban Northern Europe: Scotland and Its Neighbours c.1350-c.1650* (London, 2020), ch. 11. For the suggestion that the situation on the evening of 22 February 1452 was engineered to enable the king to plead 'chaudmelle', see Grant, A., 'Murder Will Out: Kingship, Kinship and Killing in Medieval Scotland', in Boardman and Goodare, (eds), *Kings, Lords and Men*, edd Boardman and Goodare, pp. 193–226, 220. McGladdery, *James II*, pp. 116–17,

CHAPTER THREE: THE FALL OF THE HOUSE OF DOUGLAS

conciliation of the ninth earl in supporting his marriage to his dead brother's widow can be seen as the provision of 'assythment' in a form appropriate to a king for the wrong he had committed.[125] That could even have applied to allowing the ninth earl to take the earldom title and lands when they might otherwise have been treated as forfeited for his brother's treason.

The modern reader, familiar with the whitewashing which seems often to follow modern parliamentary and other public inquiries into scandalous, disgraceful or controversial events involving public figures, may approach this late medieval example with appropriate scepticism – they would say that, wouldn't they?[126] Such scepticism is not entirely removed by Parliament's claims that its inquest (within a mere four months after the event) had been undertaken and its conclusions reached –

> with thought and great maturity, and to this end [proceeding to] another place and outwith the presence of the aforesaid most serene prince (i.e. the king), which place of the three estates being set apart, and sitting together in several houses assigned to them, and making examinations thereupon, at length, from the clear depositions and statements of the great barons, magnates, knights and nobles examined concerning the above in great number in the presence of the three estates …

The findings may, however, have been aimed primarily at an international audience, and in particular at persuading the pope and other kings that King James' killing of the treacherous earl had been justified in terms that they would understand.[127] There is a clear parallel with what happened later in

---

suggests that premeditation can be seen in the king stabbing Douglas more than once; but this simply shows intention to kill in the hot-blooded moment, not premeditation.

[125] Sellar, 'Was it Murder?', p. 137.

[126] Adapted from the famous response of Mandy Rice-Davies when at the 1963 trial of Stephen Ward defence counsel put it to her that Lord Astor denied having an affair with her or even having met her. It may also be applicable to the inquiry of General Council into the death of the duke of Rothesay in 1402: see Chapter 2 above, text accompanying note 42.

[127] See Hawes, 'Reassessing the Political Community', for discussion of the inquiry as establishing the king's version of events as 'common knowledge'.

the fifteenth century when the young James IV answered in Parliament for his rebellion against his father in which the latter 'happinnit to be slane' in the battle of Sauchieburn. The finding of the Three Estates then was that the late king had suffered from 'perverst counsale'.[128] Therefore,

> oure soverane lord that now is and the trew lordis and barouns that wes withe him in the samyne feild war innocent, quhyt and fre of the saidis slauchteris feilde and all persute of the occasioune and cause of the samyne.

The real point of the process, however, is apparent from the closing words of the verdict:

> aparte of the thre estatis forsaid, bischopis, prelattis, gret baronis and burgesis, gif thar selis herapoune to gidder withe oure soverane lordis gret sele to be schewin and producit to oure haly faider the paipe, the kingis of France, Spanye, De[n]m[ar]k and utheris realmez, as salbe sene expedient for the tyme etc.[129]

Armed with this verdict of his Parliament, the new king would be helped to avoid excommunication or otherwise become an international pariah as a parricide.

Nothing quite like these passages is to be found in the record of the proceedings of June 1452, although we know that already by early April James II had

---

On medieval understandings of the significance of provocation in homicide cases see for the canon law Küttner, S., *Kanonistische Schuldlehre von Gratian bis auf die Dekretalen Gregors IX* (Vatican City, 1935); for Germany, see Pohl-Zucker, S., 'Hot Anger and Just Indignation: Justificatory Strategies in Early Modern German Homicide Trials', in Gilbert, K. and White, S.D., (eds), *Emotion, Violence, Vengeance and Law in the Middle Ages* (Leiden, 2018), pp. 25–48; and for English law Horder, J., *Provocation and Responsibility* (Oxford, 1992), especially chs 1–4 for linkage of anger, outrage and honour; Kamali, E.P., 'The Devil's Daughter of Hell Fire: Anger's Role in Medieval English Felony Cases', *Law and History Review* 35 (2017), pp. 155–200; and Kamali, E.P., *Felony and the Guilty Mind in Medieval England* (Cambridge, 2019).

[128] See further Hawes, C., '"Perverst Counsale'? Rebellion, Satire and the Politics of Advice in Fifteenth-Century Scotland', in Rose, J., (ed.), *The Politics of Counsel in England and Scotland 1286–1707* (Oxford, 2016), pp. 117–34.

[129] *RPS*, 1488/10/51.

written to the king of France to inform him of the death of the earl of Douglas (albeit without any mention in the letter of his own part in events, which may instead have been orally transmitted by the king's messenger).[130] But with the support of Parliament's findings that the earl had refused to renounce his treasonous associations and had thereby earned the king's wrath, the latter could face the world outside Scotland with some confidence that his international standing would probably be little affected by the event. That indeed seems to have been what transpired; there is no hint in surviving sources that any papal sanction such as excommunication or the imposition of some form of penance was even contemplated, never mind actually imposed; nor were other international relations noticeably affected. In particular, even though just a year before the killing the eighth earl had been the honoured guest of the English king, the latter showed no signs of moving against his Scottish counterpart, other than the grant of a safe conduct to the dead earl's mother and widow for a visit to Canterbury, shrine of another victim of the wrath of a king.[131]

It can also surely be taken that the Parliamentary findings in June 1452 showed the Scottish political community's profound lack of sympathy for the eighth earl of Douglas, and this within a year of his supposed triumph over the king in the Parliaments of 1451. That lack of sympathy and support would transfer on to his brother and successor as earl, continue to grow, and make all but inevitable the family's ultimate fall some three years later. Even that long-time supporter of the eighth and ninth earls James lord Hamilton would abandon the latter for the king just in time in May 1455, following the failure of a mission seeking help from England; he 'couth get nane bot gif the Douglas and he wald haue bene ynglis men and maid the aith' (presumably one of fealty to the English king). He was aided in reaching his decision to change sides by his 'eme' (i.e. uncle), James Livingston, the king's chamberlain whose sister was Hamilton's mother; the event 'left the erll of douglas all begylit as men said'.[132]

When Parliament assembled in June 1455 to forfeit the house of Douglas for ever, it was with transparent awareness that a huge step was to be taken.

---

[130] *Letters and Papers Illustrative of the Wars of the English in France, temp. Henry VI*, ed. Stevenson, J. (London, 1861), i, p. 315.

[131] *Rot Scot*, ii, p. 357.

[132] *Auchinleck Chronicle* f 116v (McGladdery, *James II*, p. 267). See further McGladdery, *James II*, p. 152.

Meticulous attention had already been paid to following correct preliminary procedure in cases of this kind. The family's alienation from the rest of the political community was manifest in the attendance from all Three Estates, even larger than shown in the published records of Parliament's judgement.[133] James, lord Hamilton, was among those present as well as Malise Graham, earl of Menteith. While the ecclesiastical estate did not participate in a judgement of Parliament on a matter of blood, the seals of several bishops (the major exceptions being Aberdeen, Whithorn and Glasgow, the last probably still vacant following the death of William Turnbull in 1454), the prior of St Andrews, and 'many' abbots, were appended to the record of the forfeiture proceedings. This was 'for fuller evidence' of what had taken place. The record is not a royal document, but rather an open letter from 'the earls, magnates, nobles, barons, city and burgh commissioners in Parliament ... to all those to whose notice these present letters shall come'. It could hardly be clearer that this letter was meant to show the solidarity of the Three Estates and their determination to put an end for ever to the problems that the Douglases had increasingly posed for the kingdom over the previous fifteen years.[134]

---

[133] Names additional to those at the end of *RPS* 1455/6/6 are found in a transcript of the proceedings in NLS: Adv MS 22.1.14 f 227v–228v. Add after Lord Gray in the *RPS* list, Lords Fleming, Seton and Cathcart; then after Lord Borthwick, the seals of James Livingston and William, thane of Cawdor, as procurators of the earl of Ross. There is a gap in the transcript after the Christian name of Master John [blank] as procurator of the earl of Huntly, as in the *RPS* text; but there are several burgh seals: Edinburgh, Perth, Aberdeen, Cupar, Stirling, Linlithgow, Lanark, Peebles and only then Haddington (the only one given in *RPS*).

[134] A determination underlined again in August 1455, when Parliament particularly stated in two separate acts that nobody begotten of persons forfeited in the preceding Parliament should be able even to ask to succeed to the forfeited heritage, while anyone giving aid to the former Earl James should also be guilty of treason (*RPS*, 1455/8/3 and 1455/8/15). See also 'A Letter of James III to the Duke of Burgundy', ed. Armstrong, C.A.J., *Miscellany VIII* (Edinburgh, 1951), pp. 30–31, where *c*.1471 the king tells the duke that it does not seem to be the law of the kingdom that a sentence passed in Parliament can ever be rescinded ('*nec de jure videtur regni sentenciam in parliamento latam quovispacto posse rescindi*'). As noted above (Chapter 2 note 156), the context is the king asking the duke to cease his support of the exiled Boyds who had in their absence been sentenced to death for treason by Parliament in November 1469 (*RPS*, A1469/2). Cf however the Livingston remission, Chapter 2 above, note 155.

Chapter Four
The Coshogle Case

This and the following chapter examine in detail litigations respectively decided in January 1455 and (by way of an arbitration) in May 1465. The underlying stories of each case draw us back into the story of the fall of the Black Douglases as well as touching upon the Anglo-Scottish and the Anglo-French/Scottish wars of the preceding 150 years. The background to the cases throws further light on the ultimate lack of support for the earls of Douglas in their adversity in the 1450s, as well as the contrasting fourteenth-century rise of the kindred (and especially Archibald the Grim both before and after he became third earl) to power and landed dominance in southern Scotland. Politics and power struggles are certainly not irrelevant to either case; but a further argument, developed in the concluding Chapter 6, is that the law, which reflected, supported and guided the social system of kingship and lordship, was also a significant element in political events as well as the peaceful resolution of disputes. Our discussion seeks once more to demonstrate the value of legal analysis to gain a deeper understanding of what was going on, not only in the cases that are our points of departure, but also more generally in the world from which they emerged.

Coshogle and the Brieve of Mortancestry

Our first case is recorded in an original notarial instrument executed by Thomas de Burn, priest of Glasgow diocese and notary public.[1] It is now to be found in the Adamton charters amongst the papers of the Maxwells of

---
[1] See Appendix (c). On notaries, see Chapter 1 above, text accompanying note 67.

Monreith held in the National Library of Scotland.[2] The document records in Latin a court process about the lands of Coshogle in Dumfriesshire that took place on 22 January 1455. It has been published only in translation (but a very full and accurate one) by R.C. Reid, who also made a valiant and still useful attempt to elucidate what the case was all about.[3]

The lands under dispute in the case are today a hill farm in upper Nithsdale. The rather isolated site overlooks the deep narrow valley of the Enterkin Water as it flows west down from the Lowther Hills to join the River Nith as it emerges southward from its own tight gorge at this point. The name may be a Gaelic-Cumbric hybrid, *cois* (Gaelic 'foot') and *uchel* (Cumbric 'high'), with the Gaelic possibly having taken over from an earlier Cumbric *coes* ('leg', with the sense of 'long narrow land with a slight bend like a leg').[4] The metaphor is a reasonably accurate one for the lie of the ridge on which Coshogle sits. There are fine views, not only of the Lowther massif to the east, but also over Durisdeer to the Kirk Burn and Dalveen passes, as well as further southward down Nithsdale. While thus very well-placed to monitor traffic up and down the more northerly reaches of Nithsdale, on the routes to or from Sanquhar or Durisdeer, Coshogle itself must always have been difficult to reach. The few remaining fragments (literally) of the castle that once stood at present-day Old Coshogle are probably of sixteenth-century date.[5] But some earlier fortified residence, where the 'chief messuage' of the lands referred to in our document would most probably have been situated, seems likely.

---

[2] NLS: Acc 7043 Adamton, no. 16/2.

[3] Reid, R.C., 'An Early Coschogill Writ', *Transactions of the Dumfriesshire and Galloway Natural History and Antiquarian Society* 30 (1951–52), pp. 132–42. Coshogle is located at OS, NS 863050.

[4] Coshogle is NGR: NS 865 051. We are grateful to the late Professor Jack MacQueen for help with the derivation and meaning of the place name. If the suggested derivation is correct, it still leaves as a puzzle the Perthshire name Glenogle.

[5] See HES, Canmore ID 46310. See further Ramage, C.T., *Drumlanrig Castle and the Douglases* (Dumfries, 1876), pp. 84–85; Maxwell-Irving, A.M.T., *The Border Towers of Scotland: Their History and Architecture - The West March (Dumfriesshire & Eastern Galloway)* (Stirling, 2000), pp. 267–68; also *Scots Peerage*, vii, p. 116. The wall plaque mentioned in the Canmore, Ramage and Maxwell-Irving descriptions of Old Coshogle has been removed to Drumlanrig castle (personal communication from Buccleuch Living Heritage Trust archivist, Jan 2016).

CHAPTER FOUR: THE COSHOGLE CASE

Plate 2: NLS: Acc 7043 Adamton, no. 16/2
(Courtesy of the National Library of Scotland)

The case was raised by way of a pleadable brieve of mortancestry rather than (as Reid thought) by the retourable brieve of inquest. It was therefore a contested action between two parties (John Blair of Adamton against James Lorane) rather than the service of an heir to his lands. As we saw in Chapter 1,[6] the brieve of mortancestry was a form of action, used where the pursuer (here Blair) claimed to be the lawful and nearest heir of a close relative (in this case, his grandfather) who had died vest and in sasine as of fee (i.e. heritably) of certain lands which, however, were now being held by the defender (here, Lorane). An implication of Blair's choice of brieve was that, despite his heritable entitlement, he had never held the lands. Otherwise Lorane's

---

[6] See Chapter 1 above, text accompanying note 65.

115

presence on the land would have been the result of an ejection of Blair, for which the remedy was the brieve of novel dissasine.[7]

The mortancestry claim made by Blair was based upon the heritable sasine of Coshogle held by his grandfather Sir John on the day the latter died. The case was decided in a justiciary court, as was to be expected with a brieve of mortancestry.[8] Blair's claim was upheld by the assize of seventeen men, many of whom can be identified from their territorial designations as Nithsdale locals. Blair was thereupon duly infeft in the lands, first symbolically by the judge giving him a rod 'in token of sasine' at the place of judgement, and then by the sergeant of the court at the chief messuage of Coshogle, 'taking up earth, stone and wood as use is'. There is no suggestion of any retour to the king's chapel after the assize verdict, or of any need for the issue to Blair of a further brieve commanding that he be given sasine. The immediate implementation of the court's decision reflects this being a contested mortancestry case rather than service of an heir following upon an inquest. Blair's sasine explains why the notarial instrument recording the event was preserved in his family's muniments.

The defender, James Lorane, must previously have been in possession of Coshogle, but is unlikely to have been a mere squatter. The probability is that he had some form of apparently valid title to be there (explaining, for instance, his membership of an assize on a brieve of terce in the sheriff court of Dumfries on 8 March 1452[9]). Both parties in 1455 were represented by forespeakers – Thomas Thomson for Lorane and Thomas Graham for Blair.[10] We cannot be certain whether Thomson and Graham were professional advocates or simply intelligent and articulate individuals with a knowledge of the law by whom their principals preferred to be represented.[11]

---

[7] MacQueen, *CLFS*, chapter 5. Novel dissasine means recent dispossession from land.
[8] MacQueen, *CLFS*, 175.
[9] NRS: GD150/109.
[10] On the terminology, see Finlay, *Men of Law*, pp. 9–11.
[11] Thomas Graham of the Thornuke also acted as 'forespekare' for the pursuer in another mortancestry case heard in the justice ayre of Dumfries on 4 March 1455: see Borthwick and MacQueen, 'Three Fifteenth-Century Cases', pp. 128–30. He was also one of the assize in a service of an heir before the sheriff of Dumfries on 30 October 1454: NRAS631 (Bute MSS) Bundle A419 no.

CHAPTER FOUR: THE COSHOGLE CASE

Their debate on several points of law must have been resolved in favour of Graham, as he was thereby enabled to require that the matter be put to the assize.

Drumlanrig: Barony in Regality

The case just described has some initially puzzling features. The justiciary court was not royal, but was rather the justiciary court of Drumlanrig, 'held there in virtue of regality by James Douglas of Drumlanrig, substitute and depute of Sir Robert Crichton of Sanquhar, justiciar of the same court specially substituted and deputed by the lord thereof'.[12] But Drumlanrig from its earliest appearance in the written record is always described as a barony,[13]

---

9. On Grahams of Thornik in Wamphray parish and Dryfesdale, see Reid, R.C., 'The Border Grahams, their Origin and Distribution', *Transactions of the Dumfriesshire and Galloway Natural History and Antiquarian Society* 38 (1959–60), pp. 85–113, 94–95. There seems to have been more than one Thomas Thomson active in the 1450s onwards. Thomas Thomson, with no further designation, was auditor of causes at Parliament on 12 January 1464 (*RPS* 1464/1/1); received a fee as queen's '*causidicus*' (i.e., advocate or pleader of causes) 1462x1463 (*ER*, vii, p. 164); and witnessed an indenture made in the justiciary court at Lanark on 9 February 1465 by which yet another mortancestry process was submitted to arbitration: see further Chapter 5 below, text preceding note 19. These may all be the same as the man who acted for Lorane in the Coshogle case. Thomas Thomson, notary public, witnessed the notarial instrument recording the outcome of the March 1455 case where Thomas Graham was a party's forespeaker (Borthwick and MacQueen, 'Three Fifteenth-Century Cases', above); and also documents of 30 May 1459 and 19 July 1465 (*RMS*, ii, nos 842, 993). Thomas Thomson, burgess of Edinburgh, witnessed four documents 1466–76 (NRS: RH6/396, GD26/3/1002; *RMS*, ii, no. 1854; NRAS1100 (Roxburghe)/bundle 1950). If these are all the same man, then in many ways Thomson's profile has numerous similarities with that of the near contemporary Andrew Alanson of Aberdeen, for which see Simpson, 'Andrew Alanson'. There are also many references to Thomas Thomson, burgess of Canongate, in *Protocol Book of James Young, 1485–1515* (Edinburgh, [1952]), but he is likely someone else.

12. We are again grateful to the late Jack MacQueen for the suggestion that Drumlanrig, like Coshogle (above text at note 4), may be a Gaelic-Welsh hybrid name, the Gaelic *druim* ('back, ridge') taking over from Welsh *trum*, while Cumbric *llanerch* ('glade, clearing') persisted, albeit with metathesis.

13. The earliest reference of which we know is in an English document sent from

and baronies, unlike regalities, never had any power to hold justiciary courts.[14]

There was, however, something rather unusual about the barony of Drumlanrig. When James, second earl of Douglas, granted it to his natural, i.e. illegitimate or bastard, son William sometime between his inheritance of the earldom in 1384 and his death at the battle of Otterburn in August 1388, he reserved his regality for himself and his heirs – *regalitate eiusdem nobis et heredibus nostris reservata*.[15] Regality powers over Drumlanrig existed by virtue of a grant by David II on 12 February 1355, erecting in one over-arching regality all the lands inherited by Earl James' father William, lord of Douglas (later the first earl of Douglas), from his uncle, the Good Sir James, as well as his father, Archibald. These lands included the barony of Drumlanrig, which, it was said, the lord of Douglas had inherited from his father.[16] This also means, it should be noted, that the barony had not been included in the Douglas tailzie of 1342 under which the lands of the Good Sir James ultimately descended in 1389 to his long-lived bastard son, Archibald the Grim, third earl of Douglas.[17]

Thomas Burn's 1455 notarial instrument, however, carefully avoids identifying the lord who then held the over-arching regality. The barony had probably been held since 1444 by the third William Douglas of Drumlanrig, grandson of the second earl's grantee. James Douglas of Drumlanrig is previously linked with the fifth earl of Douglas in 1432 and, more significantly, was the ninth earl's bailie *in hac parte* and *capitaneus* of Drumlanrig on 11 November 1452.[18] He

---

'Holdetoun' in the barony of Drumlanrig on 25 February 1303 *(CDS,* ii, no. 1345). On the differences between baronies and regalities, see Grant, A., 'Franchises North of the Border: Baronies and Regalities in Medieval Scotland', in Prestwich, M., (ed.), *Liberties and Identities in the Medieval British Isles* (Cambridge, 2008), pp. 155–99 [Grant, 'Franchises'], 157–76. Drumlanrig was not a parish, in this differing from the equation of barony and parish found elsewhere; it lay within the parish of Durisdeer.

[14] Cf Grant, 'Franchises', pp. 167–68. Note also *'Discours Particulier d'Escosse, 1559/60'*, ed. McNeill, P.G.B., in *Stair Miscellany II* (Edinburgh, 1984), pp. 86–131, 90–93; MacQueen, *CLFS*, pp. 51, 53–54, 55–56, 112.
[15] *HMC 44 Report XV.8 [Buccleuch MSS]*, no. 2 (p. 8).
[16] *RMS*, i, app 1, no. 123; Fraser, *Douglas*, iii, no. 360.
[17] *RRS*, vi, no. 51; Fraser, *Douglas*, iii, no. 290.
[18] See *HMC Buccleuch*, no. 103 (p. 52) and, at slightly greater length, Fraser, *Douglas*, iii, no. 391 (p. 491); Fraser, *Buccleuch*, ii, no. 51.

may have been a younger son of the first William of Drumlanrig and brother to the second William, who succeeded his father in the barony in 1427.[19]

Douglas earls and Douglases of Drumlanrig

Sir James the Good (d.1330, d.1333) ←*brothers*→ Archibald

Archibald 'the Grim' (3rd earl) d.1400

William (1st earl) d.1384

James 2nd earl d.1388

Archibald 4th earl d.1424 — James 7th earl d.1443

William I of Drumlanrig d.1421

Archibald 5th earl d.1439

William II of Drumlanrig d.1444 — James (captain of Drumlanrig)

William 6th earl ex. 1440 — David ex.1440

William III of Drumlanrig d.1484? *

William 8th earl d.1452 — James 9th earl forfeited 1455, d.1491

Symbol indicating illegitimate birth

* The date of William III's death is disputed: he may have died in 1464 or (the view we prefer) not until 1484. See Borthwick and MacQueen, 'Three Fifteenth-century Cases', 145-6.

The justiciar Robert Crichton of Sanquhar was, however, a long-term opponent of the Douglas earls. His grant of office as sheriff of Dumfries dated 6 November 1452 reflected the royal promotion of such opponents in the aftermath of the king's killing of the eighth earl the previous February.[20] It

---

[19] See further text accompanying notes 91–93 below.
[20] *RMS*, ii, no. 790 (appointment). NRS: GD150/109, shows Crichton already

seems unlikely that he was a comital appointee to the post of justiciar in the earldom regality, or that by the time of our case in January 1455 he was using it to support the earl's interests. Appointment by the king is altogether more probable, a likelihood reinforced by Thomas Graham's charge to Crichton's substitute, James Douglas, to put the brieve of mortancestry to the assize 'in virtue of your office, as you may be willing to answer before our sovereign lord the king'. James' previous position as 'captain' of Drumlanrig may have reflected some mutually trusted intermediary role between the baron and the lord of regality, perhaps in relation to the castle as the lordship's *caput* or chief place. But it does not look as though the regality was being exercised in the earl's name any more. By that time, the view on the royalist side may well have been that Douglas regality privileges had reverted to the king.[21]

So by the time of the Coshogle case, regality jurisdiction over Drumlanrig was almost certainly being exercised in the king's rather than the earl's name. Regality jurisdiction likewise continued over Drumlanrig after the final forfeiture of the ninth earl on 10 June 1455:[22] in January 1500 the lords of council were considering a complex case of 'slaughter' that had been previously decided in the 'justice are of Drumlanerig'.[23]

The Blair Claim to Coshogle

Although Coshogle was an independent estate of the Balliols of Cavers before 1314,[24] it had clearly been absorbed into the barony of Drumlanrig by the mid-fourteenth century, being held of whoever was the lord of the latter. This emerges from another notarial instrument, this one procured by John Blair, lord

---

acting as sheriff in service of brieve of terce on 8 March 1452. See further McGladdery, *James II*, pp. 38, 103; Brown, *Black Douglases*, pp. 264, 289, 292; Borthwick, 'Council', pp. 134–35.

[21] See Chapter 3 above, text accompanying notes 108–109.

[22] *RPS* 1455/6/2, 1455/6/6.

[23] *ADC*, ii, pp. 360, 364. In a different case between the same parties less than a year later, the record refers only to the barony of Drumlanrig (*ADC*, ii, p. 463).

[24] See *RMS*, i, app 2A, no. 302 (and note 1), app 2B no (73); also *RRS*, v, no. 41; Barrow, G.W.S., *Robert Bruce and the Community of the Realm*, 4th edn (Edinburgh, 2004), p. 363; Beam, A., *The Balliol Dynasty 1210–1364* (Edinburgh, 2008), p. 168 note 278; Stell, G.P., 'Balliol, Henry de (*d.* 1246)' and 'Balliol, Alexander de (*d.* 1310?)', both *ODNB*.

of Kilwinnet in Lennox, from the leading notary Thomas Twy at Sauchie in Clackmannanshire on 8 June 1431.[25] The instrument records the production before the notary of a charter under the seal of King Robert II of good memory, the whole appearing to be in good order (that is, with all the appearance of authenticity and formal validity, so far as the notary and the four witnesses to the instrument could tell). This charter narrated the king's sight on 28 May 1374 of a charter of King David II, dated 12 April 1358, saying that he granted to his beloved James Blair, son and heir of the late Hugh Blair, all the lands of 'Corsthogill' with their pertinents in the barony of Drumlanrig.[26] David's grant (made not long after his release from eleven years of captivity in England), explains that he had granted the lands to the late Hugh by reason of the forfeiture of the late Eustace de Lorane, to be held 'of the chief lord of the said lands' (*de capitali domino de dicte terre*). Robert II's charter ratifies and confirms his predecessor's charter, perhaps signalling renewed Blair efforts to gain possession of the lands.

The charters granted by the two kings were clearly not executed by them as direct superiors of Coshogle. Instead, at least in David's case, they were filling a gap, left by whoever was the lord of Drumlanrig. By 1374 this was William, first earl of Douglas, although his hold upon the lordship may not yet have been firmly established. Whatever the position then, the question of whom the Blairs held Coshogle must have been fogged again by the second earl's grant of the Drumlanrig barony to his bastard between 1384 and 1388. By 1455 it was still the case that whoever held Coshogle did so as vassal or tenant of the lord of Drumlanrig. But for nearly 70 years there had been two such lords: the earl in regality and the descendants of his grantee in barony. Cases about these lands would be within the relevant lord's jurisdiction unless there was some specific contrary rule.[27] A mortancestry claim to the lands would not have been within the jurisdiction of the baron of Drumlanrig; but the justiciar of a lord with regality powers could take the case.

---

[25] NLS: Acc 7043 Adamton no 16/1 (Appendix (d)); see also *RMS*, i, no. 479; app 2, no. 1236. Kilwinnet is located at NGR: NS 611 792. On Twy, see Scott, 'William Cranston, Notary Public', pp. 127, 132.

[26] On Hugh and James Blair (the latter a crusader), see Penman, *David II*, pp. 121, 297, 380.

[27] See MacQueen, *CLFS*, pp. 105–14.

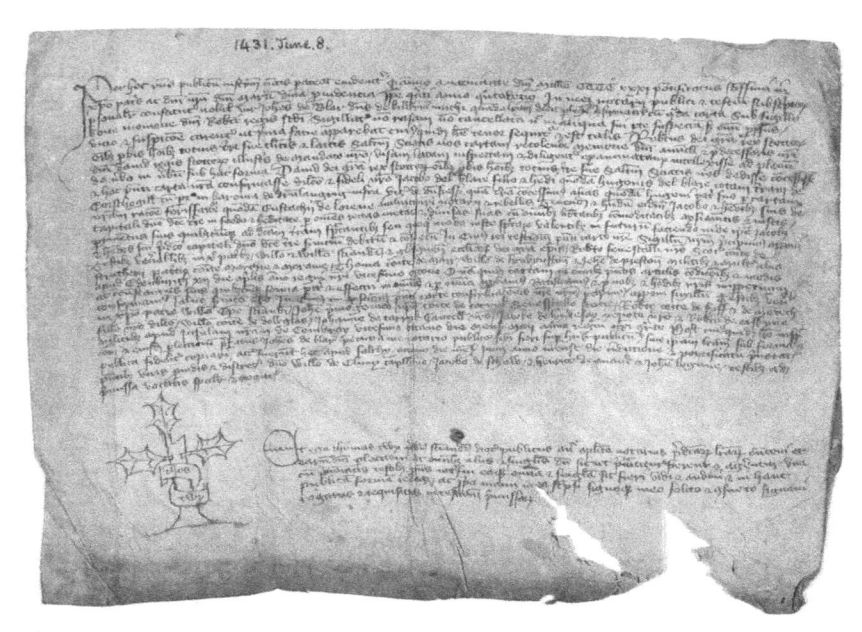

Plate 3: NLS: Acc 7043 Adamton no 16/1
(Courtesy of the National Library of Scotland)

The John Blair of the 1431 transumpt is the pursuer of 1455 rather than his father. The 1455 pursuer's grandfather was Sir John, whereas we know that the father of the 1431 John was also simply an un-knighted John. The latter was alive on 16 June 1430 but resigning the lands of Kilwinnet to his son at that point.[28] John junior may also have acquired the principal family estate of Adamton in Ayrshire from his father at the same time.[29] But it is possible to show that the father may have lived until at latest early 1443.[30] He did not

---

[28] See *RMS*, ii, no. 159.
[29] Paterson, J., *History of the County of Ayr with a Genealogical Account of the Families of Ayrshire*, 2 vols (Edinburgh, 1847–52), ii, p. 382, narrates a great seal charter of 16 June 1430 to this effect. We have not located this document amongst the Adamton papers in NLS Acc 7043/16, and Paterson may have made a mistake about the Kilwinnet charter of the same date, which he does not otherwise mention. Adamton is located at NGR: NS 379 278, close to modern Prestwick airport.
[30] See NRS: GD45/16/1517, GD45/27/76, 77 (*ER*, ix, p. 658); NRAS2516/1 (Prestwick Burgh Records).

CHAPTER FOUR: THE COSHOGLE CASE

die in sasine of Coshogle (if indeed he ever had it), since otherwise his son's claim in 1455 would have been based upon that heritable right. But while the father remained alive the son would be unable to make any claim, as he was not able to say that he was his grandfather's immediate heir.

Blairs of that ilk and Blairs of Adamton*

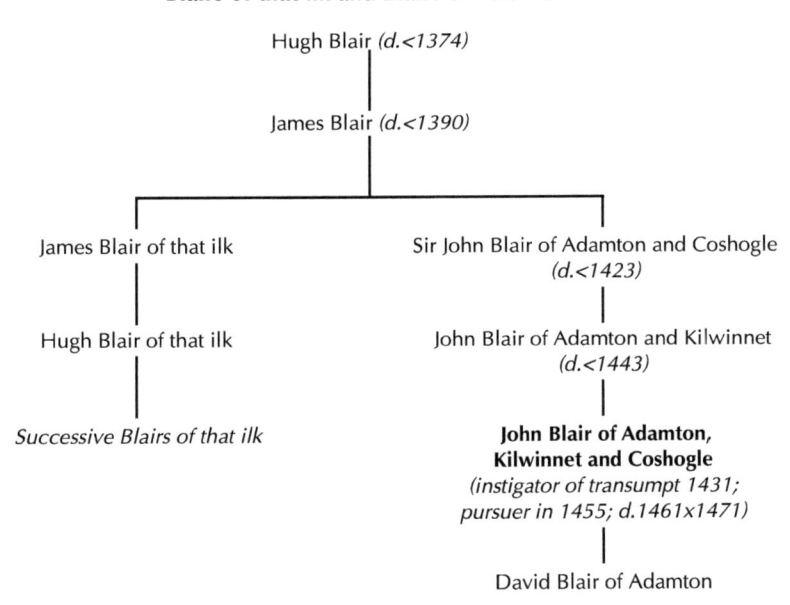

Hugh Blair *(d.<1374)*

James Blair *(d.<1390)*

├── James Blair of that ilk
│   │
│   Hugh Blair of that ilk
│   │
│   *Successive Blairs of that ilk*
│
└── Sir John Blair of Adamton and Coshogle *(d.<1423)*
    │
    John Blair of Adamton and Kilwinnet *(d.<1443)*
    │
    John Blair of Adamton, Kilwinnet and Coshogle
    (instigator of transumpt 1431; pursuer in 1455; d.1461x1471)
    │
    David Blair of Adamton

*Based upon the account of the family of Blairs of that ilk (Dalry) and the family of Blairs of Adamton (Monkton) in James Paterson, *History of the County of Ayr with a Genealogical Account of the Families of Ayrshire* (2 vols, Edinburgh 1847-52) i 413-14; ii 382-3. But documents unknown to Paterson and now available show that the Blair of that ilk lineage he provided cannot be right after the Hugh shown above.

The key point, however, is that the disinheritance of the Blairs must have occurred before 1431, probably some time before. Sir John seems to have been active as the lord of Adamton by 1390, when already he needed the consent to his grants of his son and apparent heir John, i.e. the father of the John commissioning the 1431 transumpt and raising the 1455 action.[31] John the father was lord of Adamton by 1423, however, so Sir John was dead by

---

[31] *Paisley Reg*, pp. 364–65 (11 December 1390); pp. 365–66 (26 April 1396); pp. 367–68 (29 August 1397).

123

then.³² The latter was himself a younger son of the James Blair who was the beneficiary of the grants by David II and Robert II of the lands forfeited by Eustace Lorane, and who also acquired Adamton in 1363.³³ James presumably transferred these 'conquests', or acquisitions, to his second son at some point before his own decease,³⁴ with his own firstborn son thereafter becoming the progenitor of the Blairs of that ilk based in the Ayrshire parish of Dalry.³⁵

Why then did our John have his notarial instrument drawn up in June 1431? It could simply have been an act of prudent management by a new landowner conscious of the fragility of a piece of parchment by then nearly sixty years old (after all he does not seem to have had an original of King David's 1358 charter). Alternatively, and perhaps more likely, it may have been intended for use in a future claim to Coshogle, in which the old documents would be a key piece of evidence. John the father seems to have been giving up control of the family property around 1430, and perhaps he had previously failed, through absence or disability or both, to pursue claims that might otherwise have been made. Coshogle was also some distance away from the family's other major holdings in Ayrshire and Lennox. But John the son was perhaps better placed to take action on his father's demise.

The king's arrest of the fifth earl of Douglas in mid-1431 may also have had a bearing on why John junior had his notarial instrument drawn up.³⁶ Any mortancestry claim after the death of John the father would have to be brought in the earl's regality court at Drumlanrig. Since the earl's imprisonment lasted until the end of September, the future of his regality jurisdiction was probably clouded with uncertainty throughout the summer of 1431.

---

[32] *Ayr Friars Preacher Chrs*, no. 31 (p. 47) dated 28 July 1423: seal of John Blair, lord of Adamton, procured by Ayr burgess to append to a charter for greater security, so Sir John must have died by then. John Blair of Adamton issued charters on 10 September 1425 and 26 January 1426: *Wigtown Chr Chest*, nos 714–15.

[33] *RMS*, i, no. 157; *RRS*, vi, no. 300.

[34] Possibly illustrating the relative alienability of 'conquest' (i.e. acquisition) as distinct from 'heritage': see Chapter 1 above, text accompanying note 39.

[35] Paterson, *History*, i, p. 413; ii, p. 382. Dalry is located at OS, NS 295495.

[36] *Chron Bower*, viii, p. 264.

The Loranes

Also significant in this connection is the appearance of the surname Lorane in the fourteenth-century royal charters transumed in 1431, given that the defender of 1455 was James of that ilk. Was he, or some ancestor of his, already causing problems in 1431 for the Blair claim to Coshogle? The 1455 defender was almost certainly a descendant of, or otherwise related to, the Eustace Lorane already referred to as forfeited for treason to David II before 1358.[37]

Eustace was a landholder on the Scottish side of the middle march whose allegiance seems to have swung to and fro in the period between 1329 and 1346 when Edward Balliol was seeking with powerful English support to invade southern Scotland, overthrow King David's regime and recover the crown lost by his father John in 1296. Eustace was apparently in the English king's allegiance in May 1343, when he was receiving a royal pension of 100 merks yearly until he recovered his Scottish lands.[38] But in 1346 he seems to have been in charge of Roxburgh castle on behalf of William Douglas of Liddesdale, leader of the Scottish side. He surrendered it to the English, however, after the disastrous Scottish defeat at Neville's Cross.[39] If any forfeiture before 1343 had been rescinded following apparent return to Scottish colours, events at Roxburgh clinched the ending of Eustace's career under the Scottish crown.

Forfeiture for treason theoretically entailed the permanent disinheritance of the traitor's heirs from the forfeited lands.[40] But the practical significance of this on the ground may have been non-existent between 1346 and 1357, when David II was in English captivity. Loranes, in fact, remained active in Teviotdale in the 1350s, enjoying financial support from the English Crown.[41] At least one

---

[37] See above, text surrounding note 26.
[38] *CDS*, iii, no. 1410.
[39] *Chron Bower*, vii, p. 269. See further Grant, A., 'Disaster at Neville's Cross: The Scottish Point of View', in Rollason, D. and Prestwich, M., (eds), *The Battle of Neville's Cross 1346* (Stamford, 1998), pp. 15–35; Brown, *Black Douglases*, pp. 38, 43.
[40] *Regiam Majestatem*, Book IV, title 1.
[41] See Reid, 'Coschogill Writ', pp. 140–42; Brown, *Black Douglases*, pp. 138, 169–70. See also Elliot, G.A., 'The Norman Family of Lorraine in Southern Scotland and especially in Berwickshire', unpublished typescript, NRS: F

other member of the Lorane family who held the lands of 'Hangetsyde' in the formerly Balliol barony of Cavers in Teviotdale in the sheriffdom of Roxburgh seems to have transferred his allegiance to the English king in the fourteenth century.[42] English military control of the whole region from Berwick to Annandale and beyond probably ensured that, despite Scottish forfeiture, Lorane possessions in the area held fast. The English grip on Berwickshire, Tweeddale, Teviotdale and parts of Annandale certainly remained in place, if increasingly tenuous, until the truce of 1389 which followed the Scottish victory at Otterburn the previous year.[43] Even then Jedburgh was not recovered for the king of Scots until 1409, while Roxburgh and Berwick would remain in English hands as garrison towns until 1460 and 1461 respectively. So it is conceivable that Loranes in possession in Teviotdale in the mid-fourteenth century were able to hold on for many decades thereafter.

It is in this uncertain context that Robert II's May 1374 confirmation of David II's grant to James Blair must be placed. So must Robert's own grant to James Blair, dated 23 July in the same year, of, not only 'Heroude' in the sheriffdom of Roxburgh but also other, unspecified, lands in Dumfriesshire (perhaps including Coshogle) and Ayrshire. All, it was said, had been forfeited by Eustace Lorane because he died in the peace and faith of the English king.[44] Blair's need of further royal documentation in the mid-1370s indicates continuing difficulties in making such grants effective at that time. Indeed, in some cases, they may never have become so. R.C. Reid provided a number of post-1400

375.050; *RRS*, vi, no. 130 (p. 157).

[42] See NRS: GD40/1/361 (Papers relating to the lands and barony of Fewrule, Roxburghshire), no. 9 (16th century note of writs of Hangetsyde, first a charter by James [second] earl of Douglas to Richard Hangetsyde, of the lands of Hangetsyd in barony of Cavers 'within the few of Roull' which pertained to William Loreyn who transferred his allegiance to the king of England).

[43] See Grant, A., 'The Otterburn War from the Scottish Point of View', in Goodman, A. and Tuck, A., (eds), *War and Border Societies in the Middle Ages* (London, 1992), pp. 30–64.

[44] *RMS*, i, no. 463 (original in NLS: Acc 7043 (Adamton) no. 16). See further Brown, M., 'War, Allegiance, and Community in the Anglo-Scottish Marches: Teviotdale in the Fourteenth Century', *Northern History* 41 (2004), pp. 219–38, 234. The lands of Deloraine in the Ettrick valley (NGR: NT 335 205) have nothing to do with any Lorane holding there: see Watson, W.J., *The History of the Celtic Place-Names of Scotland* (Edinburgh, 1926), p. 417.

CHAPTER FOUR: THE COSHOGLE CASE

references to Loranes in the borders, including one of 7 February 1429 mentioning Patrick Lorane's attempts to recover lands in Roxburghshire of which his father had died vest and saised as of fee: 'Homylknollis' (Hummelknows), 'Colifurde' (Colifort) and the unidentified 'Bilmeschawys'.[45] The first two of these sit on the east side of the Slitrig Water, just a mile or two south of the modern town of Hawick but in the parish, and thus also the barony of Cavers. In 1465 and 1473 John Loren or Lorane of Herwood/Harwod was on assizes for the service of heirs before the sheriff of Roxburgh, while in 1507 James Lorein of 'Herwood' served on another assize.[46] 'Heroude', 'Herwood' and 'Harwood' are all certainly the same lands, today known as Harwood, a few miles south of Bonchester Bridge at the head of the Rule Water valley.[47] In 1531 Hector Lorane, grandson of the late James Lorane (very possibly the defender of 1455), held not only Harwood but also Hawthornside (probably to be identified with the earlier 'Hangetsyde').[48]

The 1531 document says that Harwood and Hawthornside were in the barony of 'Fewrule'; but this barony was created only in 1510, as part of an erection of all the lands of Andrew, lord Herries of Terregles, as such.[49] In that and the 1531 grants the lands of Fewrule were said to be in the barony of Cavers; and there is other evidence for this as well.[50] In the later fourteenth

---

[45] See Reid, 'Coschogill Writ', p. 141 note 34 (citing *RH Supplementary Charters* without further detail, but as the citation indicates the document was then in the Scottish Record Office; it is now located in NLS: Acc 7750/1 [Rutherford of Edgerston Charters], no. 2). Hummelknowes is NGR: NT 507 127; Colifort NGR: NT 512 115.

[46] *HMC 7th report*, 728 no. 12; BL: Add Ch 16297 (for 1465 and 1473 service of heirs respectively); NLS: Acc 7750/1, no. 15 (1507).

[47] Harwood is NGR: NT 566 083. See Tancred, G., *Rulewater and its People* (Edinburgh, 1907), Chapter III. Reid, 'Coschogill Writ', p. 142, cites a sixteenth-century record of the arms of Lorene of Hairwode: argent, three laurel leaves, vert.

[48] See NRS: GD53/1. Hawthornside (OS, NT568119) lies west of Bonchester Bridge. See Tancred, *Rulewater*, pp. 50–51 (noting that the old name of Hawthornside was 'Hangingside', although not knowing when this change occurred).

[49] *RMS*, ii, no. 3446. See for the *terras* of Fewrule previously held by the Herries of Terregles *RMS*, ii, nos 2294, 2526. Note several 'rule' place-names around the Rule Water valley, including not only Bedrule but also Hallrule, Abbotrule, and Town o' Rule: see further Tancred, *Rulewater*, chs I, II, VII. The barony of Bedrule, which marched with Cavers, was one of the entailed estates of the earls of Douglas: *RMS*, i, no. 12; ibid., app 1, nos 38, 123; *RRS*, vi, no. 51.

[50] *RMS*, ii, no. 3613.

century, therefore, the Lorane lands in Teviotdale were almost certainly held at least nominally of the earl of Douglas who was the baron of Cavers (possibly taking over from Thomas, earl of Mar) until the death of Earl James in 1388.[51] Thereafter the estate was held by the earl's sister, Isabella, as his heir-general. In 1402, however, as countess of Mar, she granted Cavers to her brother's bastard, Archibald, triggering a long-running dispute about its ownership resolved eventually in favour of Archibald (who founded the dynasty of Douglas of Cavers).[52]

Once again, therefore, it was probably difficult for the earls of Douglas and their successors to translate any lordship in Teviotdale into something meaningful on the ground much before Jedburgh was regained by the Scots in 1409. The displacement of Patrick Lorane may have happened only after that, as also Sir John Blair's realisation of the grants made to him of Lorane lands in the area. But the still later evidence shows that these were not permanent settlements of the landholding position in Teviotdale, and that the Loranes in particular managed to hang on through the fifteenth and into the sixteenth century.

The Nithsdale Context

There seems no reason to doubt that, like Teviotdale, Nithsdale remained exposed to English, or English-supported, occupation after David II's return in 1357, with a confused, possibly fluid, landholding situation prevailing there as a result. In particular Loranes may have held on at Coshogle as they did in Teviotdale.

We have already seen the uncertainty on 12 April 1358 as to who was the chief lord of Drumlanrig, even although as recently as 1355 the lands had been

---

[51] For Douglas holdings of Cavers, see *RMS*, i, app 1, no. 123; *RRS*, vi, no. 227; Fraser, *Douglas*, iii, nos 19 (suggesting earlier superiority of Thomas, earl of Mar), 23, 25, 37, 77, 408 (again suggesting earlier Mar superiority). On the 'maverick' Thomas, earl of Mar, 'content to serve the crown so long as it profited him', see Penman, *David II*, pp. 159–60, 168–69, 216–18, 274–77; and Watson, 'Donald, eighth earl of Mar (1293–1332)'.

[52] For the 1402 grant and the long-running dispute over Cavers, see Boardman, *Early Stewart Kings*, pp. 288–90; Brown, *Black Douglases*, pp. 109, 120 note 31; and below text accompanying note 79.

CHAPTER FOUR: THE COSHOGLE CASE

recognised as belonging to William, lord of Douglas, by way of inheritance from his father Archibald.[53] Yet on 13 November 1357 David II confirmed to William the lands of the barony of Drumlanrig as granted to him and Margaret his wife by her brother, Thomas, earl of Mar.[54] This suggests that Thomas had been granted the barony by the king some time after 1355, perhaps as part of a package by which the earl was persuaded to throw his lot in with the still captive David. This grant may have had the consent of the lord of Douglas, whose links to Mar in the barony of Cavers have already been noted.[55] Mar yielded up any claim to Drumlanrig at the end of 1357, however, possibly marking his sister's wedding with a gift, but perhaps conceding further that the established border lord Douglas was much more likely to make the grant actually effective on the ground. The king's return to Scotland on 6 October 1357, albeit conditional on the surrender of hostages (including Mar) and the payment of ransom, foreshadowed (but did not of itself accomplish) an eventual end to English occupation of border lands such as Nithsdale, and opportunities to make good royal grants such as those of Drumlanrig and its constituent estate of Coshogle.[56]

Walter Bower, writing in the 1440s, tells us of a promise Edward III took from King David II in 1357 as a condition of his release from English captivity: destruction of the castles and fortifications of Nithsdale, identified as Dalswinton, Dumfries, Morton and Durisdeer, plus nine others unnamed.[57] Although this promise is mentioned nowhere in the surviving official documentation surrounding David's release, such destruction is not completely unlikely, for exactly the opposite reason to the one given by Bower (that these strongholds had inflicted the greatest damage on the English).

---

[53] See above, text at note 16.
[54] *RRS*, vi, no. 153.
[55] See above, text accompanying note 52.
[56] But see *Morton Reg*, ii, nos 100, 101, 130, 136, 141, 142; *RRS*, vi, nos 105, 508–09; MacQueen, *CLFS*, pp. 125, 183, for a legal process over Morton the significance of which in the present context is uncertain.
[57] *Chron Bower*, vii, pp. 304–05. Bower also tells us (ibid., p. 296) that in the 1350s the noble Roger de Kirkpatrick (presumably of Closeburn) held all Nithsdale securely in allegiance to King David but only *after* he had captured the castles at Dalswinton and Caerlaverock and cast them down to the ground. Kirkpatrick himself died violently at the hands of a James Lindsay in 1358 (Penman, *David II*, p. 208).

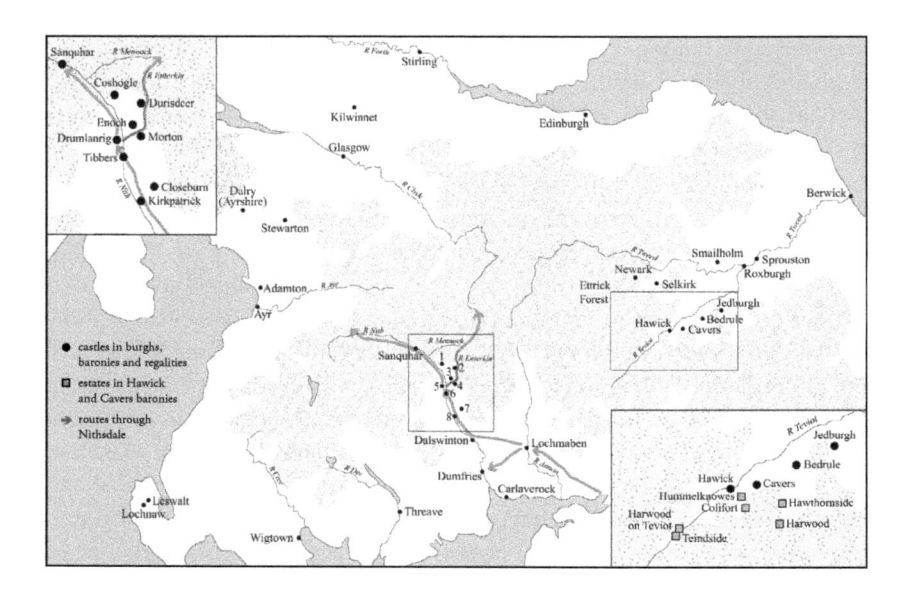

The existence of many strongholds along the length of Nithsdale, particularly in its upper reaches from Dalswinton to Sanquhar, is explained by its being a key route for much of southern Scotland. Nithsdale provided comparatively easy access from the western marches to the rest of Scotland south of Forth. Lochmaben castle, in English hands until 1384, controlled access not only to Annandale but also to Nithsdale from the south-east.[58] The valley itself was traversed by an originally Roman road from Dalswinton north, crossing the River Carron (perhaps near its confluence with the Nith at Morton Mill) before bending north-eastward to go between the other castles at Enoch and Morton and on to Durisdeer. Then it led up the valley of the Kirk Burn over into Clydesdale above Crawford. From there another formerly Roman road coming up from Annandale to Crawford divided on either side of the Clyde into east or west central Scotland. There was also a left fork at the north-eastward turn after the Carron crossing, taking another road to a ford over the Nith below the castle-mound at Tibbers. This route then passed through Drumlanrig on its way north over, ultimately, into east

---

[58] See Webster, B., 'The English Occupations of Dumfriesshire in the Fourteenth Century', *Transactions of the Dumfriesshire and Galloway Natural History and Antiquarian Society* 35 (1956–57), pp. 64–79.

CHAPTER FOUR: THE COSHOGLE CASE

Ayrshire and the country beyond. That road too was perhaps originally Roman for its entire length.⁵⁹

The Nithsdale castles thus facilitated control of the land by whoever occupied them and put, if not a stranglehold, at least severe pressure on the king of Scots whenever the occupiers leant towards the English king. De-castellation was therefore not necessarily against the Scottish king's interests so long as he could at least populate its lands with his supporters and their followings. Sandy Grant has shown that a Scottish policy of destroying castles otherwise vulnerable to English occupation went back at least to the time of Robert I.⁶⁰ The recaptured Lochmaben was also at least partially cast down in 1384.⁶¹ In Nithsdale itself there is archaeological evidence of destruction at Morton, while nothing at all remains at Durisdeer apart from the name Castlehill. We may further compare the later situation as the Scots regained Jedburgh in 1409, then Roxburgh in 1460 and Berwick in 1461. In the first two cases the town castles were destroyed after being re-taken, and only in Berwick could the English garrison be subsequently (and this time permanently) re-established. Bower's statement gains some circumstantial credibility by his further comment that many of the Nithsdale castles remained to a large extent un-rebuilt (*inedificata*) in his own time. Much of what survives of these castles today is thought to be of late fourteenth-century or subsequent construction.⁶² The earliest reference to a castle at Drumlanrig is in 1429,

---

⁵⁹ Keppie, L., *The Legacy of Rome: Scotland's Roman Remains* (Edinburgh, 2004), pp. 90–96. For an illustrative fourteenth-century English incursion by the Nithsdale route, see Nicholson, R., *Edward III and the Scots* (Oxford, 1965), pp. 205–06, 214. See too *Chron Bower*, vii, p. 270. We have also found the Roy maps of the mid-eighteenth century helpful in tracing older routes in the area: see <http://maps.nls.uk/roy/index.html>.

⁶⁰ Grant, *Independence and Nationhood*, pp. 6, 9, 45, 52. See further Cornell, D., 'A Kingdom Cleared of Castles: the Role of the Castle in the Campaigns of Robert Bruce', *Scottish Historical Review* lxxxvii (2008), pp. 233–57; Yeoman, P., 'War and (in) Pieces: Stirling Castle, June 1314', in Penman, M., (ed.), *Bannockburn 1314–2014: Battle and Legacy* (Donington, 2015), pp. 129–38, 132–34.

⁶¹ Macdonald, A.J., *Border Bloodshed: Scotland and England at War 1369–1403* (East Linton, 2000), p. 76.

⁶² G P Stell says of Morton castle that 'the upstanding structure almost certainly belongs to the Douglas [of Dalkeith] period of ownership [*i.e. after 1369/70*]' (*Exploring Scotland's Heritage: Dumfries and Galloway* (Edinburgh, 1986), p. 109). See further HES Canmore ID nos 66029 (Closeburn), 45434 (Sanquhar),

and remains of a probably fifteenth-century towerhouse exist within the present mansion.[63]

That Nithsdale in general remained a problematic zone may be a partial explanation for Archibald the Grim becoming warden of the west march by 1364 and then receiving a royal grant of all the lands of Galloway between the Rivers Cree and Nith in free barony in 1369.[64] Sandwiched between these grants, the Nithsdale baronies, especially those located on the river's west bank, must have been deliberately exposed to the weight of Archibald's growing power. This was reinforced in 1372 when he gained the earldom of Wigtown '*cum furca et fossa sok et sak toll et theme infangandtheffe et outefangandtheffe*' (i.e. with baronial jurisdiction[65]), so becoming the lord of all Galloway west of Nith.[66]

Around 1387, there was also a royal revival of the ancient lordship of Nithsdale for Archibald's bastard son William upon his marriage to Robert II's daughter Egidia.[67] This seems to have been a grant of jurisdiction more than lands: when re-suppressed in 1456, the lordship was said to have included the office of march warden within itself, and being sheriff, justiciar and chamberlain of Dumfries.[68] The march wardenship element suggests that before 1387 Nithsdale was part of the west march originally centred on Annandale, and under the jurisdiction of Archibald the Grim as warden.[69]

All this certainly confirms Nithsdale's strategic importance when warfare with the English was resurgent following the 1384 expiry of a lengthy Anglo-Scottish truce. In this context, however, the subsequent freedom of William Douglas of Nithsdale to set off on crusade in 1391, i.e. after the

---

46374 (Enoch), 65896 (Dalswinton), and 65153 (Tibbers).

[63] *HMC 44 Report XV.8 [Buccleuch MSS]*, no. 5, pp. 10–11; HES Canmore ID no. 65142 (Drumlanrig Castle).

[64] *RRS*, vi, no. 451.

[65] Grant, 'Franchises', p. 158; see also ibid., p. 171 note 75.

[66] Fraser, *Douglas*, iii, no. 327; *RMS*, i, no. 507; see further Penman, *David II*, pp. 388–89.

[67] *Chron Bower*, vii, pp. 410–14 (from which naval prowess is also evident); see further Grant, 'Franchises', p. 172; idem, 'Bastards', pp. 335–38.

[68] Fraser, *Douglas*, iii, no. 85. For inter-jurisdictional conflict in Nithsdale before 1438, see Chapter 3 above, text at note 32.

[69] Brown, 'Scottish March Wardenships', pp. 208–12.

ten-year truce which followed the Scottish victory at Otterburn in early August 1388, is significant (even if he then met his death in a fatal rammy with English fellow-crusaders at Königsberg).[70] Wardenship duties may have been less pressing in a period of truce, and perhaps it was at this time, if not later, that Sir John Blair finally succeeded in supplanting (or, perhaps, subordinating) the Loranes and gaining for himself heritable sasine of Coshogle.

The Douglases of Drumlanrig (and Hawick)

The foregoing also provides important background to the 'unusually generous' grant of Drumlanrig by James, second earl of Douglas, to his bastard son William sometime in the 1380s, not least the curious knight service which William was supposed to provide in the earl's army, but in the name of blench farm only.[71] If the earl was born after his parents married in and around 1357, he can have been only around 30 when he died at Otterburn, and any children that he had fathered surely could have been at most around half that age. His own marriage took place in 1371, perhaps as he entered minority at 14.[72] William was most probably born in the same decade. Despite his military tenurial obligations, therefore, William was probably too young to take any part in the battle of 1388. It thus may not be too much to suggest that the second earl's grant was a way of protecting the interests of his young bastard as the former set off to the long-planned renewal of border hostilities with England which would cost him his life.[73] The under-age knight service tenant and his land would then be under the wardship of the new earl, whoever that might be; while upon the youth's majority he would come into his own without liability to the casualties of ordinary military tenure.

---

[70] MacQuarrie, A., *Scotland and the Crusades 1095–1560* (Edinburgh, 1997), pp. 85–86; Ditchburn, *Scotland and Europe*, p. 70; Grant, 'Bastards', p. 337; *Chron Bower*, vii, pp. 446–48.

[71] *HMC 44 Report XV.8 [Buccleuch MSS]*, no. 2 (p. 8). The quoted comment is Grant's: 'Bastards', p. 317. He also takes note of the grant in *Independence and Nationhood*, p. 135, and in 'Service and Tenure', p. 161.

[72] For the age of marriage, see Chapter 1 above, text accompanying note 60.

[73] For the Scots' preparation in summer 1388 for the Otterburn campaign, see Grant, 'Otterburn', pp. 46–50; Macdonald, *Border Bloodshed*, chapter 3 (especially at pp. 101–09).

Two factors may have combined to undermine that plan at least for a time. One was uncertainty about who would succeed as earl, not removed until early in 1389 when Archibald the Grim was recognised as such by the king.[74] One of the other contenders for the Douglas lands, if not the title of earl, was Sir Malcolm Drummond of Concraig (through his wife, Earl James' sister Isabella). In June 1389 Drummond received a special protection from King Richard II of England with a warrant for all the border lands of the Douglas inheritance, including Drumlanrig.[75] This preceded an attempt at invasion from England in support of the Drummond claim. The young William's interests most probably lay in Earl Archibald's succession.

Further, given that Drumlanrig had been granted by Thomas, earl of Mar, jointly to his sister Margaret and the first earl, the omission of her name from Earl James' grant to his bastard was a potentially dangerous flaw in the transfer of the title. This issue probably explains a bond made on 5 December 1389 by John of Swinton and Margaret his wife, countess of Douglas and also Mar (in her own right in succession to her brother, who had died childless in 1374). By this deed the couple undertook not to move any question or controversy against William regarding Drumlanrig whenever he obtained possession, so that he might enjoy it in accordance with the charter of Earl James.[76] It appears that William had still to receive sasine from the new Earl Archibald but had settled – on what terms and with whose aid we do not know - with the first earl's widow and her new husband (a loyal Douglas man[77]).

The next direct evidence on William's claim to hold Drumlanrig is a letter of King James I, 'wrate with our proper hand' at Croydon on 30 November 1412 and sealed with the king's signet, ordering that 'oure traiste and wele belofit cosyng Schir William' is to have, not only Drumlanrig, but also Hawick and Selkirk.[78] On the same day and also in his own hand, it is worth noting, the king confirmed the barony of Cavers to Archibald Douglas, also a bastard

---

[74] See Chapter 1 above, text accompanying notes 72–75.
[75] *CDS*, iv, no. 391.
[76] *HMC 44 Report XV.8 [Buccleuch MSS]* no. 3. Since the bond bound only Swinton and the countess, there was no need for any guardian or attorney to execute it on behalf of the possibly still-minor William.
[77] On Swinton, see Brown, *Black Douglases*, p. 143.
[78] *HMC 44 Report XV.8 [Buccleuch MSS]*, no. 4 (p. 10); also in Fraser, *Buccleuch*, ii, no. 23.

CHAPTER FOUR: THE COSHOGLE CASE

of the second earl and possibly William's brother.[79] The barony of Hawick (which marched with Cavers) had been granted to Sir William in blench farm in 1407 by Archibald, the fourth earl (who had succeeded his father in 1400). The grant was followed by a confirmation from the Governor, Robert Stewart, duke of Albany.[80] The date of that grant is significantly before the Scottish recovery of Jedburgh in 1409, so the royal confirmation in 1412 may be a sign that a hitherto parchment title had finally begun to be made good on the ground.

It should also be noted here that Hawick (conjoined with the regality of Sprouston) had first been acquired for the Douglases by Archibald the Grim. This was a result of his marriage to Joanna Murray, as part of the extensive lands (including Sprouston as well as Hawick) that she had inherited from Sir Thomas Murray of Bothwell.[81] Selkirk was part of the Douglas earl's lordship in the Ettrick Forest. It is not clear, however, whether Sir William received land within the forest in the ordinary way or had been appointed to an office within the forest's administration, of which the earl was the head. Certainly Selkirk does not appear to have descended to Sir William's heirs, suggesting the latter was the case.

Sir William was also clearly a regular visitor to England at the time of the king's letter, as a member of the Scottish team of negotiators seeking the king's release and return to Scotland.[82] Earlier he was at least willing to act as hostage in England after the fourth earl's capture at Humbleton in 1402.[83] It may indeed have been as a reward for such service that William was granted Hawick by the earl in 1407, after the latter had returned to Scotland on a parole which he then broke.[84]

---

[79] *HMC 7th Report*, p. 727. See further above text accompanying note 52.
[80] NRS: AD1/31; Fraser, *Buccleuch*, ii, no. 22.
[81] See Chapter 1 above, text accompanying notes 81–82.
[82] *CDS*, iv, nos 729, 841, 872, 894; *Rot Scot*, ii, pp. 182, 197b, 200a, 204b, 207a, 219a. Earlier safe conducts for visits to England begin in 1397: ibid., pp. 138b, 175a, 177a; *CDS*, iv, p. 404. Although the index to *Rot Scot*, ii, gives several other references to William Douglas of Drumlanrig knight, these turn out to be for others of the same name, notably Sir William Douglas of Strathbrock (Uphall): ibid., pp. 104a, 105b, 106b,119b, 121a, 167a.
[83] *CDS*, iv, no. 736.
[84] See further Grant, 'Acts of Lordship', pp. 240–41, 246, 257. The relevant entries in the proposed hostage lists can be found at *Rot Scot*, ii, pp. 177, 181–82;

As befitted a knight, Sir William was a military man as well as a diplomat.[85] His holding at Hawick put him near the front line with the remaining English-controlled zone in Teviotdale, and Bower records him with his fellow-knight, Sir Gawane of Dunbar, breaking down the bridge at Roxburgh and then burning the town on 28 June 1411.[86] His chivalric inclinations are also apparent from his involvement in 'feats of arms' in England in 1405 (when his safe conduct allowed him a retinue of 24) and a licence to perform similarly against the English knight Sir John Clifford at either Berwick or Carlisle in 1414 (the safe conducts on this occasion permitted him to be accompanied by a retinue of between six and a dozen men and horses).[87]

By May 1419 Sir William had followed the fourth earl to war in France, leading a force of 400 men-at-arms and 300 archers presumably drawn from his baronies. But defeat at the hands of the English ensued under his leadership at Fresnay in the Champagne-Ardenne region in north-eastern France on 3 March 1420.[88] Later in the same year Sir William resumed a diplomatic role, receiving two safe conducts from King Henry V (dated 30 August and 7 September respectively) for himself and a *comitiva* of 20 men and horses to visit King James in France, where the latter had been taken by the English

---

CDS, iv, no. 736. A nominal annual reddendo for Hawick of one arrow *si petatur tantum* had at least some military connotation.

[85] On expectations of knighthood in fifteenth-century Scotland, see Stevenson, *Chivalry and Knighthood*, pp. 13–39. It is not known whether Drumlanrig was a knight by virtue of the military service due for his estate or had been independently dubbed. On dubbing, see Stevenson, *Chivalry and Knighthood*, pp. 41–62.

[86] *Chron Bower*, viii, p. 80. We have preferred the 'Gawane' of the source to the modern rendering 'Gavin'; the Arthurian echo in the naming was very probably deliberate. See also the comments of Clancy, T.O. and Hammond, M., 'The Romance of Names: Literary Personal Names in Twelfth- and Thirteenth-Century Scotland', in Hammond, M., (ed.), *Personal Names and Naming Practices in Medieval Scotland* (Woodbridge, 2019), pp. 166–86, 185.

[87] *CDS*, iv, nos 710, 711; *Rot Scot*, ii, pp. 209 (bis), 212a, 217b; *CDS*, v, no. 944. On duels of chivalry and tournaments, see Stevenson, *Chivalry and Knighthood*, pp. 63–80.

[88] See Forbes-Leith, W., *The Scots Men-at-Arms and Life-guards in France: from their Formation until their Final Dissolution A.D. MCCCCXVIII-MDCCCXXX* (Edinburgh, 1882), i, p. 153; Ditcham, B.G.H., 'The Employment of Foreign Mercenary Troops in the French Royal Armies, 1415–1470' (Edinburgh University PhD, 1978) [Ditcham, 'Foreign Mercenary Troops'], pp. 15, 184; Sumption, *Cursed Kings*, pp. 677, 686–87, 708.

CHAPTER FOUR: THE COSHOGLE CASE

king in his ultimately unsuccessful attempt to counter Scottish support for King Charles V of France.[89]

Sir William was twice married; a papal dispensation for his second marriage, with Jacoba Douglas (daughter of James Douglas of Dalkeith), was granted on 12 June 1410.[90] His son William II was served as heir to his father's barony of Hawick in Jedburgh sheriff court on 30 September 1427.[91] The inquest's observation that William II had failed to prosecute his inheritance rights over the previous six years suggests that his father died some time in 1421, although whether in Scotland or France is not stated.[92] Probably the issue of his father's first marriage, William II may have been born in the 1390s. He too became a hostage in England for the payment of King James I's ransom in October 1427, a situation from which he was not released until summer 1432.[93] This may in part explain, first, why William II was prompted to put his

---

[89] *Foedera*, x, pp. 18,19; *CDS*, iv, no. 897. See Chapter 1 above text accompanying notes 87–89 and Chapter 6 below, text accompanying note 45, on the significance of the Scots' refusal to obey their king.

[90] *CPL*, pp. 227–28. William I's first wife was Jean Murray. Jacoba was previously married to Sir John Hamilton of Cadzow (*Scots Peerage*, iv, p. 346; vii, p. 114).

[91] Fraser, *Buccleuch*, ii, no. 28.

[92] French sources state that a Sir William Douglas of Drumlanrig and another Sir William Douglas of 'Kyrros' were killed at the siege of Orleans on 21 October 1428, both then being buried before the high altar in the city's church of Sainte Croix, i.e. its cathedral, to which they had previously made a handsome donation. See Forbes-Leith, *Scots Men-at-Arms*, i, pp. 36, 157; Ditcham, 'Foreign Mercenary Troops', p. 61 (both citing Charles de la Saussey (Carl Sausseyo) *Annales Ecclesiae Aureliensis* (Paris, 1615), p. 596). A near-contemporary English chronicle says, however, that William Douglas of 'Danlanryk' was killed at the battle of Verneuil in 1424 (*Three Fifteenth-Century Chronicles*, ed. Gairdner, J. (London, 1880), p. 164). We think that the evidence of the 1427 inquest on the date of Sir William's death is to be preferred to these other sources, because it itself must have been based on evidence without there being any obvious motivation for falsification of what that showed, whereas others not from Scotland are themselves in conflict and may simply have been confused between the many William Douglases of the time (see also e.g. Forbes-Leith, *Scots Men-at-Arms*, i, p. 155 for a Guillaume de Douglas 'escuier' killed at the battle of Crevant on 31 July 1423).

[93] Balfour-Melville, E.W.M., *James I, King of Scots 1406–1437* (London, 1936), pp. 146–49, 202–03, 293–95 (no 51). See also *Rot Scot*, ii, p. 261b (9 Nov 1427 – arrival in London?) and *Rot Scot*, ii, p. 277a (release 20 June 1432).

affairs in order prior to his departure for an indeterminate period in England, and also why it took until 5 March 1428 for Archibald, fifth earl of Douglas, to grant him a new charter of Hawick, with the sasine that followed dated 14 February 1429.[94] Part of the story may be a negotiation between the new earl and his vassal about the non-entry fine which the latter needed to pay before he could be given sasine. Perhaps it was as reward for his service as a hostage that William II had by 1437 become a knight like his father.[95]

The uncertainties about Hawick doubtless applied also at Drumlanrig, held of the same superior but in a different sheriffdom. But further difficulties confronted William II there. On 29 May 1429, at Middleham in Yorkshire, while still a hostage, he entered an indenture with William Douglas, lord of Leswalt in Wigtownshire, under which the latter agreed to give up the castle and lands of Drumlanrig 'outane the saide landys the qwilkys he has granted him for the terym of x yhere'. William of Drumlanrig for his part quitclaimed the action he had against Leswalt. The latter was, however, to have free ish and entry to the said castle, while Drumlanrig would enjoy similar rights at Leswalt's Wigtownshire castle of Lochnaw.[96] The background to the arrangement is unclear, but it is apparent that Drumlanrig had found Leswalt in possession of his lands and was compelled to accept that position continuing until the expiry of a term of years (perhaps therefore a lease rather than a heritable grant).

This suggests that the earl of Douglas had exploited the opportunity created, perhaps first by the exercise of rights of wardship over Drumlanrig and then by the non-entry of the absent heir, to grant the otherwise vacant lands to a supporter who could immediately exploit them. There was a parallel, in other words, with the way in which the apparent pre-October 1427 vacancy at Hawick was used by one of the Douglas earls to make a grant of the East Mains of the barony to his man James Gledstanes and his wife Janet Murray.

---

[94] Fraser, *Buccleuch*, ii, no. 29 (charter to William as son and heir of Sir William); NRS: AD1/42 (sasine, taken by attorney on behalf of William).

[95] Fraser, *Douglas*, iii, no. 301, shows William II as Sir William in 1437.

[96] *HMC 44 Report XV.8 [Buccleuch MSS]*, no. 5, pp. 10–11. On William Douglas of Leswalt and his claim to Lochnaw castle, see further Brown, *Black Douglases*, pp. 171, 173, 241. Ish is a technical term in the document: from DSL (https://www.dsl.ac.uk/entry/snd/ish), 'Right or facility of exit or egress. Used gen. in phr. *ish and entry* (cf. Entry, n., 4.), of the right of an occupier of property to get access to it through the property of another.'

It took until November 1437 for William of Drumlanrig to get rid of them by way of a mortancestry action based on his father's title.[97] Perhaps he sought to make a similar claim against Leswalt in 1429, but was forced to settle because granting fixed-term leases was not beyond the powers of a superior holding property in ward or as a result of non-entry by a vassal. By 1440, however, we find William by consent of parties choosing an assize of 25 to perambulate contested marches in the barony of Sanquhar next to Drumlanrig, which would hardly have been possible had possession of his own lordship still been shaky.[98]

Hawick and Sprouston

These difficulties at Drumlanrig probably form yet further background to John Blair's 1431 notarial instrument recording the basis for his claim to Coshogle.[99] We learn no more of such uncertainty, however, until the death of Sir William II of Drumlanrig in 1444, whereupon his eldest son and heir, William III, confronted renewed difficulties in gaining entry to the barony of Hawick. Part of the problem may have been that yet again the heir was a minor, since in all probability his parents did not marry before 1427 or even 1432.[100] But additionally in 1444 the prospective superior, William, eighth earl of Douglas, had still to reach the end of his own minority, while the earl's own superior, King James II, was also still a minor who would not reach full age until October 1451.

An additional issue was that Hawick was part of the unentailed Douglas lands acquired by Archibald the Grim through his marriage with Joanna Murray of Bothwell before he became the third earl in 1389. The new eighth earl thus had no automatic inheritance claim to it.[101] Instead Margaret sister of the sixth earl inherited the superiority after the latter's execution at the 'Black Dinner' in 1440 alongside his younger brother, who would otherwise have succeeded him. The earldom and the entailed lands had then fallen to the

---

[97] Fraser, *Douglas*, iii, no. 301.
[98] NRAS1275 (Buccleuch)/Bundle 538: Crichton writs, no. 132.
[99] See above, text accompanying notes 25–26.
[100] *Scots Peerage*, vii, p. 115, states that William II's wife is 'said' to have been Janet, daughter of Sir Herbert Maxwell of Carlaverock.
[101] See Borthwick and MacQueen, 'Three Fifteenth-Century Cases', p. 140; Penman, *David II*, p. 296.

heir male, James Douglas of Balvenie earl of Avondale.[102] Margaret's 1444 marriage to the eighth earl, which followed the death of Earl James in 1443, seems to have allowed Earl William to be infeft in the lands of the barony of Hawick in 1446 (i.e. after he had attained majority).[103] Margaret herself may have only reached the marriageable age of 12 in 1444.[104]

But uncertainty persisted in Hawick. On the same day (1 March 1447) as Earl William presided at Newark over an inquest about lands in Hawick as 'baron of the regality of Sprouston' (also in Roxburghshire),[105] Oswald of Abernethy made a notarially recorded protest in the earl's court at the same place, saying that he did not claim or challenge any man as his superior in the regality of Hawick but that he would hold his lands in chief of whomsoever an inquest found to be the baron of the barony of Hawick.[106] Oswald named his lands as 'Harewode' and 'Tenside' in the sheriffdom of Roxburgh and regality of Hawick. 'Tenside' is modern Teindside, on the Teviot two miles south-west of the present town of Hawick. It is included in a 1511 list of tenandry lands (i.e. estates held of the baron) in the barony of Hawick.[107] 'Harewode' in the barony of Hawick cannot have been the Lorane estate of the same name in the barony of Cavers. But next to Teindside today is Harwood on Teviot, which can almost certainly be identified with the Over and Nether Harwood also included in the 1511 list of the tenandry lands of the barony of Hawick.[108] It thus seems highly likely that Oswald's difficulties in 1447 arose because he had his own titles from the now-deceased William II of Drumlanrig and could not get them renewed with either the still un-infeft William III or Earl William, whichever of them should now be his superior.

We saw in Chapter 2 how in January 1449, before the still-minor James II assumed the reins of government, a transumpt embodied in a royal charter

---

[102] See Chapter 1 above, text at note 96.
[103] *ER*, ix, p. 659 (index to Responde Books); Fraser, *Buccleuch*, ii, no. 38 (23 July 1446).
[104] On marriageable age, see Chapter 1 above, text accompanying note 60.
[105] NRAS1100 (Roxburghe)/bundle 702, summarised Fraser, *Douglas*, iii, no. 418. Newark (NGR: NT 418 295) was the *caput* of the Forest, and thus rather an unexpected place at which to hold the regality court of Sprouston (NGR: NT 755 353) and an inquest about lands in Hawick (NGR: NT 502 145).
[106] NRAS1100 (Roxburghe)/bundle 704, summarised Fraser, *Douglas*, iii, no. 417.
[107] NGR: NT 442 085; *RMS*, ii, no. 3576.
[108] *RMS*, ii, no. 3576. Harwood on Teviot is NGR: NT 443 094.

CHAPTER FOUR: THE COSHOGLE CASE

was made of various fourteenth-century documents lying at the root of the earl's title to various lands.[109] These included the retour of an inquest of 1320 related to the regality of Sprouston and the David II grant of Hawick with Sprouston to Thomas Murray of Bothwell in 1360.[110] That grant left ambiguous whether the undoubted regality in Sprouston also extended over Hawick. The version that survived down to 1449 seemed to say, on the one hand, that both Sprouston and Hawick were to be held of the king in free regality and then, on the other, that Hawick was held in free barony. The transumpt made no mention, however, of the fact that the heritable rights in unentailed Hawick (and Sprouston) must have been those of the earl's wife Margaret, and so pertained to him only through that marriage.[111]

It took until 6 October 1450, six years after the death of Sir William II of Drumlanrig (and over seven since the succession of the eighth earl), before William III of Drumlanrig was finally served as his father's heir in Hawick by an inquest at Jedburgh sheriff court.[112] Significantly, this was probably just after Earl William departed abroad to celebrate the papal jubilee in Rome, and also to hold diplomatic meetings en route in Burgundy, France and England.[113] But William III continued to have difficulty after the earl's return from his triumphal journey in April 1451. A notarial instrument dated 7 June 1451 records the former's request to the earl to comply with a royal brieve of sasine and the earl's reply that he could not give sasine because he stood under the king's respite.[114] As suggested in Chapter 2, this respite was most probably a royal grant of immunity from legal actions against the earl while he was absent from the kingdom on the king's business (rather than his own

---

[109] See Chapter 2 above, text accompanying notes 132–34.

[110] The David II grant of Hawick as printed in *RRS*, vi, no. 187 from NLS: Ch 951 smooths over difficult passages in the latter (itself, of course, a copy).

[111] Pre-1443 documents referring to Sprouston generally do so as a regality associated with the earls of Douglas (see e.g. *HMC* 14th Report app 3) but rarely linked with Hawick. On 10 May 1446 William, earl of Douglas and Avondale, lord of Galloway and of the regality of Sprouston grants a charter over lands in Sprouston (*HMC Roxburghe*, no. 49 – see NRAS1100 (Roxburghe) bundle 703 for the earl's full style).

[112] Fraser, *Buccleuch*, ii, no. 45. See also ibid., no. 43.

[113] See Chapter 2 above, text accompanying notes 161–73.

[114] NRS: AD1/53.

alone), and thus granted before October 1450.[115] It may, however, have been renewed in April 1451 when the earl departed again to truce negotiations in the north of England.[116]

The immediate basis for Drumlanrig's action in June may have been that, the earl being back in Scotland again to face his Parliamentary treason trial later that month, the respite should no longer hold good to delay his infeftment at Hawick. It is significant that the notarial instrument of 7 June gives its place as Edinburgh castle, where the king and the royal administration had been based since early March.[117] Drumlanrig was therefore probably seeking to exploit the deterioration of the earl's political position that had recently become apparent after his return to Scotland, culminating in the treason trial.

The Crisis of 1451 and Afterwards: Regaining Hawick and Coshogle

The outcome of the trial in June 1451 was, however, the settlement between king and earl which was discussed in detail in Chapter 3. As part of that settlement, Hawick, along with Bedrule and Smailholm, was annexed to and incorporated into the barony of Sprouston, the whole to be held by the earl in free regality.[118] There is no hint in this royal confirmation of any issues underlying or resolved by the grant. The Auchinleck chronicler thought that 'all gud scottismen war rycht blyth' about the settlement of 1451.[119] The joy may, however, not have been shared in Drumlanrig, not mentioned in any of the re-grants to the earl, or in Hawick, now firmly incorporated within the regality of Sprouston and the earl's overall superiority. To William III of Drumlanrig this latter must have seemed like a final defeat for his ambitions, if not his claims, for Hawick's independent jurisdictional status as a barony.

In June 1452, however, four months after the killing of the eighth earl, William III of Drumlanrig sought once again to exploit a changing situation

---

[115] See Chapter 2 above, text accompanying notes 163–65.
[116] See Chapter 3 above, notes 5–6, 16–20.
[117] See Chapter 3 above, text accompanying note 21.
[118] *RMS*, ii, no. 475.
[119] *Auchinleck Chronicle* f 114r (McGladdery, *James II*, p. 265).

CHAPTER FOUR: THE COSHOGLE CASE

by resigning Hawick directly to the king and seeking a new infeftment. The transaction was witnessed by Crichton of Sanquhar, enemy of the Douglas earls and William's Nithsdale neighbour.[120] But only on 11 November 1452, after the interim reconciliation of the ninth earl and the king in August, did William III finally gain infeftment in Hawick as a barony held of the earl, with no mention made of any over-arching regality or of Sprouston.[121] While this must have been a victory of a kind, it, and indeed the final forfeiture of the ninth earl in 1455, brought no end to William's difficulties in Hawick. Only ten years later, in January 1465, did he finally succeed, by way of yet another brieve of mortancestry in the justiciary court at Jedburgh, in ejecting the last of the old Douglas supporters, the Gledstanes, from demesne lands in the barony.[122]

Perhaps because there was no doubt about the earls' regality rights in Drumlanrig, it does not seem to have been caught up in anything like the difficulties that enveloped Hawick (at least until the ninth earl renounced his fealty to the king in 1452). But the difficulties about the scope of the earls' regality and superiority rights in Drumlanrig as against those of the baron, probably over at least three decades, surely provide the most convincing explanation for the presence of James Lorane on the lands of Coshogle in January 1455. He and his ancestors may always have maintained some contact with the lands forfeited by Eustace Lorane in 1346 through the troubled century and more that followed. But it does look most likely that there had been a renewal of actual possession, probably during the minority or absence in England of William II of Drumlanrig, and so very likely under either the representatives of the absent fourth earl up to 1424, or the fifth earl some time before his arrest in 1431, when John Blair took out his transumpt.

---

[120] Fraser, *Buccleuch*, ii, no. 50.
[121] Fraser, *Buccleuch*, ii, no. 51 (see further above, text accompanying note 18, for the involvement of James Douglas of Drumlanrig as the earl's bailie). On 29 March 1458 the king granted to Thomas Cranston of that ilk lands in the lordship of Sprouston which Cranston had previously resigned (having previously held the lands of the earls): see NRAS1100 (Roxburghe)/bundle 621.
[122] NRS: AD1/60 (transcribed in Borthwick and MacQueen, 'Three Fifteenth-Century Cases', pp. 136–39). Note also *RMS*, ii, no. 646 (1458 royal confirmation to the Gledstanes).

From 1424 on, as the Douglas earls apparently came under growing pressure from royal government, one response was apparently to take advantage of opportunities provided by their claimed superiority rights in places like Drumlanrig and Hawick to place and reward those willing to support them, particularly after royal pressure became downright hostility in 1452. That the Loranes benefited from this to (re-?)gain and hold possession of Coshogle between 1424 and 1452 seems highly likely. The events of 1452 in particular perhaps provided another opportunity for James Lorane to reinforce an ancient, if rather desperate, family claim in return for supporting the increasingly beleaguered earls. But all that finally came to an end in the Drumlanrig regality court on 22 January 1455, even if the Blairs, their claim at last vindicated, seem subsequently to have disburdened themselves of Coshogle and concentrated on their Ayrshire interests.[123]

---

[123] Adams, P., *A History of the Douglas Family of Morton in Nithsdale (Dumfriesshire) and Fingland (Kirkcudbrightshire) and their descendants* (Bedford, 1921), i, pp. 46–55 showing Coshogle in the hands of a cadet line of the Douglases of Drumlanrig by the late fifteenth century. See also on the Blairs of Adamton, Hunter, J., 'The House of John Blair: a Medieval Town-House in Ayr', *AANHS* 11(6) (1976), pp. 111–32. John Blair was still alive on 14 Sept 1461 (NRS: RH6/363A) but was dead by 10 February 1471 (NRS: GD236/77/1). A papal petition in 1446 shows that John Blair had lately established a chapel at Adamton dedicated to the Virgin Mary and now as patron wished to present a chaplain (*CPR*, ix, p. 548). Presumably this manifests the wealth of the Blairs, and Adamton as their principal residence.

Chapter Five
The Blarmade Case

Introduction

Sometime between 8 May and 1 June 1465, Simon Dalgleish, the precentor and official general of the diocese of Glasgow, acting at the instance of Master Robert Hamilton, chancellor of Glasgow and procurator of James Hamilton of Cambuskeith, affixed to the doors of his cathedral church a citation by way of a public edict summoning all parties having interest to hear and see the transumption of a set of documents relating to a dispute over lands in Lanarkshire. The transumpt would have the authority of the official's court interponed.[1] On 1 June, Master Hamilton duly produced the three documents in question before the court.

The first was a notarial instrument dated 5 February 1461, which narrated that Sir Robert Hamilton of Preston, as attorney of James Hamilton of Cambuskeith, had produced and had read letters of attorney, dated 18 October 1460, of King James III, naming eight men as Hamilton of Cambuskeith's attorneys. Five of these were Hamiltons, including not only Sir Robert but also James, lord Hamilton, head

---

[1] For the documents referred to here, see the Appendix to our article, 'Another Fifteenth-Century Case', in MacQueen, H.L., (ed.), *Stair Miscellany VII* (Edinburgh, 2015), pp. 133–62 (from which this chapter is extracted) and ibid, pp. 134–36. For Dalgleish as official of Glasgow 1452–70, see *Fasti Ecclesiae Scoticanae Medii Aevi Ad Annum 1638*, eds Shead, N.F. and the late Watt, D.E.R. and Murray, A.L. (Edinburgh, 2019), p. 241. See also, more generally, Ollivant, S.D., *The Court of the Official in Scotland* (Edinburgh, 1982), especially at pp. 87–88.

of the whole Hamilton kindred and one-time intimate of the eighth and ninth earls of Douglas. Sir Robert had further produced and read another instrument recording that Master Robert Hamilton, then rector of Monyabrok, acting as Cambuskeith's attorney, had petitioned Sir John Maxwell of Calderwood to give effect to a brieve from the king's chancery directed to him. This must have commanded Maxwell to give sasine to Cambuskeith. Maxwell, however, refused to comply; and the instrument quotes his response, which will be discussed further below.[2] The attorney then produced another royal brieve, dated 12 January 1461, commanding John Carmichael of that ilk, as sheriff of Lanark in that part, to give sasine to Cambuskeith of the lands of 'Blarmade' in the barony of Crawfordjohn and sheriffdom of Lanark, which had not been done by Maxwell despite the king's previous brieve. Carmichael gave the sasine as commanded.

The second document was an indenture, dated 9 February 1465, whereby the disputing parties, James Hamilton of Cambuskeith and Sir John Maxwell of Calderwood with the latter's grandson Gawane Maxwell, agreed to underlie (i.e., accept) an award of arbiters in their dispute. The third document was the consequent decree by the arbiters, in the form of a notarial instrument dated 8 May 1465, in which the ground right of the disputed lands was awarded to Hamilton of Cambuskeith.

These documents having been produced, Master Robert Hamilton next demanded that those who had not compeared[3] (presumably the Maxwells) should be held contumacious, and that the three documents should be transumed, especially because of their age and the peril of accident and loss and other causes, when by reason of the treachery of evil men and other perils from fire, water and journeys the originals could not well be carried about. The official then decerned that the persons not compearing should be reputed contumacious, and that the documents should be transumed in a public form to have the same faith as the originals in time coming. The transumption was finally carried out by John Reston, priest and notary, who also appended his notarial certification that he was acting for the official of Glasgow, together with the latter's seal of office.[4]

---

[2] See text accompanying notes 25–26 below.
[3] Compear means to appear in response to a court summons.
[4] Reston may have become commissary of Glasgow in the 1480s: *Fasti*, p. 248. But note the John Reston younger, priest, who witnesses the letters of transumpt and is perhaps a likelier candidate to have become the later commissary, since the Reston who transumed in 1465 had been active since the 1440s.

Hamilton of Cambuskeith v Maxwells of Calderwood

The proceedings on 1 June 1465 were the immediate outcome of a legal action brought earlier in the year by James Hamilton of Cambuskeith (which was part of the lordship of Kilmarnock in Ayrshire[5]) against Sir John Maxwell of Calderwood (Lanarkshire) and his grandson Gawane,[6] claiming ownership of lands called 'Blarmade'. This land formed part of the lordship of Snar, itself part of the barony of Crawfordjohn in the sheriffdom of Lanark; and this last explains why the case had to be brought within the jurisdiction constituted by the sheriffdom. Hamilton's action commenced on 9 February 1465 in the court of the king's justiciar, held in the burgh of Lanark. Presiding as 'justice for that time' was Gilbert, lord Kennedy,[7] a doubly significant figure as he was also the guardian of the minor king, since he was the latter's nearest agnate over 25 years of age (Kennedy was around 60 at the time).[8] The case had been brought with a brieve of mortancestry, a form of action which, as we have already seen, was brought by a written royal command in the court of the justiciar rather than the sheriff.[9] The brieve stated the pursuer's claim to be the lawful and nearest heir of a close relative who had died vest and in sasine as of fee (i.e. heritably) of certain lands which, however, were now being held by the defender. If the claim was upheld by an assize of the good and faithful older men of the neighbourhood, then the defender was ejected and the pursuer put in sasine in his place.

The Maxwells appear to have been representing themselves in court; certainly Sir John had the legal expertise to do so, judging from his regular appearances as an auditor of causes and complaints in parliament.[10] But Hamilton of Cambuskeith had two procurators acting on his behalf. One of these was

---

[5] For the location and history of Cambuskeith, see Borthwick and MacQueen, 'Another Fifteenth-Century Case', p. 135 note 10.

[6] We have again preferred the 'Gawane' of the source to the modern rendering 'Gavin' (see Chapter 4 note 86 above).

[7] For Gilbert as justiciar in October 1464, see MacQueen, 'Tame Magnates?', p. 109.

[8] MacQueen, H.L., 'Survival and Success: the Kennedys of Dunure', in Boardman, S. and Ross, A., (eds), *The Exercise of Power in Medieval Scotland c.1200–1500* (Dublin, 2003), pp. 67–94, at 86, 90, 92.

[9] See Chapter 1 above, text preceding note 65; also Chapter 4, text accompanying notes 6–7.

[10] *RPS* 1450/1/39, 1450/5/4, 1456/9; A1463/10/1, 1464/1/1, 1464/1/2, 1469/4; *ADA*, 8 (1469); *Wigtown Charter Chest*, no. 779.

the still rising star Master David Guthrie of Kincaldrum, a graduate in Arts of the university of Cologne who had also incepted at Paris in the late 1440s, probably for many years already a regular pleader in courts around the country and, since 1461, the king's treasurer. Many other glittering prizes of royal government still lay ahead of him in 1465.[11] The other Hamilton procurator was a churchman, Master Robert Hamilton, chancellor of the diocese of Glasgow and previously rector of 'Monyabrock' (Monieburgh in Kilsyth). As we have already seen, he played an ongoing role in the case as events unfolded from 1461 at the latest.

Master Robert was a nephew of James, lord Hamilton, and a son of Gavin Hamilton, from 1443 to 1468 provost of the collegiate church at Bothwell (founded by Archibald the Grim, third earl of Douglas, in 1398, and also his burial place upon his death in 1400).[12] Robert was thus a cousin of the pursuer. He must have had legal knowledge and skills since he had become a bachelor of decreets at Paris before 1451;[13] possibly there too he had encountered David Guthrie. Robert also accompanied his uncle and William, eighth earl of Douglas, on the latter's pilgrimage to Rome for the papal jubilee in 1450–51, and became one of the first students at the newly founded university of Glasgow from 1451/52.[14]

---

[11] See further Borthwick, A. and MacQueen, H., "Rare creatures for their age': Alexander and David Guthrie, Graduate Lairds and Royal Servants', in Crawford, B.E., (ed.), *Church, Chronicle and Learning in Medieval and Early Renaissance Scotland* (Edinburgh, 1999), pp. 227–39, especially at 229–31.

[12] *Scots Peerage*, iv, pp. 348–49; Anderson, J., *Historical and Genealogical Memoirs of the House of Hamilton, with Genealogical Memoirs of the several branches of the family* (Edinburgh, 1825), pp. 597, 636–37; *Fasti*, pp. 210, 448–49. 'Monyabrock' was in the deanery of Lennox near Kilsyth (Cowan, I.B., *The Parishes of Medieval Scotland* (Edinburgh, 1967), p. 150; to references there given add *Glasgow Reg*, i, lxvii, lxxv, no. 103; *RMS*, ii, nos 606, 3404). Monieburgh, now a small former council estate on the Stirling Road into Kilsyth, was superseded as the parish name in 1665 when Viscount Kilsyth (a descendant of a cadet line of the Livingstons of Callendar who took his title from the nearby Kilsyth Hills) founded a new town and named it for himself (Groome, F.H., *Ordnance Gazetteer of Scotland* (Edinburgh, 1901), sv 'Kilsyth'). On Archibald the Grim and Bothwell, see Brown, *Black Douglases*, p. 192.

[13] For Robert's Paris studies, see *CSSR*, v, nos 384 and 398; *CPR*, xi, pp. 318–19.

[14] See *CSSR*, v, no. 396 for the trip to Rome; and references given in Anderson, *House of Hamilton*, p. 637, for the studies in Glasgow.

CHAPTER FIVE: THE BLARMADE CASE

In attendance at the court, presumably, would have been the sheriff of Lanark and his subordinate staff, together with the usual suitors of the sheriff court, who would have been expected to attend a session of the justice ayre in their sheriffdom. From their number and perhaps others would be drawn the 'good and faithful older men of the neighbourhood' of the lands in issue who would form the assize by which the case would be determined. Also present, however, must have been the four men who witnessed the indenture soon to be struck between the Maxwells and Hamilton transferring the case from the justiciar's court to a group of men described as 'Jugis' and '*dominorum arbitrorum*' (lords arbiters) to sit later in Edinburgh. The witnesses were Sir George Campbell of Loudon, sheriff of Ayr, Duncan of Dundas, David Campbell and Thomas Thomson. Robert, lord Boyd ('eme' or uncle of Gawane Maxwell by virtue of his marriage to Marion, the sister of Gawane's father, John Maxwell[15]) may have been there, because his seal was attached to the indenture for Gawane, who 'had na sele of his awyn'. As we will see in more detail below, however, as lord of Kilmarnock, Boyd was also Cambuskeith's feudal superior and near neighbour.[16]

It is further worth noting the Ayrshire links of Sir George and (perhaps) David Campbell.[17] Gawane Maxwell's first marriage was to Agnes, daughter of Duncan of Dundas;[18] but the Dundas family of which Duncan was probably a member also had links to the Hamiltons, and in particular James, lord Hamilton.[19] Thomson is perhaps to be identified with the man of the same name who ten years earlier had acted as a forespeaker in the Coshogle case

---

[15] Gawane's father John was married to a sister of Robert, lord Boyd, so the family ties were criss-crossing and close.

[16] See further below, text accompanying notes 48–49.

[17] David Campbell did witness a resignation of lands in the barony of Dalmeny, West Lothian, by Archibald Dundas of that ilk followed by a re-grant to Philip Mowbray of Barnbougle (also West Lothian) in December 1452: NLS: Adv Ch B67–68. This transaction was, however, witnessed by Sir John Maxwell of Calderwood as well: see below, notes 81 and 91.

[18] Fraser, *Pollok*, i, p. 467. Gawane's second wife was Elizabeth Lowes (ibid., i, pp. 200–01). Her forespeaker on the latter occasion was Thomas Lowes of Manor, probably her brother (see below, note 89).

[19] Macleod, W., *Dundas of Dundas: Royal Letters and Family Papers* (Edinburgh, 1897), pp. xii–xvi; and, for earlier family links with James, lord Hamilton, see e.g. *CDS*, iv, nos 1254 (22 May 1453), 1310 (26 August 1460), 1314 (23 April 1461).

discussed in Chapter 4.[20] Care is required before any conclusions are drawn from prosopographical study of the witnesses' associations with the other participants, but it may not be going too far to suggest that they were seen as men at least balanced between the parties in their friendships and allegiances, if not actually neutral.

The presence of the witnesses, the drawing up and execution of the indenture, and the fact that there could also be named within it the seven arbiters to whose judgement the dispute would be submitted on a definite future date in Edinburgh, with the parties having to meet the costs and expenses of the arbiters (who did not all come from Edinburgh), strongly suggests that the proceedings at Lanark were a formality by which the court interponed its authority to an agreement already achieved, discharging the mortancestry process which had been going to take place. All the arrangements must have been put in place over the preceding weeks and months. The indenture was executed in counterparts: that is to say, each party executed a copy of the agreement by sealing it (and in Hamilton's case by having each of his procurators also sign it); they then exchanged their executed copies so that each had the version executed by the other side. Very possibly, the two versions of the agreement were written at either end of a single piece of parchment which was then cut up in a zig-zag fashion. This would then allow as a later test of their mutual authenticity the fitting together of the two counterparts.

The substance of the Hamilton mortancestry claim is not stated anywhere in the transumpt, so that we do not know directly upon which deceased relative's title it was based. Sir John Maxwell's claim, however, was that he held the land 'in franctenement' while his grandson Gawane held it in fee. This can probably be read as meaning that Sir John had previously held a full heritable title which he had, however, granted to Gawane while reserving to himself the *liberum tenementum* – that is, the freehold, franktenement or lifetime possession of the lands. The practice of making a grant to another while still alive but reserving what was known as the *liberum tenementum* ('franktenement' in Scots) for the remainder of the grantor's life had developed during the later fourteenth century.[21] Here, however, the use of the device may not have been so much to avoid the casualties to be paid by an incoming

---

[20] See Chapter 4 above, text accompanying note 11.
[21] See Chapter 1 above, text accompanying note 53.

CHAPTER FIVE: THE BLARMADE CASE

heir to the feudal superior or lord of whom the lands were held, so much as a way of providing land for his grandson which might otherwise have gone to another – most obviously, the son who was Gawane's father (the second John Maxwell). The grantor was thus able to continue much as before, while the grantee had the comfort of knowing there would be no relief payable on his grantor's death.

We can reasonably infer from all this that the Maxwell possession of 'Blarmade' went back some time, and that it is very unlikely to have been the result of some opportunistic seizure of lands which happened not to have been taken up by the truly entitled person at some point in the past. The Maxwells' position would have been long entrenched and probably well documented. It is significant that Hamilton's claim was initially one to hold 'Blarmade' of Sir John Maxwell, suggesting the former's recognition of some superiority entitlement of the latter, at least at that stage. Factors of this kind may have persuaded Lord Kennedy as justiciar that the case was indeed unsuitable for determination by a mortancestry assize, if indeed the parties themselves had not already agreed to it. Certainly, the indenture by which the mortancestry process was supplanted by a submission to arbitration on 9 February 1465 made clear that the judge-arbiters were not to be confined to the question raised under the brieve:

> [T]hai sall decide finaly end and deliver the grounderycht of the said mater and that dependis tharuppoun but fraud or gile eftyr thare knawlage and cunning as law Richt faith and gude conscience will fra thai have herde sene and understanding the rychtis of baith the said partis.

That the parties sought a comprehensive investigation of the merits of their respective claims without any limitation of scope is also clear from the indenture's provision that the arbiters' 'decrete sentence and deliverance [was] to have the force and effect of a brefe of rycht for evermore'. Whereas the brieve of mortancestry determined only the questions it contained, a brieve of right enabled a finding of who had 'full right' to the lands without limit as to the scope of the inquiry.[22] It was a fully proprietary remedy by which entitlements might be traced back to their roots. In contrast, a mortancestry

---

[22] MacQueen, *CLFS*, pp. 188–214.

process could only determine that the pursuer was entitled to possession as heir of a particular type of person who had died vest and saised of fee; it could not determine whether that deceased relative had been entitled to hold the fee in question. The whole arbitration process agreed by the parties thus appears akin to what was known as a 'great assize of right', apart perhaps from seeming to involve only two competing claims to the land in question and being arbitral rather than judicial in nature.[23]

The first of the three documents transumed in Glasgow in June 1465 recorded Maxwell's refusal early in 1461 to give sasine to Hamilton (represented by his appointed attorneys) despite royal brieves commanding this to be done. Hamilton's attorney then took sasine from a sheriff of Lanark appointed *in hac parte*, suggesting that the brieve addressed to Maxwell was one of *furche*, under which if the addressee did not act in accordance with the king's command, then the sheriff would.[24] But this begs the question of why further proceedings by Hamilton became necessary later. It cannot have been that Maxwell simply refused to recognise what had happened and dispossessed him, because then the action would have been one of novel dissasine. The likelihood is that Maxwell succeeded in overturning the acts of 1461, perhaps by some process of reducing Hamilton's sasine before the king's council or one of its sessions, and so compelled the latter into further litigation.[25] There may have been legal force in Maxwell's reported response to Hamilton's attorney Robert, then rector of Monieburgh: 'You are a churchman and priest and you are not able to arrange this matter of heritage with me'. Lay fees

---

[23] On the great assize of right, see ibid., p. 236 ('an action appropriate where ... there were several competing claims to a piece of land') and other examples cited in note 110 thereto. On late medieval arbitration in Scotland, see Godfrey, A.M., *Civil Justice in Renaissance Scotland: The Origins of a Central Court* (Leiden, 2009), pp. 361–93. We are grateful to Professor Godfrey for a helpful discussion of the arbitral characteristics of the 1465 process.

[24] For the brieve *furche* and near equivalents, see *Scottish Formularies*, A29, A38, E24, B56, B58–9. Other examples of the use of these brieves are given in MacQueen, *CLFS*, pp. 56–57.

[25] Thanks to the difficult political conditions resulting from the king's minority and Anglo-Scottish tensions only resolved by treaty concluded in June 1464 (see further Macdougall, *James III*, pp. 40–57), there may have been no sessions or judicial sittings of the royal council until just before or after that date: see *RPS* 1464/1/11.

were a matter for the secular arm only,[26] and Robert's involvement may have meant that the purported infeftment of James was indeed invalid.[27] He was still acting for Hamilton in 1465, but by then he was alongside the lay Master David Guthrie, so any objection to Robert had now been headed off.

The Barony of Crawfordjohn

The initial link between the events just described and the earlier parts of this book is that, as we are informed by the indenture of 9 February 1465, 'Blarmade' is part of the lordship of Snar, which in turn is part of the barony of Crawfordjohn in the sheriffdom of Lanark, half of which barony until the forfeiture of 1455 pertained to the earls of Douglas. The indenture suggests at least three levels of feudal holding or tenure beneath the king of whom the barony was ultimately held. The Douglas half of Crawfordjohn had come to Archibald the Grim with the inheritance of his wife Joanna Murray of Bothwell in the 1360s, the halving of the barony possibly indicating its having been previously co-inherited at some point by two sisters. There is an intriguing parallel, therefore, with the halving of the barony of Stewarton at some point in the fourteenth century, also part (as discussed in Chapter 3) of the Murray inheritance which had come to Archibald the Grim by virtue of his marriage.[28] When Archibald gained the Douglas earldom in 1389, the half-barony of Crawfordjohn became part of those earldom lands, albeit unentailed. The succession to Crawfordjohn of Archibald's son and grandson as fourth and fifth earls in 1400 and 1424 respectively was accordingly untroubled. William the sixth earl was, however, still a minor when his father died in 1439, and he and his lands therefore fell into the wardship of, most probably, his great-uncle, James Douglas of Balvenie, earl of Avondale, brother of the fourth earl. William never made it beyond his minority, thanks to his execution after the 'Black Dinner' in 1440.

---

[26] See further MacQueen, H., 'The King's Council and Church Courts in Later Medieval Scotland', in Dondorp, H., Hallebeek, J., Wallinga, T. and Winkel, L., (eds), *Ius Romanum – Ius Commune – Ius Hodiernum: Studies in Honour of Eltjo J H Schrage on the Occasion of his 65th Birthday* (Amsterdam, 2010), pp. 277–87, 278, 282.

[27] Note that the sasine of 'Blarmade' was taken not by Master Robert but by the lay Sir Robert Hamilton of Preston as James Hamilton's procurator.

[28] See further Chapter 1 above, text accompanying notes 81–83; Reid, T., *History of the Parish of Crawfordjohn, Upper Ward of Lanarkshire, 1153–1928* (Edinburgh, 1928), p. 32.

Also around 1440, Margaret, duchess of Touraine and countess of Galloway (and also elder sister of King James I), confirmed a charter relating to the lands of Gilkerscleuch in Crawfordjohn.[29] As the widow of the fourth earl, she may have enjoyed some lifetime rights of terce in the half-barony, akin to but not quite the same as those which she certainly held in Galloway by royal grant made after her husband's death in 1424.[30] Since terce conferred full managerial powers, Countess Margaret's position no doubt complicated the exercise of lordship in Crawfordjohn. Margaret resigned Galloway to the king for re-grant to the eighth earl before her death in 1450/51, when any terce rights in Crawfordjohn would also have ended.[31] The fee as distinct from the terce of the half-barony of Crawfordjohn would, however, have remained with the earls throughout until, with the death of the seventh earl in 1443 and still unentailed in favour of heirs male, they fell to Margaret daughter of the fifth earl, younger sister of the sixth, and, through marriage in 1444, wife to her cousin, William the eighth earl.

This last cannot have been straightforward, however, since Crawfordjohn was among the group of lands regranted to the eighth earl by the king in Parliament in July 1451.[32] As we know, this reconciliation did not last; the king killed the earl in February 1452. We have explained in the previous chapters how the ninth earl's subsequent renunciation of his obligations of homage and fealty to the king probably led to the deprivation of his inheritance, although a further reconciliation in early 1453 may have reversed this for a time.[33] But, with the final forfeiture of the ninth earl in 1455, the superiority of the Douglas earls passed definitively to the king, ending what must have been a long period of uncertainty, even turmoil, within the half-barony of Crawfordjohn. The king's superiority explains why in February 1459 he could grant lands within the barony to Walter Scott of Kirkurd as a reward for his contribution to the ultimate defeat of Earl James and his forces at the battle of Arkinholm.[34]

---

[29] *RMS*, ii, no. 255. Gilkerscleuch Mains is today a farm located at NGR: NS 897 236.
[30] *RMS*, ii, no. 47.
[31] *RMS*, ii, no. 309; Brown, *Black Douglases*, p. 288.
[32] See *RPS* 1451/6/8; *RMS*, ii, no. 464; *ER*, ix, p. 662.
[33] See Chapter 3 above, text accompanying notes 89–105.
[34] *RMS*, ii, no. 674. The lands were 'Awintoune' (Abington: NGR: NS 932 232), 'Phareholme' (see Carlisle, N., *A Topographical Dictionary of Scotland, and of the Islands in the British Seas* (London, 1813), i, sv Crawfordjohn, for Fairholm,

CHAPTER FIVE: THE BLARMADE CASE

Crawfordjohn's caput and principal castle was located where the modern village now stands, although nothing remains of that castle today.[35] Douglasdale to the north can be reached by way of a drove road. The Water of Snar runs into the barony from its heads in the Lowther massif north and west of Leadhills and Wanlockhead.[36] It then passes through a narrow valley beneath Snar Law and Sim's Hill. The Snar finally empties into the Duneaton Water, which in turn flows east-north-east under the village of Crawfordjohn and on from there to enter the River Clyde almost midway between Abington and Roberton. A castle or fortified residence of some kind stood at the modern (but now largely disused) farm steading named Snar. The castle remains are all but lost, and dating seems impossible; but this must have been the caput of the lordship of Snar.[37] At least one house, belonging to an Andrew Telfer, stood on the lands of 'Blarmade' in 1461. Here the abortive sasine of 1461 was constituted by symbolical delivery of earth and stone to the procurator of James Hamilton of Cambuskeith and the closing of the house door behind him after he had made his entry. The witnesses to this ceremony apart from the sheriff *in hac parte* – Patrick Cleland, Patrick Bell, James Somerville, Thomas Bannatyne, Alan Govan and David Dalziel – may have been other inhabitants of 'Blarmade' and Snar. Patrick Bell was also appointed as bailie, i.e. administrator of the lands. Although there is a Blairhill today north of the village of Crawfordjohn, we have found no trace of a 'Blarmade' on modern maps.[38] We think it most

---

near Netherton Hill where there was an encampment; perhaps around modern Netherhill, NGR: NS 849 217) and 'Glendonanerig' (Glendowran Hill, NGR: NS 874 205).

[35] HES Canmore ID 46443; Reid, *Crawfordjohn*, p. 43.

[36] The stream-name Snar is probably to be derived from a hypothetical Old English *snar*, 'swift', postulated for Great and Little Snoring in Norfolk (OS, TF 9434, 9533); *Cambridge Dictionary of English Place-Names* (Cambridge, 2004), svv. Snoring may be derived from *Snaringas*, 'people who live by the river Snar'. The difficulty is that there is now no river Snar in Norfolk! But an alternative derivation from Old Norse *snarr*, 'brisk', seems unlikely in both Norfolk and upper Clydesdale, while an Old English cognate is much more readily acceptable. We were helped with the place-name by the late Professor Jack MacQueen.

[37] See NGR: NS 869 221; HES Canmore ID 46452; Reid, *Crawfordjohn*, p. 43.

[38] The late Professor Jack MacQueen suggested to us that the first element in this name is Gaelic *blàr*, 'field, battle, peat-moss'. The second, almost certainly, is *madaidh*, genitive of Gaelic *madadh*, 'dog', 'mastiff', 'any wild animal of the dog species', i.e. possibly 'fox', thus the whole possibly meaning 'fox-field'.

likely to have been the relatively flat ground on either side of the Snar Water to the immediate north of Snar farm.

The Hamiltons of Cambuskeith

Our first documentary sighting of 'Blarmade' comes on 29 January 1412 when Archibald, fourth earl of Douglas, presumably acting as the direct superior of the lands, confirmed a grant of them to David Hamilton by his paternal uncle Alan of Larbert.[39] James Hamilton, son of David, was served as his heir in 1436, and can probably be identified with the pursuer in our case.[40] But this service was most likely only to the family's principal lands in Ayrshire, i.e. Cambuskeith.

The Hamiltons of Cambuskeith descended through junior lines stemming from Walter Fitzgilbert, also the progenitor in the senior line of the house of Hamilton represented by the time of the 'Blarmade' case by James, lord Hamilton.[41] The Hamiltons' descent from Walter Fitzgilbert provides an excellent illustration of Sandy Grant's observation that 'the late medieval Scottish higher nobility was extremely successful at producing sons'.[42] David Hamilton of Cambuskeith was a great-grandson of Walter.[43] An impressive kin

---

[39] Hamilton, G., *A History of the House of Hamilton* (Edinburgh, 1933), p. 213. See also ibid., pp. 42–43, 254. The confirmation is not listed among the *acta* of the fourth earl of Douglas in Grant, A., 'Acts of Lordship: The Records of Archibald, Fourth Earl of Douglas' in Brotherstone, T. and Ditchburn, D., (eds), *Freedom and Authority: Historical and Historiographical Essays presented to Grant G Simpson* (East Linton, 2000), pp. 235–74 [Grant, 'Acts of Lordship']. It comes between nos 39 and 40 in Dr Grant's list (ibid., p. 261). The original charter and its confirmation have not been traced and are therefore known only from the reference in the printed family histories. Alan Hamilton of Larbert was still alive in August 1419, when he granted a charter: see NLS: Ch 8814.

[40] Hamilton, *House of Hamilton*, p. 213.

[41] Borthwick, A.R., 'Hamilton family (*per.* 1295–1479)', *ODNB*.

[42] Grant, A., 'Extinction of Direct Male Lines among Scottish Noble Families in the Fourteenth and Fifteenth Centuries', in Stringer, K.J., (ed.), *Essays on the Nobility of Medieval Scotland* (Edinburgh, 1985), pp. 210–31, 218. Note, however, the review by Sellar, W.D.H., *Scottish Historical Review* lxvi (1987), pp. 200–03.

[43] A David Hamilton appears as a witness to a Fleming charter dated 3 November 1421: *Wigtown Charter Chest*, no. 406. But this could well be a reference to David Hamilton of Dalserf: see Hamilton, *House of Hamilton*, p. 293.

CHAPTER FIVE: THE BLARMADE CASE

solidarity is apparent in the support given to his son James from 1461 to 1465 by not only the then head of kindred, James, lord Hamilton, but also his cousins Sir Robert of Preston, Master Robert of Glasgow and others of the name.

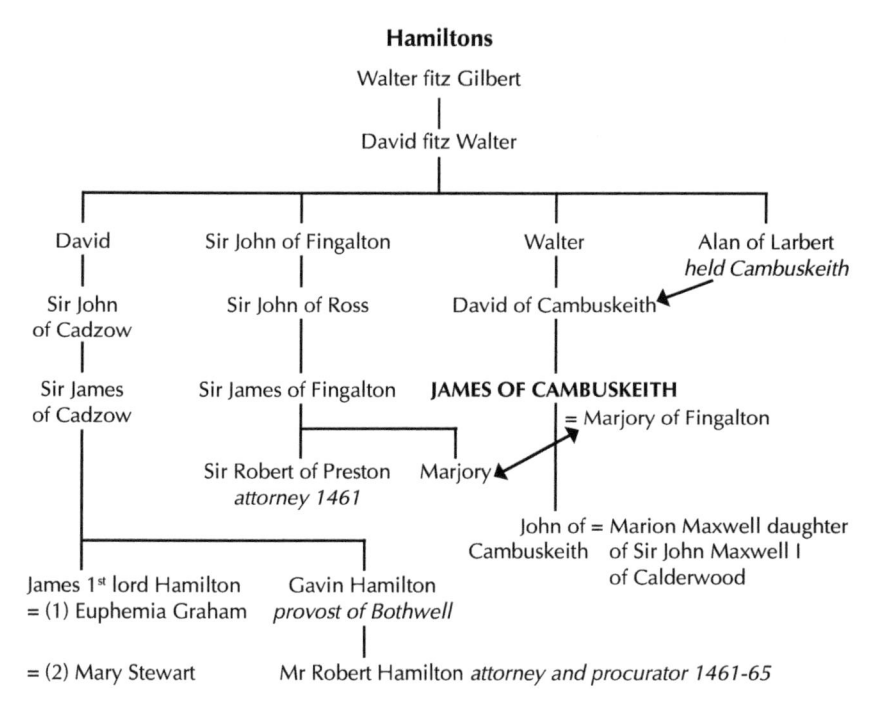

Hamiltons

Walter fitz Gilbert
|
David fitz Walter

David	Sir John of Fingalton	Walter	Alan of Larbert *held Cambuskeith*
Sir John of Cadzow	Sir John of Ross	David of Cambuskeith ←	
Sir James of Cadzow	Sir James of Fingalton	**JAMES OF CAMBUSKEITH** = Marjory of Fingalton	
	Sir Robert of Preston / Marjory *attorney 1461*	John of Cambuskeith = Marion Maxwell daughter of Sir John Maxwell I of Calderwood	
James 1st lord Hamilton = (1) Euphemia Graham = (2) Mary Stewart	Gavin Hamilton *provost of Bothwell* Mr Robert Hamilton *attorney and procurator 1461-65*		

This family tree is much simplified.

⟵⟶ *indicates that two names are one and the same person.*
⟶ *indicates the grant of "Blarmade" from Alan to David.*

There may, however, have been something of a Hamilton family tradition of changing to the winning side at critical moments. Walter, who in early 1314 held Bothwell castle in Lanarkshire for the English Crown, switched his loyalties after the battle of Bannockburn in late June and thereafter received from King Robert I the lands of Machan and the barony of Cadzow (later Hamilton) in Lanarkshire.[44] As we have already noticed briefly in Chapter 3, in July 1455, James, lord Hamilton, whose 1441 marriage to Euphemia Graham, widow

---

[44] See *RRS*, v, nos 51 (Machan) and 494 (with references there given for Cadzow).

of the fifth earl of Douglas, had 'tied him firmly to the Douglases' (which also probably helped to make him one of the earliest 'lords of parliament' in 1445), nonetheless in May 1455 surrendered the Douglas castle of Abercorn to King James II after a siege and, following a brief period of imprisonment, then received former Douglas lands and offices from the king.[45] Hamilton also kept in with the new head of the Douglas kindred, however, entering a bond of manrent with George Douglas, fourth earl of Angus, in May 1457.[46] In October 1464, just a few months before the 'Blarmade' case began in Lanark, King James III added to Hamilton's expanding portfolio the half of the lands and barony of Crawfordjohn which had previously pertained to the earls.[47] This grant, made in the king's minority at a time when government was controlled by Gilbert, lord Kennedy, as the king's tutor, is clearly significant in understanding the way in which the 'Blarmade' case developed.

We learn from a royal confirmation granted to John Hamilton of Cambuskeith on 10 October 1530 that his lands and the tower thereof were held of the lords Boyd up to their forfeiture (i.e. in 1469).[48] This document further shows not only the location of the estate in general but also that it formed part of the Boyd lordship of Kilmarnock in the bailiary of Cunningham (Ayrshire). Robert, lord Boyd, was thus closely connected to both sides in the 1465 dispute: to the Maxwells by marriage, as will be explored in more detail below, and to James Hamilton as his feudal superior and near neighbour (the chief place of the Boyds in Kilmarnock was Dean castle, a couple of miles north-east of Cambuskeith).[49] After the Boyd forfeiture, Cambuskeith was probably held of the king as steward of Scotland, explaining why the 1530 confirmation was given with consent of the king's mother (Margaret Tudor), who had received the lordship in liferent at the time of her marriage to James IV in 1503.[50]

---

[45] Borthwick, 'Hamilton family'. On the origins of lords of parliament, see Chapter 2 above, text accompanying notes 104–05.
[46] Wormald, *Lords and Men*, p. 174; Borthwick, A.R., 'Douglas, George, fourth earl of Angus (c.1417–1463)', *ODNB*.
[47] *RMS*, ii, no. 819 (24 Oct 1464).
[48] *RMS*, iii, no. 970.
[49] NGR: NS 437 398; HES Canmore ID 265333.
[50] Cameron, J., *James V: The Personal Rule, 1528–1542* (East Linton, 1998), pp. 18, 31, 44.

The Maxwells of Calderwood

We may turn now to the Maxwells of Calderwood.[51] They were a junior branch of the Maxwells of Pollok, another family further illustrating Sandy Grant's point about successful male reproduction in the Scottish higher nobility, with several other cadet lines mushrooming through the fourteenth century.

The first Maxwell of Calderwood, Sir Robert, was a second son whose father, the lord of Pollok, settled extensive lands (mostly in Lanarkshire) upon him in 1400–01.[52] The property from which Robert and his descendants took their territorial designation was Calderwood, like most of his other lands, in or near modern East Kilbride.[53] These were not, in other words, very proximate to the Douglas heartlands in upper Clydesdale, albeit closer at hand to the later acquisitions of Archibald the Grim lower down the Clyde at Bothwell and Drumsagard. Robert's marriage to Elizabeth Danielston brought him the lands of Finlayston (Renfrewshire) and Stanley (Perthshire). His talents extended to diplomacy; he negotiated in England for the release from captivity of not only King James I but also Murdoch Stewart, son of the Governor of Scotland in the king's absence, Robert duke of Albany. Robert Maxwell also undertook military service in France in support of the French king against the English, although he was under the leadership of John Stewart, earl of Buchan, (the Governor's younger son) rather than the earl of Douglas, who led other Scottish forces in France at the time.[54] Robert died in France, having made his will at Chinon on 7 September 1420 and probably breathing his last sometime shortly afterwards. The will directed that he be buried in the church of the Friars Minor at Angers.[55]

---

[51] See generally Fraser, *Pollok*, i, pp. 462–67.

[52] Fraser, *Pollok*, i, p. 139; see ibid., nos 19–23. Note earlier grants of Jackton in the 1390s: ibid., nos 16 and 17.

[53] The others in Lanarkshire were Dripps, Jackton, Allerton, Newlands, Greenhills and the over lordship of a quarter of Thornton. The two Aikenheads (Meikle and Little) were in what is now the King's Park district in Cathcart parish on the south side of Glasgow. In Tweedsmuir, Robert received Hawkshaw, Finglen and Carterhope.

[54] See Ditcham, 'Foreign Mercenary Troops', especially at pp. 182–83; Brown, *Black Douglases*, pp. 210–26.

[55] Fraser, *Pollok*, i, no. 28.

Maxwells of Calderwood

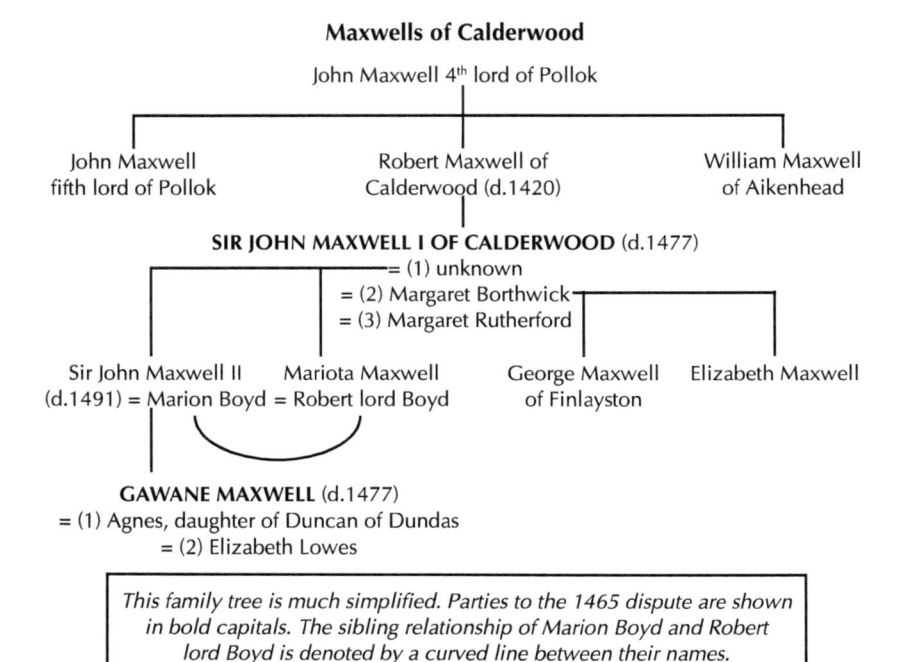

John Maxwell 4th lord of Pollok

- John Maxwell fifth lord of Pollok
- Robert Maxwell of Calderwood (d.1420)
- William Maxwell of Aikenhead

SIR JOHN MAXWELL I OF CALDERWOOD (d.1477)
= (1) unknown
= (2) Margaret Borthwick
= (3) Margaret Rutherford

- Sir John Maxwell II (d.1491) = Marion Boyd
- Mariota Maxwell = Robert lord Boyd
- George Maxwell of Finlayston
- Elizabeth Maxwell

GAWANE MAXWELL (d.1477)
= (1) Agnes, daughter of Duncan of Dundas
= (2) Elizabeth Lowes

> *This family tree is much simplified. Parties to the 1465 dispute are shown in bold capitals. The sibling relationship of Marion Boyd and Robert lord Boyd is denoted by a curved line between their names.*

Robert's will is a fascinating document. For present purposes, however, its most interesting (and most tantalising) bequests are three in favour of Alan of Hamilton: first, twenty golden nobles, Robert's black horse and a fother of lard (*unam foderatum de saygnes*), together with a supplication to his heir not to allow either Alan or his wife to fall into need for the whole of their lives; next, an assignation to Alan of Robert's reversionary right in ten merks of land granted, presumably in security for some debt, to Fergus Kennedy;[56] and lastly, in relation to another ten merks' worth of land possessed by Robert which were formerly of the said Alan, a pure and free cession of his right to the said Alan and his heirs, acquitting the lands from all pactions or contracts made by Robert about the said lands

---

[56] Whether this Fergus is to be identified with the Fergus Kennedy who was keeper of Loch Doon castle in 1434 must remain conjectural: MacQueen, H.L., 'The Kin of Kennedy, Kenkynnol and the Common Law', in Grant, A. and Stringer, K., (eds), *Medieval Scotland: Crown, Lordship and Community: Essays Presented to G W S Barrow* (Edinburgh, 1993), pp. 274–96, 291.

for him and his heirs so long as Alan and his heirs remained the men of his son and his heirs.

This seems to suggest some previous dispute between the two men about land which, perhaps, Alan should hold of Robert. If Robert's beneficiary can be identified with the Alan Hamilton of Larbert who had granted 'Blarmade' to his nephew David eight years earlier, then just conceivably that grant was the trigger for the dispute between Robert and Alan. Perhaps already in 1412 Maxwell of Calderwood had some sort of claim to superiority over 'Blarmade' which had been ignored or bypassed in Alan's grant to David and its confirmation by the fourth earl. But it is more likely, given the final decision of the dispute against the Maxwells in 1465, that the earl intruded Robert as a mid-superior after Alan's grant to David, causing an angry reaction and claim of warrandice from Alan's now demoted grantee.[57] Whatever, it is clear that Alan was on Robert's conscience as he confronted his own mortality and the destiny of his soul.

It is entirely possible, of course, that the Alan Hamilton who troubled Robert's mind in 1420 was quite different from the one who granted 'Blarmade' in 1412, and that it is pure coincidence to find that name in conjunction with a Maxwell of Calderwood forty years before the legal clash with the Hamiltons of Cambuskeith which is the main object of our discussion. Nor were any of the grants his father made to Robert in Lanarkshire in the vicinity of Crawfordjohn. Robert would have to have made an independent form of acquisition from the earl of Douglas before or (more probably) not very long after 1412. There was, however, at least one earlier, if tenuous, link between the Maxwells and the earls: Robert's stepmother had held the lands of Whitchester in the barony of Hawick of Archibald the third earl in and before 1399.[58] But the only evidence of any direct interaction between the fourth earl and Robert is an outright alienation by the former to the latter in 1416, under which Robert received from the earl the lands of Nether Calderwood in the barony of Kilbride, presumably thereby completing his holding of the Calderwood estate. This, it was said, was for the service and

---

[57] For such conduct by a superior as a wrong to the vassal in rendering the conditions of the latter's tenure more onerous, see Chapter 6, notes 59–64.
[58] Fraser, *Pollok*, i, no. 18. The second marriage of Sir John Maxwell of Pollok to Elizabeth of Whitchester was the probable occasion of this transaction (ibid., i, p. 14).

counsel with which Robert had provided the earl.[59] It may therefore have reflected some existing relationship rather than being simply a bit of tidying-up of landholdings on each side.

Nearly a quarter of a century later, Robert's eldest son and successor, Sir John Maxwell of Calderwood, the first defender of 1465, was more evidently linked with the earls of Douglas. A striking feature is that these links survived the rapid turnover in the earldom resulting from the sudden but natural death of the fifth earl in June 1439, the execution of the still-minor sixth earl after the Black Dinner in November 1440, and the succession to the earldom of the sixth earl's great-uncle, James Douglas of Balvenie, earl of Avondale. So, in July 1438, John Maxwell was, with others including Thomas Boyd of Kilmarnock and George Campbell of Loudon (later one of the witnesses to the 1465 indenture), a commissioner of the fifth earl to relax a recognition of disputed lands in the earl's regality of Lauder.[60] In February 1440, the second-named witness to a charter by the sixth earl of lands in Roxburghshire was John Maxwell of Calderwood.[61] The witness-list position suggests some closeness to the young earl at that point which may have stemmed from the prior link with the latter's father, the fifth earl. However that may have been, and perhaps despite it, Maxwell further witnessed an undated charter of James Douglas as earl of Douglas and Avondale which must have been granted between November 1440 and March 1441, i.e. within months, if not weeks, of the Black Dinner.[62] Maxwell was also present in March 1441 when Robert Fleming, son and heir of the executed Malcolm, attempted to obtain brieves of inquest with which to be served heir to his unforfeited father's lands.[63] There

---

[59] Fraser, *Pollok*, i, no. 27. On the basis of this single instance, Grant makes Robert a member of the fourth earl's affinity to whom he granted lands or offices or annuities, but in its 'outer' rather than its 'inner circle', i.e. the group made up of persons to whom individually the earl made relatively few such grants: 'Acts of Lordship', pp. 248–49.

[60] *Laing Chrs*, no. 117.

[61] Fraser, *Douglas*, iii, no. 303 (p. 374) (18 Feb 1440 at Edinburgh) (original at Floors Castle, Roxburghe MSS, bundle 702 [41/4]).

[62] *HMC Hamilton, additional charters*, no. 131. The charter antedates the remarriage of the fifth earl's widow, Euphemia Graham, to Sir James Hamilton of Cadzow, i.e. the later James, lord Hamilton. The charter is also notable for the consent given by the seventh earl's beloved firstborn son and heir Sir William (eighth earl from March 1443).

[63] NLS: Ch 15,554.

CHAPTER FIVE: THE BLARMADE CASE

is, however, no evidence to suggest that Maxwell continued his links to the Douglas earls after the death of the seventh earl in 1443.

Maxwell's place in the circle of the Douglas earls may have been connected with the position he had earlier gained in the counsels of King James I. Although John was still a minor when he succeeded his father Robert in 1421, by 1423 he was following in the paternal footsteps as one of the commissioners appointed to treat for the release of King James I from his English captivity. On the king's release in 1424, Maxwell was a hostage in England for the payment of the royal ransom, but was quite quickly released.[64] Although there are few other references to him in the 1420s and early 1430s,[65] by March 1436 he had apparently been knighted, when he in the company of many other leading Scots sailed to France with the king's daughter Margaret for her marriage to the Dauphin.[66] After the king's assassination at Perth on 21 February 1437, a royal supporter probably had little difficulty in adhering to Archibald, fifth earl of Douglas, lieutenant-general of the kingdom as the nearest agnate of the minor King James II.[67] Another important link formed by John Maxwell during the reign of James I was the one already noted with the Boyds of Kilmarnock. Possibly as early as March 1435 (though the date is uncertain), John's eldest son John was of an age to agree to marry the daughter of Thomas Boyd of Kilmarnock, reflecting what was evidently already a significant link between the two families, since Thomas had been godfather to Maxwell junior at his baptism.[68] In

---

[64] Fraser, *Pollok*, i, pp. 463–65.
[65] He issued or witnessed some charters (see e.g. *RMS*, ii, nos 9, 10, 65, 66, 186; *Laing Chrs*, no. 105).
[66] See *Chron Bower*, viii, p. 249; the event is dated June 1435 in Fraser, *Pollok*, i, p. 465.
[67] McGladdery, *James II*, p. 13.
[68] See NRS: GD8/1012 (bond by Thomas Boyd of Kilmarnock, to John Maxwell, lord of Calderwood, of 550 marks because of marriage of the said John Maxwell's son to the said Thomas's daughter) (printed in Fraser, *Pollok*, i, p. 466). The document is damaged, and the date cannot therefore be ascertained. The marriage needed a papal dispensation dated 9 July 1440, the possible impediment being Thomas's godfatherhood of the younger John Maxwell: see *CPR*, ix, p. 110. John junior was able to be a witness to a document dated 27 June 1446: see Glasgow City Archives: T-PM 2/3. Thomas Boyd was killed by Alexander Stewart 'buktuth' and others on 7 July 1439 (see *Auchinleck Chronicle* f 109r (McGladdery, *James II*, p. 261).

addition, Sir John's daughter Marion married Robert, first lord Boyd, eldest son of Thomas Boyd.

After the death of James, seventh earl of Douglas, in March 1443, John Maxwell's Douglas links seem to have come to an end, and there is also little evidence of his activities during the remainder of the royal minority.[69] But he came back to prominence when James II assumed active control of royal government in 1449, with the legal and judicial skills to which we have already referred seeming to be the primary cause. He was one of the baronage representatives as an auditor of causes at the January 1450 parliament, and again at the General Council in May 1450.[70] He was chosen to be one of the baronage auditors in October 1456,[71] and again in July 1460.[72] This was followed by an already mentioned host of appearances among the lords auditors in the 1460s.[73] He was also chosen in June 1454 as one of the ambassadors extraordinary to negotiate a peace with England.[74] Maxwell's services were not only valued in royal government. In April 1449, he witnessed a charter of the bishop of St Andrews, and in February 1450 he witnessed a resignation made before the bishop.[75] In October 1449, he received a three-year safe conduct to go on pilgrimage to Rome;[76] but, given his other appearances around this time in Scotland, maybe he never went. In December 1452, he witnessed a resignation made in presence of George Crichton, earl of Caithness;[77] and in March 1454 he witnessed a Caithness charter.[78] There is no sign of particular royal favour for Maxwell under James II other than the grant of a licence in January 1452 for the construction of a tower on his lands in the barony of Finlayston in Renfrewshire, acquired by his father on his marriage to Elizabeth Danielston.[79]

---

[69] At the June 1441 General Council, he was the pursuer in a legal case: *RPS* 1441/6/1.
[70] *RPS* 1450/1/39; 1450/5/4.
[71] *RPS* 1456/9.
[72] Angus Archives: M/W1/10/1 (not in RPS).
[73] See above, note 10.
[74] *Foedera*, xi, p. 349.
[75] NRS: GD97/2/13; GD18/422.
[76] *CDS*, iv, no. 1217.
[77] NLS: Adv Ch B67.
[78] Fraser, *Caerlaverock*, ii, pp. 433–34; original in Hull History Centre, DD EV/80/23.
[79] NRS: GD162/6/1/3. The grant of such licences, which began in the fourteenth

CHAPTER FIVE: THE BLARMADE CASE

Sir John himself was married at least thrice.[80] This led to a number of transactions in which he was clearly looking to balance the interests of the eldest sons of each of the first two marriages. In October 1452, John, the eldest son of his first marriage, issued a bond obliging himself never to gainsay his father's resignation to the king of Finlayston and Stanley in favour of the children to be borne between his father and Margaret Borthwick, the son's 'gude-mother', i.e. stepmother, and therefore Sir John's second wife.[81] Margaret was the daughter (most probably) of William, first lord Borthwick.[82] Crown confirmation of John's resignation was dated 3 April 1454. Clearly this move had later consequences: in December 1472, the son, now also Sir John (having been knighted in his own right), and his son and heir Gawane renounced any rights they might have in the said lands to Sir John junior's brother George. He must have been a half-brother of Sir John junior, due to inherit Finlayston as the son of Margaret Borthwick. The bond is very neatly signed by both Sir John junior and Gawane – a sign of good education, surely, and perhaps not untypical of a family background with an interest in legal business. A crown charter dated 7 January 1477 of the lands of the barony of Finlayston to George, designed son and heir of Sir John Maxwell

---

and was not uncommon in the fifteenth century, does not appear to have been the subject of systematic study apart from Mackay Mackenzie, W., *The Mediaeval Castle in Scotland* (London, 1927), pp. 76–78 and Appendix A. Mackenzie's list is evidently incomplete: it does not mention this grant for Finlayston, for example, or another for Guthrie in 1468 (NRS: GD188/1/1/2). See further Borthwick, A.R. and MacQueen, H.L., "Rare creatures for their age': Alexander and David Guthrie, Graduate Lairds and Royal Servants', in Crawford, B.E., (ed.), *Church, Chronicle and Learning in Medieval and Early Renaissance Scotland* (Edinburgh, 1999), pp. 227–39, 231.

[80] Fraser, *Pollok*, i, p. 465, misses the first of Maxwell's marriages and reverses the order of the last two.

[81] All documents referred to here and below are in NRS, GD162/6/1. The bond is witnessed by the son's three brothers, Alexander, Patrick and James: not mentioned in Fraser, *Pollok*, i, p. 465. Note also *RMS*, ii, no. 1346 (James III confirmation dated 19 January 1478 of charter by Sir John Maxwell of Calderwood dated 1 February 1464 for the daughter Elizabeth born between him and spouse Margaret Borthwick; the witnesses to the latter include Margaret's father, William, lord Borthwick, and Archibald Dundas of that ilk). In July 1454, Maxwell's eldest son received land from his father in the barony of Mauldslie (Fraser, *Pollok*, i, no. 45).

[82] See Borthwick, A.R., 'Borthwick family (*per.* c.1400–c.1515)', *ODNB*.

of Calderwood knight, followed on his parents' resignation; and there was a follow-up confirmation on 22 January 1478 (Sir John the father having died between the dates of the two charters). On 12 March 1478, the new Sir John of Calderwood and Gawane issued another bond obliging them never to trouble George in his peaceful possession of Finlayston, under a £1,000 penalty – suggesting that perhaps the death of the long-lived patriarch left the junior line represented by George feeling its position to be less secure than before; or that the senior line of the late Sir John's descendants had not been fully at ease with what they may have seen as an exclusion from their inheritance. The first Sir John's relict Margaret Rutherford was still claiming terce in 1492:[83] she must have been his third and final wife.

This material also makes clear that, through his second wife Margaret Borthwick, Sir John senior was related to her father William, first lord Borthwick. In January 1465, Borthwick was with William, lord Abernethy, in Rothiemay conducting the general justice ayre south of Forth;[84] and his Maxwell connection may explain why Gilbert, lord Kennedy, had to step in, as head of the minority government, and be 'justice for that time' at Lanark in February when the 'Blarmade' case came on for decision. It may also be one of the factors which led Hamilton of Cambuskeith and the Maxwells of Calderwood to decide that their dispute should be submitted to arbitration by persons who were 'unsuspect', that is, clearly impartial as between them both, rather than to any assize before the justiciars south of Forth.

What Lay behind the Litigation in the 1460s?

A tentative reconstruction of what happened to bring about the 1465 case may start with the 1436 service of James Hamilton as heir to his father David. This cannot have included 'Blarmade'. As we have seen, a mortancestry action such as James raised in the 1460s was based on a claim that, although an ancestor had died vest and saised as of fee in the disputed lands, the raiser of the action had never gained entry to them because someone else intruded. James must therefore have been unable to enter 'Blarmade' from at latest 1436, and quite possibly earlier, depending on exactly when his father died. The crucial point

---

[83] *ADC*, i, pp. 238–39.
[84] MacQueen, 'Tame Magnates?', p. 110.

CHAPTER FIVE: THE BLARMADE CASE

is that James's claim can only have been based on his father being in heritable possession on his death; he could not have gone back to his great-uncle Alan of Larbert, who had given the lands away while still alive, and whose relationship with James was not within the scope of a brieve of mortancestry. If James's claim was to hold 'Blarmade' of the Maxwells of Calderwood, the latter must therefore have held the superiority by 1436, having been granted it at some point by one of the earls of Douglas. We cannot, however, say for certain that this superiority stemmed from being the lords of Snar, since this designation is not given to the Maxwells in our documents. We must also note the figure of George Weir of Snar, who in 1455 was a member of an assize in the Coshogle case discussed in the previous chapter.[85] Was George merely an inhabitant of the lordship, or its lord?

If we carry as far as we dare speculation about the references to a dispute with Alan Hamilton in Robert Maxwell's will of 1420, perhaps the latter was granted a claim to the immediate superiority over 'Blarmade', despite Alan and his grantee seeing themselves as successive tenants of the earl. The resultant tensions between the families may have never been fully resolved after 1420 despite Robert's testamentary hopes to the contrary. It may not have helped that his heir John (one of the two defenders in 1465) succeeded as a minor, with his lands being managed by his uncle William of Aikenhead as tutor until he reached majority, possibly around 1423.[86] A continuing stand-off may have led to James's refusal to seek entry with the Maxwells when his father died in the mid-1430s while, perhaps, he was unable to gain entry from the string of Douglas earls between 1439 and 1455.

When the Douglas earldom lands were forfeited in 1455, the king became the superior of the Douglas half of Crawfordjohn, and the tenurial grade of all other holders of land in the half-barony rose by one. King James II clearly exercised his superiority directly for some years. Perhaps it was only after the king's accidental death at Roxburgh in 1460 that Hamilton of Cambuskeith gave up the argument that he now held 'Blarmade' directly of the king. There may have been pressure in that direction from the head of his kindred, James, lord Hamilton, who

---

[85] NLS: Acc 7043/16/2 (Adamton).
[86] Fraser, *Pollok*, i, p. 464. In July 1424, King James I confirmed John's charters in favour of his uncle, suggesting that by then John was of full age (*RMS*, ii, nos 9, 10). William may have received Aikenhead from his brother Robert (see above, note 53).

'briefly became a regular at court'[87] in the government of the minor King James III, and who stood to gain the Douglas half-barony of Crawfordjohn. Certainly, Cambuskeith's push for infeftment in the lands gathered momentum during the first phase of the king's minority: first the attempt to get Maxwell to admit him in 1461; then the mortancestry action in February 1465 (presumably a step in contemplation and preparation throughout 1464 at latest); and finally the submission to the arbitration from which Cambuskeith emerged at last triumphant on 8 May 1465.

We learn little substantive from the transumpt record of the actual arbitration proceedings in the Edinburgh tolbooth. The arbiters were John, lord Lindsay of the Byres, Gilbert, lord Kennedy, William Murray of Polmaise, Alexander Stewart of Galston, John Shaw younger, Thomas Lowes of Manor in Peebles-shire, and George Greenlaw, burgess of Edinburgh. Of these, Lindsay of the Byres had become a lord of parliament in May 1452 and justiciar north of Forth in 1457, as well as being an ambassador abroad and sitting judicially on the king's council. He would be the northern justiciar again in 1466.[88] He may have taken the lead among the arbiters; it is notable that his name precedes that of the king's guardian Kennedy in their listing. The others named, while by no means insignificant figures in their time, were certainly much less prominent in the politics of the period.[89] But, like Lindsay and Kennedy, they must have been free of any suspicion of possible partiality on either side of the dispute. There seems no reason to doubt their collective claim to have decided the case unanimously, 'the meritis and the grund of the matir and caus be ws riply avisit and undirstandyn eftyr law

---

[87] Borthwick, 'Hamilton family', *ODNB*.

[88] MacQueen, 'Tame Magnates?', pp. 108–09.

[89] William Murray of Polmaise (also of Touchadam) was sheriff of Stirling by 16 January 1461 (Borthwick, 'Council', p. 502) and was also at the same time for a couple of years constable or keeper of Stirling castle (*ER*, vii, pp. 7, 59, 65, 187). Alexander Stewart of Galston (Ayrshire) was brother of John, lord Darnley (*Scots Peerage*, v, p. 348). John Shaw younger was probably of the Shaw of Sauchie line from Clackmannanshire. Thomas Lowes of Manor was probably brother of Gawane Maxwell's second wife Elizabeth Lowes; but this marriage must have been after 1465, as otherwise Thomas would have been suspect as partial to the Maxwell side and so unacceptable to the Hamiltons. See above note 17 and Buchan, J.W., *A History of Peebles-shire* (Glasgow, 1927), iii, pp. 554–55. George Greenlaw features among the lords of the articles in parliament and in other financial roles in the 1460s, as well as sitting once on a 'session' administering justice: *RPS* 1464/10/1, 1467/10/5, 1468/9, 1468/10, 1473/7/19.

rycht faith gude conscience our knawlage and cunning We hawande God be for Ee'.[90] Cambuskeith was again represented by Master David Guthrie and Master Robert Hamilton; but Sir John Maxwell of Calderwood compeared alone, his grandson Gawane 'nocht comperande bot contumacily absentand hym'. The younger man may well have seen this as his grandfather's fight. Nevertheless the struggle was, if we believe the record, a keen one, with the arbiters noting that the parties (and, presumably, Cambuskeith's procurators) were 'be ws oft and mony tymis remowit and agane incallit'. If the proceedings began as planned at 9am on 25 April and did not finish until 8 May, they were also lengthy. An audience may have watched the contest unfold, namely those who witnessed the arbiters' sealed document formally articulating their decision. These were led by two lords of parliament, at least one of whom (James, lord Hamilton) had a direct interest in the outcome. The other was Maxwell's father-in-law, William, lord Borthwick, who was accompanied by his son and heir (also William, and a knight in his own right). Further names among the witnesses were Robert Colville of that ilk, Archibald Dundas of that ilk, Alexander Lindsay of Dunrod, Patrick Colquhoun, Duncan of Dundas (also a witness to the indenture at Lanark by which the 'Blarmade' case had been submitted to arbitration, and the younger brother of Archibald of that ilk[91]), Alexander Hamilton (another relative of the pursuer?), John Mowbray of Hoppringle,[92] Herbert Murray and 'mony othirez'. It was perhaps the best show in town on 8 May 1465.

Conclusions

The Edinburgh victory was consolidated by Master Robert Hamilton in the proceedings in the Glasgow official's court on 1 June 1465 with which we

---

[90] See *http://www.dsl.ac.uk/entry/dost/ee_n* for the usage meaning 'having God before our eye(s)'.

[91] See Fraser, *Pollok*, i, no. 62; NRS: GD75/4; above, text accompanying note 19. The Dundases of Dundas in West Lothian had earlier been closely linked with the Douglas earls but moved into royal circles after 1452: see Grant, 'Acts of Lordship', pp. 246, 252–53; Brown, *Black Douglases*, pp. 115, 121 note 44, 176, 286; Dunlop, *Bishop Kennedy*, pp. 221–22, 235 note 3. Archibald Dundas of that ilk, for whom see also note 81 above, was sheriff of Linlithgow by mid-1454 (Borthwick, 'Council', pp. 500–01) and remained in that office on 22 April 1465 (NRS: RH6/382).

[92] This must be a transcription error for 'Barnbougle', since the Mowbrays owned that estate, not Hoppringle.

began. In some ways, this entirely ecclesiastical process seems to show the religious arm being invoked to give force to the secular decision – rather the reverse of the usual picture in these matters.[93] But it all seems a very heavyweight set of processes for a claim to what must have been a relatively insignificant piece of land of small if any economic or other value. Setting aside Cambuskeith's initial attempt to gain sasine with the apparent support from the government of the royal minority in 1461, the process in 1465 began before the king's guardian (Gilbert lord Kennedy) and along the way involved a number of the other leading figures in the kingdom at the time: Robert, lord Boyd, John, lord Lindsay of the Byres and David Guthrie, for example. There must have been some symbolic or political explanation for all of this.

The end result probably suited not only Hamilton of Cambuskeith but also his kinsman James, lord Hamilton. It cleared his new property of half of Crawfordjohn, at least in part, of a man in Sir John Maxwell who may have had too much of a past association with the forfeited earls of Douglas for his complete comfort.[94] But, from a political perspective, while Lord Hamilton's 'star seems to have waned' later in the royal minority,[95] and the Maxwells of Calderwood were clearly close to the Boyds of Kilmarnock, neither Robert, lord Boyd's, July 1466 coup against Gilbert, lord Kennedy, to take over the guardianship of the young king, nor Boyd's own eventual fall and exile in 1469, seems to have affected the 1465 outcome.[96] Lord Hamilton, continuing to display the family ability to adapt to changing circumstances, was sufficiently in favour with the adult James III in 1474 to marry the king's sister Mary (widow of Thomas Boyd, earl of Arran, executed brother of the exiled Robert). On his own death in 1479, Hamilton's holding in Crawfordjohn was inherited by his minor heir, eventually to form part of a barony of Hamilton

---

[93] But cf. Ollivant, *Official*, p. 87.

[94] The Maxwells of Calderwood still had at least one other estate in the barony of Crawfordjohn in June 1492, namely 'Mekle Blackburn': *ADC*, i, p. 239. Blackburn lies north of the village of Crawfordjohn, but it is not possible to say in which half of the barony it stood.

[95] Borthwick, 'Hamilton family', *ODNB*.

[96] Contrast the mortancestry case between Gilbert, lord Kennedy, and Robert, lord Fleming, decided in favour of the former in April 1466, where the result seems to have been reversed very rapidly after the Boyd coup: see MacQueen, 'Kin of Kennedy', especially at p. 277. For the Boyd coup and downfall, see Macdougall, *James III*, pp. 68–72, 81–85.

erected in 1513 for that son (who had become earl of Arran in 1503).[97] At the next level down in the tenurial chain, that of the Hamiltons of Cambuskeith, the son and heir of the 1465 pursuer married Marion, daughter of the 1465 defender Sir John Maxwell, so that the tensions between the fathers did not carry over into the next generation.[98] There seems no reason to doubt that the decision on the title to 'Blarmade' held good until the end of the fifteenth century at least.

We would suggest that the reason for the 1465 process shifting from one of mortancestry to one considering the 'ground right' of the lands was because it became clear in the run-up to the proceedings at Lanark in February that Hamilton of Cambuskeith was raising not so much his own entitlement to inherit as the question whether his holding was to be of the Maxwells of Calderwood or of the king (and thus from late 1464 of James, lord Hamilton, his head of kin). The process was therefore one of invalidating any formal title held by the Maxwells, which must have come originally from the earls of Douglas. This was a strong step indeed, justifying elaborate process. The doubt over the validity of the Maxwell titles is most likely to have been about the legitimacy of interposing a mid-superior so that a tenant lost his direct tenurial connection to the earl. Whatever the legal rule on that matter, the assize had been directed to decide not only according to law but also in accordance with 'Richt faith and gude conscience'; and clearly altogether they favoured the Hamiltons. It may even be their acceptance of the invalidity of the Maxwell title deeds which explains the complete absence of any such documentation today.

---

[97] *RMS*, ii, nos 2311, 3803. The other half-barony of Crawfordjohn was held by the Barclays of Kilbirnie (see *RMS*, ii, nos 2490, 2491); the two halves were eventually re-united by the Hamilton earls of Arran early in the sixteenth century: for the story of Hamilton reunification and possession of the barony down to c.1793, see Reid, *Crawfordjohn*, pp. 33–42, 89–90.

[98] Hamilton, *House of Hamilton*, p. 213. For marriage as a weak means of settling feud, see Wormald, *Lords and Men*, 79. We are inclined to see it as a stronger tool in the pursuit of peace between kin groups. See also Cathcart, A., ''Inressyng of Kyndnes, and Renewing Off Thair Blud': The Family, Kinship and Clan Policy in Sixteenth-Century Scottish Gaeldom', in Ewan, E. and Nugent, J., (eds), *Finding the Family in Medieval and Early Modern Scotland* (Aldershot, 2008), pp. 127–38.

Chapter Six
Conclusions

Violence, Law and Society

On 8 July 1455, just over two months after the battle of Arkinholm, King James II sent a letter to King Charles VII of France narrating at some length how he had dealt with the treasonous rebellion of James, the former earl of Douglas, and his brothers and accomplices.[1] The king himself had besieged the Douglas castle of Abercorn since Easter, reducing it to collapse and arresting its inhabitants. But James Douglas had escaped to England, leaving behind his three brothers, Archibald, earl of Moray, Hugh, earl of Ormond, and John Douglas of Balvenie. Their forces had been defeated in a lethal conflict in the marches of the kingdom on 1 May (i.e. Arkinholm). The earl of Moray was killed on the field of battle and beheaded, his head then sent to the king at Abercorn. Ormond had been captured and sentenced to death (a sentence probably carried out after the Parliament in June 1455). Balvenie, however, had escaped to England. The Douglas castle at Threave had been destroyed, but those at Douglas itself and at Strathaven were spared in response to the inhabitants' appeal for the king's mercy.

This book has argued for the additional significance of law and legal analysis in probing more deeply into the nature of late medieval government and landed society.[2] The king's letter confirms, however, that law and legal

---

[1] Pinkerton, *History*, i, pp. 486–88.
[2] See also Borthwick and MacQueen, 'Three Fifteenth-Century Cases'; Grant, A., 'To the Medieval Foundations', *Scottish Historical Review* 73 (1994), pp. 4–24, 6.

analysis is far from the whole story when it comes to understanding the medieval polity. Brute force and military might were also vital, and not just to enable a king to deal with rebels but also to enforce justice. The story of Earl Archibald's head conjures up images from a much less ordered state of affairs: for example, the severed heads that are apparently the trophies of battle as depicted on the pre-1000 CE Sueno's Stone by Forres; the heads of the defeated MacWilliam insurgents that were displayed before the young Alexander II at Kincardine in the summer of 1215; and, in our own times, the widely condemned executions of some of its hostages by the Middle Eastern group known as ISIS or Daesh. Perhaps the most extreme historical example took place in England after the Restoration of 1660, when the body of Oliver Cromwell was exhumed from its burial place in Westminster Abbey, hanged at Tyburn and beheaded, with the head thereafter displayed on a spike at Westminster Hall until 1685.[3] Yet it must also be remembered that even after the later middle ages an element of 'public ritual' in legal process continued to be the display in prominent public places of the heads and other body parts of traitors executed after trial.[4]

This kind of display was, of course, meant as an example *pour descourager les autres*, a grim way to inform and reinforce 'common knowledge' in the public domain.[5] In Scotland as recently as 1437, the body of the *proditoris regis* Robert Stewart, who had surreptitiously admitted to the Perth Blackfriars after midnight the band of men who then assassinated James I, was quartered; one of the parts was exhibited in Ayr, while the traitor's head was displayed above the gates of Perth itself.[6] The heads of co-conspirators Walter Stewart,

---

[3] Morrill, J., 'Oliver Cromwell (1599–1658)', *ODNB*.

[4] A notable example is the first Marquess of Montrose, executed in 1650: see Stevenson, D., 'Graham, James, first marquess of Montrose (1612–1650)', *ODNB* ('Execution'). His body was, however, reassembled as far as possible after the Restoration and buried in state in St Giles Kirk, Edinburgh.

[5] For 'public ritual', 'common knowledge' and the 'public domain', see Hawes, C., 'Reassessing the Political Community: Politics and the Public Domain in Fifteenth-Century Scotland', unpublished paper delivered at the Colloquium on *Legal Culture in Medieval and Early Modern Scotland*, held on 16–17 December 2019. An earlier version was delivered at the Scottish Legal History Group meeting on 1 October 2016.

[6] Brown, *James I*, p. 197 (citing *ER*, v, p. 25 and Connolly, '*Dethe of the Kyng of Scotis*', p. 64).

CHAPTER SIX: CONCLUSIONS

earl of Atholl, and Christopher Chambers, burgess of Perth, were likewise placed on spikes in Edinburgh.[7]

Authorised retributive violence and the display of its results were thus important elements of the legal process; but not the only ones. While executions were not uncommon in the period, especially during the reign of James I – obvious examples then are the duke of Albany and his sons, and the earl of Lennox in 1425[8] – there are also numerous examples where that did not happen and individuals who had been arrested at the king's command were perhaps not even put on trial before being released. Amongst those also arrested but freed in 1424 were Malcolm Fleming of Cumbernauld (later one of the victims of the Black Dinner executions in 1440), Thomas Boyd, younger of Kilmarnock, Robert Graham (leading assassin of James I in 1437, also executed for that role), Sir John Montgomery of that ilk, Alan Otterburn, Isabella countess of Lennox and Mary Leslie countess of Ross (mother of Alexander lord of the Isles).[9] Later in the reign of James I, we can point to the further examples of Alexander lord of the Isles himself in 1428 and 1429 and Archibald fifth earl of Douglas in 1431.[10] In the reign of James II, the fall of the Livingstons in 1449 prompted some executions; but in 1452 the still-surviving leaders of the family, including the previously exiled Alexander Livingston of Callendar and his son James, were granted a comprehensive remission of their offences, and James went on to become royal chamberlain from 1454 to 1467.[11]

---

[7] Connolly, '*Dethe of the Kyng of Scotis*', p. 68. The other conspirators probably suffered a similar fate; they were certainly all tortured, hanged, drawn and disembowelled before final execution.

[8] *Chron Bower*, viii, pp. 244–45 (where other executions at the time are also noted). See ibid., pp. 260–61, for the executions in 1428 of Alexander Macruarie of Garmoran, John MacArthur and James Campbell.

[9] *Chron Bower*, viii, pp. 240–43.

[10] *Chron Bower*, viii, pp. 258–63, 264–65. Note the role of the Queen in interceding with the king to have mercy on each of the Lord of the Isles and Douglas, comparable with her successor's role in the treason trial of the eighth earl of Douglas in 1451 (above, Chapter 2, text accompanying note 174, and Chapter 3, text accompanying note 110). The fate of John Kennedy of Dunure, arrested at the same time as Douglas, remains mysterious: he is said in one slightly later source to have escaped his captivity and gone into exile (*Liber Pluscardensis*, i, p. 377; ii, p. 284).

[11] For the remission, see NLS: Adv Ch B.1316 and 1317; for it and the previous fall of the Livingstons see above Chapter 2, text accompanying notes 153-56;

The first three chapters of this book sought to highlight less violent law and legal process at work in fourteenth- and fifteenth-century Scotland. Perhaps the fundamental reason for doing so was best expressed long ago by the greatest of all British legal historians, F. W. Maitland: 'Legal documents, documents of the most technical kind, are the best, often the only evidence that we have for social and economic history, for the history of morality, for the history of practical religion'.[12] He might have added political history to his list. The very fact that such documents were regularly, indeed constantly, drawn up is indicative of the centrality and importance of law in this society or, more concisely, of its 'legal consciousness'.[13] They were and are also the pre-eminent markers of late medieval noble society's 'common legalities', those 'widespread practices aimed at producing explicitly legal effects'.[14] Even if Robert, duke of Albany and governor of Scotland, complained that their length and prolixity opened such documents up to the frivolous exceptions of pleaders (*causidicos*) in court by which the words themselves were defeated,[15] they are a more reliable guide to what was going on than the sometimes lurid accounts of chroniclers, both contemporaneous and (especially) later. By paying close attention to what the crucial documents – statutes, charters, notarial instruments – actually say and were meant to achieve in law, we can propose re-interpretations of a number of key moments in the later medieval history of Scotland.

Regency

Thus, for example, royal government in the period between 21 February 1437 and 26 October 1451 must be understood in terms of the conditions of regency prevailing during the long minority of James II. Throughout that time what went on followed the principles of regency as they had developed in

---

and Appendix (b). For James Livingston's post-1452 career as chamberlain, lord of parliament and counsellor to James II, see Borthwick, 'Council', pp. 157, 203–06, 491.

[12] Maitland, F.W., 'Why the History of English Law is Not Written', in Fisher, H.A.L., (ed.), *The Collected Papers of Frederic William Maitland, Downing Professor of the Laws of England*, 3 vols (Cambridge, 1911), vol 1, p. 486.

[13] See Chapter 1 above, text accompanying notes 14–18.

[14] Johnston, T., *Law in Common: Legal Cultures in Late-Medieval England* (Oxford, 2020), p. 7.

[15] *Chron Bower*, vii, pp. 410–11.

Scotland since at least 1286. In the absence of a regent nominated in advance by the dead James I, the nearest available agnate – Archibald, fifth earl of Douglas – took office, but was appointed by and subject to the supervision of the Three Estates. When that appointee himself died, the Three Estates assumed responsibility and the solution adopted appears akin to that of the Guardians appointed in 1286 and the various appointments made in the 1330s before Robert Stewart came of age and, as the king's nearest agnate and heir-presumptive, took up the guardianship to which he was entitled.[16]

The innovation in 1439 seems to have been the creation of a somewhat fluid group of counsellors who were, however, 'such persons as for the time were best suited to represent the realm or carry out the needs of the time'.[17] By contrast with 1286 and the 1330s, there was no challenge to the young king himself, nor was he absent from the kingdom. There was also no external threat to its independence given the nine-year truce with England from 1438 to 1447 and the fact that England was still embroiled in a losing war with France.[18] The main aim in establishing a conciliar form of regency from 1439 on must therefore have been the achievement of a reasonable balance between the various internal interests that would best enable proper oversight and control of the royal estates, prevent abuse of royal resources, protect the king's rights and continue the administration of justice. There may also have been some sense of the possible exposure of any regent to the ultimate fate of the second Albany Governor and his family in 1425 if the king, once he came of age, found or had reason to find there to have been treasonous maladministration. The idea that the sixth earl of Douglas could prove to be a suitable replacement for his late father upon achieving majority may also have been significant to the course of action finally taken.

Alexander Livingston's intervention against the queen mother in 1439 propelled him into the inner group of counsellors as one who had acted decisively for the good of the king and the realm in a moment of crisis. But the aggrandisement of himself, his family and his associates that took place through the 1440s was to be their undoing in 1449, their ousting taking place

---

[16] See Chapter 2 above, text accompanying notes 11–15.
[17] McNeill, 'Scottish Regency', p. 131 (quoted above Chapter 2, text accompanying note 10).
[18] For English weakness in the later 1430s and 1440s, see Powell, 'Lancastrian England', pp. 466–71.

with the acceptance and approval of the Three Estates, albeit seemingly *ex post facto*. It is more difficult, however, to know what lay behind the execution of the sixth earl of Douglas and his brother in November 1440. James Douglas of Balvenie, earl of Avondale, had already done well out of the regency, possibly as his nephew's right-hand man in his short-lived lieutenancy, and becoming an earl in his own right as well as justiciar. But pure greed and ambition for himself and his son and heir William as earls of Douglas cannot be altogether ruled out as a cause of the Black Dinner and its aftermath. But if so, Avondale must also have had support within the Three Estates in the regency. The threat apparently posed to the king by the sixth earl, his brother and their older friend Malcolm Fleming must have seemed very real in order to justify the executions meted out to all three men. At the same time, the non-forfeiture of their estates so that their heirs could take the land must mean that, if the law was being followed, either their offences were not treason or the whole business was subsequently recognised as a major miscarriage of justice requiring reversal so far as it was possible to do so. Support for that possibility can be found, not only in the 1441 judicial decision that Fleming had been unlawfully killed, but also in the undoubted 1452 reversal of the forfeiture of Alexander Livingston of Callendar and his son and heir James.

The Eighth Earl's Conduct 1444–51

The arrival of William, eighth earl of Douglas, in the inner councils of the regency at least coincides with what appears its least settled period, namely 1444 to 1447, the early part of which can be said to amount to a small civil war. A particularly significant event at that time was the removal of William Crichton as chancellor, which may have been, or have had, the result of ill-feeling between him and Earl William. Whether the young earl was immediately and absolutely at the forefront of the inner council seems improbable, however; and what is quite clear is that for him another major issue was the reunification of the Douglas earldom estates, splintered after the death of the sixth earl by the continuing effects of the tailzie of 1342 while the lands descended from the independent holdings of Archibald the Grim remained open to female inheritance. There may too have been a concern to emphasise his position as the rightful inheritor of all the past Douglas glories in Scotland

and beyond. This is suggested, not only by his grandiose trip to Rome in 1450–51 when he claimed to be the guardian of the kingdom, but also, and perhaps more so, by the splendid tomb he (presumably) had erected for his father the seventh earl in the Douglas parish kirk of St Bride's, alongside those of the family's famous progenitor, the Good Sir James, and the fifth earl, who had led the kingdom as lieutenant-general from 1437 to 1439 and whose effigy shows him as duke of Touraine.[19]

The extent to which the eighth earl used his council position in furtherance of the reunification objective is not entirely clear. His marriage to his cousin required papal rather than conciliar dispensation. He seems to have been able quite soon after his succession to the earldom to persuade his mother and his aunt to step aside in his favour from their lands of Stewarton and Galloway respectively, as well as taking a title to his wife's estate of Hawick. All these lands were also covered by the 1449 transumpt, and some of them were confirmed to the earl in the Parliament of 1450. Chapter 3 shows, however, that the earl's previous dealings in these matters were part of the case against him in June 1451 for misuse of power in the regency, especially where they extended his jurisdiction from barony to regality or beyond without any royal sanction. If the 1449 transumpt began life as part of an inquiry by the minority government into the landholding titles of the earl of Douglas with the aim of helping him fulfil his ambitions of a grand reunification of his estates, perhaps that process was turned against him during his absence abroad in the autumn and winter of 1450–51 (or even after his return to Scotland in April) by those now advising the king (perhaps including Chancellor Crichton and Bishop Turnbull, both of whom continued in royal government after the end of the minority).[20]

---

[19] See Brydall, R., 'The Monumental Effigies of Scotland, From the Thirteenth to the Fifteenth Century', *Proceedings of the Society of Antiquaries of Scotland* 29 (1894), pp. 329–410, at 337, 367–68, 378–79; Stevenson, *Chivalry and Knighthood*, pp. 126, 128. The seventh earl's tomb bears a double effigy showing the earl and his wife (Beatrix Sinclair). Since she died in exile in England around 1463 after the forfeiture of her sons in 1455, it seems unlikely that the effigies were carved after her death; most likely, therefore, the eighth earl was planning and executing a grand memorial to both his parents from his father's death in 1443 on.

[20] Durkan, *William Turnbull*, pp. 28–33, 46–51.

There can also be little doubt that the administration of the Forest and of the wardenship of the west and middle march by the fourth and fifth earls as well as Earl William had overreached its authority and jurisdiction, appropriating power seen as pertaining only to the king himself. In the Forest, finally, the council and, indeed, the Three Estates in Parliament with the king had been prepared in January 1450 to grant Earl William, not just regality, but regalian powers that in effect excluded the king and severely reduced his resources. Such a transaction benefiting a member of the regency government at the expense of their royal charge was precisely of a kind to invite suspicious subsequent review, and the Three Estates seem to have done just that in the summer of 1451 as the king approached formal majority.

Apart from the Forest, all the lands and offices seriously under review in 1451 were acquisitions made by Archibald the Grim and therefore formed part of the unentailed inheritance of the Douglases, i.e. they pertained to Earl William only by virtue of his 1444 marriage with Margaret the Fair Maid of Galloway. A further issue here might have been that, while that marriage had had papal sanction, it had certainly never had the blessing of a fully adult king or, probably, the council or Three Estates. Margaret's own consent, or its validity to constitute marriage, might even have been in doubt as well. But there was no reversal or adjustment in 1451 of the 1450 grant of her *maritagium*, and it seems unlikely that Margaret's possible claim to the Crown was much of an issue in 1451. This is probably confirmed by the fact that after Earl William's death, she was allowed quite quickly to marry his brother, James the ninth earl (albeit that marriage, like her first one, remained childless). The king and his advisers, concerned as they must have been about the royal succession ahead of the birth of a male heir in May 1452, clearly saw no threat in Margaret's marriages with her cousins. They probably saw no greater threat when in 1453 Malise Graham, earl of Menteith, returned to Scotland from captivity in England, by when a royal son had been added to the daughter born in 1451 and the risk of failure to produce a male heir was increasingly reducing.

But the parliamentary proceedings against the eighth earl in the summer of 1451 were neither the beginning of the end for the Douglases, nor any kind of humiliation for the king. The earl had made overweening claims during the royal minority, seeking to reunite the family's ancestral lands and to augment

CHAPTER SIX: CONCLUSIONS

its hereditary offices, and for that he was brought to book in the appropriate forum. But the objective of the king in pursuing the 'legal ritual' of a treason trial in Parliament was, not to destroy Douglas power, but rather to show it firmly under royal control; and in that he succeeded. It was most likely the earl who felt humiliated and fearful of the king's wrath again in future, as shown by his need of the king's guarantee of his safety before he would come to the subsequent royal gathering at Stirling in February 1452.

The killing that followed, we would suggest, was not part of any plot or conspiracy against the earl. The king had no need to engage in that sort of activity, given his control of the machinery of the law, and a conspiracy to kill the earl made little political sense. Instead, an argument possibly inflamed by the consumption of alcohol where the parties also bore lethal weapons ended as all too many such have done, in the sudden and violent death of one of them.

Calling the King to Account

The proceedings that followed in Parliament in June 1452, by which the king sought to clear his name, and his conciliation of the dead man's publicly vengeful brother, show his awareness of having made a major political blunder and his effort to repair the damage that had done to what had been a central plank of royal policy.[21] But the proceedings also show Parliament as a forum where the king's conduct as well as those of his regents could be brought under review, however unlikely it might be that royal misbehaviour would be sanctioned with anything like the severity visited upon, for example, the Livingstons in 1449–50.[22] The reported words of Sir Robert Graham as he undertook his unsuccessful attempt to arrest James I in a 1436 Parliament show how he at least, as 'a man of great elloquens and subtille witte, and wele-lurnid in the lawe', saw the forum as the right place to review the conduct of the king:

> I arrest you, sir, in the name of the three astattes here nowe assembled in the present perlement, for right as your liege peple

---

[21] For analysis of this as a battle between king and ninth earl to establish 'common knowledge' in the public domain, see Hawes, 'Reassessing the Political Community', unpublished.

[22] Further on this aspect of parliamentary authority see Brown, 'Public Authority', pp. 123–25, 144.

ben bounden and sworne unto your mgeste roialle, in the same wyesse be ye sworne and enseured your peple to kepe and governe your lawe, so that ye doo [t]hem noo wronge but in alright maytiene and defende [t]hemm.²³

Graham's action failed; he clearly did not have the political support from the Three Estates that he needed to succeed.²⁴ After the failure of his attempt at parliamentary procedure, he renounced his allegiance to the king and declared 'by worde and writyng' his intention to defy him, before going on to plot his assassination.²⁵ The renunciation looks like a *diffidatio*, a vassal's declaration that he was no longer bound by his sworn obligation of fealty to the king, comparable in this regard with the actions taken by James Douglas at Stirling and Edinburgh in 1452 following the killing of his brother the eighth earl.²⁶ Graham was said to be 'a gret legister of bothe lawes [*i.e. of canon and civil law*], and specially in civille', and he may have studied in Paris in the 1390s.²⁷ His perception of a mutuality of obligation arising from the reciprocal oaths of king and people that Parliament could in some way enforce against a defaulting king may not have been altogether wide of the mark.

---

[23] Connolly, '*Dethe of the Kynge of Scotis*', pp. 52–53. See also Brown, M.H., '"I have thus slain a tyrant": *The Dethe of the Kynge of Scotis* and the Right to Resist in Early Fifteenth-Century Scotland', *Innes Review* 47 (1996), pp. 24–44; Tanner, R., '"I arest you, sir, in the name of the three astattes in perlement"': The Scottish Parliament and Resistance to the Crown in the Fifteenth Century', in Thornton, T., (ed.), *Social Attitudes and Political Structures in the Fifteenth Century* (Stroud, 2000), pp. 101–17; Tanner, *LMSP*, pp. 68–71.

[24] See also Weiss, R., 'The Earliest Account of the Murder of James I of Scotland', *English Historical Review* 52 (1937), pp. 479–91. Instead, Graham's lands were forfeited (presumably as those of a traitor) and he was outlawed.

[25] Connolly, '*Dethe of the Kynge of Scotis*', p. 53.

[26] See Brown, '"I have thus slain a tyrant"', p. 33; Chapter 3 above, text accompanying notes 89–90.

[27] Connolly, '*Dethe of the Kynge of Scotis*', p. 66. The claim is verified to some extent by Brown, '"I have thus slain a tyrant"', p. 38; Tanner, *LMSP*, p. 70. Graham may thus have been one of the earliest 'graduate lairds', for which see Borthwick, A. and MacQueen, H., '"Rare creatures for their age': Alexander and David Guthrie, Graduate Lairds and Royal Servants', in Crawford, B.E., (ed.), *Church, Chronicle and Learning in Medieval and Early Renaissance Scotland* (Edinburgh, 1999), pp. 227–39.

CHAPTER SIX: CONCLUSIONS

The arrest of Robert II by David Fleming and others on 7 February 1388, perhaps triggered by the king's reluctance to undertake hostilities with England, is one possible precedent from that period for Graham's action.[28] A further later example is the arrest of James III by a group of his nobles on 22 July 1482 at a gathering at Lauder in the Scottish borders, from where he was taken into incarceration at Edinburgh castle.[29] In this as in the cases of Robert II and James I the king was accused of misgovernance of the realm, including putting it in danger of 'a major battle [with English forces] whose outcome looked grim' when the English army was otherwise bound to disband by 11 August.[30]

There are also at least signs of mutuality in the oaths thought to have been given by the clergy and barons (which included one of fealty by the latter) in reciprocation for that sworn by the young James II in Parliament in June 1445, by which they were to give the king good counsel and protect him from harm in return for his governance according to law.[31] The form of these oaths may have gone back at least to fourteenth-century coronation services.[32] A possible explanation for why eight years after his coronation James took his oath to govern –

> ... eftir the lawis and custumis of the realm; the law, custume and statutis of the realm neyther to eik nor to myniss without the consent of the thre estaits, and na thing to wirk na use tuiching the commoun proffit of the realm bot consent of the thre estaits; the law and statutis maid be my forbearis keip and use in all punctis, at all my power, till all my leigis in all things...[33]

– may be the end of his pupillarity the previous year, leading to the renewal (or perhaps his taking for the first time) oaths that he would scarcely have understood at the age of 6. But despite suggestions to the contrary, the king had not previously declared himself of full age[34] and he may still have been

---

[28] On this see Chapter 2 above, text accompanying note 24.
[29] See Macdougall, *James III*, ch 7, for a full account.
[30] Macdougall, *James III*, pp. 198–200 (quotation at 196).
[31] *RPS* 1445/4-6. See Chapter 2 above, text accompanying note 114.
[32] Lyall, R.J., 'The Medieval Scottish Coronation Service: Some Seventeenth Century Evidence', *Innes Review* 28 (1977), pp. 3–21.
[33] *RPS* 1445/3.
[34] See Borthwick, 'Council', pp. 189–90 and Appendix F; followed by Tanner, *LMSP*, p. 111, noting earlier views to the contrary.

regarded as too young to lead the defence of the kingdom, the other major royal duty to which he might have been expected to swear. But, as we will now suggest, there was otherwise nothing in the content of his oath out of line with long-established expectations of Scottish kingship.

We note first that similarly mutual obligations to govern in accordance with law may also have been commonly made incumbent by oath, not only upon those exercising authority on behalf of incapable kings, but also by those whom they were to govern. Thus in 1318 the community of the realm, ecclesiastical and lay, took a great oath to uphold both the tailzie of the Crown and the guardianship arrangements made by Robert I in Parliament in the event of his dying while his nominated heirs were minor.[35] John, earl of Carrick, and his advisory council certainly swore mutual oaths in 1385 as Carrick assumed responsibility for the administration of justice in the realm, and he lost his position because he had ceased to be capable of either leading the kingdom's defence or governing its internal affairs.[36] Oaths of fealty, presumably echoing those that would have been made to the king himself, were to be taken to the earl of Fife on his appointment as royal guardian in 1388 while, according to Bower (writing 50 years later), Fife himself also took an oath upon his appointment, presumably to govern and defend the kingdom.[37] The justification for the arrest of David, duke of Rothesay, in 1402 was his failure to fulfil that which he had sworn to do as lieutenant in 1399.[38] There was also lack of reciprocity involved here, however, in that the advice of the council appointed and 'sworne til gife hym [i.e. Rothesay] lele consail for the comoun profite nocht hafande ee to fede na freydschyp' had been ignored, while Bower adds that the appointed council resigned to the king (*quitabit se regi*) as a result of Rothesay spurning their advice (*spreto proborum consilio denuo*).[39]

This is not the place to embark upon a full analysis of 'the right to resist' (or the correlative rights and duties to give and take 'good counsel') in later medieval Scotland. That has been ably and persuasively discussed by Lynn

---

[35] See Chapter 2 above, text accompanying note 5.
[36] See *RPS* 1384/11/16, 17 and Chapter 2 above at note 20.
[37] See Chapter 2 above, text accompanying note 28.
[38] See Chapter 2 above, text accompanying note 39.
[39] *RPS* 1399/1/3; *Chron Bower*, viii, pp. 38–39.

Kilgallon with special reference to Robert Graham's failed attempt to arrest the king; but, however, and like those who have written on this subject before her, without making any reference to the mutual oaths of king (or his lieutenants or guardians) and his counsellors for the good governance of the realm discussed above.[40] The possibility of bringing the king to account on this basis may even explain the fifteenth-century interest in the Declaration of Arbroath and its 'deposition clause', manifested particularly by the inclusion of full texts in Bower's *Scotichronicon* (written in the 1440s) and (twice) in the *Liber Pluscardensis* (written in 1461).[41] Further, the parliamentary processes which in England preceded the deposition and abdication of Edward II in 1327 and the deposition of Richard II in 1399 were well-known to Fordun, Wyntoun, Bower and the author of the *Liber Pluscardensis*, and were doubtless also of some precedential value in this regard in Scotland.[42] Notably, the

---

[40] See Kilgallon, L., 'Communal Authority, Counsel and Resistance in the Reign of James I: A Conceptual Approach', *Scottish Historical Review* 100 (2021), pp. 1–24, also citing Wormald, J., 'National Pride, Decentralised Nation: The Political Culture of Fifteenth-Century Scotland', in Clark, L. and Carpenter, C., (eds), *Political Culture in Late Medieval Britain* (Woodbridge, 2004), pp. 181–94; Mason, R.A., *Kingship and the Commonweal: Political Thought in Renaissance and Reformation Scotland* (East Linton, 1998), pp. 8–35; Brown, '"I have thus slain a tyrant" (note 23 above); *The Politics of Counsel in England and Scotland 1286–1707*, ed. Rose, J. (Oxford, 2016).

[41] *Chron Bower*, vii, pp. 4–9; *Liber Pluscardensis*, ii, pp. 201–05, 252–54. See further Cowan, E.J., *The Declaration of Arbroath: 'For Freedom Alone'* (Edinburgh, 2020), pp. 88–93; Broun, D., 'The Declaration of Arbroath and Contractual Kingship: Reading the Deposition Clause in the Middle Ages', in Müller, K.P., (ed.), *Scotland and Arbroath 1320–2020: 700 Years of Fighting for Freedom, Sovereignty, and Independence* (Berlin, 2020), pp. 91–109, especially at 93–95, where the incorporation of the Declaration in several other fifteenth-century documents shows that 'the Declaration was not only copied regularly but, presumably, it was also read often.' Cf however, Mason, R.A., 'Beyond the Declaration of Arbroath: Kingship, Counsel and Consent in Late Medieval and Early Modern Scotland', in Boardman, S. and Goodare, J., (eds), *Kings, Lords and Men in Scotland and Britain, 1300–1625: Essays in Honour of Jenny Wormald* (Edinburgh, 2014), pp. 265–82.

[42] The replacement of Edward II whilst still living by his son and heir Edward III is referred to in *Chron Bower*, vii, pp. 32–35, while a full account of the deposition and abdication of Richard II is given at *Chron Bower*, vii, pp. 22–29. See also on the depositions *Chron Fordun*, i, p. 351 (ii, p. 343) (Edward II); *Chron Wyntoun*, ii, pp. 372–73 (Edward II), iii, pp. 70–76 (Richard II); and *Liber Pluscardensis*, i, p.

deposition of Richard was for breach of his coronation oath to uphold the kingdom's laws.[43] In addition, parliamentary procedures, including an Act of Accord on the royal succession for subsequent breach of which the king was then held to have forfeited the throne, led to the anyway mentally unfit Henry VI's long-drawn out fall from power in England in 1460–61. He was ultimately succeeded by Edward IV, previously earl of March and not Henry's heir, while Henry, perhaps following an example set previously by Richard II, sought refuge in Scotland;[44] so his situation would have been particularly well-known north of the border.

It may, however, be accepted that deposition (as distinct from arrest) of the king was not a remedy ever seriously attempted in later medieval Scotland. When James I under the sway of Henry V king of England tried to order the Scottish armies in France in 1419 and 1420 to cease their military activities, he may from a Scots point of view have come dangerously close to subjecting his kingdom to the English and thus to deserve to be 'driven out as our enemy and a subverter of his own right and ours' so that 'we would make some other man who was able to defend us our king'.[45] But only his specific orders needed to

---

256 (Edward II), pp. 332–37 (Richard II). See further Valente, C., 'The Deposition and Abdication of Edward II', *English Historical Review*, 113 (1998), pp. 852–81; Lane, S., 'The Bishops and the Deposition of Edward II', *Studies in Church History* 56 (2020), pp. 131–51; Theilmann, J.M., 'Caught between Political Theory and Political Practice: 'The Record and Process of the Renunciation and Deposition of Richard II'', *History of Political Thought* 25 (2004), pp. 600–19; Fletcher, C.D., 'Narrative and Political Strategies at the Deposition of Richard II', *Journal of Medieval History* 30 (2004), pp. 323–41; *The Deposition of Richard II: "The Record and Process of the Renunciation and Deposition of Richard II"(1399) and Related Writings*, ed. Carlson, D.R. (Toronto, 2008).

[43] See Baker, Sir John, *The Reinvention of Magna Carta 1216–1616* (Cambridge, 2017), p. 63.

[44] See Griffiths, R.A., 'Henry VI (1421–1471)', *ODNB*; Johnson, L., *The Shadow King: The Life and Death of Henry VI* (London, 2019), chapters 31–33. There was a brief 'readeption' of the king in 1470, but this lasted little more than seven months, and Edward IV was then restored to the throne. Walter Bower narrates Richard's exile in Scotland and eventual death at Stirling in 1419 (*Chron Bower*, vii, pp. 28–29, 64–67, 114–15); see further Nicholson, *Scotland: The Later Middle Ages*, pp. 222, 247 ('Mammet'); Boardman, *Early Stewart Kings*, pp. 240–41, 246 ('the Richard II imposter').

[45] We have followed the translation of the Declaration in Cowan, *'For Freedom Alone'*, pp. 146–49, 148. For the refusal of his subjects to obey James I, see

CHAPTER SIX: CONCLUSIONS

be disobeyed; his eventual return to Scotland does not seem to have led to any immediate issues for his kingship. Again, even when James III was replaced by his heir in 1488, it was because the king 'happinnit to be slane' on the field of Stirling, not because he had previously been misled by the 'peruerst counsale of diverse persouns beand with him for the tym, quhilkis counsalit and assistit to him in the inbringinge of Inglismen and to the perpetuale subjeccione of the realm'.[46] Rather, the perverse counsel had justified his subjects in rising against him to bring him back to the paths of good governance.

The whole problem of incapable and absent kings, recurrent since 1329, along with the issues created by unfit and possibly incompetent lieutenants such as Carrick and Rothesay, may also have shown that the greatest issues for Scottish governance lay, not just in avoiding or courting subjection to the English, but also in ensuring the internal peace, justice and law which only strong leadership and good example could secure.[47] For that reason James II was himself subjected to a form of trial in Parliament in 1452 for killing the earl of Douglas, and the verdict applied to his case the common law principles of forethought felony and slaughter by chance medley.[48] The king was not above the law, as hinted by the probably deliberate omission in *Regiam Majestatem* of the famous statement by the Roman jurist Ulpian included in the treatise's exemplars, Justinian's *Institutes* and *Glanvill*: '*sed et quod principi placuit legis habet vigorem*' (what pleases the prince has the force of law).[49] The enacting formulae in Scottish legislation from the reign of Alexander II (1214–49) on show consistently that while the king's authority made the law it did so only with the presence, advice and assent of his counsellors, whether in Parliament or General Council, thus confirming the position sworn to by James II in 1445.[50] This also confirms the validity of

---

Chapter 1 above, text accompanying notes 87–89; Chapter 4 above, text accompanying note 89.
[46] RPS 1488/10/51. See Chapter 3 above, text accompanying notes 128–29.
[47] See Cowan, 'For Freedom Alone', pp. 94–95.
[48] See Chapter 3 above, text accompanying notes 122–31.
[49] *Digest*, 1.4.1 (Ulpian); Justinian, *Institutes*, 1.2.6; *Glanvill*, prologue (at p 2). See Neilson, G., 'Magna Carta Re-Read', *Juridical Review* 17 (1905), pp. 128–44, 128–29; MacQueen, H.L., 'Magna Carta, Scotland and Scots Law', *Law Quarterly Review* 134 (2018), pp. 94–116, 106.
[50] Godfrey, A.M., 'Parliament and the Law', in Brown, K.M. and MacDonald, A.R., (eds), *The History of the Scottish Parliament volume 3: Parliament in Context*

Chief Justice Fortescue's observation, quoted above in Chapter 1, that the king of Scots reigned 'by the wisdom and counsel of many'.[51] Indeed, it was the law that made the king ('the succession to his right according to our laws and customs which we shall maintain to the death', according to the Declaration of Arbroath).[52] As the thirteenth-century English jurist *Bracton* further put it, the king ought to follow the law, but was subject only to the petition of his subjects to correct and amend his ways, which failing 'it is punishment enough for him that he await God's vengeance'.[53] *Bracton* may be compared on this with the Scottish jurist Thomas Craig of Riccarton, writing around 1600, who made clear that the general rule of mutual fidelity extended to king as well as people, he having duties to them to govern in accordance with the divine law and laws conform thereto; to protect them from violence, wrong and oppression; to ensure that the administration of justice is incorrupt; and, crucially, not to violate his oath to respect the honour and dignity of all amongst his people.[54] Parliament or General Council were then the principal forums in which the king (or those acting in his stead) might be held to account on the performance of his duties and allowed or persuaded to pass new laws and rectify any wrongs that he might have committed.

Law and Tenure in the Localities

With the case studies in Chapters 4 and 5, we move away from the centre of royal government to the operation of in what we may for convenience call the localities. The studies show that the localities were not simply the scenes of the bloody feuds and killings suggested by the Auchinleck chronicle.[55]

1235–1707 (Edinburgh, 2010), pp. 157–85, 158, 169, 172. Enacting formulae may be examined in *RPS*; see also *Laws of Medieval Scotland*, pp. 572–73, 576–77, 580–83, 616–19, 620–21.

[51] See Chapter 1 above, text accompanying note 9.

[52] Cowan, *'For Freedom Alone'*, p. 147. There was also the statutory tailzie of the Crown in 1373 which governed the succession from Robert II on: see Chapter 1, text accompanying note 40.

[53] *Bracton*, ii, p. 33.

[54] Craig, *Jus Feudale*, 2.11.33 (London, 1655, p. 215; Leiden, 1716, pp. 394–95; Edinburgh, 1732, p. 294; Clyde translation 1933, i, p. 607), also cited in Chapter 3 above, note 89.

[55] *Auchinleck Chron* ff 109r, 109v, 110v, 111v, 112r, 121v (McGladdery, *James II*, pp. 261–64, 269, 274), recording various homicides in the 1440s.

They demonstrate instead that appreciation of the law of procedure, landholding, succession and legitimacy underlying such disputes can lead on to much wider inquiries the conclusions of which throw new light on the power relations of the factor common to them both, those of the earls of Douglas in the fourteenth and fifteenth centuries.[56] The stories challenge Michael Brown's analysis of Douglas lordship as being essentially about the creation of networks based on personal friendship, loyalty and military prowess rather than land tenure.[57] They show that land tenure still mattered in later medieval lordship relations: not only to secure service and loyalty from the lord's point of view, but also, from the tenant's, to provide security of possession and inheritance.[58] If neither was certain, stability and support were fatally undermined.

The Douglas earls were not, at least after 1420, very good superiors for the Douglases of Drumlanrig, the Blairs of Adamton or the Hamiltons of Cambuskeith. Their long-drawn out and, in the case of Drumlanrig at least, repeated difficulties in gaining entry to their inheritances can have done nothing to promote any feelings of friendship or loyalty to the earls; rather the opposite. Further damage must have been done if, as happened to the Blairs and the Hamiltons, the earls inserted new mid-superiors between themselves and their tenants. At the turn of the sixteenth and seventeenth centuries, having explained as a general principle of feudal law the mutuality of obligation between superior and vassal, Craig wrote of Scots law in his *Jus Feudale*:

> By our law, we permit the alienation of a superiority by a lord so long as the position of the vassal is not thereby worsened, i.e. so long as another superior is not interposed between the lord and the vassal; and this kind of alienation is prohibited, for multiplication of lords by which all the services of the vassal increase counts as greater hardship for the vassal.[59]

---

[56] See also Borthwick and MacQueen, 'Three Fifteenth-Century Cases', for further illustration of the role played by law in dispute resolution.

[57] Brown, *Black Douglases*, pp. 157–82.

[58] Grant, 'Service and Tenure', pp. 170–75.

[59] Craig, *Jus Feudale,* 2.11.35 (London, 1655, p. 216; Leiden, 1716, p. 396; Edinburgh, 1732, p. 295; Clyde translation 1933, i, p. 609). The Latin is as follows: '*Nostro jure, alienationem superioritatis permittimus dominis, dummodo vassalli conditio in ea non sit deterior, i.e. dummodo alium*

There is nothing so specific in the texts of earlier Scots law, although the mutuality principle on which it is based is also highlighted in *Regiam Majestatem*.⁶⁰ But the *Libri Feudorum*, to which reference was made in fourteenth-century Scottish courts, did spell out that if a lord granted to a third party land already pertaining to a vassal holding in military tenure, the grant was invalid.⁶¹ In England *Bracton* discussed the problem in some detail, distinguishing, however, between the homage owed by the vassal, which with some exceptions could not be transferred to another lord, and the vassal's services, which with some exceptions, *could* be transferred.⁶² Maitland was doubtful about how far any of this reflected actuality:

> On the whole we have little reason to suppose that the rights of the tenants had ever in this country been a serious obstacle to alienations by the lords. ... It would be a mistake to suppose that the lofty feudal ladders which we find in the thirteenth century, had been always, or even generally, manufactured only by the process of adding new rungs at their nether ends; new rungs were often inserted in their middles.⁶³

---

superiorem non interposuerit inter se et vassallum; et hoc casu alienatio prohibetur, ne multiplicatis dominis, in quorum omnium servitia vassallus totetur, duriores fiant vassalli partes.'

⁶⁰ *Regiam Majestatem*, II, p. 62 (*APS*, i, p. 621; Stair Society vol 9, II, p. 67). According to the *Practicks of Sir James Balfour of Pittendreich*, ed. McNeill, P.G.B. (Edinburgh, 1962–63), i, p. 126 (c V), the mutuality principle was also stated in the *Liber de Judicibus*, c 135. For the *Liber*, see *Laws of Medieval Scotland*, pp. 55–56, 71, 97, 106, 110, 127, 132, 152, 165, 177, 188, 199, 205, 251–53, 326–27, 352.

⁶¹ See *Libri Feudorum: Vulgata,* transcribed by A. Stella, in *Civil Law, Common Law, Customary Law Project Publications*, St Andrews, 2019 [https://clicme.wp.st-andrews.ac.uk/online-texts/libri-feudorum-vulgata], 1.26[27–28], §1. The text is also available in the Ames Foundation Digital Collection of Harvard Law School: see http://amesfoundation.law.harvard.edu/digital/CJCiv/CJCivMetadataNov.html#t5frlf. For references to the *Libri* in Scottish courts, see MacQueen, *CLFS*, p. 53.

⁶² *Bracton*, ii, pp. 237–39; discussed in Pollock, F. and Maitland, F.W., *The History of English Law before the Time of Edward I*, 2nd edn (Cambridge, 1898, repr 1968), i, pp. 346–39.

⁶³ Pollock and Maitland, *History of English Law*, i, pp. 348–49.

CHAPTER SIX: CONCLUSIONS

But nonetheless Craig's statement of Scots law may well reflect something of medieval attitudes towards lordly alienations and their adverse effects upon tenants, whether or not there was an actual legal prohibition against them. Oswald of Abernethy's 1447 protest in Hawick, saying that he did not claim or challenge any man as his superior in the regality of Hawick but that he would hold his lands in chief of whomsoever an inquest found to be the baron of the barony of Hawick,[64] may provide an example. His grievance must have been echoed by others in Hawick and in Drumlanrig. In those cases, of course, the problem was not so much the insertion of mid-superiors as the earls granting others baronies while continuing to claim their own regality jurisdictions. But here too Craig's discussion of feudal law principle highlighted how a superior could only grant away the whole of whatever jurisdiction he held by virtue of his lordship; to do less was wrongfully to prejudice the affected vassal.

In Drumlanrig, however, the earls also exercised residual rights of superiority to infeft tenants of their own (the Loranes) within lands already apparently granted absolutely to a different tenant. In Hawick, the earls' claim to exercise superior regality jurisdiction within another's barony probably did not promote the baron's goodwill for his lord (even if such an arrangement was long established in Drumlanrig). In both cases the earls at the time of acting may have been more concerned about their need for immediate support than about feudal principle or the rights of those already in place below them, and were therefore ready to seize opportunities that seemed to be available through wardship, regality and the like. But the longer-term costs of such short-term benefits may have been considerable. That is apparent in the aftermath of the fall of the Douglas empire, as illustrated by the 'Blarmade' case, where those who had survived the collapse contested what had been left behind.[65]

---

[64] NRAS1100 (Roxburgh)/Bundle 704, summarised Fraser, *Douglas*, iii, no. 417.

[65] Note too that on 19 May 1455 (i.e. only a couple of weeks after Arkinholm) Countess Elizabeth Dunbar of Moray in her widowhood attempted to confirm a grant she and her husband Earl Archibald had previously made to her illegitimate half-brother Alexander of Westfield, while her elder sister Countess Janet engaged in similar confirmations later that year, to receive royal confirmation in 1457 NRS: GD466 (formerly NRAS3094). Elizabeth's confirmation preceded by one day her entry into a marriage contract with the son and heir of the earl of Huntly (for which see Chapter 3 above at note 120).

The rapid turnover of the earls through the deaths of the fifth in 1439, the sixth in 1440 and the seventh in 1443 did nothing to promote stability of tenure either, in that those holding land of them had to seek new entry and confirmation of title with each successor earl in turn. The sixth and the eighth earls coming in while still minors introduced further uncertainty in each case, since full entry with them could not be assured until they reached the age of 25. This insecurity amongst those who held of the earls is surely part of the explanation for the falling away of their support in the early 1450s, even despite the terrible circumstances, amounting to betrayals of trust in the name of royal government, in which the sixth and the eighth earls met their deaths.[66]

There must also be a question mark about the earls' administration of their sprawling empire. How could it have operated on the basis of personal links alone across such a vast array of estates? The fourth earl's younger brother, James Douglas of Balvenie, played a significant managerial role when the former was captive in England between 1402 and 1407.[67] The rules of the law, on services, inheritance, and casualties, pointed the way to justifiable outcomes in individual cases arising during any prolonged gap in the top management. But during the later lengthy absences of the earl and his heir as leaders of armies in France between 1419 and 1424, what actually happened 'back home'? Absence of the earl or not, there must always have been dependence – over-dependence, perhaps – on the proper application of these rules by the men who acted as stewards, bailies and other officers in the many different localities over which the earls held sway: the Gledstanes in Lauderdale and Teviotdale and the Maxwells of Carlaverock in Annandale, for example.[68] How were they brought to account for what they did in the name of the earl?

---

[66] See also Borthwick, 'Council', pp. 158–68 (commenting that loyalty to the earls of Douglas was 'difficult and unrewarding' (ibid., p. 162) and that 'the eventual overthrow of the Douglases may well have been a loss of loyalty towards them amongst former adherents' (ibid., p. 166), while also acknowledging that Crown pressure also played a part in leading Douglas adherents to switch away from the earls).

[67] Brown, *Black Douglases*, p. 234.

[68] On the Gledstanes, see Borthwick and MacQueen, 'Three Fifteenth-century Cases', p. 145; Brown, *Black Douglases*, p. 168; Fraser, *Douglas*, i, pp. xlv–xlix. For the lords of Carlaverock as stewards of Annandale, see *RMS*, ii, no. 242.

CHAPTER SIX: CONCLUSIONS

From time to time the accidents of succession also forced together the previously distinct administrations of different lords: as when Archibald the Grim, already the holder of a massive estate, gained the earldom lands in addition in 1389; or when in 1440 James Douglas of Balvenie, earl of Avondale, added the Douglas earldom to his already widely scattered personal holdings in Clydesdale, West Lothian and the north-east. Such growth by chance acquisition probably added to the stresses and strains on overall lordly governance over time, and to the likelihood of things going wrong. Sandy Grant has contrasted the 'uniquely businesslike' Sir James Douglas of Dalkeith (d. 1420), who made cartularies and inventories of his muniments to let him know what he had and to what he was entitled from his substantial estates, while 'his contemporaries ... usually bundled the documents they wanted to keep into 'charter-chests''.[69] Such unsystematic practices explain, for example, the difficulties Archibald the Grim had in 1388–89 in locating the tailzie of 1342 which gave him the earldom and its lands, and the reason why, once it was found, he then had it transumed to provide an authentic copy for use should need arise again.[70] The tailzie itself may have been an attempt to impose order on incipient chaos amidst the troubles of 1330–57, as was also the case with the 1355 consolidation of the twin strands of the Douglas inheritance as a regality.[71] Any uniformity of arrangement thereby achieved broke down again when Archibald the Grim's great collection of lands and offices, itself perhaps never fully consolidated outside Galloway and the west march, was added to the mix in 1389.

In the investigation and re-granting of the earldom titles which clearly began to take place within royal government early in 1449, there is apparent a desire to sort out a chaotically uncertain and variable situation in Archibald's former territories in particular. This was evident, as we have shown, in the question about the lordship of Hawick and its relation to the regality of Sprouston. But there may have been similar questions about the other lands

---

[69] Grant, 'Service and Tenure', p. 148. See too MacQueen, *CLFS*, pp. 260–61, on the litigiousness of James Douglas of Dalkeith and, for his ownership of *libros statutorum regni Scocie* and/or *libros civiles et statuta regni Scocie* (books of the civil, i.e. Roman, law as well as Scottish statutes?), *Morton Reg*, ii, nos 193, 196.

[70] See notes to *RRS*, vi, no. 51 and Fraser, *Douglas*, iii, no. 290 (both based on notarial transumpt of 8 March 1391 now held in NRAS859 (Earls of Home), Box 92/2/290).

[71] Grant, 'Franchises', p. 196.

under investigation in the crisis of 1451, especially those which, like Hawick and Sprouston, had been mentioned in the 1449 transumpt, and were also the subject of parliamentary consideration in January and February 1450.[72]

None of this denies the likely significance of personal relationships between lord and man, or, indeed their lack when, thanks to the rules on inheritance, only some purely formal tenurial link bound the individuals concerned. It certainly looks as though the relationship between the fourth earl and Sir William I of Drumlanrig was not replicated in the immediately following generations of their families. Nor did the actors in the dramas discussed here move only in conformity with lawyers' advice or the law. In numerous instances – above all when the king killed the eighth earl in February 1452 – this was clearly not the case. We might also consider, for example, the dubious manouevres at the Black Dinner leading to James Douglas of Balvenie, earl of Avondale, succeeding to the Douglas earldom. But at the same time, it is to be observed that the earldom descended over a century in accordance with the rules and practice governing inheritance, while the kingship did likewise despite successive kings' prolonged minorities, incapacities and absences in England.

The 'Blarmade' dispute and its resolution shows the interaction that was possible between forms of action at common law, purely secular arbitration and ecclesiastical processes. We can see in action laymen of the landed classes who were literate and able to represent themselves or others in litigation and arbitration, and also a churchman acting on behalf of a layman in his legal business. Notaries clearly played a vital role in producing documents which could thereafter be taken as authentic records, whether of an event that had occurred, such as Hamilton of Cambuskeith's request for sasine of 'Blarmade' from Sir John Maxwell of Calderwood, or of another document the survival of which could not be guaranteed against the inevitable hazards to which it might be exposed. In the case of the transumpt of the arbitration outcome made on 1 June 1465, there was the additional guarantee that anyone acting contrary to what it recorded would be exposed to ecclesiastical censure, whatever other consequences there might be in the secular arena. In none of this, however, or indeed in the Coshogle case, is there any evidence of

---

[72] See *RMS*, ii, nos 308, 309, 315. This also suggests that small regalities were not merely 'honorific': cf Grant, 'Franchises', p. 198.

CHAPTER SIX: CONCLUSIONS

interpersonal violence or feud over the disputed lands, despite the long-running nature of both disputes.[73]

We cannot say, therefore, that the stories in Chapters 4 and 5 are of only legal or local significance, however unimportant the land in question between the parties. They are rather evidence of a society rooted in the rule – the common knowledge and the public ritual – of law and 'legal consciousness'. They also show how incomplete is still our understanding of post-Douglas earldom politics – and indeed of politics before 1455. None of the main protagonists in the Coshogle or 'Blarmade' cases features largely or indeed at all in the standard political histories of the period. Yet each of them was vitally affected by, and played a role in, what was going on throughout the period covered by this book. The Blairs of Adamton and the Loranes, as well as the Douglases of Drumlanrig, were all closely connected with the Douglas earls, yet survived their fall (even the Loranes). The Hamiltons of Cambuskeith and Maxwells of Calderwood related not only to the earls of Douglas but also, in the 1450s and 1460s, to the increasingly significant Boyds of Kilmarnock and other families close to the heart of royal government. But, despite the dangers inherent in such relationships, the Hamiltons and the Maxwells waxed and prospered throughout the fourteenth and fifteenth centuries, surviving the fall not only of the earls but also of the Boyds when they too overreached themselves in the later 1460s.

The setback for the Maxwells of Calderwood in the 1465 case thus appears as no more than that, viewed in the overall context of the family's fortunes in the fifteenth century, and may well have been seen by them in just that light. Such a phlegmatic response to events helps to explain the means and manner of their survival and success in the complex conditions of their Scotland. Alongside that in their and other similarly placed families must go things like the survival instinct and kin solidarity displayed by the Hamiltons, and, in a different way, by the Maxwells, as well in their care across several generations to provide not only for the heir but also for younger sons and daughters and the subsequent generations which these in turn produced. Well-judged and

---

[73] For further discussion, see Godfrey, A.M., 'Rethinking the Justice of the Feud in Sixteenth-Century Scotland', in Boardman, S. and Goodare, J., (eds), *Kings, Lords and Men in Scotland and Britain, 1300–1625: Essays in Honour of Jenny Wormald* (Edinburgh, 2014), pp. 136–54.

timely marriages, often more than one on each side of the gender divide, are also part of this kin-focused picture. But surely at least as critical was awareness, understanding and, where needed, exploitation of the law and legal process (including arbitration) by shrewd, literate and capable people not invariably disposed to violence or merely political gain. All these elements must be brought into account if we are fully to comprehend the workings of political and landed society in the later medieval kingdom of the Scots.

We began this chapter with the beheading of traitors, including at least one of the Douglases (i.e. Archibald, earl of Moray). It is perhaps right to finish by noting that when the exiled Earl James was captured by the Scots at Lochmaben in 1484, after nearly thirty years in the active service of the English Crown, he was simply held for the remaining seven years of his life at the abbey of Lindores in Fife, not really imprisoned and certainly not executed as a traitor. By 1484 he was clearly no longer seen as any kind of threat to the king of Scots, and there was no perception of any need to wreak public vengeance against an aged man whose kindred had been effectively destroyed long before. And no doubt he himself was weary after half a lifetime of mainly military activity. The career of the literate James Douglas, who had matriculated in Arts at the university of Cologne around 1440 with a view to achieving high-level ecclesiastical positions, and who had subsequently gone in pursuit of secular honour and glory, whether as a tournament knight or in making a splendid progress to Rome in the company of his elder brother or in avenging the 'foule slauchter' of that same brother by the king, illustrates very well how difficult it is to comprehend the individual acts, motivations and understandings that went together to make up noble society as a whole in the Scotland of his time.[74]

---

[74] See generally Borthwick, 'Douglas, James, ninth earl of Douglas and third earl of Avondale c.1425–1491'.

Appendix

General Editorial Principles

The aim in creating these transcripts has been to provide a readable text while reproducing the wording of the originals as closely as possible. All punctuation is editorial, and capitalisation is limited to modern conventions. Abbreviated words have been silently expanded. Editorial notes have been kept to a minimum. As the scribes seem to have used word forms like "gracia", "pertinenciis" and "audiui", they have been so rendered uniformly, except on the rare occasions when a different spelling is clear. There are a few occasions when a word is split between lines. When that happens, the word is hyphenated at the end of the line where the split word occurs.

(a) NLS: Ch. 951

See Plate 1. For discussion of and comment upon this transumpt to be dated 20 January 1449, see Chapter 2, text accompanying notes 132–46. For a summary see Wigtown Charter Chest no 30. The document is badly damaged: in the middle, there is a significant hole from top to bottom, and the text towards the right-hand edge of the document has worn in places. The damage has made the text difficult to read in places, especially (for example) in lines 28 and 29 below where there will be a few words missing (noted as "lacuna" in this transcript).

The text as given here is therefore a composite one, drawn from the following sources (to which reference may be had for further editorial notes): (1) the principal source, which has been heavily relied upon by the editors of the so-far published volumes of Regesta Regum Scottorum, is the transcript made by Maitland Thomson (1847-1923), Curator of Historical Records at the former Scottish Record Office (now National Records of Scotland), within his notebook NRS: GD212/1/10 – however, though it is a very good transcript, Thomson did accidentally omit a few words; (2) other transcripts of some of the confirmed charters, also by Maitland Thomson, are within NRS: GD212/1/126; and (3) the versions published in RRS, v and vi, and RMS, i, as referred to in the footnotes below. Very occasionally, this transcript does not follow every letter of the published versions, as a better reading of certain letters is possible with the benefit of a zoomable digital image. In the interest of providing a readable text, this transcript also omits all the square brackets in the published versions denoting presumed readings. It is unclear if the transumpt was more legible when Thomson prepared his transcript, or (as seems likely) he expanded his transcript into the areas most damaged or worn based on his long experience of reading charters, therefore surmising the most likely words which are now invisible or entirely lost. Even Thomson's transcript fails at the points where the word "lacuna" is given, however.

The charter is one of transumpt by King James II, 20 January 1449, of the following charters: (1) King David II, 20 January 1367, to Thomas Fleming restoring to him the earldom of Wigtown, as held by the late Malcolm Fleming, earl of Wigtown, but without the rights of regality; (2) King Robert II, 7 October 1372, confirming the charter of Thomas Fleming, earl of Wigtown, 8 February 1372, by which he sold the earldom of Wigtown to Sir Archibald Douglas, lord of Galloway; (3) King Robert II, 9 March 1372, confirming the agreements made between Sir Archibald Douglas and Thomas Fleming, earl of Wigtown; (4) King David II, 18 September 1369, to Sir Archibald Douglas of all royal lands in Galloway between the Cree and the Nith in free barony, just as the king's late uncle, Edward Bruce, held them; (5) King David II, 5 June 1358, to Thomas Murray, pantler of Scotland, of the baronies of Hawick and Sprouston, in the sheriffdom of Roxburgh, Sprouston in free regality and Hawick in free barony; (6) King Robert I, 31 January 1321, inspecting the record of an inquest, 2 August 1320, into the royal liberties by which the lord de Vescy held Sprouston, in the sheriffdom of Roxburgh, under King Alexander III, and granting them to Robert Bruce, his son; (7) King Robert I, 26 February 1322, to William Murray of half of Stewarton in Cunningham. The great seal of James II was applied along with the seals of five witnesses for the further strengthening of the transumpt.

In the transumpt, the first word of the charters issued by Kings Robert and David has been deliberately put in larger letters by the scribe: here, to mimic *the scribe's intentions in making the different documents transcribed easier to locate, the initial word of each separate document has been given in bold.*

1. **Jacobus** Dei gracia rex Scotorum omnibus probis hominibus tocius terre sue clericis et laicis salutem. Sciatis nos quasdam cartas inclitissimorum antecessorum nostrorum regum Scocie eorum magnis sigillis sigillatas sanas integras non rasas non abolitas non cancellatas nec in aliqua sui parte suspectas set omni prorsus vicio et suspicione carentes
2. inspexisse vidisse et ad plenum intellexisse tenores infrascriptos continentes. **David** Dei gracia rex Scotorum omnibus probis hominibus tocius terre sue clericis et laicis salutem. Sciatis nos dedisse concessisse et hac presenti carta nostra restituisse et confirmasse Thome Fleming comiti de Wigtoune totum comitatum de Wigtoune cum pertinenciis.
3. Tenendum et habendum eidem Thome et heredibus suis de nobis et heredibus nostris in feodo et hereditate per omnes rectas metas et diuisas suas cum omnibus et singulis libertatibus commoditatibus asyamentis et iustis pertinenciis suis quibuscumque ad dictum comitatum spectantibus seu quoquomodo iuste spectare valentibus in futurum, adeo libere et quiete plenarie integre et honorifice
4. in omnibus et per omnia sicut quondam Macolmus Fleming comes de Wigtoune auus predicti Thome dictum comitatum cum pertinenciis liberius quiecius plenius et honorificencius tenuit seu possedit. Salvo quod regalitatem aut ius regalitatis in ipso comitatu non habeat aut ipsa regalitate utatur quam ex certa causa in suspenso remanere volumus quousque aliud super hoc
5. duxerimus ordinare. In cuius rei testimonium presenti carte nostre sigillum nostrum precepimus apponi. Testibus venerabilibus in Christo patribus Willelmo episcopo Sanctiandree, Patricio episcopo Brechinensi cancellario nostro, Roberto senescallo Scocie comite de Stratherne nepote nostro, Willelmo comite de Douglas, Roberto de Erskyn, Archibaldo de Douglas, Waltero de Haliburtone
6. et Willelmo de Dischingtone, militibus. Apud Perth vicesimo die Januarii anno regni nostri tricesimo septimo.[1] **Robertus** Dei gracia rex Scotorum omnibus probis hominibus tocius terre sue clericis et laicis salutem. Sciatis quod cum Archibaldus de Douglas miles consanguineus noster

---

[1] 1366-67; *RMS*, i, no 250; *RRS*, vi, no 368.

carissimus de mandato nostro ad hoc summonitus et ad nostram vocatus presenciam nobis ostenderit et

7   exhibuerit in pleno nostro concilio tento apud Strivelyn ibidem propter hoc specialiter congregato, cartam Thome Fleming alias comitis de Wigtone de et super vendicione et alienacione comitatus eiusdem prefato Archibaldo confectam, cum aliis evidenciis pro jure ipsius Thome Fleming et prefati Archibaldi in hac parte facientibus; nos eandem cartam sic nobis exhibitam et ostensam

8   ibidem de mandato nostro visam lectam inspectam et diligenter examinatam per nos et dictum nostrum concilium, sigilloque dicti Thome Fleming sigillatam, non cancellatam non viciatam non rasam non abolitam nec in aliqua sui parte suspectam set omni vicio prorsus et suspicione carentem de verbo in verbum intelleximus sub hac forma. Omnibus hanc cartam visuris vel

9   audituris Thomas Fleming comes de Wigtone salutem in domino sempiternam. Noveritis me non vi aut metu ductum nec errore lapsum set mera et spontanea voluntate mea in magna necessitate urgente et inevitabili constitutum, et precipue propter magnas et graves discordias et inimicicias capitales alias inter me et maiores indigenas comitatus predicti

10 exortas, vendidisse ac titulo vendicionis imperpetuum concessisse nobili et potenti viro domino Archibaldo de Douglas militi, domino Galwidie ex orientale parte aque de Creth, totum comitatum meum de Wigtone supradictum cum pertinenciis ac totum jus et clameum quod michi heredibus vel assignatis meis in dicto comitatu cum pertinenciis competit seu competere poterit

11 quomodolibet in futurum in prefatum Archibaldum pure simpliciter absolute et imperpetuum transtulisse pro una certa et notabili summa pecunie michi in mea magna et urgente necessitate predicta pre manibus persoluta, de qua summa fateor me bene et integre persolutum. Tenendum et habendum prefato Archibaldo heredibus suis vel suis assignatis in feodo et hereditate per

12 omnes rectas metas et diuisas suas, in pratis pascuis et pasturis moris marresiis viis semitis aquis stagnis molendinis et multuris, cum bondis et bondagiis ac eorum sequelis aucupacionibus venacionibus et piscariis, ac cum ecclesiarum advocacionibus, cum furca et fossa sok et sak thol et theme infangandtheif et outefangandtheif, cum feodis et forisfacturis

13 et eschaetis, cum wardis releuiis et maritagiis ac liberetenencium seruiciis; necnon cum omnibus aliis et singulis libertatibus commoditatibus asiamentis iustis pertinenciis et liberis consuetudinibus ad dictum

comitatum spectantibus vel quomodolibet spectare valentibus quoquo titulo sive jure, adeo libere et quiete plenarie integre et honorifice in omnibus et per omnia sicut ego

14 Thomas predictus dictum comitatum de Wigtone liberius quiecius plenius integrius et honorificencius tenui et possedi seu aliqui predicessorum meorum dictum comitatum tenuerunt et possiderunt. In cuius rei testimonium sigillum meum presentibus est appensum. Datum apud Edynburgh octauo die mensis Februarii anno domini millesimo trecentesimo septuagesimo primo. Hiis

15 testibus, Waltero Dei gracia abbate Sancti Nemoris, Willemo Monypeny rectore ecclesie de Cambuslang, Nigello de Cuninghame, Thoma de Rate et Nicholao Smerles, burgensibus de Drumfres et multis aliis. Quam quidem cartam sic nobis exhibitam et ostensam in omnibus punctis condicionibus articulis et circumstanciis universis forma pariter et effectu per omnia ratifica-

16 mus approbamus et pro nobis et heredibus nostris imperpetuum confirmamus, saluo servicio nostro. In cuius rei testimonium presenti carte confirmacionis nostre nostrum precepimus apponi sigillum. Testibus venerabilibus in Christo patribus Willemo et Patricio Sanctiandree et Brechinensi ecclesiarum episcopis, Johanne primogenito nostro comite de Carric senescallo Scocie, Roberto comite de Fyf et

17 de Mentethe filio nostro dilecto, Willemo comite de Douglas, Johanne de Carric cancellario nostro, Hugone de Eglingtone et Roberto de Erskyn, militibus. Apud Strivelyn septimo die mensis Octobris anno regni nostri secundo.[2] **Robertus** Dei gracia rex Scotorum omnibus probis hominibus tocius terre sue salutem. Sciatis nos concessisse et hac presenti carta

18 nostra confirmasse illas conuenciones condiciones sive contractus initos inter Archibaldum de Douglas militem ex parte una et Thomam Fleming comitem de Wigtoun ex parte altera. Tenendas seruandas et complendas ex utraque parte earundem adeo libere inuiolabiliter et firmiter sicut indenture littere sive carte inter ipsas partes inde confecte in se juste continent plenius et

19 proportant, saluo seruicio nostro. In cuius rei testimonium presenti carte confirmacionis nostre nostrum precepimus apponi sigillum. Testibus

---

[2] 1372; *RMS*, i, no 507; text of Thomas Fleming's charter summarised in *Wigtown Charter Chest*, no 7.

venerabili patre Willelmo episcopo Sanctiandree, Johanne primogenito nostro comite de Carric et senescallo Scocie, Roberto comite de Fyff et de Mentethe dilecto filio nostro, Willelmo comite de Douglas consanguineo nostro, Johanne de Carric

20 canonico Glasguensi cancellario nostro, Hugone de Eglintone et Roberto de Erskyn, militibus. Apud Sconam nono die mensis Marcii anno regni nostri secundo.[3] **David** Dei gracia rex Scotorum omnibus probis hominibus tocius terre sue clericis et laicis salutem. Sciatis nos dedisse concessisse et hac presenti carta nostra confirmasse dilecto speciali et fideli

21 nostro Archibaldo de Douglas militi pro suo diligenti labore et grato seruicio nobis efficaciter et effectuose impenso omnes terras nostras Galwidie existentes videlicet inter aquam de Creiche et aquam de Nythe pro quarum pacificacione et justificacione idem Archibaldus sumptus fecit non modicos et labores in persona propria sustinuit vehementes. Tenendas et habendas

22 eidem Archibaldo et heredibus suis de nobis et heredibus nostris in feodo et hereditate per omnes rectas metas et diuisas earundem in unam integram et liberam baroniam, in boscis et planis in pratis et pascuis in moris et marresiis in viis et semitis in aquis et stagnis molendinis multuris et eorum sequelis in aucupacionibus venacionibus et piscariis, cum burgis et libertatibus

23 burgorum existentibus in eisdem terris, cum tenandiis et seruiciis liberetenencium cum ecclesiarum aduocacionibus, cum bondis bondagiis natiuis et eorum sequelis, cum furca et fossa cum sacco et socca thol et theme et infangandtheif, necnon et cum omnibus aliis et singulis libertatibus commoditatibus asiamentis et justis pertinenciis suis quibuscumque ad dictas terras

24 spectantibus seu quoquomodo juste spectare valentibus in futurum, adeo libere et quiete plenarie integre et honorifice sicut bone memorie Edwardus de Broys auunculus noster carissimus predictas terras dum vixit liberius quiecius plenius et honorificencius tenuit seu possedit. Reddendo inde annuatim nobis et heredibus nostris dictus Archibaldus et heredes

25 sui unam rosam albam apud castrum nostrum de Drumfres in festo Sancti Petri quod dicitur aduincula nomine albe firme pro warda releuio maritagio sectis curie ac pro omnibus aliis seruiciis exactionibus seu demandis

---

[3] 1372; not fully printed anywhere so far as noted.

que de dictis terris exigi poterunt seu requiri. In cuius rei testimonium presenti carte nostre sigillum nostrum precepimus apponi. Testibus venerabilibus in Christo patribus

26 Willelmo episcopo Sanctiandree et Patricio episcopo Brechinensi cancellario nostro, Roberto Senescallo Scocie nepote nostro, Johanne Senescallo comite de Carric, Georgio comite Marchie, Roberto de Erskyn, Jacobo de Douglas, Waltero de Lesly, Waltero de Haliburtona, Alexandro de Lyndesay et Johanne Heris, militibus. Apud Edynburgh decimo octauo die Septembris anno regni nostri quadragesimo.[4]

27 **David** Dei gracia rex Scotorum omnibus probis hominibus tocius terre sue salutem. Sciatis nos dedisse concessisse et hac presenti carta nostra confirmasse dilecto nostro Thome de Morauia panitario nostro Scocie baroniam de Hawic et baroniam de Sprowystone cum pertinenciis infra vicecomitatum de Roxburgh. Tenendam et habendam predictam baroniam de Sprowystone cum pertinenciis

28 predicto Thome et heredibus suis de nobis et heredibus nostris in feodo et hereditate in liberam regalitatem adeo libere et quiete in omnibus et per omnia sicut [*lacuna*] baroniam de Hawic eidem Thome et heredibus suis de nobis et heredibus nostris in feodo et hereditate in liberam baroniam, per omnes rectas metas et diuisas suas cum feodis et forisfactu-

29 ris cum seruiciis omnium liberetenencium et ecclesiarum aduocacionibus et cum omnimodis aliis libertatibus commoditatibus asiamentis et justis pertinenciis [*lacuna*] cum pertinenciis spectantibus seu quouismodo iuste spectare valentibus in futurum. Faciendo nobis et heredibus nostris ipse Thomas et heredes sui seruicia de predictis baroniis debita et

30 consueta. In cuius rei testimonium presenti carte nostre sigillum nostrum precepimus apponi. Testibus venerabilibus in Christo patribus Willelmo episcopo Sanctiandree, Patricio episcopo Brechinensi cancellario nostro, Roberto senescallo nostro Scocie comite de Stratherne, Patricio comite Marchie et Morauie, Thoma comite de Marre, Willelmo de Keth marescallo nostro Scocie, Willelmo

31 de Leuingstone et Roberto de Erskyn, militibus, ac multis aliis. Apud Edynburgh quinto die Junii anno regni nostri vicesimo octauo.[5] **Robertus** Dei gracia rex Scotorum omnibus probis hominibus tocius terre sue

---

[4] 1369; *RMS*, i, no 329; *RRS*, vi, no 451.
[5] 1358; *RRS*, vi, no 187.

salutem. Sciatis nos inspexisse ac veraciter intellexisse inquisicionem de mandato nostro coram vicecomite nostro de Roxburgh per probos et fideles
32 homines eiusdem vicecomitatus super libertatibus consuetudinibus et seruiciis dominii de Sproustone factam et ad capellam nostram retornatam in hec verba. Inquisicio facta apud Roxburgh die Sabati proxime post festum beati Petri aduincula anno gracie millesimo tricentesimo vicesimo, videlicet cum quibus libertatibus consuetudinibus liberisque seruiciis dominus de Vescy inte-
33 grum tenementum de Sproustone olim tenuit, per Willelmum de Rule, Adam de Rule, Petrum de Aldroxburgh, Johannem de Lilliscleif, Robertum de Wodfurde, Patricium de Langneutone, Thomam fullonem, Willelmum de Sprowistone, Johannem filium Ade, Galfridum clericum, Radulphum Fossart, Adam de Cauertone et Alexandrum de Chattow. Qui
34 iurati unanimiter dicunt quod totum tenementum de Sproustone olim tenuit dominus de Vescy regaliter per easdem libertates quas dominus Alexander rex Scocie dudum alias terras suas eiusdem regni tenuit; et per consuetudines quod nulli homines sui de tenemento de Sproustone infra burgos Scocie pro bonis suis propriis vendendis vel ad proprium usum
35 suum emendo tallagium dabunt set tamen si dicti homines aliquod vendiderint vel ad proprium usum emerint et illud idem pro commodo suo mercando vendiderint tallagium dabunt; et quod dictus dominus de Vescy habebit in dicto tenemento de Sproustone justiciarium suum, camerarium, cancellarium, coronatores, seruientes ad habendum dicto
36 domino de Vescy ad modum regis, et eciam mensuras suas quascunque per se ad modum dicti domini regis Scocie manutenendas. In cuius rei testimonium sigillum vicecomitis de Roxburgh unacum sigillis Willelmi de Roule, Alexandri de Chattow, Hugonis de Roule, Galfridi clerici, qui dicte inquisicioni interfuerunt est appensum. Nos igitur dominium
37 tocius tenementi de Sprowistone predictum ad nos pertinens ad Robertum de Broys filium nostrum acceptare volentes dictum dominium eidem Roberto damus concedimus et hac presenti carta nostra confirmamus. Tenendum et habendum sibi et heredibus suis de corpore suo legitime procreandis, adeo libere et quiete plenarie et honorifice cum omnibus libertatibus commoditatibus
38 liberis seruiciis consuetudinibus et asiamentis in omnibus et per omnia sicut inquisicio suprascripta liberius quiecius plenius aut honorificencius plenius proportat et testatur. Faciendo nobis et heredibus nostris dictus

Robertus et heredes sui predicti seruicium inde debitum et consuetum temporibus predecessorum nostrorum regum Scocie. In cuius rei testimonium presenti carte nostre sigillum

39 nostrum precepimus apponi. Testibus Bernardo abbate de Abirbrothoc cancellario nostro, Thoma Ranulphy comite Morauie domino Vallis Anandie et Mannie, Waltero senescallo Scocie, Jacobo domino de Douglas, Alexandro de Setone et Roberto de Lawedre, militibus. Apud Berwicum super Tuedam ultimo die Januarii anno regni

40 nostri quinto decimo.[6] **Robertus** Dei gracia rex Scotorum omnibus probis hominibus tocius terre sue salutem. Sciatis nos dedisse concessisse et hac presenti carta nostra confirmasse Willelmo de Morauia consanguineo nostro dilecto pro homagio et seruicio suo mediatatem tocius tenementi de Stywardstone in Cunyngham, quam quidem mediatatem idem Willelmus nunc

41 tenet per suas rectas metas et diuisas factas inter ipsum Willelmum ex parte una et Patricium de Morauia fratrem suum seniorem. Tenendam et habendam eidem Willelmo et heredibus suis de nobis et heredibus nostris seu assignatis libere quiete plenarie et honorifice in feodo et hereditate sine aliquo retinemento in perpetuum cum omnibus libertatibus commod-

42 itatibus asiamentis et justis pertinenciis in omnibus et per omnia ad predictam mediatatem terre spectantibus seu de jure spectare valentibus in futurum quoquomodo. Faciendo idem Willelmus et heredes sui medietatem seruicii unius militis tantum. In cuius rei testimonium presenti carte nostre sigillum nostrum precepimus apponi. Testibus Bernardo abbate

43 de Abirbrothot cancellario nostro, Thoma Ranulphy comite Morauie domino Vallis Anandie et Mannie, nepote nostro, Jacobo domino de Douglas, Gilberto de Haya constabulario nostro, et Roberto de Kethe marescallo nostro, militibus. Apud Are vicesimo sexto die Februarii anno regni nostri sextodecimo.[7] Quas

44 quidem cartas coram notario et subscriptis testibus ad futuram rei memoriam transumi mandavimus volentes atque mandantes tantam fidem huic presenti transumpto [*lacuna*] insertis ubique fore adhibendam. In cuius rei testimonium presenti transumpto magnum sigillum nostrum apponi precepimus. Testibus reverendo in Christo patre Willelmo

---

[6] 1320-21; *RRS*, v, no 172.
[7] 1321-22; *RRS*, v, no 205.

45 episcopo Glasguensi, dilecto consanguineo nostro Alexandro comite de Craufurd, Alexandro de Leuingstone de Calendar, militibus, Magistro Jacobo de Lyndesay preposito ecclesie collegiate de Linclouden, et Roberto de Leuingstone nostrorum compotorum rotulatore, quorum testium presenti transumpto in ipsius maiorem roboracionem sigilla sunt appensa. Apud [*lacuna*] vicesimo die

46 mensis Januarii anno domini millesimo quadringentesimo quadragesimo octavo et regni nostri duodecimo.[8]

There are seven tags for the appending of seals remaining on the document, but no seals remain. Six of the tags are more or less complete; the seventh is a fragment. In addition, one tag has completely disappeared. As there are only five witnesses named, it is not clear why there should be as many as eight seal tags.

(b) NLS Adv Chs B. 1316, 1317

For discussion of and comment upon this text (which survives in two copies, NLS Adv Chs B. 1316 and 1317, both to be dated 27 August 1452), see Chapter 2, text accompanying notes 153-6. The text is a remission by King James II in favour of Alexander Livingston of Callendar, knight, James Livingston, his first-born son, the late Alexander Livingston, late son of Livingston [elder] and brother german of James, the late James Dundas of that ilk, Duncan Dundas, his brother, Robert Bruce, brother of John Bruce of Clackmannan, and the late Robert Livingston, burgess of Linlithgow. The King notes their services in his tender age, and because of their future service, out of his benevolence and special grace, and with the advice and consent of the Three Estates in the parliament at Edinburgh, 26 August 1452, all civil and criminal actions by them in former times are remitted; the judicial sentences passed against them at the parliament at Edinburgh, 21-22 January 1450, are annulled; the said persons are received back into royal favour, and they are restored to their lands, castles, possessions, offices etc as described in their charters, and are restored to worldly honours; all this notwithstanding any parliamentary acts against them, especially an act stating that any who lays hands on the person of the king, queen, prince or the king's castles would commit treason without prospect of remission. Confirmed by the appending of the king's great seal, along with the seals of five bishops, of the chancellor

---

[8] 1448-49.

and four other barons, of the burgh commissioners of three burghs, [and of the abbot of Holyrood], in the name of the Three Estates, at Edinburgh 27 August 1452.

1 Jacobus Dei gracia rex Scotorum omnibus et singulis ligiis et subditis nostris et aliis quibuscunque ad quorum noticias presentes nostre littere peruenerint salutem. Quia sicut
2 considerauimus et ad mentem nostram reduximus magnos et indefessos labores variasque solicitudines ac seruicia laudabilia nobis in nostra teneritate temporibus euolutis factis et ex-
3 hibitis per Alexandrum de Levingstoun[9] de Calenter militem, Jacobum de Levingstoun ipsius filium primogenitum, quondam Alexandrum de Levingstoun filium quondam Alexandri et [fratrem][10] germanum Jacobi
4 predictorum, quondam Jacobum de Dundas de eodem, Duncanum de Dundas fratrem eiusdem, Robertum Bruce fratrem Johannis Bruce de Clakmanane, et per quondam Robertum de Levingstoun bur-
5 gensem de Lithqw temporibus etiam retroactis multiformiter nobis impensis, necnon propter eorum grata seruicia temporibus profuturis impendenda, ex nostris beneuolencia fauore
6 et gracia speciali, cum auisamento et consensu nostrorum trium statuum in nostro parliamento tento apud Edinburgh sabbato xxvi°[11] die mensis Augusti anno domini millesimo
7 quadringentesimo quinquagesimo secundo et regni nostri xvi°[12], remisimus et presencium tenore remittimus predictis personis et eorum cuilibet omnes et singulas actiones criminales
8 et ciuiles nobis temporibus preteritis per ipsos aut ipsorum quemlibet quomodolibet perpetrates; ac adnullamus, cassamus et irritamus omnes et singulas iudicia, sentencias et pro-
9 cessus et inde secuta in contrarium predictorum personarum vel alicuius earundem latas seu fulminatas in parliamento nostro tento apud Edinburgh xxi° et xxii° diebus mensis Ja-

---

[9] NLS Adv Ch B.1316 always spells *Levingstoun* with an *e* at the end.
[10] Read into the original for it to make sense.
[11] Written out fully in NLS Adv Ch B.1316.
[12] Ditto.

10 nuarii anno domini m⁰ cccc⁰ xlix⁰ et regni nostri xiii⁰ [13]. Sic quod nuncquam temporibus profuturis sentencie, iudicia et processus vim effectum vel vigorem in iudicio vel extra

11 directe vel indirecte quomodolibet habebunt seu quouismodo optinebunt sed cassanda, irritanda, adnullanda et nullius valoris seu efficacie reputanda erunt

12 imperpetuum per presentes. Insuper recepimus predictas personas et quamlibet earum superstitem ipsorum heredes et successores in nostris fauore et gracia specialibus, et declaramus

13 ipsos et ipsorum quemlibet nostros legios homines et fideles, ipsosque et eorum quemlibet ac eorum heredes et successores restituimus in omnibus et singulis terris, redditibus, castris, tur-

14 ribus et possessionibus, officiis, firmis et assedationibus iuxta et secundum tenores cartarum et evidenciarum suarum infeodationibus antiquarum, necnon mundanis honoribus

15 dignitatibus et bone fame restaurando ac penitus et omninino restituendo; adeo libere, plenarie et honorifice sicut predicte persone aut earum quelibet predicte ante prolacionem predictorum

16 iudiciarum, processuum et sentenciarum habuerunt seu quomodolibet possiderunt; et omnem infamie notam si quam propter quamcunque actionem criminalem racione dicti nostri processus, iudicii

17 vel sentencie inantea factam incidebant vel aliquis eorum incidebat autoritate nostra regia auferimus, ammouemus, relaxamus et ipsos et eorum quemlibet de plenitudine

18 nostre regie maiestatis suis honori et bone fame sicut prius reintegramus, habilitamus ac dispensatione restituimus ac per presentes restitimus pro perpetuo, ita quod omnes

19 actus legittimos exercere legittime poterunt in futurum. Non obstantibus quibuscunque actis seu decretis in concilio [sic] generalibus seu parliamentis inantea editis seu factis,

20 et presertim in quoddam acto siue decreto alias edito in quo continebatur quod quicunque imponeret manus in personam nostram, regine aut principis aut nostris castris quibuscunque

21 quod eo facto proditoriam absque ulla remissione committeret tradicionem. Quodquidem actum siue decretum preiudicium nullatenus generare volumus personis predictis aut eorum alicuis

---

[13] Ditto.

22 suis heredibus aut successoribus temporibus profuturis. Mandantes propterea uniuersis et singulis ligiis et subditis nostris cuiuscunque gradus, sexus, condicionis aut nacionis
23 extiterint ne ipsi nec aliquis ipsorum ausum temerario presumant seu presumat contra predictas personas vel earum aliquam heredes vel successores occasione premissorum
24 opprimere questionem seu demandam facere penes ipsorum honores, bonam famam seu dignitates vel contra tenorem nostre gracie et deliberacionis huiusmodi nostri parlia-
25 menti devenire audeant seu audeat sub pena plenarie forisfacture. In quorum omnium et singulorum premissorum magnum sigillum nostrum et sigilla reverendorum in
26 Christo patruum Jacobi, Willelmi, Thome, Johannis et Thome, Sanctiandree Glasguensi, Dunkeldensi, Morauiensi et Candidecase ecclesiarum episcoporum, et dilectorum consanguineorum nostrorum
27 Willelmi domini Crethton[14] cancellarii nostri, Alexandri comitis de Huntlee domini le Gordoun, Willelmi domini le Somervil, Andree domini le Gray, et Roberti domini le Lyle, ac sigilla
28 commissariorum burgorum nostrorum de Edinburgh, Hadington et Coupir nomine trium regni nostri statuum presentibus sunt appensa. Apud Edinburgh vicesimo septimo die
29 mensis Augusti anno domini millesimo quadringentisimo quinquagesimo secundo et regni nostri decimo sexto supradictis. Ac etiam sigillum venerabilis in Christo patris abbatis
30 monasterii Sancte Crucis de Edinburgh[15].

Signed by the king himself.[16]

---

[14] These names spelt slightly differently in NLS Adv Ch B.1316. In that version, Huntly precedes Crichton.
[15] The abbot of Holyrood is not listed as a witness in NLS Adv Ch B.1316.
[16] The King's signature is not written on NLS Adv Ch B.1316. On Adv Ch B.1317, there are eight seals surviving, which are all rather damaged. Three appear to be episcopal, round seals; four are heraldic, presumably baronial, seals. The King's great seal is the other one, and is a mere fragment. There is one tag now without a seal attached. There are no missing tags. NLS Adv Ch B.1316 bears only the tag for the now-missing great seal.

(c) NLS: Acc 7043 Adamton charters No 16/2

See Plate 2. For discussion of and comment upon this notarial instrument to be dated 22 January 1455, see Chapter 4, text accompanying notes 1-11. R C Reid provides a translation of the document (with which he was assisted by Dr Gordon Donaldson, as he then was), in 'An Early Coschogill Writ', Transactions of the Dumfriesshire and Galloway Natural History and Antiquarian Society 30 (1951-2) 132-42, 132-4. The instrument (written by Thomas Burn, notary public), 22 January 1455, records the proceedings in a justiciary court of Drumlanrig, held by James Douglas of Drumlanrig, depute of Sir Robert Crichton of Sanquhar, specially deputed by the lord thereof as justiciar of the court. The forespeaker of John Blair of Adamton, pursuer, led a brieve of mortancestry concerning the lands of Coshogle, in the barony of Drumlanrig and sheriffdom of Dumfries, against James Lorane, defender. After legal arguments, Blair's forespeaker requested Douglas to convoke an assize to determine the issue of the brieve. The assize was elected and stated as their conclusion that the late Sir John Blair, grandfather of the pursuer, died last vest and saised in the lands, and that John the pursuer is his heir, whereupon Douglas instructed the sergeand of the court to give the pursuer his sasine.

1. In Dei nomine amen per hoc presens publicum instrumentum cunctis pateat euidenter quod anno ab Incarnacione domini millesimo quadringentesimo quinquagesimo quarto mensis vero Januarii die vicesimo
2. secundo indictione secunda pontificatusque sanctissimi in Christo patris ac domini domini nostri Calisti divina providencia pape tercii anno primo. In mei notarii
3. publici et testium subscriptorum presencia personaliter constitutus nobilis vir Thomas de le Grahame prolocutor Johannis de Blare de Adamtoune actoris ab una
4. in placito breuis de morteantecessoris super terris de Costhogil infra baroniam de Drumlangrig et vicecomitatum de Drumfres jacentibus et per dictum Johannem impetrati. Quiquidem
5. Thomas post nonnullas altercaciones et legis questiones inter ipsum dictum Thomam et Thomam Thome prolocutorem Jacobi Lorane rei ab altera super terminacione
6. dicti breuis motas in quadam curia justiciarie de Drumlangrig per spacium xl^a dierum ante proclamata vigore regalitatis tenta ibidem per honorabilem virum

7 Jacobum de Douglas de Drumlangrig substitutum et deputatum Roberti de Crechtoune de Sanchar militis justiciarii dicte curie per dominum eiusdem specia-
8 liter substituti et deputati in talibus verbis dixit ad Johannem Irland seriandum curie: Ego Thomas de le Grahame prolocutor Johannis de Blare princi-
9 palis actoris in hac causa ex parte ipsius dico quod placitum breuis dictarum terrarum de Costhogil certis ex causis per me superius assignatis debet isto
10 die ad recognicionem asise admitti; et ad hoc affirmandum inuenio plegium in manu tua et aliud plegium super hoc pro maiori habundancia[17] quod primum plegium
11 per me inuentum est juridicum et sufficientis roboris et valoris pro et ex eo quod nec dictus Jacobus Lorane nec aliquis alius ex parte ipsius aliquid
12 dicit juridice vel in forma juris plegium meum legitime recontrariando vel contradicendo quod de jure plegium meum in aliquo poterit diminuere vel derogare.
13 Et hiis ut premissum est per dictum Thomam de le Grahame dictis, propositis et allegatis ipse dictus Thomas ad Jacobum de Douglas reuerenter dixit:
14 Domine substitute et deputate vos audistis quot raciones, allegaciones et proposiciones ex parte dicti Johannis de Blar et pro defensione et terminacione sue
15 cause dicti breuis in vestra condigna presencia proposui et allegaui, et nullus pro parte aduersa comparet qui aliquod impedimentum opponit in contrarium mee alle-
16 gacionis, quin placitum dicti breuis secundum probata et per me allegata poterit legitime isto die ad recognicionem asise admitti et ab asisa ulterius non repelli; Quare[18]

---

[17] For this reading of an obscure word in the original (see Plate 2), see Adriano Capelli, *Lexicon abbreviaturarum: Dizionario di abbreviature latine ed italiane usate nelle carte e codici specialmente del medio-evo* (6th edn, Milan, 1987) p. 166 (a reference for which we are indebted to John Hudson). Reid/Donaldson translate the word as 'security' but the context is one of affirming by way of a second pledge, i.e. more than required by law, that the pursuer's brieve should now be put to the recognition of an assize. For usual procedure on a brieve of mortancestor see *Quoniam Attachiamenta* ed David Fergus (Stair Society vol 44, 1996) 216-9.

[18] This word is not well-written. Reid/Donaldson's lengthy translation renders it as "wherefore", which makes sense in the context, and the word "Quare" is perhaps the best fit.

17 vobis supplico domine substitute et deputate ac virtute vestri officii stricte vos omnino sicuti coram suppremo domino nostro rege volueritis respondere quatenus placitum dicti breuis
18 ad recognicionem asise admittatis, fidelem asisam eligendo que veritatem ambiguitatis dicti breuis isto die juridice et iuste poterit terminare. Quiquidem
19 Jacobus de Douglas requisicionem dicti Thome iustam fore intelligens, secundum suum intellectum et per consilium curie instructus et informatus fecit conuocari
20 asisam de fidedignioribus patrie ibidem pro tunc congregatis quorum nomina subsecuntur videlicet: Robertus de Dalzel de eodem, Gilbertus Makmath de Dalpeter,
21 Johannes Boile de Wamfray, Cuthbertus Molmorsone de Arestroane, Johannes Blak Patonsone de Blakwod, Patricius Blak de Templand, Georgius de
22 Douglas, Johannes le Menzeis de Achincol, Georgius Were de Snar, Rothaldus de Dalzel, Gilcristus Grersone, David de Jhonstoune, Fergusius
23 Donaldsone, Ricardus Edgar de Inglischtoune, Alanus Makrath, Rothaldus de Banachtine et Jacobus Braune de Dalvene. Quiquidem homines
24 prescripti et in asisam electi et jurati, intellectis et conceptis omnibus per dictum Thomam de le Grahame pro terminacione dicti breuis sibi propositis, foras exierunt et ibidem per certum
25 tempus expectantes et que in dicta causa terminanda erant mature decernentes, rimantes et discucientes in omnibus unanimiter concordauerunt, et
26 sic cum sua declaracione ad asisam intrauerunt. Et Rothaldus de Dalzel cancellarius asise, pro se et suis sociis qui dicte asise intererant pro finali
27 conclusione tocius dicte cause, dixit quod Johannes olim de Blar miles, auus dicti Johannis de Blar prosecutoris huius breuis, obiit ultimo vestitus et sasitus
28 ut de feodo ad pacem et fidem domini nostri regis de dictis terris de Costhogil cum pertinenciis; et quod dictus Johannes de Blar prosecutor dicti breuis est legitimus et propin-
29 quior heres dicti olim domini Johannis de Blar militis aui sui de dictis terris cum pertinenciis; et quod est legitime etatis. Quibus auditis dictus Thomas de le Graham
30 onerauit Johannem Russel sectatorem curie ut ipse perageret officium suum. Et dictus Johannes Russel ad preceptum dicti Thome de le Graham dedit

31 pro judicio ut dictus Johannes de Blar haberet talem et consimilem sasinam in et de dictis terris de Costhogil cum pertinenciis qualiter Johannes
   olim de Blar miles
32 auus dicti Johannis habuit in dictis terris illo die quo fuit vivus et mortuus.
   Quo judicio in forma sic dato dictus Jacobus de Douglas dedit virgam
33 dicto Johanni de Blar in signum sasine dictarum terrarum cum pertinenciis, precipiens seriando curie Johanni Irland quatenus sine dilacione
   personaliter accederet ad capitalem
34 messuagium dictarum terrarum, et ibidem personaliter existens sasinam
   hereditariam dictarum terrarum dicto Johanni vel suo certo actornato
   exhiberet. Et hiis dictis
35 prefatus Johannes Irland accessit ad capitalem messuagium dictarum terrarum, et ibidem cum assumptis terra, lapide et ligno ut est moris sasinam
36 hereditariam dictarum terrarum cum pertinenciis dicto Johanni de Blar
   tradidit et deliberauit et inuestiuit in eisdem. Super quibus omnibus et
   singulis premissis ipse dictus
37 Thomas de le Graham a me notario subscripto pro future rei memoria sibi
   fieri peciit cum instancia presens publicum instrumentum. Acte fuerant
38 hic publice apud Drumlangrig hora quasi secunda post meridiem sub
   anno die mense indictione et pontificatus supradictis. Presentibus ibidem
   honorabilibus
39 viris videlicet Edwardo de Crechtoune, Symone Ker, Donaldo Huntar,
   Georgio de Dalzel, Georgio Were de Carkow, Alexandro de Abernethy,
40 armigeris, dominis Johanne Bel, Johanne Gerland, Archibaldo Cuke,
   Thoma Quhelp, capellanis et Roberto Ker cum multis aliis testibus ad
   premissa vocatis.

[Notarial sign of Thomas Burn]

> Et ego Thomas de Burn presbiter Glasguensis dyocesis imperiali
> auctoritate publicus notarius premissis omnibus et singulis
> dum sic ut premittitur fierent dicerentur et agerentur una cum
> prenominatis testibus presens interfui eaque omnia et singula sic
> fieri vidi et audiui in notam recepi et in hanc publicam formam
> redegi tam supra quam subtus manu mea propria scripsi presens
> publicum instrumentum exinde confecti me et nomen meum
> subscribendo signisque meis solitis et consuetis signaui rogatus

specialiter et requisitus in fidem et testimonium omnium et singulorum premissorum; interlineacione unius verbi videlicet sasine approbando.

There are the remains of a seal tag, but no seal.

(d) NLS Acc 7043 Adamton No 16/1

See Plate 3. For discussion of and comment upon this notarial copy to be dated 8 June 1431, see Chapter 4, text accompanying notes 25-36. It is written by Thomas Twy, notary public, at request of John Blair, lord of Kilwinnet, 8 June 1431, for copy of a charter by King Robert II, 28 May 1374, confirming a charter by King David II, 12 April 1358, in favour of James Blair, son and heir of the late Hugh Blair, of the land of Coshogle, in the barony of Drumlanrig and sheriffdom of Dumfries, which had been previously been granted by the king to Hugh after the forfeiture of the late Eustace Lorane.

1 Per hoc presens publicum instrumentum cunctis pateat euidenter quod anno a natiuitate domini millesimo CCCC° xxxi pontificatus sanctissimi in
2 Christo patris ac domini nostri domini Martini diuina prouidencia pape quinti anno quartodecimo.[19] In mei notarii publici et testium subscriptorum
3 personaliter constitutus nobilis vir Johannes de Blar dominus de Kilwynnet michi quamdam litteram dedit perlegendam confirmacionis cum quadam carta sub sigillo
4 bone memorie domini Roberti regis secundi sigillata non rasam non cancellatam nec in aliqua sui parte suspectam set omni prorsus
5 vicio et suspicione carentem ut prima facie apparebat, cuius quidem littere tenor sequitur et est talis: Robertus Dei gracia rex Scottorum
6 omnibus probis hominibus tocius terre sue clericis et laicis salutem. Sciatis nos cartam recolende memorie domini auunculi et predecessoris nostri

---

[19] News of Pope Martin V's death on 20 February 1431 after 13 years and 101 days in office had evidently not reached Twy on 8 June 1431. Martin was succeeded by Pope Eugenius IV on 3 March 1431. Twy was probably over 60 years of age when he wrote this instrument: see W Scott, 'William Cranston, Notary Public c.1395 to 1425, and Some Contemporaries', in *Miscellany VII*, ed H L MacQueen (Edinburgh: Stair Society vol 62, 2015), 125-32, 127, 132.

7 domini David regis Scottorum illustris de mandato nostro visam lectam inspectam et diligenter examinatam intellexisse ad plenum

8 de uerbo in uerbum sub hac forma: David Dei gracia rex Scottorum omnibus probis hominibus tocius terre sue salutem. Sciatis nos dedisse concessisse

9 et hac presenti carta nostra confirmasse dilecto et fideli nostro Jacobo del Blare filio et heredi quondam Hugonis del Blare totam terram de

10 Corschogill cum pertinenciis in baronia de Drumlangrig infra vicecomitatum de Dumfress, quam terram concessimus alias quondam Hugoni patri suo per cartam

11 nostram racione forisfacture quondam Eustachii de Lorene inimici nostri notarii [sic] et rebellis. Tenendam et habendam eidem Jacobo et heredibus suis de

12 capitali domino dicte terre in feodo et hereditate per omnes rectas metas et diuisas suas cum omnibus libertatibus commoditatibus aysiamentis et iustis

13 pertinenciis suis quibuscunque ad dictam terram spectantibus seu quoquo modo iuste spectare valentibus in futurum. Faciendo inde ipse Jacobus

14 et heredes sui predicto capitali domino dicte terre seruicium debitum et consuetum. In cuius rei testimonium presenti carte nostre sigillum nostrum precipimus apponi.

15 Testibus venerabilibus in Christo patribus, Willemo et Willemo Sanctiandree et Glasguensi ecclesiarum Dei gracia episcopis, Roberto senescallo nostro Scocie comite de

16 Strathern, Patricio comite Marchie et Morauie, Thoma comite de Marr, Willemo de Lynvynstoun, et Johanne de Prestoun, militibus, et multis aliis.

17 Apud Edenburgh xii die Aprilis anno regni nostri vicesimo octauo.[20] Quam quidem cartam in omnibus punctis articulis condicionibus et modis

18 ac circumstanciis suis quibuscunque forma pariter et effectu in omnibus et per omnia approbamus ratificamus et pro nobis et heredibus nostris imperpetuum

19 confirmamus, saluo seruicio nostro. In cuius rei testimonium presenti carte confirmacionis nostre nostrum precipimus apponi sigillum. Testibus venerabili

---

[20] This is 12 April 1358; the charter would therefore be placed between *RRS*, vi, nos 180 and 181.

20 in Christo patre Willelmo episcopo Sanctiandree, Johanne primogeniti nostro comite de Carryk senescallo Scocie, Roberto comite de Fyff et de Menteth,
21 filio nostro dilecto, Willelmo comite de Dowglas, Johanne de Carryk cancellario nostro, Jacobo de Lyndesay nepote nostri, et Roberto de Erskyne,
22 militibus. Apud Insulam nostram de Combray vicesimo octauo die mensis Maii anno regni nostri quarto.[21] Post cuius quidem littere inspec-
23 tionem et euisdem perlectionem prefatus Johannes de Blar peciit a me notario publico sibi fieri super hiis publicum siue [sic] ipsam litteram sub forma
24 publica fideliter copiari. Acta fuerunt hec apud Salchy octauo die mensis Junii anno mense die indictione et pontificatu prenotatis.[22]
25 Presentibus viris prouidis et discretis, domino Willelmo de Cluny capellano, Jacobo de Schaw, et Henrico de Anand et Johanne Logane, testibus ad
26 premissa vocatis specialiter et rogatis.

[Notarial sign manual of Thomas Twy]

> Et ego Thomas Twy presbiter Sanctiandree diocesis publicus auctoritate apostolica notarius predictarum litterarum ostencionem et earundem perlectionem ac omnibus aliis et singulis dum sic ut premittitur fierent et agerentur una cum prenominatis testibus presens interfui eaque omnia et singula sic fieri vidi et audiui et in hanc publicam formam redegi ac propria manu mea scripsi signoque meo solito et consueto signaui rogatus et requisitus in testimonium premissorum.

---

[21] For an abbreviated text see *RMS*, i, no 479.
[22] There does not seem to be a pre-noted indiction, perhaps an oversight by Twy.

Bibliography

(a) Unpublished Primary Sources

Angus Archives
M/W1/10/1
M/W1/4/11

Bodleian Library, Oxford
MS Fairfax 23

British Library
Add Ch 16297
Harleian MS 4694
Royal MS 17 DXX

Edinburgh University Library
MS DC.7.63 (John Law, *De Cronicis Scotorum Brevia*; extracts printed in *ER*, v,
    pp. lxxxv–vi)

Glasgow City Archives
T-PM 2/3

Lambeth Palace Library
MS 167

National Library of Scotland
Acc 7043/16 (Adamton Charters)
Acc 7750/1 (Rutherford of Edgerston Charters)
Acc 12189 (Westraw and Pettinain Cartulary)
Adv Ch B 67
Adv Ch B 1316
Adv Ch B 1317
Adv MS 22.1.14
Adv MS 25.4.15
Ch 951 (Neilson Collection)
Ch 8814 (Callendar Papers)
Ch 15,554 (Fleming of Wigtown Muniments)

Dep.175 Box 184 no. 2 (Gordon Cumming of Altyre and Gordonstoun)
MS 1010 (Winton Cartulary)

National Records of Scotland
AD1/31, 42, 53 (printed Borthwick and MacQueen, *Juridical Review* (1986)), 60 (printed Borthwick and MacQueen, *Juridical Review* (1986)) (Lord Advocate's Department: Miscellaneous Charters)
CS7/430 (Register of Acts and Decreets)
GD8/1012 (Boyd Papers, Burgh of Kilmarnock)
GD10/14 (Murray of Broughton and Cally)
GD18/422 (Clerk of Penicuik)
GD25/1/33, 53, 61 (Ailsa Muniments)
GD26/3/1002 (Leven and Melville Muniments)
GD40/1/361 (Marquesses of Lothian (Newbattle Muniments), papers relating to the lands and barony of Fewrule, Roxburghshire)
GD44/13/10/3 (Dukes of Richmond and Gordon (Gordon Castle))
GD45/16/1517, 45/27/76, 77 (Dalhousie)
GD53/1 (Papers of the Elliot Family of Harwood, Roxburghshire)
GD75/4 (Dundas of Dundas)
GD86/9 (Fraser Charters)
GD97/2/13 (Edmondstone of Duntreath)
GD150/109 (Morton Muniments)
GD158/72 (Hume of Polwarth/Earls of Marchmont)
GD162/6/1/3 (Belhaven Muniments)
GD188/1/1/2 (Guthrie of Guthrie)
GD212/1/10, 126 (Maitland Thomson Papers)
GD236/77/1 (Dundas & Wilson CS)
GD350/1/949 (Borthwick of Borthwick)
GD466, formerly NRAS3094 (Dunbar of Westfield papers)
RH6/321, 325, 363A, 382, 396 (Register House Charters)
SP7/13/1 (Treaties with Norway, etc)

National Register of Archives for Scotland
NRAS387 (Kinloch-Smythe of Balhary), unsorted MSS.
NRAS631 (Bute)/Bundle A419
NRAS859 (Home)/Box 92/2 and Box 131/1
NRAS1100 (Roxburgh)/Bundles 621, 702, 703, 704, 1950
NRAS1275 (Buccleuch)/Bundle 538 (Crichton writs)
NRAS2516/1 (Prestwick Burgh Records)

(b) Published Primary Sources

Acta Dominorum Auditorum: The Acts of the Lords Auditors of Causes and Complaints, ed. Thomson, T. (Edinburgh, 1839)

BIBLIOGRAPHY

Acta Dominorum Concilii: The Acts of the Lords of Council in Civil Causes, eds Thomson, T. and others (Edinburgh, 1839, 1918, 1993)

Acts of the Lords of the Isles, eds Munro, J. and R.W. (Edinburgh, 1986)

Acts of the Parliaments of Scotland, eds Thomson, T. and Innes, C. (Edinburgh, 1814–75)

Annales Ecclesiae Aureliensis, by de la Saussey, Charles (Carolo Sausseyo) (Paris, 1615)

Auchinleck Chronicle, ed. McGladdery, C., Appendix, *James II*, 2nd edn (Edinburgh, 2015), pp. 261–76

Bracton De Legibus et Consuetudinibus Angliae, ed. Woodbine, G.E., trans. Thorne, S.E. (Cambridge, MA, 1968–77)

Buke of the Howlat, ed. Hanna, R. (Woodbridge, 2014)

Calendar of Documents relating to Scotland, eds Bain, J. and others (Edinburgh, 1881–1986)

Calendar of Papal Letters to Scotland of Benedict XIII of Avignon: 1394–1419, ed. McGurk, F. (Edinburgh, 1976)

Calendar of Papal Registers Relating to Great Britain and Ireland, eds Bliss, W.H. and others (1893-)

Calendar of Scottish Supplications to Rome, eds Lindsay, E.R. and others (Edinburgh and Glasgow, 1934, 1956, 1997, 2017)

Calendar of the Laing Charters 854–1837, ed. Anderson, J. (Edinburgh, 1899)

Charter Chest of the Earldom of Wigtown, ed. Grant, F.J. (Edinburgh, 1910)

Charters of the Friars Preachers of Ayr, ed. Cochran-Patrick, R.W. (AHCAG, 1881)

Charters and Writs concerning the Royal Burgh of Haddington. 1318–1543, ed. Wallace-James, J.G. (Haddington, 1895)

Charters and other Documents relating to the Royal Burgh of Stirling AD 1124–1707, ed. Renwick, R. (Glasgow, 1884)

Court Book of the Barony of Carnwath 1523–1542, ed. Dickinson, W.C. (Edinburgh, 1937)

David Hume of Godscroft's The History of the House of Douglas, ed. Reid, D., 2 vols (Edinburgh, 1996)

Deposition of Richard II: "The Record and Process of the Renunciation and Deposition of Richard II" (1399) and Related Writings, ed. Carlson, D.R. (Toronto, 2008)

'*The Dethe of the Kynge of Scotis*: A New Edition', ed. Connolly, M., *Scottish Historical Review* lxxi (1992), pp. 46–69

'*Discours Particulier d'Escosse*, 1559/60', ed. McNeill, P.G.B., in *Stair Miscellany II* (Edinburgh, 1984), pp. 86–131

Dundas of Dundas: Royal Letters and Family Papers, ed. Macleod, W., (Edinburgh, 1897)

Edward I and the Throne of Scotland 1290–1296: An Edition of the Record Sources for the Great Cause, eds Stones, E.L.G and Simpson, G.G. (Glasgow, 1978)

Exchequer Rolls of Scotland, eds Stuart, J. and others (Edinburgh, 1878–1908)

Foedera, Conventiones, Litterae et Cuiuscunque Generis Acta Publica, ed. Rymer, T., Record Commission edn (London, 1816–69)

Fraser, W., *The Scotts of Buccleuch* (Edinburgh, 1878)

———, *The Book of Carlaverock* (Edinburgh, 1873)

———, *The Douglas Book* (Edinburgh, 1885)

———, *The Melvilles Earls of Melville, and the Leslies Earls of Leven* (Edinburgh, 1890)

———, *The Red Book of Menteith* (Edinburgh, 1880)

———, *Memoirs of the Maxwells of Pollok* (Edinburgh, 1863); OR Fraser, W., *The Cartulary of Pollok-Maxwell* (Edinburgh, 1875)

Genealogical Deduction of the Family of Rose of Kilravock, ed. Innes, C. (Aberdeen, 1848)

History and Cronicles of Scotland by Robert Lindesay of Pitscottie, ed. Mackay, A.J.G., 3 vols (Edinburgh, 1899)

Illustrations of the Topography and Antiquities of the Shires of Aberdeen and Banff, ed. Robertson, J. (Aberdeen, 1847–69)

Issues of the Exchequer being payments made out of His Majesty's revenue from King Henry III to King Henry VI inclusive (1216–1461) with an appendix, Record Commission (London, 1837)

Jean de Wavrin, *Recueil des Chroniques et Anchiennes Istories de la Grant Bretagne à present nommé Engleterre*, eds Hardy, W. and E.P.C.L. (London, 1864–91, repr Cambridge, 2012)

Johannis de Fordun, *Chronica Gentis Scotorum*, ed. Skene, W.F. (Edinburgh, 1871–72)

BIBLIOGRAPHY

Joannis de Fordun Scotichronicon cum Supplementis et Continuatione Walteri Boweri Insulae Sancti Columbae Abbatis, ed. Goodall, W. (Edinburgh, 1759)

Jus Feudale Tribus Libris Comprehensum by Thomas Craig of Riccarton (Edinburgh, 1655; Leipzig, 1716; Edinburgh, 1732); trans. Lord Clyde (Edinburgh, 1933). Note a new edition ed. and trans. L. Dodd has begun with the publication of Book I (Edinburgh, 2017)

Laws of Medieval Scotland: Legal Compilations from the Thirteenth and Fourteenth Centuries, ed. Taylor, A. (Edinburgh, 2019)

'Letter of James III to the Duke of Burgundy', ed. Armstrong, C.A.J., in *Scottish History Society Miscellany VIII* (Edinburgh, 1951)

Letters and Papers Illustrative of the Wars of the English in France, temp. Henry VI, ed. Stevenson, J. (London, 1861)

Liber de Judicibus, as cited in *Practicks of Sir James Balfour of Pittendreich* (below), i, p. 126 (c V)

Libri Feudorum: Vulgata, transcribed by Stella, A., in *Civil Law, Common Law, Customary Law Project Publications*, St Andrews, 2019 [https://clicme.wp.st-andrews.ac.uk/online-texts/libri-feudorum-vulgata]

Original Chronicle of Andrew of Wyntoun, ed. Amours, F.J. (Edinburgh, 1903–14)

Orygynale Cronykil of Scotland by Androw of Wyntoun, ed. Laing, D. (Edinburgh, 1872–79)

Practicks of Sir James Balfour of Pittendreich, ed. McNeill, P.G.B. (Edinburgh, 1962–63)

Protocol Book of James Young, 1485–1515, ed. Donaldson, G. (Edinburgh,1952)

Regesta Regum Scottorum, eds Barrow, G.W.S. and others (Edinburgh, 1960–)

Regiam Majestatem (*APS*, i, pp. 597–641; *Regiam Majestatem and Quoniam Attachiamenta*, ed. Cooper, T.M. (Lord) (Edinburgh, 1947)

Registrum de Dunfermelyn, ed. Innes, C. (Edinburgh, 1842)

Registrum Episcopatus Glasguensis, ed. Innes, C. (Edinburgh, 1843)

Registrum Honoris de Morton, eds Thomson, T. and others (Edinburgh, 1853)

Registrum Magni Sigilli Regum Scotorum, eds Thomson, J.M. and others (Edinburgh, 1882–1914)

Registrum Monasterii de Passelet, ed. Innes, C. (Glasgow, 1832; Edinburgh, 1877)

Rotuli Scotiae in Turri Londinensi et in Domo Capitulari Westmonasteriense Asservati, eds Macpherson, D. and others (London, 1814–19)

Scotichronicon by Walter Bower, eds Watt, D.E.R. and others (Aberdeen and Edinburgh, 1993–98)

Scottish Formularies, ed. Duncan, A.A.M. (Edinburgh, 2011)

Statutis and Use of Merchis in Tym of Were, APS, i, pp. 714–16

Three Fifteenth-Century Chronicles, ed. Gairdner, J. (London, 1880)

Tractatus de Legibus et Consuetudinibus Regni Anglie qui Glanvilla Vocatur, ed. Hall, G.D.G. (London, 1965)

Wigtownshire Charters, ed. Reid, R.C. (Edinburgh, 1960)

(c) Reference Works and Websites

Cambridge Dictionary of English Place-Names, eds Watts, V.E. and others (Cambridge, 2004)

Dictionaries of the Scots Language (DSL), accessible at *https://dsl.ac.uk/*

Fasti Ecclesiae Scoticanae Medii Aevi Ad Annum 1638, revised edn, eds Watt, D.E.R. and Murray, A.L. (Edinburgh, 2003)

Groome, F.H., *Ordnance Gazetteer of Scotland: A Graphic and Accurate Description of Every Place in Scotland*, new edn (Edinburgh, 1901)

Historic Environment Scotland, Canmore, accessible online at *https://www.historicenvironment.scot/archives-and-research/archives-and-collections/national-record-of-the-historic-environment/*

Internet Archive, accessible online at *https://archive.org/*

Medieval and Early Modern Sources Online (MEMSO), accessible online at *https://tannerritchie.com/memso/* (subscription service)

Oxford Dictionary of National Biography (*ODNB*), accessible online at *https://www.oxforddnb.com/* (subscription service)

The Parishes of Medieval Scotland, ed. Cowan, I.B. (Edinburgh, 1967)

The Parliaments of Scotland: Burgh and Shire Commissioners, ed. Young, M.D. (Edinburgh, 1992–93)

Records of the Parliaments of Scotland (*RPS*), accessible online at *https://www.rps.ac.uk/*

Roy Maps, accessible online at *http://maps.nls.uk/roy/index.html*

The Scots Peerage, ed. Balfour Paul, Sir J (Edinburgh, 1904–14)

Stell, G.P., *Exploring Scotland's Heritage: Dumfries and Galloway* (Edinburgh, 1986)

Topographical Dictionary of Scotland, and of the Islands in the British Seas, ed. Carlisle, N. (London, 1813)

(d) Secondary Sources

Adams., P, *A History of the Douglas Family of Morton in Nithsdale (Dumfriesshire) and Fingland (Kirkcudbrightshire) and their descendants* (Bedford, 1921)

Armstrong, J.W., '"Malice" and motivation for hostility in the burgh courts of late medieval Aberdeen', in Armstrong, J.W. and Frankot, E. (eds), *Cultures of Law in Urban Northern Europe: Scotland and Its Neighbours c.1350–c.1650* (London, 2020), pp. 207–23

Anderson, J., *Historical and Genealogical Memoirs of the House of Hamilton, with Genealogical Memoirs of the several branches of the family* (Edinburgh, 1825)

Baker, Sir John, *The Reinvention of Magna Carta 1216–1616* (Cambridge, 2017)

Balfour-Melville, E.W.M., *James I, King of Scots 1406–1437* (London, 1936)

Barrow, G.W.S., *Robert Bruce and the Community of the Realm*, 4th edn (Edinburgh, 2004)

Beam, A., *The Balliol Dynasty 1210–1364* (Edinburgh, 2008)

Blakeway, A., *Regency in Sixteenth Century Scotland* (Woodbridge, 2015)

Boardman, S., 'The Man Who Would Be King: The Lieutenancy and Death of David, Duke of Rothesay, 1378–1402', in Mason, R. and Macdougall, N., (eds), *People and Power in Scotland; Essays in Honour of T C Smout* (Edinburgh, 1992), pp. 1–27

———, *The Early Stewart Kings: Robert II and Robert III 1371–1406* (East Linton, 1996)

———, 'Lordship in the North-East: The Badenoch Stewarts I: Alexander Stewart, Earl of Buchan, Lord of Badenoch', *Northern Scotland* xvi (1996), pp. 1–29

———, 'Coronations, Kings and Guardians: Politics, Parliaments and General Councils, 1371–1406', in Brown, K.M. and Tanner, R.J., (eds), *The History of the Scottish Parliament volume I: Parliament and Politics in Scotland 1235–1560* (Edinburgh, 2004), pp. 102–22

———, 'Stewart, David, Duke of Rothesay, (1378–1402)', *Oxford Dictionary of National Biography* (Oxford, 2004) [*https://doi.org/10.1093/ref:odnb/26468*]

———, 'A Saintly Sinner? The Martyrdom of David, Duke of Rothesay', in Boardman, S. and Williamson, E., (eds), *The Cult of Saints and the Virgin Mary in Medieval Scotland* (Woodbridge, 2010), pp. 87–104

Borthwick, A.R., 'The King, Council and Councillors in Scotland, c.1430–1460', 2 vols (Edinburgh University PhD, 1989)

———, 'Borthwick family (*per. c.*1400–*c.*1515)', *Oxford Dictionary of National Biography* (Oxford, 2004) [*https://doi.org/10.1093/ref:odnb/54135*]

———, 'Crichton, William of that ilk, first lord Crichton (*d.*1453)', *Oxford Dictionary of National Biography* (Oxford, 2004) [*https://doi.org/10.1093/ref:odnb/6701*]

———, 'Douglas, George, fourth earl of Angus (c.1417–1463)', *Oxford Dictionary of National Biography* (Oxford, 2004) [*https://doi.org/10.1093/ref:odnb/7884*]

———, 'Douglas, James, ninth earl of Douglas and third earl of Avondale c.1425–1491', *Oxford Dictionary of National Biography* (Oxford, 2004) [*https://doi.org/10.1093/ref:odnb/7892*]

———, 'Hamilton family (*per.* 1295–1479)', *Oxford Dictionary of National Biography* (Oxford, 2004) [*https://doi.org/10.1093/ref:odnb/54222*]

———, 'Livingston, Alexander, of Callander (*b.*c.1375, *d.* in or before 1456)', *Oxford Dictionary of National Biography* (Oxford, 2004) [*https://doi.org/10.1093/ref:odnb/16800*]

Borthwick, A. and MacQueen, H., 'Three Fifteenth-Century Cases', *Juridical Review* 31 (1986), pp. 123–51

———, ''Rare creatures for their age': Alexander and David Guthrie, Graduate Lairds and Royal Servants', in Crawford, B.E., (ed.), *Church, Chronicle and Learning in Medieval and Early Renaissance Scotland* (Edinburgh, 1999), pp. 227–39

———, 'Another Fifteenth-Century Case', in *Stair Miscellany VII*, ed. MacQueen, H.L. (Edinburgh, 2015), pp. 133–62

———, 'Law, Tenure and Douglas Lordship: A Fifteenth-Century Case Study', in Boardman, S., and Ditchburn, D., (eds), *Kingship, Lordship and Sanctity in Medieval Britain: Essays in honour of Alexander Grant* (Woodbridge, 2022), pp. 176-209

Brown, M., *James I* (Edinburgh, 1994)

———, 'Regional Lordship in North-East Scotland; The Badenoch Stewarts II: Alexander Stewart Earl of Mar', *Northern Scotland* xvi (1996), pp. 31–53

———, '"I have thus slain a tyrant": The Dethe of the Kynge of Scotis and the Right to Resist in Early Fifteenth-Century Scotland', *Innes Review* 47 (1996), pp. 24–44

———, *The Black Douglases: War and Lordship in Late Medieval Scotland 1300–1455* (East Linton, 1998)

———, 'Public Authority and Factional Conflict: Crown, Parliament and Polity, 1424–1455', in Brown, K.M. and Tanner, R.J., (eds), *The History of the Scottish Parliament volume I: Parliament and Politics in Scotland 1235–1560* (Edinburgh, 2004), pp. 123–44

———, 'War, Allegiance, and Community in the Anglo-Scottish Marches: Teviotdale in the Fourteenth Century', *Northern History* 41 (2004), pp. 219–38

———, 'Cameron, John (d.1446)', *Oxford Dictionary of National Biography* (Oxford, 2004) [*https://doi.org/10.1093/ref:odnb/4443*]

———, 'Douglas, James, of Balvenie [*called* James the Gross], seventh earl of Douglas and first earl of Avondale (d. 1443)', *Oxford Dictionary of National Biography* (Oxford, 2004) [*https://doi.org/10.1093/ref:odnb/7891*]

———, 'Graham, Malise, third Earl of Strathearn and first Earl of Menteith (1406x13–1490)', *Oxford Dictionary of National Biography* (Oxford, 2004) [*https://doi.org/10.1093/ref:odnb/54217*]

———, 'French Alliance or English Peace? Scotland and the Last Phase of the Hundred Years War, 1415–53', in Clark, L., (ed.), *The Fifteenth Century VII: Conflicts, Consequences and the Crown in the Late Middle Ages* (Woodbridge, 2007), pp. 81–99

———, 'The Scottish March Wardenships (c.1340–c.1480)', in King, A. and Simpkin, D., (eds), *England and Scotland at War, c.1296–c.1513* (Leiden, 2012), pp. 203–29

———, 'The Great Rupture: Lordship and Politics in North-east Scotland', *Northern Scotland* 5 (2014), pp. 1–25

———, 'The Lanark Bond', in Boardman, S. and Goodare, J., (eds), *Kings, Lords and Men in Scotland and Britain, 1300–1625: Essays in Honour of Jenny Wormald* (Edinburgh, 2014), pp. 227–45

———, '"Lele consail for the comoun profite': Kings, Guardians and Councils in the Scottish Kingdom, c.1250–1450', in Rose, J., (ed.), *The Politics of Counsel in England and Scotland 1286–1707* (Oxford, 2016), pp. 45–61

———, 'War, Marriage, Tournament: Scottish Politics and the Anglo-French War, 1448–1450', *Scottish Historical Review* xcviii (2019), pp. 1–21

Buchan, J.W., *A History of Peebles-shire* (Glasgow, 1927)

Cameron, J., *James V: The Personal Rule, 1528–1542* (East Linton, 1998)

Cathcart, A., '"Inressyng of Kyndnes, and Renewing Off Thair Blud': The Family, Kinship and Clan Policy in Sixteenth-Century Scottish Gaeldom', in Ewan, E. and Nugent, J., (eds), *Finding the Family in Medieval and Early Modern Scotland* (Aldershot, 2008), pp. 127–38

Clancy, T.O. and Hammond, M., 'The Romance of Names: Literary Personal Names in Twelfth- and Thirteenth-Century Scotland', in Hammond, M., (ed.), *Personal Names and Naming Practices in Medieval Scotland* (Woodbridge, 2019), pp. 166–86

Cornell, D., 'A Kingdom Cleared of Castles: the Role of the Castle in the Campaigns of Robert Bruce', *Scottish Historical Review* lxxxvii (2008), pp. 233–57

Cowan, E.J., *The Declaration of Arbroath: 'For Freedom Alone'* (Edinburgh, 2020)

Cox, J., 'The Lindsay Earls of Crawford: The Heads of the Lindsay Family in Late Medieval Scottish Politics, 1380–1453' (Edinburgh University PhD, 2009)

Crawford, B.E., *The Northern Earldoms: Orkney and Caithness from AD 870 to 1470* (Edinburgh, 2013)

Dickinson, W.C., 'An Inquiry into the Origin and Nature of the Title Prince of Scotland', *Economica* 11 (1924), pp. 212–20

———, 'Freehold in Scots Law', *Juridical Review* 57 (1945), pp. 135–51

Ditcham, B.G.H., 'The Employment of Foreign Mercenary Troops in the French Royal Armies, 1415–1470' (Edinburgh University PhD, 1978)

Ditchburn, D., *Scotland and Europe: The Medieval Kingdom and Its Contacts with Christendom, 1214–1560* (East Linton, 2000)

Donaldson, G., *Scottish Kings* 2nd edn (London, 1977)

Downie, F., "'La voie quelle menace tenir': Annabella Stewart, Scotland, and the European Marriage Market, 1444–56', *Scottish Historical Review* lxxviii (1999), pp. 170–91

———, *'She is but a woman': Queenship in Scotland 1424–1463* (Edinburgh, 2006)

Dunlop, A.I., *The Life and Times of James Kennedy Bishop of St Andrews* (Edinburgh, 1950)

Durkan, J., *William Turnbull Bishop of Glasgow* (Glasgow, 1951)

———, 'The Early Scottish Notary', in Cowan, I.B. and Shaw, D., (eds), *The Renaissance and Reformation in Scotland: Essays in Honour of Gordon Donaldson* (Edinburgh, 1983), pp. 22–40

Finlay, J., *Men of Law in Pre-Reformation Scotland* (East Linton, 2000)

Fisk, C.L., '&: Law_Society in Legal History Research', in Dubber, M.D. and Tomlins, C., (eds), *The Oxford Handbook of Legal History* (Oxford, 2018), ch 26 (DOI: 10.1093/oxfordhb/9780198794356.013.26)

Fletcher, C.D., 'Narrative and Political Strategies at the Deposition of Richard II', *Journal of Medieval History* 30 (2004), pp. 323–41

Forbes-Leith, W., *The Scots Men-at-Arms and Life-guards in France: from their Formation until their Final Dissolution A.D. MCCCCXVIII–MDCCCXXX* (Edinburgh, 1882)

Giddens, A., *The Constitution of Society* (Cambridge, 1984)

Gilbert, J.M., *Hunting and Hunting Reserves in Medieval Scotland* (Edinburgh, 1979)

Godfrey, A.M., *Civil Justice in Renaissance Scotland: The Origins of a Central Court* (Leiden, 2009)

———, 'Parliament and the Law', in Brown, K.M. and MacDonald, A.R., (eds), *The History of the Scottish Parliament volume 3: Parliament in Context 1235–1707* (Edinburgh, 2010), pp. 157–85

———, 'Rethinking the Justice of the Feud in Sixteenth-Century Scotland', in Boardman, S. and Goodare, J., (eds), *Kings, Lords and Men in Scotland and Britain, 1300–1625: Essays in Honour of Jenny Wormald* (Edinburgh, 2014), pp. 136–54

Gordon, R.W., 'Critical Legal Histories Revisited: A Response', *Law & Social Inquiry* 37 (2012), pp. 200–15

———, 'Critical Legal Histories', *Stanford Law Review* 36 (1984), pp. 57–126

Grant, A., 'The Higher Nobility in Scotland and their Estates, c.1371–1424' (University of Oxford DPhil, 1975)

——, 'Earls and Earldoms in Late Medieval Scotland (c.1310–1460)', in Bossy, J. and Jupp, P., (eds), *Essays presented to Michael Roberts* (Belfast, 1976), pp. 24–40

——, 'The Development of the Scottish Peerage', *Scottish Historical Review* lvii (1978), pp. 1–27

——, 'The Revolt of the Lord of the Isles and the Death of the Earl of Douglas, 1451–1452', *Scottish Historical Review* lx (1981), pp. 169–74

——, *Independence and Nationhood: Scotland 1306–1469* (London, 1984)

——, 'Extinction of Direct Male Lines among Scottish Noble Families in the Fourteenth and Fifteenth Centuries', in Stringer, K.J., (ed.), *Essays on the Nobility of Medieval Scotland* (Edinburgh, 1985), pp. 210–31

——, 'Scotland's 'Celtic Fringe' in the Late Middle Ages', in Davies, R.R., (ed.), *The British Isles 1100–1500: Comparisons Contrasts and Connections* (Edinburgh, 1988), pp. 118–41

——, 'The Otterburn War from the Scottish Point of View', in Goodman, A. and Tuck, A., (eds), *War and Border Societies in the Middle Ages* (London, 1992), pp. 30–64

——, 'The Wolf of Badenoch', in Sellar, W.D.H., (ed.), *Moray: Province and People* (Edinburgh, 1993), pp. 143–61

——, 'To the Medieval Foundations', *Scottish Historical Review* 73 (1994), pp. 4–24

——, 'Disaster at Neville's Cross: The Scottish Point of View', in Rollason, D. and Prestwich, M., (eds), *The Battle of Neville's Cross 1346* (Stamford, 1998), pp. 15–35

——, 'Acts of Lordship: The Records of Archibald, Fourth Earl of Douglas', in Brotherstone, T. and Ditchburn, D., (eds), *Freedom and Authority: Historical and Historiographical Essays presented to Grant G Simpson* (East Linton, 2000), pp. 235–74

——, 'Service and Tenure in Late Medieval Scotland, 1314–1475', in Curry, A. and Matthew, E., (eds), *Concepts and Patterns of Service in the Later Middle Ages* (Woodbridge, 2003), pp. 145–79

——, 'Franchises North of the Border: Baronies and Regalities in Medieval Scotland', in Prestwich, M., (ed.), *Liberties and Identities in the Medieval British Isles* (Cambridge, 2008), pp. 155–99

———, 'Murder Will Out: Kingship, Kinship and Killing in Medieval Scotland', in Boardman, S. and Goodare, J., (eds), *Kings, Lords and Men in Scotland and Britain, 1300–1625: Essays in Honour of Jenny Wormald* (Edinburgh, 2014), pp. 193–226

———, 'Royal and Magnate Bastards in the Later Middle Ages: The View from Scotland', in Bousmar, É., Marchandisse, A., Masson, C., and Schnerb, B., (eds), *La bâtardise et l'exercice du pouvoir (XIIIe–début XVIe siècle)* (Lille, 2015), pp. 313–67

Griffiths, R.A., 'Henry VI (1421–1471)', *Oxford Dictionary of National Biography* (Oxford, 2004) [https://doi.org/10.1093/ref:odnb/12953]

Halliday, S., 'After Hegemony? The Varieties of Legal Consciousness Research', *Social and Legal Studies* 28 (2019), pp. 859–78

Hamilton, G., *A History of the House of Hamilton* (Edinburgh, 1933)

Hannay, R.K., 'On 'Parliament' and 'General Council'', *Scottish Historical Review* xviii (1921), pp. 157–70, reprinted in *The College of Justice: Essays by R K Hannay*, ed. MacQueen, H.L. (Edinburgh, 1990), pp. 217–30

Hawes, C., ''Perverst Counsale'? Rebellion, Satire and the Politics of Advice in Fifteenth-Century Scotland', in Rose, J., (ed.), *The Politics of Counsel in England and Scotland 1286–1707* (Oxford, 2016), pp. 117–34

Helmholz, R.H., 'The Medieval Canon Law in Scotland: Marriage and Divorce', in Godfrey, A.M., (ed.), *Stair Miscellany VIII* (Edinburgh, 2020), pp. 95–112

The History of the Scottish Parliament volume I: Parliament and Politics in Scotland 1235–1560, eds Brown, K.M. and Tanner, R.J. (Edinburgh, 2004)

Hudson, J., *The Oxford History of the Laws of England Volume II 871–1216* (Oxford, 2012)

Hunt, K., 'The Governorship of Robert Duke of Albany (1406–1420)', in Brown, M. and Tanner, R., (eds), *Scottish Kingship 1306–1542: Essays in Honour of Norman Macdougall* (Edinburgh, 2008), pp. 126–54

Hunter, J., 'The House of John Blair: a Medieval Town-House in Ayr', *AANHS* 11(6) (1976), pp. 111–32

An Introduction to Scottish Legal History, ed. Paton, G.C.H. (Edinburgh, 1958)

Johnson, L., *The Shadow King: The Life and Death of Henry VI* (London, 2019)

Johnston, T., *Law in Common: Legal Cultures in Late-Medieval England* (Oxford: Oxford University Press, 2020)

Kennedy, C., 'Sociology of Law and Legal History', in Přibáň, J., (ed.), *Research Handbook on the Sociology of Law* (Cheltenham, 2020), pp. 31–42

Keppie, L., *The Legacy of Rome: Scotland's Roman Remains* (Edinburgh, 2004)

Kilgallon, L., 'Communal Authority, Counsel and Resistance in the Reign of James I: A Conceptual Approach', *Scottish Historical Review* 100 (2021), pp. 1–24

Kings, Lords and Men in Scotland and Britain, 1300–1625: Essays in Honour of Jenny Wormald, eds Boardman, S. and Goodare, J. (Edinburgh, 2014)

Laing, D., 'Historical Notices of the Family of King James the First of Scotland, Chiefly from Information Communicated by John Riddell, Esq, Advocate', *Proceedings of the Society of Antiquaries of Scotland* 3 (1862), pp. 88–101

Lane, S., 'The Bishops and the Deposition of Edward II', *Studies in Church History* 56 (2020), pp. 131–51

Lyall, R.J., 'The Medieval Scottish Coronation Service: Some Seventeenth Century Evidence', *Innes Review* 28 (1977), pp. 3–21

McAndrew, B., 'Heraldic Investigations anent Early Murray Genealogy', *Proceedings of the Society of Antiquaries of Scotland* 140 (2010), pp. 145–64

Macdonald, A.J., *Border Bloodshed: Scotland and England at War 1369–1403* (East Linton, 2000)

———, 'Profit, Politics and Personality: War and the Later Medieval Scottish Nobility', in Brotherstone, T. and Ditchburn, D., (eds), *Freedom and Authority: Historical and Historiographical Essays presented to Grant G Simpson* (East Linton, 2000), pp. 118–30

Macdougall, N., *James III*, 2nd edn (Edinburgh, 2009)

McGladdery, C., 'Seton family, per c.1300–c.1510', *Oxford Dictionary of National Biography* (Oxford, 2004) [https://doi.org/10.1093/ref:odnb/54318]

———, 'The Black Douglases, 1369–1455', in Oram, R.D. and Stell, G.P., (eds), *Lordship and Architecture in Medieval and Renaissance Scotland* (Edinburgh, 2005), pp. 161–87

———, *James II*, 2nd edn (Edinburgh, 2015)

Mackay Mackenzie, W., *The Mediaeval Castle in Scotland* (London, 1927)

McNeill, P.G.B., 'The Scottish Regency', *Juridical Review* 12 (1967), pp. 127–48

MacQuarrie, A., *Scotland and the Crusades 1095–1560* (Edinburgh, 1997)

MacQueen, H.L., *Common Law and Feudal Society in Medieval Scotland* (Edinburgh, 1993, repr 2016)

———, 'The Kin of Kennedy, Kenkynnol and the Common Law', in Grant, A. and Stringer, K., (eds), *Medieval Scotland: Crown, Lordship and Community: Essays Presented to G W S Barrow* (Edinburgh, 1993), pp. 274–96

———, 'Survival and Success: the Kennedys of Dunure', in Boardman, S. and Ross, A., (eds), *The Exercise of Power in Medieval Scotland c.1200–1500* (Dublin, 2003), pp. 67–94

———, 'The King's Council and Church Courts in Later Medieval Scotland', in Dondorp, H., Hallebeek, J., Wallinga, T., and Winkel, L., (eds), *Ius Romanum – Ius Commune – Ius Hodiernum: Studies in Honour of Eltjo J H Schrage on the Occasion of his 65th Birthday* (Amsterdam, 2010), pp. 277–87

———, 'Tame Magnates? The Justiciars of Later Medieval Scotland', in Boardman, S. and Goodare, J., (eds), *Kings, Lords and Men in Scotland and Britain, 1300–1625: Essays in Honour of Jenny Wormald* (Edinburgh, 2014), pp. 93–117

———, 'Magna Carta, Scotland and Scots Law', *Law Quarterly Review* 134 (2018), pp. 94–116

Madden, C., 'Royal Treatment of Feudal Casualties in Late Medieval Scotland', *Scottish Historical Review* lv (1976), pp. 172–94

Maitland, F.W., 'Why the History of English Law is Not Written', in Fisher, H.A.L., (eds), *The Collected Papers of Frederic William Maitland, Downing Professor of the Laws of England*, 3 vols (Cambridge, 1911), i, pp. 480–97

Marshall, S., *Illegitimacy in Medieval Scotland 1100–1500* (Woodbridge, 2021)

Mason, R.A., *Kingship and the Commonweal: Political Thought in Renaissance and Reformation Scotland* (East Linton, 1998)

———, 'Beyond the Declaration of Arbroath: Kingship, Counsel and Consent in Late Medieval and Early Modern Scotland', in Boardman, S. and Goodare, J., (eds), *Kings, Lords and Men in Scotland and Britain, 1300–1625: Essays in Honour of Jenny Wormald* (Edinburgh, 2014), pp. 265–82

Maxtone Graham, R.M., 'Showing the Holding', *Juridical Review* 2 (1957), pp. 251–69

Maxwell-Irving, A.M.T., *The Border Towers of Scotland: Their History and Architecture - The West March (Dumfriesshire & Eastern Galloway)* (Stirling, 2000)

Munro, R., *The James Plays* (London, 2014)

Neilson, G., 'Magna Carta Re-Read', *Juridical Review* 17 (1905), pp. 128–44

Neilson, G., 'The March Laws', in *Stair Miscellany I* (Edinburgh, 1970), pp. 12–77

Nicholson, R., *Edward III and the Scots* (Oxford, 1965)

———, 'Feudal Developments in Late Medieval Scotland', *Juridical Review* 18 (1973), pp. 1–21

———, *Scotland: The Later Middle Ages* (Edinburgh, 1974)

Ollivant, S.D., *The Court of the Official in Scotland* (Edinburgh, 1982)

Oram, R.D., 'The Making and Breaking of a Comital Family: Malcolm Fleming, First Earl of Wigtown, and Thomas Fleming, Second Earl of Wigtown', *International Review of Scottish Studies* 42 (2017), pp. 1–58

Parker, H., ''In all gudly haste': The Formation of Marriage in Scotland, c.1350–1600' (University of Guelph PhD, 2012)

———, 'Family, Finance and Free Will: Marriage Contracts in Scotland, c.1380–1500', *Scottish Archives* 18 (2012), pp. 10–24

———, ''At thair perfect age': Elite Child Betrothal and Parental Control, 1430–1560', in Nugent, J. and Ewan, E., (eds), *Children and Youth in Premodern Scotland* (Woodbridge, 2015), pp. 173–86

Paterson, J., *History of the County of Ayr with a Genealogical Account of the Families of Ayrshire*, 2 vols (Edinburgh, 1847–52)

Penman, M., *David II, 1329–71* (East Linton, 2004)

———, '*Diffinicione successionis ad regnum Scottorum*: Royal Succession in Scotland in the Later Middle Ages', in Lechaud, F. and Penman, M., (eds), *Making and Breaking the Rules: Succession in Medieval Europe, c.1000-c.1600* (Turnhout, 2008), pp. 43–59

———, *Robert Bruce King of the Scots* (New Haven, 2014)

———, 'The Lion Captive: Scottish Royals as Prisoners of England, c.1070-c.1424', *Quaestiones Medii Aevi Novae* 20 (2015), pp. 413–34

Pinkerton, J., *The History of Scotland from the Accession of the House of Stuart to that of Mary; with Appendices of Original Papers* (London, 1797)

The Politics of Counsel in England and Scotland 1286–1707, ed. Rose, J. (Oxford, 2016)

Pollock, F. and Maitland, F.W., *The History of English Law before the Time of Edward I*, 2nd edn (Cambridge, 1898)

Powell, E., 'Lancastrian England', in Allmand, C.T., (ed.), *The New Cambridge Medieval History VII c.1415-c.1500* (Cambridge, 1998), pp. 457–76

Ramage, C.T., *Drumlanrig Castle and the Douglases* (Dumfries, 1876)

Reid, N.H., 'Margaret 'Maid of Norway' and Scottish Queenship', *Reading Medieval Studies* viii (1982), pp. 75–96

———, *Alexander III 1249–1286: First Among Equals* (Edinburgh, 2019)

Reid, N. and Penman, M., 'Guardian-Lieutenant-Governor: Absentee Monarchy and Proxy Power in Scotland's Long Fourteenth Century', in Pechaud, M. and Penman, M., (eds), *Absentee Authority Across Europe* (Woodbridge, 2017), pp. 191–218

Reid, R.C., 'An Early Coschogill Writ', *Transactions of the Dumfries-shire and Galloway Natural History and Antiquarian Society* 30 (1951–52), pp. 132–42

———, 'The Border Grahams, their Origin and Distribution', *Transactions of the Dumfries-shire and Galloway Natural History and Antiquarian Society* 38 (1959–60), pp. 85–113

Reid, T., *History of the Parish of Crawfordjohn, Upper Ward of Lanarkshire, 1153–1928* (Edinburgh, 1928)

Scotland and the Flemish People, eds Fleming, A. and Mason, R. (Edinburgh, 2019)

Scott, W., 'William Cranston, Notary Public c.1395 to 1425, and Some Contemporaries', in MacQueen, H.L., (ed.), *Stair Miscellany VII* (Edinburgh, 2015), pp. 125–32

Sellar, W.D.H., 'Review of *Essays on the Nobility of Medieval Scotland* ed K J Stringer (1985)', *Scottish Historical Review* lxvi (1987), pp. 200–03

———, 'Forethocht Felony, Malice Aforethought and the Classification of Homicide', in Gordon, W.M. and Fergus, T.D., (eds), *Legal History in the Making: Proceedings of the Ninth British Legal History Conference, Glasgow 1989* (London, 1991), pp. 43–59

———, 'Marriage by Cohabitation with Habit and Repute: Review and Requiem?', in Carey Miller, D.L. and Meyers, D.W., (eds), *Comparative and Historical Essays in Scots Law: A Tribute to Professor Sir Thomas Smith QC* (Edinburgh, 1992), pp. 117–36

———, 'Marriage, Divorce and the Forbidden Degrees: Canon Law and Scots Law', in Osborough, W.N., (ed.), *Explorations in Law and History: Irish Legal History Society Discourses, 1988–1994* (Blackrock, 1995), pp. 59–82

———, *Continuity, Influences and Integration in Scottish Legal History: Select Essays of David Sellar*, ed. MacQueen, H.L., (Edinburgh, 2022)

———, 'Was it Murder? John Comyn of Badenoch and William, Earl of Douglas', in Kay, C.J. and Mackay, M.A., (eds), *Perspectives on the Older Scottish Tongue* (Edinburgh, 2005), pp. 132–38

———, 'Succession Law in Scotland – A Historical Perspective', in Reid, K.G.C., de Waal, M. and Zimmermann, R., (eds), *Exploring the Law of Succession: Studies National, Historical and Comparative* (Edinburgh, 2007), pp. 49–66

Simpson, A.R.C., 'Men of Law in the Aberdeen Council Register? A Preliminary Study, circa 1450–1460' *Juridical Review* [2019], pp. 136–59

———, 'Andrew Alanson: Man of Law in the Aberdeen Council Register, c.1440-c.1475?', in Armstrong, J.W. and Frankot, E., (eds), *Cultures of Law in Urban Northern Europe: Scotland and Its Neighbours c.1350-c.1650* (London, 2020), pp. 247–66

———, 'Earth and Stone: History, Law and Land through the Lens of Sasine', in Combe, M. M., Glass, J. and Tindley, A., (eds), *Land Reform in Scotland: History, Law and Policy* (Edinburgh, 2020), pp. 113-53

Smith, J. Irvine, 'Succession', in Paton, G.C.H., (ed.), *An Introduction to Scottish Legal History* (Edinburgh, 1958), pp. 208–21

Stell, G.P., 'Balliol, Henry de (d. 1246)', *Oxford Dictionary of National Biography* (Oxford, 2004) [*https://doi.org/10.1093/ref:odnb/1207*]

———, 'Balliol, Alexander de (d. 1310?)', *Oxford Dictionary of National Biography* (Oxford, 2004) [*https://doi.org/10.1093/ref:odnb/1203*]

Stevenson, D., 'Graham, James, first marquess of Montrose (1612–1650)', *Oxford Dictionary of National Biography* (Oxford, 2004) [*https://doi.org/10.1093/ref:odnb/11194*]

Stevenson, K., *Chivalry and Knighthood in Scotland, 1424–1513* (Woodbridge, 2006)

Sumption, J., *Cursed Kings: The Hundred Years War IV* (London, 2015)

Sumption, Lord, 'Anglo-Scottish Relations, 1290–1513, and the Beginnings of International Law', in Godfrey, A.M., (ed.), *Stair Miscellany VIII* (Edinburgh, 2020), pp. 1–12

Tancred, G., *Rulewater and its People* (Edinburgh, 1907)

Tanner, R., '"I arest you, sir, in the name of the three astattes in perlement": The Scottish Parliament and Resistance to the Crown in the Fifteenth Century', in Thornton, T., (ed.), *Social Attitudes and Political Structures in the Fifteenth Century* (Stroud, 2000), pp. 101–17

———, *The Late Medieval Scottish Parliament: Politics and the Three Estates, 1424–1488* (East Linton, 2001)

Taylor, A., *The Shape of the State in Medieval Scotland, 1124–1290* (Oxford, 2016)

Theilmann, J.M., 'Caught between Political Theory and Political Practice: 'The Record and Process of the Renunciation and Deposition of Richard II', *History of Political Thought* 25 (2004), pp. 600–19

Tomlins, C., 'Historicism and Materiality in Legal Theory', in Del Mar, M. and Lobban, M., (eds), *Law in Theory and History: New Essays on a Neglected Dialogue* (Oxford, 2016), pp. 57–83

Tytler, P.F., *The History of Scotland from the Accession of Alexander III to the Union* (Edinburgh, 1887)

Valente, C., 'The Deposition and Abdication of Edward II', *English Historical Review*, 113 (1998), pp. 852–81

Watson, F., 'Donald, eighth earl of Mar (1293–1332)', *Oxford Dictionary of National Biography* (Oxford, 2004) [*https://doi.org/10.1093/ref:odnb/18021*]

Watson, W.J., *The History of the Celtic Place-Names of Scotland* (Edinburgh, 1926)

Webster, B., 'The English Occupations of Dumfriesshire in the Fourteenth Century', *Transactions of the Dumfries-shire and Galloway Natural History and Antiquarian Society* 35 (1956–57), pp. 64–79

Weiss, R., 'The Earliest Account of the Murder of James I of Scotland', *English Historical Review* 52 (1937), pp. 479–91

Willock, I.D., *The Origins and Development of the Jury in Scotland* (Edinburgh, 1966)

Wormald, J., *Lords and Men in Scotland: Bonds of Manrent 1442–1603* (Edinburgh, 1985)

———, 'National Pride, Decentralised Nation: The Political Culture of Fifteenth-Century Scotland', in Clark, L. and Carpenter, C., (eds), *Political Culture in Late Medieval Britain* (Woodbridge, 2004), pp. 181–94

Yeoman, P., 'War and (in) Pieces: Stirling Castle, June 1314', in Penman, M., (ed.), *Bannockburn 1314–2014: Battle and Legacy* (Donington, 2015), pp. 129–38

(e) Unpublished Secondary Sources

Elliot, G.A., 'The Norman Family of Lorraine in Southern Scotland and especially in Berwickshire', unpublished typescript, NRS: F 375.050

Hawes, C., 'Reassessing the Political Community: Politics and the Public Domain in Fifteenth-Century Scotland', unpublished paper delivered at the Colloquium on *Legal Culture in Medieval and Early Modern Scotland*, held on 16–17 December 2019 (earlier version delivered at the Scottish Legal History Group meeting on 1 October 2016)

Neville, C.J., 'The Manuscript Tradition of the Medieval *Leges Marchiarum* Treatise', unpublished paper delivered at the Colloquium on *Legal Culture in Medieval and Early Modern Scotland*, held on 16–17 December 2019

Index

NB: page locators in **bold** denote text in family trees.

A

Abercorn, castle of (Linlithgow), 158, 173
Abernethy in Rothiemay, William, 166
Abernethy, Oswald of, 140, 191
Abington ('Awintoune') (Lanark), 155
Adamton (Ayr), 122–24
Aikenhead, William of, **160**, 167
Aikenhead, Little (Lanark), 159n53
Aikenhead, Meikle (Lanark), 159n53
Albany governors, 47-48, 50, 53
    Murdoch duke of Albany, **14**, 48, 159
        execution, 50, 177
    Robert duke of Albany, **14**, 89, 184
Alexander II (king of Scots 1214-1249), 174, 187
Alexander III (king of Scots 1249-1286), 4, 9, 39
Allerton (Lanark), 159
Anglo-Scottish truces, 73–74, 76–79, 102, 106n121
Annandale (Dumfries), 28
    claims to terce, 64
    English control, 126, 130
    Nithsdale, relationship with, 132
arbiters, 146, 149–51, 167–69

arbitration, 20
    Blarmade case, 166, 167–69, 194–95
    mortancestry, 117n11, 151–52
Archibald third earl of Douglas, *see* Douglas, Archibald "the Grim" (third earl of)
Archibald fourth earl of Douglas, *see* Douglas, Archibald (fourth earl of)
Archibald fifth earl of Douglas, *see* Douglas, Archibald (fifth earl of)
Argyll
    royal lieutenancy in, 52n70, 52–53, 54, 57
Arkinholm, battle of (1455) (Dumfries), 98, 106n120, 154, 173, 191n65
Arnold duke of Gueldres, 67
arrest of the king, 42
    James I, unsuccessful attempt, 181–82, 185
    James III, 183
    Robert II, 183
arrest of the queen mother, 54–55, 58, 71
assassinations and executions
    Archibald, earl of Moray, 173
    Black Dinner executions

237

David Douglas, 3, 27–28, 30, 33–34, 62, 64, 139, 153, 162, 178
William Douglas (sixth earl), 3, 27–28, 30, 33–34, 62, 64, 139, 153, 162, 178
Malcolm Fleming, 3, 27, 29–30, 33–34, 175, 178
James I, 3, 29, 35, 51–52, 94, 107, 163, 174, 175, 182
Livingston family, 58, 82, 175
Murdoch of Albany, 50, 177
public display of bodies, 174–75
Robert Fleming, 162, 175
Thomas Boyd, 170, 175
assizes
brieve of terce, 116–17
contested marches, 139
Coshogle case, 167
Lorane case, 127
mortancestry assize, 19, 116, 120, 151
John Blair of Adamton v James Lorane, 115–17
Hamilton of Cambuskeith v Maxwells of Calderwood, 147, 149, 166, 171
Auchinleck chronicle, 2–3, 72, 76–77
auditors of causes
Maxwell of Calderwood, Sir John, 147, 164
Ayr
Robert Stewart's body, 174
Ayrshire, 130–31
Blair family holdings, 124, 126, 144
Campbell family links, 149–50
see also Adamton; Ayr; Cunningham; Kilmarnock, lordship of; Stewarton

B

Balfour, Sir James, of Denmilne (antiquarian), 105–6
Balliol of Cavers family, 120–21
Balliol family, 39
Edward, 125
John (king of Scots 1292-1296), 11
Bannatyne, Thomas (in 'Blarmade'), 155
Bannockburn, battle of (1314), 157
Barclay of Kilbirnie family, 171n97
baronial jurisdiction, 121, 179
cum furca et fossa jurisdiction, 87–88, 132
Ettrick and Selkirk Forest, 85–86, 180
Hawick, 142
Middle and Western Marches, wardenship of, 83–84, 84n34, 97, 180
Wigtown, earldom of, 87–88, 89
Basle, Council of, 31–32, 56, 67n142, 72
bastards, *see* illegitimacy
bastardy as a legal status, 16–17
Beaufort, Joan (queen to James I)
arrest and incarceration of, 54–55, 58, 71
custody rights, 53–54
Bedrule (Roxburgh), 127n49, 142
Bell, Patrick (in 'Blarmade'), 155
Berwick
English control, 126, 131
Scottish control, 131
Berwickshire, 125–26
see also Berwick; Roxburgh
Black Dinner (1440)
executions
David Douglas, 3, 27–28, 30, 33–34, 62, 64, 139, 153, 162, 178

INDEX

William Douglas (sixth earl), 3,
  27–28, 30, 33–34, 62, 64,
  139, 153, 162, 178
Malcolm Fleming, 3, 27,
  29–30, 33–34, 175, 178
James "the Gross" Douglas' role,
  27–29, 30, 33–34
treason and conspiracy, 28–30
Blackburn (Lanark), 170n94
Blair, Hugh, 121, **123**
Blair, James, 121, **123**, 124, 126–27
Blair of Adamton family, **123**, 189, 195
  John, of Adamton and Kilwinnet,
    120–24
  John, of Adamton, Kilwinnet, and
    Coshogle
    1455 Coshogle case, 115–17,
      120, 122–24, 139, 143,
      144n123
  Sir John Blair of Adamton and
    Coshogle, 122–24, 128, 133
Blair of that ilk family (Dalry), **123**, 124
Blairhill (Lanark), 155–56
Blarmade (Lanark) lands dispute,
  169–71
  arbitration, 166, 167–69, 194–95
  Archibald Douglas (fourth earl),
    156, 161–62
  Crawfordjohn, barony of, 153–56
  Hamiltons of Cambuskeith, 156–
    58, **157**
    dispute with Maxwells of
      Calderwood, 147–53
  Hamilton family, 156–58, 167–68,
    169, 170–71
  indentures, 146
  James III, 158
  letters of attorney, 145–46
  Maxwells of Calderwood, 159–66,
    160
  dispute with Hamiltons of
    Cambuskeith, 147–53
  reasons for litigation, 166–69
  sasine of Blarmade, 146, 152, 170,
    194
  witnesses, 155–56
blench ferme, 15–16, 133, 135
Bonchester Bridge (Roxburgh), 127
Borthwick family
  Margaret, **160**, 165–66
  William (first lord), 166, 169
  Sir William, 169
Bothwell (Lanark)
  castle, 157
  collegiate church, 148
  estate, 25
Bower, Walter (chronicler), 6–7, 43,
  47, 129, 131–32, 136, 184–85
Boyd of Kilmarnock family, 71n156,
  112n134, 162–64, 195
  Marion, **160**
  Robert, lord of Kilmarnock, 149,
    149n15, 158, **160**, 170
  Thomas, earl of Arran, 170–71
  Thomas, (younger of Kilmarnock),
    162–63, 163n68, 175
Bracton, Henry de (English jurist), 6,
  188, 190
Brechin, battle of (1452), 106,
  106n120
brieves
  brieves, pleadable, 23, 23n75, 115
  brieves, royal, 141–42, 146, 152
  brieves of *furche*, 152, 152n24
  brieves of inquest, 15, 23, 29, 107,
    162
  retourable brieves, 115
  brieves of mortancestry, 19, 120,
    126–27, 143, 147, 150–52,
    166–67, 168

239

Coshogle, 113–17
brieves of novel dissasine, 115–16
brieves of perambulation, 63n125, 139
brieves of right, 151–52
brieves of sasine, 141
Brown, Michael (historian), 49, 59, 78, 103, 189
Bruce, Christian, 39
Bruce, James (bishop), 57n95
Burgundy
diplomatic meetings with William Douglas, 72, 141
Philip duke of, 13, 67
Burn, Thomas de, 113–14

C

Cadzow, barony of (later Hamilton) (Lanark), 18n62, **157**, 157–58
Calderwood (Lanark), 161–62
  see also Maxwells of Calderwood family
Cambuskeith, estate of (Ayr), 149, 168–69
  see also Hamiltons of Cambuskeith family
Cameron, John (bishop), 67n142
Campbell, David, 149, 149n17
Campbell, Duncan, of Lochawe, 52–53, 54, 57
Campbell, Sir George, of Loudon, 149, 162
canon law, 10
forbidden degrees of affinity, 62
legitimacy, 16
marriage, 16
Canterbury (Kent), 111
Carlisle (Cumberland), 136
Carmichael, John, of that ilk, 146

Carrick, earldom of
Steward of Scotland, 94–95
title of king's male heir-apparent, 33n115, 38
Robert II's heir, 40–42, 93, 184, 187
Robert III's heir, 44, 47–48
Carron, River, 130
Carterhope (Selkirk), 159n53
castles
Abercorn castle, 158, 173
Bothwell castle, 157
Craig Douglas castle, 75–76
Crawfordjohn caput and principal castle, 154–55
Dalswinton castle, 129n57, 129–30
Dean castle, 158
Douglas, castle of, 158, 173
Dumfries castle, 129
Durisdeer castle, 129, 131
Edinburgh castle, 3, 78, 142, 183
Enoch Castle, 130
Lochmaben castle, 130, 131
Lochnaw castle, 138
Morton castle, 129, 131, 131n62
policy of destruction, 129n57, 131
David II, 129
Edward III (king of England), 129
Roxburgh castle, 125
Stirling castle, 2, 53
Strathaven castle, 173
Threave castle, 63, 90, 95n77, 173
Tibbers castle, 130
casualties (feudal), 15–16, 133, 150–51, 192
Cavers, barony of (Roxburgh), 120–21, 125–28, 129, 134–35, 140
chamberlain ayres, 83–84

INDEX

chamberlain of Dumfries, 132
Chambers, Christopher, 174–75
Charles V (king of France 1364-1380), 136–37
Charles VII (king of France 1422-1461), 64, 173
Church
  forbidden degrees of affinity, 62
  legitimacy, 16
  marriage, 16
  Schism of the Church (1439), 31–32, 56, 57
  spiritual and legal authority, 10
Clackmannan, sheriffdom of, 93–94
Cleland, Patrick (in 'Blarmade'), 155
Clerisone, Andrew (in Pettinain), 97
Clifford, Sir John (English knight), 136
Clyde, River, 130, 155
Clydesdale (Lanark), 130, 155n36, 159, 193
Colifort ('Colifurde'), barony of Cavers (Roxburgh), 127
Cologne, university of, 32, 148, 196
Colquhoun, Patrick, 169
Colville of that ilk, Robert, 169
common knowledge, 8–9, 19, 174–75, 195
common legalities, 9, 176
conjunct infeftment
  succession of land, 17, 19
    Stewarton and Pettinain, 95–96
conquest, land acquired by, 11
  alienability, 124n34
Coshogle (Dumfries) litigation, 113
  assizes, 167
  Blair claim, 115–17, 120–24, **123**, 124, 139, 143, 189, 195
  brieve of mortancestry, 113–17
  David II, 121, 124, 126
  Douglases of Drumlanrig, 133–39
  Drumlanrig, 117–20
  Hawick and Sprouston, 139–42
    regaining Hawick, 142–43
  Lorane claims, 125–28
    regaining Coshogle, 143–44
  Nithsdale, 128–33
  notarial instruments, 113–14, 116
    Blair claim, 120–21, 124, 139
    Drumlanrig claim, 118–19
  Old Coshogle, 114, 114n5
    regaining Coshogle, 143–44
  sasine of Coshogle, 116, 122–23, 133
courtesy, 17
Craig Douglas castle (Selkirk), 75–76
Craig, Thomas, of Riccarton, 188, 189–90
Cranston, Sir William, 54
Cranston, Thomas, of that ilk, 143n121
Crawford (Lanark), 130
Crawfordjohn, barony of (Lanark), 146, 147, 153–54, 158, 161, 167–68, 170–71
  caput and principal castle, 154–55
  village of, 155–56
Cree, River, 25–26, 62, 63, 65, 68, 79, 81, 87–88, 90, 132
  see also Wigtown, earldom of; Galloway
Crichton, Sir George, 164
Crichton, Sir James, 61, 99
Crichton, Sir Robert, of Sanquhar, 117, 119–20, 143
Crichton, Sir William (lord), chancellor, 29, 33–34, 57–58, 59–60, 67, 71, 75, 98, 178–79
Cromwell, Oliver, 174
Cunningham (Ayr), 94, 158

D

Dalmeny (Linlithgow), 149n17
Dalswinton, castle of (Dumfries), 129n57, 129–30
Dalveen Pass (Dumfries), 114
Danielston, Elizabeth, 159, 164
Dauphin of France, 12, 163
David I (king of Scots 1124-1153), 36–37
David II (king of Scots 1329-1371), 9, 51
   Coshogle, 121, 124, 126
      Lorane family, 125
   destruction of castles, 129
   Douglas tailzie 1342, 21–23, 28, 33, 61–62, 118, 178–79, 193
   Drumlanrig, 118, 129
   Ettrick and Selkirk Forest, 85
   Hawick and Sprouston, 141
   Pettitain, 92, 92n66
   regency, 37–40
   Wigtown, earldom of, 65, 87–88
Dean castle, Kilmarnock (Ayr), 158
Declaration of Arbroath, 185, 188
Deloraine, lands of (Selkirk), 126n44
Dickinson, William Croft (historian), 94–95
dispute resolution, 8–9, 19–21, 188–96
   see also 'Blarmade' lands dispute; Coshogle (Dumfriesshire) litigation
Donald, earl of Mar, 39
Douglas earls, **22**
   authority of the king, 154
   Blairs of Adamton, relationship with, 195
   Douglases of Drumlanrig, relationship with, **119**, 189, 195
   Loranes, relationship with, 195
   Maxwell of Calderwood, relationship with, 162–63, 167
   see also individual earls
Douglas (Lanark) parish kirk of St Bride, 179
Douglas regality grant 1354, 22
Douglas tailzie 1342, 21–23, 28, 33, 61–62, 118, 178–79, 193
Douglas, Sir Archibald
   guardian, 21, 39
Douglas, Archibald, earl of Moray, 7, 60–61, 173–74
Douglas, Archibald "the Grim" (third earl of), 21–22, **22, 93, 119**
   land acquisition, 65–66, 132, 180, 193
   Crawfordjohn, 153
   Drummond, land dispute with, 23–25
   Hawick and Sprouston, 135, 139
   Isabella of Mar, land dispute with, 23–25
   Middle and Western Marches, wardenship of, 25, 82, 132
   Wigtown, earldom of, 25, 62–63, 65, 87–90
   marriage, 25
   power and influence, 24–25
   tailzie of 1342, 23–25, 62, 178
Douglas, Archibald (fourth earl of), **22**, 26–28, 64, **93, 119**
   Blarmade case, 156, 161–62
   capture at Humbleton, 135
   Drumlanrig, 62–63
   duke of Touraine, 26, 64
   Galloway, 63, 68
   Hawick, 135
   steward of Scotland, 92–93

INDEX

Stewarton, 92, 94–95
Middle and Western Marches, wardenship of, 82
Wigtown, earldom of, 87, 88–89
Douglas, Archibald (fifth earl of), **22**, 26–27, **119**
  arrest, 124, 143, 175
  Crawfordjohn, 153–54
  death, 27, 162
  Drumlanrig, 118
  Ettrick and Selkirk Forest, 85–86, 98, 180
  Hawick, 137–38
  lieutenant-general, 27, 52–54, 77–78, 179
  Middle and Western Marches, wardenship of, 82–84, 180
  Wigtown, earldom of, 88, 89
Douglas, Archibald, of Cavers, 128, 134
Douglas, castle of (Lanark), 158, 173
Douglas, David
  execution at Black Dinner, 3, 27–28, 30, 33–34, 62, 64, 139, 153, 162, 178
Douglas, Elizabeth, countess of Buchan, **93**
  Stewarton, 92–93, 95
Douglas, George (first earl of Angus), 33
Douglas, George (fourth earl of Angus), 12–13, 78, 158
Douglas, Hugh (the Dull), 21–22
Douglas, Hugh, earl of Ormond, **22**, 59–60, 99, 173
Douglas, Isabella, 23–24, 128, 134
Douglas, Jacoba, 137, 137n90
Douglas, James (second earl of), **22**, 23, 42, **119**
  Drumlanrig, 118, 121, 133–35

Douglas, James "the Gross" of Balvenie (seventh earl of), 27–28, 28n94
  earl of Avondale, 28, 56–57
  justiciar, 27, 29–30, 56–57
  role in Black Dinner executions, 27–30, 33, 57
Douglas, James (ninth earl of), **22**, 32, **93**, 99, **119**
  Anglo-Scottish truce, involvement in, 77–79, 102
  capture 1484 and held at Lindores, 196
  Drumlanrig, 118–20
  fealty to the king, 99–100, 142–43, 154
  Henry VI, meetings with, 73–74, 77–78
  Lanark bond, 101
  papal dispensation to marry, 18–19, 31–32, 101, 108–9, 180
  papal jubilee in Rome, 32, 36, 72–73, 102, 141, 148, 164, 178–79, 196
  Stewarton, 100–1
  support for English king, 99–100
  Wigtown, earldom of, 100–2
Douglas, James, of Drumlanrig, 117–18, 120
Douglas, John, of Balvenie, 173
Douglas, Margaret
  untailzied estates, 30–31, 62, 63–64, 180
  transumpt of 1449, 68
Douglas, Sir James (the Good Sir James), 21–22, **22**, **119**
  Drumlanrig, 118
  Ettrick and Selkirk Forest, 85
  guardianship, 37

243

Douglas, Sir James, of Dalkeith, 137, 193, 193n69
Douglas, Sir James, of Ralston, 77n12
Douglas, William (first earl of), 21–23, **22**, 118, **119**, 121
Douglas, William (sixth earl of), **22, 119**
   execution at Black Dinner, 3, 27–28, 30, 33–34, 62, 64, 139, 153, 162, 178
   treason and conspiracy, 28–29, 177–78
   wardship, 153, 177
Douglas, William (eighth earl of), **22, 93, 119**
   abuse of regency power, 98, 103, 179
   assassination, 1–3, 30–31, 103–12, 119–20, 142–43, 181, 192, 194
   Crawfordjohn, 154
   England
      Henry VI, meeting with, 73–74, 77–78
   Hawick, 139–40
   lord of Galloway, 62, 63–64, 68
   papal dispensation to marry, 18–19, 31–32, 62, 179
   papal jubilee in Rome, 32, 36, 72–73, 102, 141, 148, 164, 178–79, 196
   regency government
      Douglas dominance, 59–64
      reunification of Douglas lands, 61–64
   resignation of Stewarton, 95
   rupture from king James II, 75–79, 103–7, 178–81
      assassination of William Douglas (eighth earl of), 103–12
      Ettrick and Selkirk Forest, 85–86, 180
      Middle and Western Marches, wardenship of, 82–84
      settlement of 1451, 79–82
      Stewarton, 90–98, 104
      treason trial, 98–103
      Wigtown, earldom of, 86–90, 104
   status abroad, 72–74
   transumpt of 1449, 67–68, 179
      Ettrick and Selkirk Forest, 68–69
      Galloway lands, 68
      land acquisition, 67–69
   treason, 98, 106–9
Douglas, William (son of the Good Sir James), 21
Douglas, William, of 'Danlanryk', 137n92
Douglas, Sir William, of 'Kyrros', 137n92
Douglas, William, lord of Leswalt, 138–39
Douglas, William, of Liddesdale, 125
Douglas of Dalkeith family, 131 n62
Douglas of Drumlanrig family, **119**, 189, 195
   grant of Drumlanrig, 133–39
   James, 117, 118–19
   Sir William (I), 69, 72, 133–37, 137n92, 194
   Sir William (II), 118, 137–39, 140, 141
   William (III), 118, 139, 140, 141–43
Douglasdale (Lanark), 155
Dripps (Lanark), 159n53
Drumlanrig (Dumfries)
   Archibald Douglas (fourth earl), 62–63

INDEX

Archibald Douglas, (fifth earl), 118
barony and regality of, 117–20
David II, 118, 129
Douglas earls and Douglases
   of Drumlanrig, relationship
   between, **119**, 189, 195
Douglases of Drumlanrig family,
   119
   grant of Drumlanrig, 133–39
   James, 117, 118–19
   Sir William (I), 69, 72, 137n92
   Sir William (II), 118, 138–39
   William (III), 118
   James Douglas (second earl), 118,
      121, 133–35
   James Douglas (ninth earl), 118–20
   regality court of, 124, 144
Drummond, Sir Malcolm
   Archibald "the Grim", land dispute
      with, 23–24, 134
Drumsagard (Lanark), 159
Dumfries castle
   destruction of castles, 129
Dumfries sheriff court, 116, 116n11
   Robert Crichton of Sanquhar,
      119–20
Dumfriesshire, 126
   see also Coshogle litigation
Dunbar family
   Elizabeth, 61, 100n92, 106n120,
      191n65
   Sir Gawane of, 136
   Janet, 61, 99
Dundas of Dundas family, 169n91
   Agnes, **160**
   Duncan of, 149–50, 169
   forfeiture of estates, 70
   James, 69–70
Dundas of that ilk, Archibald,
   149n17, 165n81, 169

Duneaton Water, 155
Dunlop (Ayr), 93–95
Dupplin Moor, battle of (1333)
   (Perth), 39
Durham (Northumberland), 78
Durisdeer (Dumfries), 114, 130
   castle of, 129, 131

E

earls, belting of, 23–24
Edinburgh
   castle, 3, 78, 142, 183
   tolbooth, 168
Edward III (king of England
   1327-1377)
   destruction of Scottish castles, 129
Enoch, castle of (Dumfries), 130
Enterkin Water, 114
Ettrick and Selkirk Forest
   Craig Douglas castle, 75–76
   grant of 1451, 85–86
   in regaliam, grants, 68–69, 86
   rupture between Douglases and
      James II, 85–86, 180
   transumpt of 1449, 68–69
Eugenius IV (Pope), 67n142
Exchequer Rolls, 56

F

feats of arms, 136
fees
   heritage
      brieves of mortancestry, 19,
         115, 126–27, 147, 150–52,
         166–67, 168
      Ettrick and Selkirk Forest, 85
      Stewarton, 91
   lay fees, 152–53
   queen's *causidicus*, 117n11
   terce distinguished, 154

245

Felix V (anti-Pope), 31
female inheritance, *see* succession of women
'Fewrule', barony of (Roxburgh), 127–28
Fife, Robert Stewart, earl of, **14**, 24–25
 royal guardian, 43–45, 184
Finglen (Selkirk), 159n53
Finlayston (Renfrew), barony of, 159, 164–66
Fitzgilbert, Walter, 156–57
Fleming family
 David, 42, 183
 John, lord, of Cumbernauld, earl of Wigtown, 90
 Malcolm, earl of Wigtown, 87, 88n49
 Sir Malcolm, of Biggar and Cumbernauld, 175
  execution (Black Dinner), 3, 27, 29–30, 33–34, 178
  treason and conspiracy, 29–30
 Sir Robert, of Biggar and Cumbernauld
  brieve of inquest, 29–30, 162–63
 Thomas, second earl of Wigtown, 65, 88n49
forbidden degrees of marriage, 18–19, 31–32, 62
forespeakers, 116, 149–50
forest jurisdiction and courts, 85–86, 135, 180
forest rights, 85–86, 98
forfeiture
 Boyd family, 158
 Douglas family
  Archibald, earl of Moray, 99–100
  James (seventh earl), 30–31

  James (ninth earl), 97, 103, 111–12, 120, 143, 154, 167–68
  Sir James, 100
  William (sixth earl) (absence of forfeiture), 28–30, 33–34, 62
  William (eighth earl) (crimes giving rise to forfeiture), 81–82, 103
  William (eighth earl) (grant of forfeited lands), 69–70, 104–5
 Eustace de Lorane, 121, 124, 125–26, 143
 Herbert Maxwell, 92n66
 James of Dundas, 69–70
 Livingston family, 105, 178
Fortescue, Sir John
 exile to Scotland, 4–5
France
 Arnold duke of Gueldres, 67
 Charles V (king of France 1364–1380), 136–37
 Charles VII (king of France 1422–1461), 64, 173
 Crevant, battle of (1423), 137 n92
 Dauphin of France, 12, 163
 diplomatic meetings, 72, 141
 Francis duke of Brittany, 12
 Fresnay (Champagne-Ardenne), battle of (1420), 136
 Philip duke of Burgundy, 13, 67
 Robert Maxwell of Calderwood's death, 159
 Scottish support for French king, 26–27, 88, 136–37, 159, 186–87, 192
 Orleans, siege of (1428), 137n92
 Verneuil, battle of (1424), 26, 95, 137n92
Francis duke of Brittany, 12

frank tenement, 15, 96, 150–51
free holdings, 15, 96, 150–51

G

Galloway
  annexed to the Crown, 90
  grant of 1450, 68, 81, 87
  lordship of
    Archibald "the Grim", 25, 62, 88, 132, 193
    James (ninth earl) Douglas, 101
    William (eighth earl) Douglas, 62–63, 68, 87, 89–90, 97–98
  Margaret Stewart's liferent, 89, 95n77, 154, 179
  settlement of 1451, 79–80, 87
  transumpt of 1449, 65
Garter King of Arms, 73, 77, 102n107
General Council
  Carrick's position, 41–42
  Fife's conduct, 43
  Parliament distinguished, 51n64
  queen mother's rights of custody, 54–55
  relationship with the king, 47–48
  regency appointments, 38–39
    king David II, 39–40
    king James II, 52–54
    king Robert II, 40–44
    king Robert III, 44–48
  right to oversee minority governments, 56–59, 187–88
  Rothesay's lieutenancy, 46–48, 109n126
  see also Parliament; Three Estates
Gilbert, John (historian), 85–86
Gilkerscleuch (Lanark), 154
Glasgow
  cathedral church, 145
  university, 148
Gledstanes family (Hawick), 143, 192
Gledstanes, James, 138
Glendowran ('Glendonanerig') (Lanark), 155n34
Gordon, Alexander, earl of Huntly, king's lieutenant, 13, 106n120
Gordon, George, master of Huntly, 191n65
Govan, Alan (in 'Blarmade'), 155
governance
  good governance
    Parliament, role of, 183–84
    royal authority, 9–10, 43, 185, 187
  law, relationship with, 5–6, 35–36
  see also governors and governorships; guardians and guardianship; lieutenants and lieutenancies
governors and governorships
  Albany Governors
    Murdoch Stewart duke of Albany, 53n71, 159, 177
    Robert Stewart duke of Albany, 43n27, 48–50, 89n52, 92–93, 135, 176
  terminology, 36–37
  see also guardians and guardianship; lieutenants and lieutenancies
Graham, Euphemia, **14**
  wife (1) of Archibald Douglas (fifth earl), **14**
  wife (2) of James lord Hamilton, **14**, 18n62, **157**, 157–58, 162n62
Graham, Malise (earl of Menteith), **14**, 24n78, 51–52, 76, 102–3, 112, 180

Graham, Sir Robert
  arrest attempt on James I, 181, 184–85
  assassination of James I, 3, 29, 35, 51, 94, 107, 163, 174, 175, 182
Grant, Alexander (historian), 4–5, 24, 89
Gray, Patrick
  role in assassination of William Douglas (eighth earl of), 1–3
great assize of right, 151–52
great seal, 50, 51, 57
  register of, 67n142, 79
  transumpt of 1449, 66–67
Greenhills (Lanark), 159n53
Greenlaw, George (burgess of Edinburgh, arbiter), 168
ground rights, 146, 171
Guardian, (Great) of the kingdom of Scotland
  William Douglas (eighth earl) self-designated as, 73, 179
guardians and guardianship
  Sir Alexander Douglas, 33n115
  appointment by the community, 39–40
  Gilbert lord Kennedy, 147, 168, 170
  king striking down detrimental transactions by, 87
  origins, 176–77, 184
  Robert Stewart, earl of Fife, 24–25, 43–46, 89n52
  terminology, 36–37, 40, 47–48
  terms of office, 51
  Thomas Randolph, 37–39
  see also governors and governorships; lieutenants and lieutenancies

Gueldres, Mary of (queen to James II), 13, **14**, 67, 70
Guthrie, Master David, of Kincaldrum, 147–48, 153, 169–70

H

Halidon Hill, battle of (1333) (Berwick), 21, 33n115, 39
Hamilton (Cadzow), barony of (Lanark), 157
Hamilton earls of Arran, 171n97
Hamilton family, **157**
  Alan, of Larbert, 156, 161, 166–67
  Alexander, 169
  Blarmade case, 156–58, 167–68, 169, 170–71
  David, 156
  Dundas family links, 149–50
  Gavin, 148
  Sir James (lord), **14**, 18n62, 72, 102, 111–12, 145–46, 156, **157**, 158, 167–68, 170–71
  Sir John, of Cadzow, 18n62
  Master Robert, 145–46, 148, 169–70
  Sir Robert, of Preston, 145, 153n27
Hamilton of Cambuskeith, 156, **157**, 158, 189, 195
  David, 156–57, 166
  James, 145–46, 147–53, 166–69, 170–71, 194
  John, 158
Harwood ('Heroude', 'Herwood', 'Harwood') (Roxburgh), 127, 140
Harwood on Teviot ('Harewode', 'Over and Nether Harwood') (Roxburgh), 140
Hawes, Claire (historian), 8–9, 19
Hawick, barony of (Roxburgh), 62–63
  court action for, 72, 134–39, 139–44

East Mains of, 138
Margaret Stewart, 68
Oswald of Abernethy, 191
regality of, 142, 191
transumpt of 1449, 66, 69, 179, 194
Hawkshaw (Selkirk), 159n53
Hawthornside ('Hangetsyde') (Roxburgh), 127–28
Henry V (king of England 1413-1422), 136–37, 186
Henry VI (king of England 1422-1461/1470-1471)
　Anglo-Scottish truce, 73–74, 77–78
　exile to Scotland, 4–5
　mental incapacity, 186
Heriot, John, of Trabroun, 88n50
heritage, 11, 23n75
　fee and heritage
　　brieves of mortancestry, 19, 115, 126–27, 147, 150–52, 166–67, 168
　　Ettrick and Selkirk Forest, 85
　　Stewarton, 91
　forfeited heritage, 112n134
　see also female inheritance; succession to land; succession to the Crown; succession to title of honour
Herries, Andrew lord, of Terregles, 127
hierarchies of succession
　illegitimate children, 16–17
　succession to land, 10–11
　　non-royal landowners, 15
　succession to the Crown, 11–12
　women
　　succession to land, 11
　　succession to the Crown, 12–13

'Holdetoun' (Dumfries), 117n13
Holland, Anne, 31
Holyrood
　coronation of James II, 51
homage and fealty, 60, 154
homicide
　by forethocht felony, 107–8, 108n124
　chaudmelle (in hot blood), 108, 108n124
hostages in England for king's ransom, 129
　Douglas of Drumlanrig, William II, 137–38
　Graham, Malise (earl of Menteith), 24n78, 52
　Maxwell of Calderwood, John I, 163
　Murray, Sir Andrew, 40
Hudson, John (historian), 8
Humbleton Hill, battle of (1402) (Northumberland), 135
Hume, Alexander, 91, 96
Hume, David, of Godscroft
　History of the House of Douglas, 97–98
Hummelknows ('Homylknollis'), 127
Hundred Years War, 26–27, 55–56
Hunt, Karen (historian), 49–50

I

illegitimacy
　succession to land and titles, 16–17
incapacity of kings, 9–10, 40–41, 186
　see also governors and governorship; guardians and guardianship; lieutenants and lieutenancies
in liberam varrenam, 85

in liberam regalitatem seu regaliam grants, 94
in regaliam grants
  Ettrick and Selkirk Forest, 68–69, 86
indentures
  James and Archibald Douglas, 32, 62n122, 69
  James Hamilton of Cambuskeith and Sir John Maxwell of Calderwood, 146, 149–51, 153
  Douglas of Drumlanrig, William II and William Douglas of Leswalt, 138
inter-dependence of king and aristocracy in Scotland, 4–5
  James II regency government
    Douglas dominance, 59–64
    reunification of Douglas lands, 61–64
interpretation of documentary sources, 3–4
Isabella of Lennox, 175
Isabella (sister of James II), **14**, 23–24, 134
  as heir presumptive, 12–14, 128
  see also Douglas, Isabella

J

Jackton (Lanark), 159n53
James I (king of Scots 1406-1437), 1
  assassination, 3, 29, 35, 51, 94, 107, 163, 174, 175, 182
  English captivity, 48
    Scottish denial of James' kingship, 26–27
James II (king of Scots 1437-1460)
  coronation, 51, 60
  death, 9
  Douglas dominance, 59–64
  reunification of Douglas lands, 61–64
  heirs, 71
  majority and full authority, 69–70
    avenging arrest of queen mother, 71
    overthrow of Livingston family, 70–71
  regency, 51
    Archibald Douglas (fifth earl), 52–54
  role in Black Dinner executions, 1–3, 27–28
  rupture from William Douglas (eighth earl of), 75–79
    assassination of William Douglas (eighth earl of), 103–12
    Ettrick and Selkirk Forest, 85–76
    Middle and Western Marches, wardenship of, 82–85
    settlement of 1451, 79–82
    Stewarton, 90–98
    trial, 98–103
    Wigtown, earldom of, 86–90
James III (king of Scots 1460-1488), 13, **14**
  arrest, 183
  Blarmade case, 158
  Prince of Scotland, 94
  replacement, 187
James IV (king of Scots 1488-1513), 109–10, 158
James VI (king of Scots 1569-1603), 36–37
James second earl of Douglas, *see* Douglas, James (second earl of)
James seventh earl of Douglas, *see* Douglas, James "the Gross" of Balvenie (seventh earl of)

James ninth earl of Douglas, *see* Douglas, James (ninth earl of)
Jedburgh, 126, 128, 131, 135
  sheriff court, 74, 137, 141, 143
Johnstone, Matthew, of Pettinain, 97–98
jurisdiction
  baronial jurisdiction, 121, 179
    cum furca et fossa jurisdiction, 87–88, 132
    Hawick, 142
    Wigtown, earldom of, 87–88, 89
  forest jurisdiction and courts, 85–86, 135, 180
  justiciars
    mortancestry claims, 121, 147
    wardens compared, 84
  Parliament and General Council distinguished, 51n66
  regality jurisdiction, 68, 179–80, 191
    Drumlanrig, 120, 121, 124
  wardens of the marches, 77, 81, 82–84, 180
justice ayres, 149, 166
justiciars, 44, 56–58, 166
  Alexander Livingston of Callendar, 58
  Alexander, lord of the Isles, 57–58
  Alexander Stewart earl of Buchan, 44
  David Stewart earl of Carrick, 44
  Gilbert lord Kennedy, 151
  James "the Gross" Douglas (seventh earl of), 27, 56–57, 178
  John lord Lindsay of the Byres, 168
  Sir Robert Crichton of Sanquhar, 117, 119–20
  William Sinclair earl of Orkney, 97
justiciary courts, 116, 143
  Drumlanrig regality, 117–18

K

Kennedy, Fergus, 160, 160n56
Kennedy, Gilbert lord (of Dunure), 96, 100
  arbiter, 168–69
  justice for that time at Lanark, 147, 166
  justiciar, 151
  king's guardian, 170–71
  king's tutor, 158
Kennedy, James, bishop of St Andrews, 32
Kennedy, John, of Dunure, 175n10
Kilconquhar, Adam of, 38
Kilmarnock, lordship of (Ayr), 147, 149, 158
  see also Boyd of Kilmarnock family
Kincardine (Mearns), 174
kings, arrest of,
  James I (attempted arrest), 181–82, 184–85
  James III, 183
  Robert II, 42, 42n24, 183
king's chapel, 116
king's council, 152, 168
  striking down inquest decisions, 15
  use of royal seal by regents, 43–44
king's lieutenant in the north
  Alexander, earl of Mar, 53
  Alexander, lord of the Isles, 57
  earl of Huntly, 13, 106n120
  see also lieutenants and lieutenancies
king's lieutenant for the marches, 84n34

251

see also lieutenants and lieutenancies
Kintyre and Knapdale (Argyll), *custodes* of, 52–53
Kirk Burn pass (Dumfries), 114, 130
Kirkpatrick, Roger de, 129n57
knight service, 133
Königsberg (Prussia), 133

L

Lalain, Jacques de, 32
Lanark
   burgh of Lanark, 147
   Lanark bond, 101
   sheriff court, 149
   sheriff *in hac parte*, to give sasine, 152, 155
   sheriffdom, 97, 146, 147, 148–49, 153
land acquisition
   Archibald "the Grim"
      Douglas lands, 23–25
      Galloway, 26
      Isabella of Mar, land dispute with, 23–25
      Sir Malcolm Drummond, land dispute with, 23–25
      Middle and Western Marches, 25, 82
      Murray of Bothwell lands, 25
      Wigtown, 25, 87–89
   William Douglas (eighth earl of)
      alienations and forfeiture, 81–82
      Ettrick and Selkirk Forest, 68–69, 85–86
      Galloway lands, 68
      Middle and Western Marches, 82–84
      rescinded grants, 81
      settlement of 1451, 79–80
      Stewarton, 90–98
      transumpt of 1449, 67–68
      trial, 98–103
      variations of grants, 81
      Wigtown, earldom of, 86–90
landownership
   Blarmade, *see* Blarmade (Lanark) land dispute
   Coshogle, *see* Coshogle (Dumfries) litigation
   law and landownership, 8–9
   majority, 17–18
   Nithsdale, 114–17
   succession to land
      absence of son, 10–11
      division of lands, 11
      hierarchy of succession, 10–15
      illegitimate children, 16–17
      inherited land and conquest land, 11
      law, role and importance of, 10–11
      legal capacity, 17
      loss upon marriage, 11
      non-royal landowners, 15
      superior landholders, 16
      twins, 10
      wardship, 17
      women, 11, 21–23, 30–31, 68, 139–41, 154
   succession to land (women), 11
      Douglas tailzie 1342, 21–23
      impact of Black Dinner executions, 30–31
      Margaret Douglas, 30–31, 68, 139–41, 154
      untailzied Douglas estates, 30–31, 139–41, 154
   see also land acquisition; tailzies

INDEX

Langshaws, barony of (Ayr), 91
Lauder (Berwick), 162, 183
Lauderdale (Berwick), 192
law
  common knowledge, 8–9
  common legalities, 9
  contrasted with 'rycht faith gude conscience', 151, 168–69, 171
  criminal and political setting, 8
  customary law, 8–9
  ecclesiastical authority, 10
  governance, relationship with, 5–6, 35–36
    good governance, 5–6
  law and justice
    general peace, 7–8
    law enforcement, 6–7
  law and politics, 8
    absent kings, 9–10
    age-related incapacity of kings, 9
    lack of suitable heir, 9–10
    mental incapacity of kings, 9–10
  law and society, 6
  law of the marches, 77, 81, 82–84, 180
  legal consciousness, 5–6, 176, 195
  lese majeste, 46, 108
  non-criminal law, 8–9
  role of, 5, 8–9
  Salic law, 64
  social practices, influence of, 8
  succession to land, 10
    see also succession to land
Law, John (chronicler), 72, 98n88
lawyers, 19–20
Leadhills (Lanark), 155
legal consciousness, 5–6, 176, 195
legal representation, 19–20

legal rituals, 8, 181
lese majeste, 46, 108
Leswalt (Wigtown), 138–39
letters of attorney
  Blarmade case, 145–46
Liber Pluscardensis, 185–86
liberum tenementum, 15, 96, 150–51
Libri Feudorum, 190
lieutenants and lieutenancies
  Archibald Douglas (fifth earl) lieutenant-general of the kingdom, 51, 56–57, 77–78, 83–84, 163, 178, 179
  Argyll lieutenancy, 52–53, 54
  David duke of Rothesay, 44–47, 184
  incompetency, 187–88
  king's lieutenants
    Argyll lieutenancy, 52–53, 54
    king's lieutenant for the marches, 84n34
    king's lieutenant in the north, 13, 53, 57, 106n120
  king's lieutenant for the marches, 84n34
  king's lieutenant in the north
    Alexander, lord of the Isles, 57
    Alexander Gordon, earl of Huntly, 13, 106n120
    Alexander Stewart, earl of Mar, 53
    Robert II, under, 40–41, 49
    Robert III, under, 49
    terminology, 36–37, 40–41, 49
  see also guardians and guardianship; governors and governorship
Lincluden (Dumfries), collegiate church of, 67
  march laws declared at, 83–84

253

Lindores (Fife), abbey of, 196
Lindsay of the Byres, John lord, 168–69, 170
Lindsay family
  Alexander (fourth earl of Crawford), 66–67,106, 106n121
  Alexander, of Dunrod, 169
  David (first earl of Crawford), 46
  Mr James, 67, 129n57
  Jean, 64
  Sir William, of Rossie, 46
Linlithgow, 29, 42, 47
Livingston revolution, 58, 67
Livingston family
  Sir Alexander, of Callendar, 29, 30, 54, 58–59, 70, 175, 177–78
  fall from favour, 69–71
  James (lord), 70–71, 102, 105, 111
  Robert, 67
Lochmaben, castle of (Dumfries), 130, 131
Lochnaw, castle of (Wigtown), 138
London
  Anglo-Scottish truce negotiations, 76–77
Lorane family
  Eustace de, 121, 124, 125, 126, 143
  Hector, of Harwood and Hawthornside, 127
  James, 115, 116–17, 143–44
  Patrick, 126–27, 128
Lorein, James, of Harwood, 127
lords of parliament, 58–59
  appointment, 60
  George Seton, 97
  Lindsay of the Byres, 168
  support for inner council, 59
  prevalence of Douglases, 59–60, 158

Louis, count of Geneva, 13
Lowes, Elizabeth, 149n18, **160**
Lowes, Thomas, of Manor (arbiter), 149n18, 168, 168n89
Lowther Hills (Dumfries), 114, 155

M
MacArthur, John, 175n8
MacDonald, Alexander, lord of the Isles, earl of Ross; king's lieutenant in the north, 54, 57–58, 175
MacDonald, John, lord of the Isles and earl of Ross, 105
Machan, estate of (Stirling), 157
Macruarie, Alexander, of Garmoran, 175n8
Maitland, F. W. (legal historian), 176, 190
majority, age of, 17
  David II, 33n115
  Douglas, William (eighth earl), 62–63, 89, 140
  Douglas, William (sixth earl), 28, 177
  James I, 48
  James II, 180
  James VI, 37
  regents, 40
manrent, bonds of, 84n34, 101, 158
Mantel, Hilary (historical novelist), 1
marches,
  'statutis ordanit' for (1430), 82–83
  'statutis and use of merchis in tym of were' (Lincluden 1449), 82–83
Mar, Margaret of, 18–19
Margaret of Norway (queen-designate of Scotland), 48n48
maritagium, 63–64, 69, 180
Marjorie, countess of Carrick, 38

INDEX

Marquess of Montrose, 174n4
marriage,
  age of, 17–18
  cohabitation with habit and
    repute, 16n57, 54n79
  consanguinity as impediment to,
  marriage *per verba de futuro*
    subsequente copula, 16, 54n79
  marriage *per verba de praesenti*,
    16, 18
  means to settle feud, 16–17
  marriage to dead brother's widow
    dispensation for, 18–19, 31–32
  papal dispensations
    forbidden degrees of
      consanguinity, 18–19,
      31–32, 62
  relationships of affinity and
    consanguinity, 18–19, 31–32, 62
Mauldslie, barony of (Lanark),
  165n81
Maxwell, Eustace, 92n66
Maxwell, Herbert, 92n66
Maxwell, Janet, 139n100
Maxwell of Calderwood family, 159,
  160, 167, 171, 194–95
  Gawane, 146, 147, 149–51, 165–
    66, 169
  George, 165–66
  John, 151, 163
  Sir John (I), 146, 147, 150–52,
    157, 162–69, 171, 194
  Sir John (II), 149, 151, 163n68,
    163–66
  Marion, 149, **157**, 164
  Sir Robert, 159–62
Maxwell of Carlaverock family, 192
Maxwell of Monreith family, 113–14
Maxwell of Pollok family, 159–61,
  160

McGladdery, Christine (historian), 59
McNeill, Peter (legal historian), 48–50
  categories of regency, 36–38, 52,
    53–54
messuage (chemys), 91, 97–98, 114,
  116
Middle and Western Marches,
  wardenship of, 73, 77, 81, 90
  Archibald "the Grim" (third earl
    of), 25, 82, 132
  Archibald Douglas (fourth earl of),
    82
  Archibald Douglas (fifth earl of),
    82–84, 180
  baronial jurisdiction, 83–84,
    84n34, 97, 180
  limitation of power, 84
  William Douglas (eighth earl of)
    rupture from king James II, 82–84
Middleham (Yorkshire), 138
military service (tenure), 17, 136n85
minority government
  Blarmade case, 166
  Douglas domination of, 59–60
    abuse of powers, 71, 73
    transumpt of 1449, 64–71, 179
  General Council, relationship
    with, 56
  James I, 6–7, 53
  royal seals, 57
Monieburgh ('Monyabrock') (Kilsyth)
  (Stirling), 148, 148n12, 152–53
Montgomery of that ilk, Sir John, 175
Morton (Dumfries)
  castle of, 129, 131, 131n62
  Mill, 130
Mowbray, Philip, of Barnbougle,
  149n17
Mowbray, John, of Hoppringle (*recte*
  Barnbougle), 169

Mowbray, Roger, of Barnbougle and
   Dalmeny, 82
Munro, Rona (dramatist), 1–2, 3
Murray family
   Christian, 39
   Elizabeth, of Stewarton and
      Pettinain, **93**, 95–96
   Herbert, 92n66, 169
   Janet, 138–39
   Jean, 137n90
   Joanna, of Drumsagard, 25
   Patrick, 92, **93**
   William, 66, 91–92, **93**
   William, of Polmaise (Touchadam),
      168, 168n89
Murray of Bothwell family
   Sir Andrew (guardian), 39
   Joanna (wife of Archibald "the
      Grim" (third earl of Douglas)), **93**
   land brought to marriage, 25,
      66, 92, 139, 153
   Sir Thomas, 25, 92, **93**, 135, 141
Murray of Cockpool family, 92
mutual obligations
   divine law, 188
   feudal law, 189–90
   king and barons, 183
   king and clergy, 183
   king and people, 182, 189–90
   oaths sworn, 183–85

N

Nether Calderwood (barony of
   Kilbride) (Lanark), 161
Neville's Cross, battle of (1346)
   (Northumberland), 125
Newark, castle of (Selkirk), 140
Newcastle (Northumberland), 76, 78,
   80
Newlands Lanark), 159n53

Nith, River, 114, 130–31
   see also Galloway
Nithsdale (Dumfries), 83, 128–32
   Annandale, relationship with, 132
   baronies, 132–33
   land disputes, 114–17
   lordship of, 97
   warden of, 83–84, 97
non obstantibus clause (grants of
   1451), 81–82, 87, 89, 90
non-entry fines, 16, 138–39
notarial instruments, 20, 72, 141–42,
   176
   Blarmade case, 145–46
   Coshogle case, 113–14, 116
      Blair claim, 120–21, 124, 139
      Drumlanrig claim, 118–19
   incapacity of kings, 40n18, 52n70,
      52n70
notaries public, 20, 194–95

O

oaths, 7, 29, 37, 41, 43, 43n28,
   45–46, 46n39, 188
   mutuality of oaths, 59–61, 182–86
official of Glasgow, 145, 146
   official's court, 145, 169–70
Ormsheuch (Ayr), 92, 93–95
Otterburn, Alan, 175
Otterburn, battle of (1388)
   (Northumberland), 23, 42, 118,
   126, 133
Otterburn, Nicholas, 32, 67n142

P

papal dispensation to marry
   forbidden degrees of
   consanguinity, 18–19, 31–32
papal jubilee (1451), 32, 36, 72–73,
   102, 141, 148, 164, 178–79, 196

INDEX

papal supplications, 73
Paris, university of, 148, 182
Parliament
   Archibald "the Grim"'s land
     claims, 23
   auditors of causes and complaints,
     147–48, 164
   censure of kings, 181–88
   General Council distinguished,
     51n64
   James II's oath, 7, 59–60
   lords of parliament, 58–59
     appointment, 60
     George Seton, 97
     Lindsay of the Byres, 168
     support for inner council, 59
     prevalence of Douglases,
       59–60, 158
   regency appointments, 38–39
     for king David II, 39–40
     for king James II, 52–54
     for king Robert II, 40–44
     for king Robert III, 44–48
   succession to the Crown, 11–12
   William Douglas (eighth earl of)
     1451 settlement, 79–82, 85–86
     inquiry into death, 107–12, 181
     land claims, 63–64, 68–69,
       70–71, 74, 78–79, 179–80
     treason trial of, 98–103, 103–4,
       180–81
   see also General Council; Three
     Estates
Penman, Michael (historian), 40
perambulation, 63n125, 139
Perth
   assassination of James I, 3, 29, 35,
     51, 94, 107, 163, 174, 175,
     182
   Blackfriars, 174

Pettinain (Lanark), 91, 92, 92n66,
   96–98
Philip duke of Burgundy, 13, 67
pleadable brieves, 23, 23n75, 115
pre- or pro-locutors, 20
prerogative, *see* royal prerogative
Prince of Scotland, 47n47, 94
Principality of Scotland, 94
procurators, 20, 147–48, 150, 155, 169
professional lawyers, 20
public domain, 8, 174
public good, 46
public ritual, 174, 195

Q

queens and queen mothers
   influence of, 52, 79, 103
     interceding with the king to
       show mercy, 175

R

Ralston, John (bishop), 67n142
Ramornie, Sir John, 46
Randolph, John, earl of Moray
   (guardian), 39–40
Randolph, Thomas (guardian), 37–39
regality and regalian powers
   1354 grant of regality
     lands of Sir James Douglas, 22
   Drumlanrig,
     barony and regality of, 117–20
     regality court of, 124, 144
   Galloway, 63n125
   Hawick, 140, 142, 191
   in regaliam distinguished, 68–69
   justiciary courts
     Drumlanrig regality, 117–18
     Lauder, 162
     Sprouston, 66, 135, 140, 141, 142,
       193

regents and regency
    appointment by Three Estates,
        38–39
        for king David II, 39–40
        for king James II, 52–54
        for king Robert II, 40–44
        for king Robert III, 44–48
    Douglas dominance, 59–61
        reunification of Douglas lands,
            61–64
        for king David II, 37–40
        for king James II, 52–54
        for king Robert II, 40–44
        for king Robert III, 44–48
    nearest agnates, 38
        king Robert II, 40–44
    nomination of regents, 37–38
        king David II, 37–38
    powers, 49–50
        in name of king, 50
        in own name, 50
    regency council, 46–49, 55–59
    terminology, 36–37
        guardian nomenclature, 40
        lieutenancy nomenclature,
            40–41
    terms of office, 50–51
Regiam Majestatem, 6, 28–29, 187,
    190
Reid, Norman (historian), 4–5
Reid, R. C. (historian), 114–15,
    126–27
remissions
    Alexander Livingston of Callendar,
        70–71, 175
    James Livingston, 70–71, 175
    William Douglas (eighth earl of),
        79, 81–82, 103
respite, royal letters of, 72, 104, 107,
    141–42

Reston, John, 146, 146n4
Richard II (king of England 1377-
    1399), 134, 185–86
Robert I (king of Scots 1306-1329),
    21, 37–38, 51, 82
    charters, 85 (The Forest), 91
        (Stewarton)
Robert II (king of Scots 1370-1390),
    14
    arrest, 183
    incapacity, 9, 24, 40–44
    regency, 40–44, 49, 53
    as Stewart, Robert
        guardian, 38, 40
        lieutenant, 40
    Wigtown, earldom of, 87
Robert III (king of Scots 1390-1406),
    14
    absent heir, 48
    death, 48
    incapacity, 9, 44–48
    regency, 44–48, 49
    steward of Scotland, 94
    as Stewart, John, earl of Carrick,
        41–42, 93
    Stewarton, 94
Roberton (Lanark), 155
Roman roads, 130–31
Rome
    papal jubilee, 32, 36, 72–73, 102,
        141, 148, 164, 178–79, 196
Ross, Countess of (wife of the Lord of
    the Isles), 175
Roxburgh, 131, 136
    castle, 125
    death of James II, 167–68
    sheriffdom of, 125–26, 127, 140
Roxburghshire, 66, 127, 162
    see also Hawick; Sprouston
royal prerogative

appointing earls, 23–24, 23n76, 24n77–80, 33, 89
 using seals, 50
Rule Water, 127
Rutherford, Margaret, **160**, 166

S

Salic law, 64
Sanquhar (Dumfries), 114, 130
 contested marches, 139
sasine, 15–16, 19
 brieves of mortancestry, 115–16, 147
 brieves of *furche*, 152
 brieves of novel dissasine, 15–16
 notarial instruments, 145–46
 royal brieves of sasine, 141–42, 146
 royal estates, 97–98, 137–38, 141–42, 152
 sasine of Blarmade, 146, 152, 155–56, 170, 194
 sasine of Coshogle, 116, 122–23, 133
 sasine of Drumlanrig, 134, 141–42
 sasine of Hawick, 138
 sasine of Pettinain, 97–98
 sasine of Stewarton, 97
Sauchie (Clackmannan), 121, 168n89
Sauchieburn, battle of (1488) (Stirling), 110
Schism of the Church (1439), 31–32, 56, 57
Scott, Walter, of Kirkurd, 154
seals
 great seal register, 67n142, 79
 great seals
  gubernatorial, 50
  royal, 50, 51, 57, 66–67, 67n142
 privy seals, 32, 57, 66–67, 104
Selkirk, 135,
 see also Ettrick and Selkirk Forest
sessions, 168n89, 152, 152n25
 sessions of the justice ayre, 149
Seton, Sir George (first lord), **93**, 95, 95n77, 97
Shaw, John, younger, 168
Sigismund the Rich, duke of Austria-Tyrol, 13
Sim's Hill (Lanark), 155
Sinclair, Beatrix, 96–97
 grants of Stewarton and Pettinain, 96
Sinclair, William (third earl of Orkney), **93**, 95n77, 95–97
Slitrig Water, 127
Smailholm (Roxburgh), 142
Snar, lordship of (Lanark), 147, 153, 155n36, 155–56, 167
 see also Blarmade land dispute
Snar Law, 155
Snar Water, 155–56
Snowdon Herald, 77–78
Somerville, James (in 'Blarmade'), 155
Sprouston, regality of (Roxburgh), 66, 68–69, 72, 135, 139–42, 142–43, 193–94
Stanley (Perth), 159, 165
Steward of Scotland (*senescallo Scotiae*), 91, **93**, 94, 92–96, 158
Stewart family
 Alexander (elder twin of James II), 10
 Alexander, 'buktuth', 163n68
 Alexander, earl of Buchan, 33, 33n116, 41n18, 44
 Alexander, earl of Mar, 33, 53–54, 95
 Alexander, of Galston, 168, 168n89

259

Annabella, 12–13, **14**
David, duke of Rothesay, 44
   arrest and death, 46–47
   lieutenant, 44–46
Egidia, 83–84, 97, 132
Eleanor, 12–13, **14**
Euphemia, **14**, 51
Isabella, 12–13, **14**
James, 'Black Knight' of Lorne, 54–55
Joanna, 12–13, **14**
John, earl of Atholl, 31
John, earl of Buchan, **14**, 88, 159
   Stewarton, 92, **93**, 95
Margaret (daughter of John Stewart and Elizabeth Douglas), **93**, 95
Margaret (daughter of James I), **14**
Margaret (sister of James I) **14**, 89
Mary (daughter of James I), **14**
Mary (daughter of James II), **14**
Murdoch (duke of Albany)
   governor of Scotland, **14, 48**, 53n71, 159
Robert (later King Robert II), 37–48, 40
Robert (duke of Albany)
   governor of Scotland, guardian, 43–44
   lieutenant, 47–48
Robert, *proditoris regis*, 174
Sir Thomas, **93**, 95
Walter (earl of Atholl), 37, 51, 174–75
Stewarton (Ayr), 93
   divided lordship, 91–92
   Douglas family
      lack of clarity, 90–91
   Elizabeth Murray, 96
   John Stewart, 92–94
   le Mote de Castletoun, 91

Steward of Scotland, 94
William Douglas (eighth earl of),
   regrant, 97–98
   resignation, 95–96
Stirling
   castle, 2, 53
   town cross, 99, 104
Strathaven, castle of (Lanark), 173
succession to land, 32–33
   absence of son, 10–11
   hierarchy of succession, 10–11
      non-royal landowners, 15
      women, 11
   illegitimate children, 16–17
   inherited land and conquest land, 11
   law, role and importance of, 10–11
   legal capacity, 17
   wardship, 17
   twins, 10
   women, 11
      division of lands, 11
      loss upon marriage, 11
   see also tailzies
succession to the Crown, 11–12
   tailzie of 1373, 11–12
   women, 12–13
succession to title of honour, 32–33
   daughters, 12
   illegitimate children, 16–17
   sons, 11–12
succession of women
   succession to land, 11
      Douglas tailzie 1342, 21–23
      impact of Black Dinner executions, 30–31
      Margaret Douglas, 30–31, 68, 139–41, 154
      untailzied Douglas estates, 30–31, 139–41, 154

succession to the Crown, 12–13
  tailzie of 1373, 11–12
Swinton, John of, 134

T

tailzies, 11, 19
  Douglas tailzie 1342, 21–23, 28,
    33, 61–62, 118, 178–79, 193
  female succession to the Crown,
    11–12
Tanner, Roland (historian), 53–54,
  56–57, 59–60
Taylor, Alice (historian), 4
Teindside ('Tenside') barony of
  Hawick (Roxburgh), 140
Telfer, Andrew (in 'Blarmade'), 155
terce, 17, 64, 154, 166
  brieves of terce, 116–17
Teviot, River, 140
Teviotdale (Roxburgh), 125–28, 128–
  29, 136, 192
Thomas, earl of Mar, 128–29, 134,
  128n51
Thomson, Thomas, 116–17, 117n11,
  149
Threave castle (Dumfries), 63, 90,
  95n77, 173
Three Estates
  authority, 28, 53–54, 55–56, 59,
    103, 110, 112
  appointment of regent, 39–51,
    52, 53–55, 73, 177–78
  grants of land to Douglases,
    68–69, 71, 81–82, 86–87,
    90–91, 98, 180
Tibbers, castle of (Dumfries), 130
Tillicoultry, barony of (Clackmannan),
  93–94
Traboyack (Ayr), 93–95
Trabroun (Berwick), 88n50

transumpt of 1449, 64–69, 79, 87–88,
  90, 91, 140–41, 179, 193–94
treason
  assassination of James I, 3, 29, 35,
    51, 94, 107, 163, 174, 175,
    182
  Black Dinner, 3, 27–30, 33–34,
    62, 162
  forfeiture for treason, 81–82, 103,
    125–26
  James Douglas (ninth earl), 111–
    12, 112n134
  march laws (Lincluden 1449), 83
  Sir Malcolm Fleming, 29–30
  treason trials, 60
  William Douglas (eighth earl
    of), 98–103, 142, 175n10,
    181
  wardens' powers, 84
  William Douglas (sixth earl of),
    28–29, 30, 177–78
  William Douglas (eighth earl of),
    81–82, 98–103, 106–9, 111
truces, Anglo-Scottish, 73–74, 76–79,
  102, 106n121
Tudor, Margaret (queen to James IV),
  158
'Tulchfraser' (Stirling), 93–94
Turnbull, William (bishop), 57, 66–67,
  98, 112, 179
tutors and tutoring, 17, 61, 158, 167
  appointment of tutors, 19
Tweeddale, 126
Tweedy, James, of Drummelzier,
  84n34
Twy, Thomas, 120–21
Tyburn (London), 174

V

van Borselen, Wolfaert, 13, 24n77

W

Wanlockhead (Dumfries), 155
wardens and wardenship
    deputes and officers, appointment of, 78n16
    jurisdiction and courts, 83–84, 97
    lieutenants of, 83n30, 84n34
    Middle and Western Marches, 25, 73, 77, 81, 82–84, 90, 132–33
    limitation of power, 84
    Nithsdale, 83–84, 97, 132–33
wardship, 133, 138
    succession to land, 17, 153, 191
Weir, George, of Snar, 167
West Lothian, 169n91, 193
west march, *see* Middle and Western Marches, wardenship of
Westminster
    Anglo-Scottish truce, 102, 106n121
    Westminster Abbey, 174
    Westminster Hall, 174
Whitchester (barony of Hawick) (Roxburgh), 161
Whitchester, Elizabeth of, 161n58
Wigtown, earldom of
    1451 grant to William Douglas (eighth earl of), 86–90
    legitimacy of claim, 87–88
    baronial jurisdiction, 87–88, 132
    Archibald "the Grim" (third earl), 87–89
    non obstantibus clause, 87
Wigtown, sheriffdom of, 86–90
William first earl of Douglas, *see* Douglas, William (first earl of)
William sixth earl of Douglas, *see* Douglas, William (sixth earl of)
William eighth earl of Douglas, *see* Douglas, William (eighth earl of)
women, *see* succession of women

Lightning Source UK Ltd.
Milton Keynes UK
UKHW021348010822
406675UK00010B/2234